DOES COLLEGE MATTER?

Some Evidence on the Impacts of Higher Education

*Proceedings of a Conference
on the Benefits of Higher Education
Held at Woods Hole, Massachusetts, July 16–19, 1972*

DOES COLLEGE MATTER?

SOME EVIDENCE ON THE IMPACTS OF HIGHER EDUCATION

Edited by

LEWIS C. SOLMON and *PAUL J. TAUBMAN*

Board on Human Resources
National Research Council
Washington, D.C.

Department of Economics
Wharton School of Finance
and Commerce
University of Pennsylvania
Philadelphia, Pennsylvania

Panel on the Benefits of Higher Education
Board of Human Resources
National Academy of Sciences—National Research Council

1973

ACADEMIC PRESS   New York and London
A Subsidiary of Harcourt Brace Jovanovich, Publishers

ACADEMIC PRESS, INC.
111 Fifth Avenue, New York, New York 10003

United Kingdom Edition published by
ACADEMIC PRESS, INC. (LONDON) LTD.
24/28 Oval Road, London NW1

Library of Congress Cataloging in Publication Data
Main entry under title:

Does college matter?

Conference held at Woods Hole, Mass., July 16-19,
1972, sponsored by the Panel on the Benefits of Higher
Education.
Includes bibliographies.
1.   Education—Economic aspects—United States—
Congresses.   2.   Education, Higher—Aims and objectives—
Congresses.   3.   Education, Higher—United States—
1965-   —Congresses.   4.   Universities and
colleges—United States—Finance—Congresses.
I.   Solmon, Lewis C., ed.   II.   Taubman, Paul J., ed.
III.   National Research Council. Office of Scientific
Personnel. Board on Human Resources. Panel on the
Benefits of Higher Education.
LC66.D63   301.5'6   73-7443
ISBN 0–12–655050–6

CONTENTS

Part II.   Income-Related Effects on the Educated

Part III.   Effects on the Educated: Emerging Areas of Study

Contents

Part IV.   **Public Aspects of Higher Education**

LIST OF CONTRIBUTORS

Numbers in parentheses indicate the pages on which the authors' contributions begin.

C. Arnold Anderson (393), Comparative Education Center, University of Chicago, Chicago, Illinois

Alexander W. Astin (104, 107), Office of Research, American Council on Education, Washington, D.C., and Graduate School of Education, University of California, Los Angeles, California

Mary Jean Bowman (381), Comparative Education Center, University of Chicago, Chicago, Illinois

Barry R. Chiswick (151), National Bureau of Economic Research, New York, New York, and Department of Economics, Queens College, City University of New York

Kenneth E. Clark (317), College of Arts and Sciences, University of Rochester, Rochester, New York

Thomas J. Cottle (175), Education Research Center, Massachusetts Institute of Technology, Cambridge, Massachusetts

Andre Daniere (365), Institute of Human Sciences, Boston College, Chestnut Hill, Massachusetts

Stephen P. Dresch (335), National Bureau of Economic Research, New Haven, Connecticut, and Research in the Economics of Higher Education, Yale University, New Haven, Connecticut

Anne Ellison (35), Office of the Dean for Student Affairs, Massachusetts Institute of Technology, Cambridge, Massachusetts

Richard B. Freeman (321), Department of Economics, University of Chicago, Chicago, Illinois

EDMUND W. GORDON (251), Department of Education, Teachers College, Columbia University, New York, New York

W. LEE HANSEN (329), Department of Economics, University of Wisconsin, Madison, Wisconsin

ROBERT W. Hartman (271), The Brookings Institution, Washington, D.C.

ROBERT M. HAUSER (102, 129), Department of Sociology, University of Wisconsin, Madison, Wisconsin

MACK H. JONES (239), Department of Political Science, Atlanta University, Atlanta, Georgia

CARL KAYSEN (147), The Institute for Advanced Study, Princeton, New Jersey

FRITZ MACHLUP (353), Department of Economics, Princeton University, Princeton, New Jersey, and Department of Economics, New York University, New York, New York

DAVID S. MUNDEL (293), John Fitzgerald Kennedy School of Government, Harvard University, Cambridge, Massachusetts

ELLIS B. PAGE (159), The Bureau of Educational Research, University of Connecticut, Storrs, Connecticut

MICHELLE PATTERSON (225), Department of Sociology, Brandeis University, Waltham, Massachusetts, and Department of Sociology, University of California, Santa Barbara, California

GERALD M. PLATT (341), Department of Sociology, University of Massachusetts, Amherst, Massachusetts

BENNETT SIMON (35), Education Research Center, Massachusetts Institute of Technology, Cambridge, Massachusetts, and The Cambridge Hospital, Harvard Medical School, Cambridge, Massachusetts

LEWIS C. SOLMON (13, 77, 403), Board on Human Resources, National Research Council, Washington, D.C., and National Bureau of Economic Research, New York, New York

PAUL J. TAUBMAN (1), Department of Economics, Wharton School of Finance and Commerce, University of Pennsylvania, Philadelphia, Pennsylvania

CHARLES V. WILLIE (231), Department of Sociology, Syracuse University, Syracuse, New York

DAEL WOLFLE (65), Graduate School of Public Affairs, University of Washington, Seattle, Washington

FOREWORD

The Board on Human Resources of the National Research Council, under whose auspices this book is published, is the direct successor to the Commission on Human Resources and Advanced Education, which began after World War II under the sponsorship of the Conference Board of the Associated Research Councils. During its more than 20-year history the Commission produced a number of publications dealing with the ways in which this nation identifies, educates, and utilizes its resources of human talent. The two most notable of these publications are the classic volume by Dael Wolfle, *America's Resources of Specialized Talent* (New York: Harper, 1954) and the recently published book by John K. Folger, Helen S. Astin, and Alan E. Bayer, *Human Resources and Higher Education* (New York: Russell Sage Foundation, 1970), which brings up to date many of the Wolfle findings and examines some additional issues in the area of talent development and utilization.

This book represents something of a shift or expansion of the interests of the Board in the direction of the costs and benefits of varying types and amounts of higher education. Costs and benefits are properly seen to include both monetary and nonmonetary expenditures and benefits that accrue both to individuals and to the larger society. Essentially, the book is a series of papers that resulted from an interdisciplinary conference on the benefits of higher education, held at Woods Hole, Massachusetts, during the summer of 1972. The conference was arranged by the Board's newly created Panel on the Benefits of Higher Education and was attended mainly by economists and sociologists, but participants included representatives from psychiatry, psychology, education, and history as well.

The featured papers for the first day of the conference were prepared by Lewis C. Solmon, who reviews and assesses the literature on the effects of schooling on subsequent success primarily by examining the influence of amount and quality of education on earnings when socio-economic origins and ability are taken into account, and by Anne Ellison and Bennett Simon, who provide a social-psychiatric overview of research in higher education, stressing the social-psychological costs and benefits of higher education. Various scholars were asked either to comment on these papers or to develop ideas related to these topics. For the most part they developed their own, somewhat independent, papers. Dael Wolfle and Alexander W. Astin each prepared commentaries that extend the evidence on the relationship between family background, ability, quality of education, and earnings, a topic that Solmon covered in his original paper but has expanded into a new paper in this volume. Robert M. Hauser provides new evidence on the relationship between this same set of variables but takes into account several methods of measuring interaction effects. Carl Kaysen discusses the intellectual issues and policy matters that gave rise to interest in costs and benefits of education and suggests that the human capitalists may have already mined most of the pay dirt in this area. He suggests that future work might well be directed toward the intensive study of careers—including recruitment patterns into various careers, career income distributions, lifetime earnings patterns in different careers, and how the people in various occupations spend their time. Barry R. Chiswick considers the questions involved in the relationship of schooling, screening, and income and presents evidence that tends to refute the "sheepskin hypothesis," by showing that the larger payoff from schooling received by graduates compared to drop-outs is due to productivity differences. Ellis B. Page presents the rationale for a new measure of general educational advancement called the "bentee" or "benefit T-score"—a normalized, equal-interval scale, adjusted for a norm of some relevant comparison group, e.g., seniors in high school—and gives examples of its utility in evaluation programs. Michelle Patterson brings together findings on the monetary returns to higher education for women, pointing out that most studies have ignored women or, if women are included, that the data and the analysis have been inadequate to answer the important questions.

Four papers that were not included in the conference deliberation have been added to round out the coverage and increase the treatment of important concerns: Edmund W. Gordon traces the development of higher education for minorities and suggests important new directions for future efforts. Mack Jones discusses the development of the black colleges in America and indicates the ways in which they now fail to meet their responsibilities to the black community. Charles V. Willie discusses some of the problems of college education for blacks and the meaning of their education for the majority and minority populations of the United States. Finally, Thomas J. Cottle presents three intensive life studies of the varying effects of college on the lives of individuals.

On the second day of the conference, attention centered on the responsibility of government and the student or his family in meeting the costs of higher education. The major papers were by Robert W. Hartman and by David S. Mundel. Hartman's paper is devoted to a summary and examination of the arguments for and against greater public subsidy for higher education. He concludes that there are good *a priori* reasons for, and no empirical evidence to invalidate, policies that would (1) target existing subsidies at both federal and state levels on low-income students, (2) increase research and innovation in higher education, and (3) encourage moves toward relative prices for higher education that reflect relative costs. Mundel's paper attempts to state the appropriate role of government in higher education in a free society. He argues that the appropriate and effective bases for social support and intervention in a free market are (a) public goods and social benefits, e.g., economic growth, (b) externalities, e.g., lower crime rates, and (c) market imperfections, e.g., the imperfections on the capital market. After examining each of these justifications, he concludes that the evidence indicates that social policy efforts should be focused on students from lower- and moderate-income families.

Several economists then comment on the Hartman and Mundel papers. Richard B. Freeman is skeptical about the effects of public subsidization of higher education, arguing that its social benefits may be less than commonly thought and that a regressive income redistribution may result. W. Lee Hansen directs his remarks to the problems of how to better estimate the scope and magnitude of external benefits and, in using these estimates, to determine the appropriate financial arrangement among different levels of government and the students and their parents. Gerald M. Platt discusses how best to finance higher education so that more of the poor may obtain the kinds of postsecondary education that will increase their cognitive competence, not just their vocational skills. Andre Daniere briefly reviews the issues that have occupied students of the economics of higher education during the last decade, emphasizing the shift in interest from concern with "rates of return" to social investment in education to equity or equality of the distribution of education among social groups, and pointing out some of the challenging research and policy issues resulting from the two approaches.

Before the close of the conference several participants availed themselves of the opportunity to either comment in general on the major issues of the conference or to emphasize particular issues that they felt had been omitted or needed further emphasis. Fritz Machlup addresses himself to several issues, including, among others, the problems involved in using parents' socioeconomic characteristics in the explanation of students' attainments, the possibility that the positive income differentials associated with additional postsecondary education in the past may have vanished for current graduates, the need to examine more completely the nonpecuniary benefits of postsecondary education, and the factors that attract or deter people from taking postsecondary education. Mary Jean Bowman raises questions about the noncognitive effects of education and the subsequent significance of such learning, the importance of analysis of careers, and makes a number of assertions concerning income redistribution, the importance of increasing the educational levels of minority groups, screening, on-the-job learning, social mobility, and the discrepancies between social and private benefits. C. Arnold Anderson, in discussing the results of interdisciplinary research on outcomes of higher education, comments about the nature of educational improvements, the nonvocational goals of higher education, equality of opportunity and equity, universalistic principles for allocating schooling and jobs, similarities and differences in the sociological and economic approaches to education, comparative perspectives on social mobility, and the need for microanalytic studies. Finally, the volume closes with a statement on the prerequisites for further research by Solmon. In this essay, written after the conference, he lays out some of the issues in the study of costs and benefits of higher education, attempts to elaborate on some of the important conceptual problems that arose during the deliberations, and indicates how some of our research methods and conclusions need to be qualified.

WILLIAM H. SEWELL

Department of Sociology
University of Wisconsin
Madison, Wisconsin

PREFACE

This book is the result of a conference on higher education held July 16–19, 1972, under the auspices of the Panel on the Benefits of Higher Education of the Board on Human Resources, National Research Council. The meeting was the Panel's first attempt to bring together scholars and other interested parties from a wide range of disciplines and professions, who are concerned with higher education, to answer some of the questions of interest to the Panel. The positive and negative benefits of higher education can come in many forms and are studied differently by people in various disciplines, but too often research conducted on one front is unknown to researchers in other areas. By continuing to stimulate interdisciplinary discussions and by making important research findings resulting from these widely known, the Panel hopes to increase the awareness on the part of many researchers of complementary studies by colleagues in other fields and thereby improve the quality of research in a number of disciplines. Research on higher education can no longer be one-dimensional. Quantitative work must acknowledge factors not subject to measurement, and those interested in the humanistic side of higher education have to realize that statistical constructs are not necessarily irrelevant.

The first two papers by Solmon, as well as the papers by Ellison & Simon, Hartman, and Mundel, were commissioned before the conference, and a number of scholars were invited to comment on them at the conference. Some of the discussants prepared formal papers, which appear in the volume. Other discussants were less formal. Their tape-recorded comments were turned back to them to be revised and rewritten for inclusion in the volume. At this point some of the discussants decided to write papers of varying lengths, expressing their views on the invited papers and on subjects discussed at the conference. Others felt their comments should more directly reflect the conference atmosphere and more explicitly respond to the issues developed there. The editors have allowed the participants freedom regarding the structure of their own papers, and this explains the varying degrees of formality in the volume.

The Panel felt it would be a disservice to readers if the volume did not contain a more balanced discussion of even the limited impacts of higher education that appeared in the papers prepared and discussed at the conference. To that end we have taken several steps. People who study higher education use a wide variety of techniques, but the case study and personal interview approaches were virtually ignored at the conference. This omission was particularly upsetting to scholars who believe that you cannot really understand the effects of higher education on, for example, blacks, unless you spend time at an institution that admits blacks, or unless you study a variety of institutions that admit a larger or smaller proportion of blacks, or, indeed, unless you are black yourself. In redressing this particular imbalance, the editors were fortunate to be able to include some of Dr. Tom Cottle's work. We selected three of his essays that emphasized the tremendous diversity in effects of the college experience. The first piece describes the impact of the higher education experience on a black youth; the second, its effects on a student who fails out of college; and the third, the adjustment of an older man who goes to college. Certainly these interviews provide a different perspective than a regression coefficient, and they confirm that the effects of college can be negative as well as positive. Since we are concerned with the effects of college on different individuals, we invited Dr. Mack Jones and Dr. Edmund Gordon to contribute papers to the volume that deal specifically with the impacts of higher education on blacks.

Finally, several of our Panel members expressed a desire to comment, as individuals, on either specific contributions in the volume or on the general flavor of the volume as a whole. Since we are anxious that this volume express as many points of view as possible, we welcome these comments.

In summary, we hope that this volume represents a more or less well-balanced first cut at analyses of certain impacts of higher education. In places it very clearly reflects the flavor of our conference. In other places we have made explicit attempts to balance the tone of the conference with additional materials so that the book might be more useful. The Panel must acknowledge the cooperation and commitment of all participants at the conference. Many thoughtful papers were prepared with rather short notice, and sincere effort was made to communicate ideas to an audience that did not have the training and tools possessed by the groups usually addressed by the participants. The desire to get one's views clearly on the table was demonstrated by each speaker, as was the effort to learn from others.

It should be very clearly and explicitly stated that this book does not represent the opinions of the Panel on the Benefits of Higher Education or the Board on Human Resources as a whole. The members of these groups who have written for the volume have done so under their own name, and their comments are personal only and not those of any organization with which they are affiliated. Though our Panel and Board members learned a great deal from the conference and their future activities will be aided by it, this book should not be interpreted as being representative of the future plans or objectives of the Panel.

Basic support for the Board and its Panel has come from the Russell Sage Foundation, the James McKeen Cattell Fund, the National Endowment for the Humanities, and the National Academy of Sciences. Dr. William C. Kelly, director of the National Research Council's Office of Scientific Personnel, has been an advisor and strong supporter of the conference and this volume from the start; his contribution is gratefully acknowledged. The administrative aspects of the conference were exceptionally well handled by Marianne Graves and Diane Haspel. The tedious job of editing the widely diverse set of contributions was done cheerfully and most competently by Joan Tapper. The burden of typing the manuscript has fallen upon Elizabeth Class and Marianne Graves. Completion of the task has been no mean accomplishment in such a short time. A volume of this magnitude can only develop out of the combined efforts of a large number of highly competent people. The editors acknowledge all of these.

DOES COLLEGE MATTER?

Some Evidence on the Impacts of Higher Education

INTRODUCTION

Paul J. Taubman

The benefits of higher education can take many forms (some negative, perhaps) and range widely through areas that concern several academic disciplines. It was partly for this reason that an interdisciplinary Panel on the Benefits of Higher Education was formed in spring 1972. A second reason was to aid in communication, so that publications on this topic in one field would not be overlooked by members of another.

The conference held at Woods Hole, July 16–19, 1972, was the first sponsored by the Panel. Intensive as this conference was, it was obvious that a discussion of all the benefits from higher education was impossible. Therefore, a conscious decision was made in the beginning to try to limit the material to a few particular subjects. The Panel does not intend to imply that the benefits discussed are the only ones, or those that it is most interested in, or that the methodologies employed in the papers presented at the conference are the only or best ones to use. Indeed, to indicate the value of alternative approaches, and to make the volume more representative, papers by Thomas Cottle, Edmund Gordon, and Mack Jones are included in this volume (pp. 175–224, 251–268, 239–250).

At the first conference the Panel planned to focus on the general question: What do we know about the effects of different types of higher or postsecondary education on different kinds of individuals and on society? Answers to this sort of problem are very relevant, at least to

1

economists, in determining whether the individual or society should be asked to pay the major portion of the bill for college attendance. Because of this connection, and because of the substantial current interest in this problem, a portion of the meeting was devoted to this financing question.

The conference did reach some conclusions. On the positive side, the evidence presented by both Anne Ellison & Bennett Simon (pp. 35–63) and by Lewis Solmon (pp. 13–34; 77–102) strongly supports the notion that a college education changes an individual's personality, attitudes, motivation, and values and adds to a white male's earning potential. (Partly because of the lack of data, similar evidence is not available for nonwhites and for women.) This might seem like a trivial conclusion, but, in fact, there are many people who have maintained that average differences observed on an attitudes test between college and high school graduates are *not* caused by the college experience but existed before the individual went to college. While the evidence in these papers is never drawn from an ideal sample in which "everything else" has been controlled, in the best studies many of the most obvious things have been held constant. Thus, it seems clear that college does "matter."

The Panel had hoped to accumulate information on the effect of different kinds of postsecondary education on different types of people. While a few studies have begun to examine this area, there are many gaps in our knowledge. Solmon, for example, summarizes the available evidence on how monetary returns vary with intelligence level. The answers vary by study and perhaps by measures of intelligence. Solmon then presents some new and intriguing evidence that monetary benefits vary by quality of college attended. However, it is not clear whether his results arise from differences in the education at the various schools or because of some unmeasured differences in the students at different institutions. This last view cannot be easily rejected, given Alexander Astin's findings (pp. 107–127) that the *increase* in some types of general knowledge or cognitive skills does not depend on the type of college attended, though there are differences in the average *level* of skills by school.

Robert Hauser (pp. 129–145) examines how monetary returns vary by the respondent's socioeconomic status (SES). Of course, he finds, as practically all other researchers have, that SES affects earnings given years of schooling and mental ability. But he also finds that monetary returns are constant at various levels of SES. While this factor is a reasonable proxy for various peer-group and family effects, it also may well be a substitute for other capacities that are genetically inheritable. Thus, his results may have an even broader scope.

Ellison & Simon's paper presents an overview of the literature of the effects of education on affective and cognitive development. They conclude that college changes scores on thinking introversion and complexity scales and on nonauthoritarianism and social maturity scales. However, once individual characteristics are held constant, the type of school has no additional impact. Nevertheless, the type of person may have an impact, since there is some evidence that the emotionally rich improve even more from going to college.

With the exception of papers by Ellison & Simon and Michelle Patterson, the conference offered little evidence about the benefits of higher education for women. Other studies do exist and should probably be reexamined more thoroughly in the future (Mincer, 1970; Welch, 1972). Some of the benefits for blacks are contained in the papers by Gordon, Jones, and Willie.

The conference also came to some useful negative conclusions. Expressed more openly in discussion than in the papers was the widespread feeling that "years of schooling" was a highly aggregate and imperfect measure of what postsecondary education was about. The measure is imperfect because it implies that an education at Princeton and Podunk are the same thing, because it tends to make people think that education comes only from schooling and that schooling automatically produces education, and because it does not indicate how or why college attendance increases various aspects of a person's cognitive and affective development. A second, though related, point is the fact that no good explanation of what in particular education does to make a person more productive is available. This is an important question. If the deciding factor is not a person's extra knowledge or increased ability to think but his ability to get along with others or to be socially correct, then the structure, hiring, and promotion policies of colleges and universities, for example, are called into question.

The papers dealing with the relationship between student and government in paying for education are interesting and informative. Their major conclusion is that both the policy makers and the taxpayers are in an untenable position: While, as far as many economists are concerned, the general criteria necessary to answer the questions are known, little solid empirical research has been done. Thus, policy makers have little information on which to decide issues, and the taxpayer has no means to determine if wise programs are being followed.

It was stated earlier that an important purpose of the Panel is to encourage interdisciplinary communication. An explanation of why so many of the papers were prepared by economists is, therefore, in order: Before the Panel met formally, a decision was made to use the first summer of its existence to hold a conference, leaving most of the details to the chairman and staff director. We chose to focus on the material we knew best; and while such a choice partly reflected familiarity, it also reflected a feeling that one way to communicate is to concentrate on only a few disciplines at a time.

One unexpected difficulty arose from this decision; the economists did not fully define all their terms, since, after all, other economists would understand them. Thus, as an aid to the reader, an overview of the framework used in all conference papers follows, rather than a summary of each paper.

There is a basic framework underlying all the disciplines. An individual is considered to possess various skills, traits, and attributes that somehow produce such things as mental capacity, personality, and other cognitive and affective skills. These, in turn, help determine a person's economic, social, and psychological status. The skill levels, however, are not predetermined at conception but, in general, can be changed by peer-group influences, schooling, on-the-job training, and television, newspapers, and so on.

To isolate the effect of higher education, one can observe the variance in, for example, earnings of people who differ only with respect to education. This is accomplished in practice either by using regression analysis to "hold constant" some things while obtaining an average difference by education level, or by studying representative individuals.

The various disciplines begin to diverge here. Economists, for example, tend to think of education in terms of a model of "human capital," defining capital as an item purchased currently, but whose benefits are realized partly in the future. Thus, education is capital because it increases earnings, art appreciation, and so on in the future. This analysis is very useful to economists, since it largely allows us to treat human capital like other types of capital.

Up to this point economists and sociologists would be in agreement. But some economists, led by Theodore Schultz, Gary Becker, and Jacob Mincer, have forcefully argued that an economic man should invest in more education till his rate of return on the last dollar of investment just equals his interest cost paid to finance his investment. The theoretical investment model has been analyzed in great detail; many of its predictions have been found to be roughly consistent with observed data, and relatively few of its predictions have been refuted.

This particular investment model is an extremely powerful analytical and descriptive tool. For example, Mincer (1970) has demonstrated that under certain circumstances the model implies that people receive larger incomes as they age, because they "paid" for on-the-job training by accepting low wages early in their work career. Mincer then presents some evidence that suggests that about three fourths of the variation in (white male) earnings is due to either variation in years of schooling or on-the-job training. Since the on-the-job training model argues that such training alters the pattern of lifetime earnings, but not its average level (when discounted to the present), this version of the human capital model implies that much of lifetime income inequality is due to educational differences that could be eliminated. These results are largely derivable because it has been assumed that people invest rationally in education. Some economists, including this author, accept the capital concept but don't believe that a rational investment model is a valid description of how people behave. Thus, we dispute—at times in a heated and arcane manner—the above conclusions and findings. However, it is extremely difficult to find information that would conclusively disprove the model.

Sociologists who examine earnings functions also presume that there is some connection between a person's skills and the income he receives. But a primary focus of their studies is socioeconomic status. The SES concept combines a great many things, including skills taught and tastes molded in the household, peer-group influences, and also (as a proxy) some inheritable skills. What is somewhat surprising about the research in this area is that economists and sociologists have been allowed to measure it as they have. It would seem that we've been using the crudest type of information when we say "it's the father's or the mother's education" or "the father's occupation" that makes the difference. After all, a Berkeley graduate who is a business owner can be making leather belts and selling them on a street corner, living in a commune, and raising a child in one particular way, or he can be a corporate executive who's raising a child in a totally different manner and perhaps never even seeing him. As with education, it would seem that a disaggregation of socioeconomic status into measures of input or output would be an important step.

There is another approach to this problem, exemplified in some of the work that Simon reported on. Rather than looking at the effects of schooling by examining a person's earnings, it is possible to try and measure the actual skills he has—whether of a physical or mental nature—and how they have changed with education.

One consequence of schooling, apparently, is change in an individual's personality, his attitudes, and his values. These things can be valued for themselves, but they certainly can also affect a person's earning capacities. It should be possible to integrate the material discussed in the psychological and other literature into a person's earnings function;

such an approach might have very important implications. For example, if college primarily changes the affective behavior of individuals, the relevant characteristics of a college would be different from a type in which the cognitive abilities of a person are altered. That is, for the socialization of students you would want a different type of teacher, living environment, and peer group within the college, and you probably would want to retire me to a research institute.

As a researcher, I would like to point out a technical problem that does influence some work on these subjects. The use and the insistence upon variables such as the Duncan occupational status scale in some sociological studies is difficult to understand. Certainly, there are occupational differences in status that can have rather important implications in terms of the welfare of the individual, power structure, and so on, and to create an index of this arrangement is not an irrelevant task. But it must be realized that it is what the economists call an ordinal index. On such a scale the difference between two numbers does not measure how much better off one person is than another. To use absolute differences that are meaningless as a dependent variable in an equation doesn't tell very much. Nor is it very useful in explaining income, because there's no necessary relationship between income and some arbitrarily scaled set of numbers. But despite this technical problem, it is possible to integrate the sociological literature, the personality development literature, and the economics literature in order to better understand what determines a person's earnings.

The above discussion, like the conference, often emphasized earnings. Yet it is trite, but true, that man does not live by bread alone; people don't get higher education just to achieve more income in the future. Nor should we examine education only to describe what is going to happen to the distribution of income. Colleges are intended to serve other functions, including the transmission of cultural values and knowledge, the broadening of opportunities, and the creation of a new individual. These are important goals but the reader may conclude from the material presented that the economists at the conference would not pay very much attention to them. Of course, some of these nonmonetary aspects can be included in an economics framework. It is possible to write an equation that says spirit is a function of various things and to derive a demand function for spirit. But that's not the most relevant question. What is crucial is the extent to which the nonmonetary goals of college relate to the other types of questions we are asking. One way of focusing on this is to ask what types of education are going to be relevant to the production of a well-rounded individual, one that realizes his full potential. To answer this we would want a different type of an educational system than the one that we've been discussing here. If reading and grasping Shakespeare's message are important, you don't necessarily want a community college that concentrates purely on vocational skills. It's also clear that we must not be parochial about how "education" is produced. Adult education, educational TV, newspapers, and so on are certainly ways of transmitting culture and knowledge. Thus, it is very relevant to know if we really want to transmit culture at the college level.

To digress for a minute, an economist concerned with the allocation of resources automatically asks himself if there is market failure: It can be shown rigorously that when markets operate well (that is, don't fail) the prices established by supply and demand will allocate goods to produce the maximum value of any output—whether economic goods or anything else—that will be available to society. In other words, the price system eliminates the need for the government to grant subsidies or to intervene in general. But it has been well recognized for at least 40 years that one of the reasons markets can fail is that an individual does not capture all the benefits from a particular action. Thus, as long as his actions are based only on his private benefits and costs, the (decentralized) market will not provide an optimal distribution. The papers in Part III focus on the particular question of whether the individual will capture all the benefits.

It is important to determine whether the framework I have sketched above rules out society's helping an individual to achieve a more rounded personality, more culture, or more nonincome activity. I don't believe it does, and I don't believe Robert Hartman (pp. 271–292) says it does. He suggested essentially two or three reasons why one would simply reject either the social-versus-private-benefit framework or the particular conclusion that more culture should not be subsidized: It may be true that the value of culture to society is more than its value to any individual, that is, the distinction between private and social benefits exists. However, the idea that efficiency should be thought of only in terms of level of income, while equity should be thought of primarily in terms of income distribution, was implicit in the discussion of his paper. Economists often say this and then add that, since income redistribution can be achieved in other and better ways, only efficiency should be discussed. Even from an economics viewpoint, this set of conclusions need not be accepted. Education and nonincome values can be "merit" goods; it may be an inalienable right for every individual in this society to have the opportunity to fulfill himself. Another criticism of this approach is that when there are many goals and many distributional criteria, the use of any one, or a weighted average of them, will be an arbitrary decision. Why should individuals in society, acting together or separately, be involved in arbitrarily excluding some individual from having this opportunity? In other words, rather than use a pure efficiency criteria, we may be willing to lose some income in order not to have arbitrary discrimination.

There is one other way of viewing this problem. As Kenneth Clark pointed out (pp. 317–320), if education is partly related to income distribution, partly to social and cultural values, and partly to the better man, a proper choice should be made, given all these consequences. But if one aspect is overridingly important, that determines the choice, and there is only a restricted or second-best decision made on the other goals. Some would argue that economic efficiency should be in the second-best category. I think, however, that Clark's point is based on the feeling that the educational effects are relatively small on income but very large on other aspects of human behavior. In other words, if differences in education account for 5 or 10 percent of the differences in income, but for a great deal more in terms of human happiness and human dignity, then it doesn't make sense to worry about the 5 or 10 percent. Of course the percentage may be higher. Some people who work in the area of human capital claim that education accounts for a major portion of the differences in *lifetime* earnings. Still, the choice between one or another goal certainly involves such questions as: How much income and how much material and nonmaterial wealth do you already have? People deciding to go to college are no longer people living in abject material poverty. If, however, they are still living in spiritual poverty, one can argue that the emphasis should switch from the income to the nonincome aspects of the question.

Finally, I would like to summarize several areas of controversy that arose during the conference. One important issue was the existence of benefits not captured by the individual. These are listed explicitly and distinguished from nonmonetary benefits in the papers by David Mundel (pp. 293–315) and Robert Hartman. Yet the comment was made that if the papers had been written 10 years ago, they would have included essentially the same categories of social benefits, the same economic framework, and the same conclusion—that we didn't really know how important any of the social benefits were. In fact, if the economic framework were excluded, the same arguments would probably be found in the letters of Benjamin Franklin and Thomas Jefferson. It is time for the social sciences to see if there are indeed reasons to justify various types of higher education subsidies. As Dresch points out (pp. 335–340), even assuming subsidies will exist, it is relevant to ask how to structure this financing to get the most out of the system and to eliminate institutions that are no longer useful. However, to answer this question, we must know what different types of schools do to the individual.

I have a final comment about the screening controversy that arose here and that I have been concerned with in my research. I agree with Carl Kaysen (pp. 147–150) that, in fact, we do not necessarily observe an equilibrium outcome in the world of occupational choice, that often people are excluded from jobs that they could well hold on the basis of testing or other credentials. The material that Barry Chiswick presented (pp. 151–158), while interesting, is, I think, a somewhat distorted view of what the screening hypothesis is. The concept is an extremely important issue that should be approached from a number of different viewpoints. As Andre Daniere noted (pp. 365–379), if screening does occur, a number of important consequences follow: For example, one can demonstrate that screening based on education causes income redistribution—from those that don't have education to those that do. This has implications in terms of how many people should be educated and in calculations of how much society will benefit from education. Moreover, even if everyone were college educated, screening could be based on whether or not one went to Harvard. While it is important to determine whether screening exists, it is difficult to fully demonstrate what is happening in this area in economics.

In conclusion, I found the conference very fruitful and feel that, despite the language problems, its interdisciplinary goals have been met.

REFERENCES

Mincer, J. The distribution of labor incomes: A survey with special reference to the human capital approach. *Journal of Economic Literature,* 1970, 8: 1–26.

Welch, F. Black–white differences in returns to schooling. Unpublished manuscript, National Bureau of Economic Research, 1972.

Part I

REVIEWS OF THE LITERATURE

SCHOOLING AND SUBSEQUENT SUCCESS

The Influence of Ability, Background, and Formal Education

Lewis C. Solmon

Although formal schooling has a wide variety of impacts on those educated and on others in society, much research by economists and sociologists has concentrated upon the effects on occupational achievement. It is important to review some of the studies that examine the relationship between education and two specific measurable benefits to the educated—income and occupational status. These are realized over the whole postschool career and, for reasons that will become apparent below, may not be evident during the first few years of full-time employment.

The literature to be summarized ignores, for the most part, work by psychologists and others who focus on changes in students that occur during the college years. A few of these studies will be cited in an attempt to show how they relate to the other studies and how each focus can benefit from the other. A complete understanding of the workings of higher education awaits a fuller integration of these approaches. For example, occupational attainment, if affected by formal schooling, must depend upon changes in cognitive and affective behavior that occur during the college years.

Some research dealing with effects of educational attainment below the college level is also noted at the beginning. Although not central to the task at hand, these studies suggest rationales for some of the results observed in the studies of college students. For example, although teacher traits are important determinants of success of elementary school children, these are not the characteristics usually accompanying higher salaries. Moreover, years of schooling is a poor measure of attainment when there are wide variations in days schools are open each year. These results lead to particular perspectives in my own studies of college impact (pp. 77–102).

Eric Hanushek (1972, pp. 108–110) has studied two data sets: a single California school system and a sample of urban schools in the Northeast and the Great Lakes region. Both analyses concentrate on elementary education and, in particular, on the production of achievement levels or cognitive ability. Hanushek summarizes his findings as follows:

> There is no doubt that family background has a pervasive and powerful impact on student achievement; higher socioeconomic status is systematically related to higher achievement. . . . The importance of the quantity and quality of school inputs is more interesting than the importance of family backgrounds. The analyses indicate that differences among teachers have a significant impact upon the achievement of students. . . . [However], factors which are purchased by the school systems are not for the most part the characteristics of schools and teachers which are important in determining achievement levels. The bulk of instructional expenditures go toward the purchase of three classes of inputs: class size, teacher experience, and teacher graduate education. . . . The characteristics of teachers which appear important in the estimated models include teacher verbal ability . . . , recentness of teacher educational experiences, and proportion of non-white teachers (which may be interpreted as a measure of the quality of educational experiences of non-white teachers).

Hanushek points out that, based on these findings, differences in per pupil expenditures will not be systematically related to differences in student achievement, because school funds are not spent to purchase those inputs that have the important effects on student achievement. Therefore, to measure quality of higher educational institutions merely by expenditures per student misses the point. We must know where these expenditures are made—whether to acquire the "proper attributes" of faculty or other productive aspects of the school environment. Obviously, the school with the large expenditure per student, if it is used to finance a football program, is not going to be a quality institution.

Finis Welch (1972) attempts to explain black–white differences in returns to schooling, negating the conclusion in his earlier work that schooling was a poor investment for a southern, rural black. He argues that the quality of schooling was not considered in the first paper.

The majority of the black, adult population in 1959 had last attended school in the decades of the 20's and 30's. During those periods Negroes attended school only about two-thirds as many days as whites. . . . Also, southern schools spent a little more than three times as much on white as on black pupils. In this context, it should not be surprising that schooling contributed much less to black income than to white. . . . Through time, the relative quality of black schooling has risen rapidly. This has been one of the major reasons for recent gains in relative black incomes.

Although Hanushek accounts for the initial ability of individual students, and hence measures output as the *net* change in aptitude scores effected by the schools themselves, Welch does not introduce ability into his discussion. In explaining black–white income differences, there are no measures of aggregate differences in initial ability of the two groups. However, we can conclude from these very different studies that school inputs do have an effect on the school system output, whether measured in terms of changes in achievement scores or ultimately in income differentials. We now turn to related studies that deal with higher education.

Alexander Astin (1968) tries to determine the effects of certain traditional indices of institutional excellence on the intellectual achievement of the undergraduate student by using scores on the area tests of the Graduate Record Examination (GRE). His sample deals with students at colleges that require all seniors to take the area test; therefore, student self-selection, which occurs in the GRE national program for graduate school selection, is not a factor. Astin controls for initial ability of the students by using their scores on the National Merit Scholarship Qualifying Test (taken before entering college) as an independent variable. A wide array of other student input control measures are also used.

Astin's analysis fails to confirm the hypothesis that the students' achievement in social sciences, humanities, or natural sciences is facilitated by the intellectual level of his classmates, the level of academic competitiveness, or the financial resources of his institution. Similarly, the evidence does not support the contention that the bright student benefits more than the average student from exposure to these assumed indices of institutional "quality." Astin also finds that differences in student achievement during the senior year are much more highly dependent on variations in student characteristics that existed before entrance into college than on the characteristics of the undergraduate college attended.

A subsequent study by Centra & Rock (1971) investigates selected features of the college environment presumed to be related to students' achieving significantly more or less than predictable from their aptitude at entrance. Contrary to the Astin study, these results do suggest that college environmental features are related to student achievement. In particular, students appear to learn more than might be expected if they feel that instructors are readily accessible, interested in teaching, and interested in students as individuals. Also related to overachievement are college environments in which students have freedom in choosing courses and can try out a variety of courses before selecting a major. High scores on the cultural facilities factor of a university, which indicate excellent facilities in music and art, as well as what the students view as rich cultural programs, are related to overachievement in the humanities but underachievement in the natural sciences tests.

The Centra & Rock study used a sample of 27 colleges, generally small, liberal arts institutions, that might be expected to emphasize educational output as measured by the GRE Area Tests. The students studied took the GRE's in their senior year by their own choosing, implying that the sample was a rather select group with at least some interest in doing postcollege work.

A study by Paul Heist & associates (1961) concludes that the students of high ability attending highly productive institutions have a pattern of traits, values, and attitudes more closely related to serious intellectual pursuits than have students of high ability attending less productive institutions. This research was done in conjunction with a study of college productivity (quality), measured by the number of BA's who go on to win PhD's. The high productivity of some schools is attributed not only to student input quality or to the college itself but to a fortunate combination of faculty and student expectations, interests, and values.

Although the Astin work is differently enough conceived from the other two studies that one need not spend a large amount of time reconciling the results, it appears that the outcomes are not inconsistent. The work by Taubman & Wales (1972) and my own work (pp. 77–102) indicate that the effects of college quality are not linear; that is, in general, high-ability students get more out of "good" schools than do students with less ability. The Astin study examines a rather general group of college students and finds little impact of college quality on achievement. The Centra & Rock and the Heist studies analyze much more selective groups of students and find that attributes of the college have an effect. In other words, if we combine the results, the implication is that if colleges matter, they matter to better students.

In a review article on the determinants of effectiveness in higher education, Robert Berls (1969) points out that tests of academic potential or cognitive achievement probably represent only a partial description of the likelihood of real-life accomplishment in those professions requiring above-average mental ability. The relationship between verbal intelligence and creativity is curvilinear, but at about 120 IQ the slope of the curve drops sharply. Thus, the two variables, while still correlated, are less so than at lower points in the IQ range. This implies that changes in attitudes or aptitudes due to the school experience are of value only to the extent that subsequent success is altered by the changes in these characteristics. In other words, we must measure success or contribution of the schooling experience by its contribution to success in later life, which, in turn, might be measured by income or by occupational status. (Others might argue that it should be measured by happiness or, preferably, by the expansion of choices available to the graduate.)

Recent work by Ellis Page (1972, pp. 33–34) acknowledges these kinds of problems and relationships:

> Educational research and development have repeatedly run aground in the fog of undefined goals. Long-range human goals, such as "happiness," "adjustment," or "equality," seem too remote from curriculum to be useful in educational planning. . . . Lack of an overall *effectiveness criterion*, therefore, makes it difficult to apply management science techniques in education.

Page proposes a method for reducing student profiles to single scores, in a unit known as the bentee, hoping to obtain a reasonably strong consensus of what constitutes sound education for the graduating high school senior. We then would be able to relate college inputs to output measured in bentees. Even with this more general unit of educational output, the same problem remains: What is the value of educational output measured upon completion of the educational experience in terms of subsequent success in life?

As with interest in the immediate effects of higher education, studies of the relationship between educational inputs and longer-run outputs, such as income or occupational status, are not recent phenomena. Donald Bridgman (1930) attempted to explain the success, defined as salary adjusted for number of years' experience, of American Telephone & Telegraph Company employees by their experiences in college. In general, he concludes that rank in class, campus achievements, and early graduations, in that order, are significant indices of success in the Bell system. He acknowledges that he had no control for individual ability. (It should be noted that some people use rank in class as a proxy for ability.)

Sometime later, in a classic study of superior high school graduates, Dael Wolfle & Joseph Smith (1956) observe that, although there were substantial geographic differences among three regions studied, within each region and for the three combined, those students who ranked closest to the top of their high school classes reported the largest annual incomes. In this study men are classified according to the education each received after finishing high school. The difference in income was greatest for the college graduates and less for those of lesser education. In a similar analysis, using scores on an intelligence test rather than rank in class, Wolfle & Smith find that for men of a given range of intelligence, incomes are higher for those who have more education. Among men with the same amount of education, higher incomes go to those who make higher scores on intelligence tests. The income differential associated with levels of intelligence, like that associated with high school rank, is smaller than the differences associated with varying amounts of education. Both sets of results from this study suggest an interaction between years of schooling and individual ability, measured by scores on IQ tests or rank in class.

Wolfle & Smith also use their sample to analyze the effect of father's occupation on the probability of entering a profession. They find that this variable has little effect. Among those who attain any particular academic level there is little relation between father's occupation and the percentage of the sample in the professions. Within each educational group, however, the sons of professional men have larger incomes than the sons of other men. They also find that college graduates are much more likely to be professional than those who are not graduates.

The studies by Bridgman and by Wolfle & Smith are limited due to the specificity of the samples, lack of data on important variables, and rather primitive statistical techniques (two by two classification tables rather than regression analysis). Nevertheless, they show at least the seeds of the kind of analysis that underlies current discussion of the relationships between educational inputs and outputs.

A very impressive study was the doctoral dissertation, done in 1963, by Shane Hunt (1963) at Yale University. Hunt's data was collected by the Time Survey, drawn from alumni records of nearly all the four-year colleges and universities in the United States and including college graduates of all ages. He used multivariate regression analysis to explain income of graduates by a constructed measure of ability from grades in college, extracurricular activities, socioeconomic background variables, years elapsed since graduation, and some purported measures of college quality, such as number of students enrolled and expenditures per pupil. Hunt finds the relationship between income and ability, experience, and size of college significant but sees less support for the argument that prestige of college affects income with individual student ability con-

trolled. Expenditures per pupil were a positive, relatively weak determinant of individual incomes. Hunt also examines interactions among
various of the income determinants by looking at cross-product terms.
His study brings into the discussion many of the qualifications and reser-
vations that are necessary when generalizing results from a microeconomic data set. The work is even more impressive when we realize
that almost all of the writings of the "human capital school" had not
appeared at the time this research was undertaken.

Following the fundamental work of Schultz (1963), Becker (1964),
and Mincer (1970), which established both theoretically and empirically
the concept of expenditures for education, health, etc., as investments
in human capital, a great outpouring of more or less sophisticated statistical studies analyzed income-generating functions, including measures
suggested by the human capital approach. These studies attempted to
find the extent to which the relationship between years of schooling
completed and income must be modified to account for the fact that
people with different numbers of years of schooling have different innate
abilities, family backgrounds, and quality of schools attended. Research
on these topics is reviewed by Dael Wolfle (pp. 65–74), but the papers
by Weisbrod & Karpoff (1968); Hines, Tweeten, & Redfern (1970);
Reed & Miller (1970); Daniere & Mechling (1970); Ashenfelter &
Mooney (1968); Hansen, Weisbrod, & Scanlon (1970); Morgan & David
(1963); and Rogers (1967) should be mentioned here. As Taubman
& Wales (1972) point out, each of these articles suffers from one or
more of these serious problems: poor measures of education and ability,
small and inadequate sample size, improper statistical technique, or too
specialized a sample from which to form generalizations.

However, several studies not subject to most of these criticisms have
appeared in the last year or so. Research by John Hause (1972),
Griliches & Mason (1972), and Taubman & Wales (1972) deserve a
more detailed analysis. At least part of each of these three studies uses
a sample of World War II veterans. Hence, scores on the Armed Forces
Qualifying Test (AFQT) are available for all members of the samples.
The Hause and Taubman & Wales sample (a group of white males
in the upper half of the ability distribution) was resurveyed in 1955
and 1969; the Griliches & Mason sample was followed up in 1964 and
is a less exclusive group.

If education and ability are positively associated, then a measure of
educational contribution to income that ignores the ability variable will
be biased upward. Griliches & Mason investigate the magnitude of this
bias by the estimation of income-generating equations containing mea-

sures of education without including ability and with it. The inclusion of ability leads to another bias due to the correlation of ability with the quality of schooling variable, which is not included. The new bias, partially a function of the magnitude of the correlation between quantity of schooling and ability, is solved by concentrating on that part of schooling occurring after or during military service. This turns out to be almost entirely uncorrelated with Griliches & Mason's measure of ability and, thus, not subject to this type of bias. Moreover, since the intelligence test available in their data was administered prior to entering service, performance on it cannot be affected by the schooling increment after military service

Griliches & Mason conclude that schooling is apparently of strong economic and statistical significance in the explanation of observed differences in income. Their results indicate a relatively low independent contribution of measured ability. Holding age, father's status, region of origin, length of military service, and the AFQT score constant, an additional year of schooling would add about 4.6 percent to income in their sample. At the same time, a 10 percent improvement in the AFQT score would add only about 1 percent to income. Paul Taubman (1972) criticizes the Griliches & Mason paper for several reasons. First, the authors do not attempt to discern any interactions among the various determinants of income. Second, the measure of IQ used apparently is not the optimal one, according to Taubman's own work.

The work by John Hause certainly cannot be charged with ignoring interaction effects between ability and schooling. Hause suggests two hypotheses to be considered empirically (1972, p. S111). First, schooling and ability have a significant complementary effect on earnings:

> Let us suppose that schooling is measured in time units and that the opportunity cost of foregone earnings is a significant part of the investment costs of schooling. The strong, positive relationship between schooling attainment and measured ability suggests that there is a greater incentive for persons of more ability to obtain more schooling. If the marginal products of ability and years are independent, it implies that people of low ability have a greater incentive to invest in schooling. The increase in earnings from an increment of schooling is the same for all, regardless of ability, but the foregone earnings are lower for those with less ability. This argument implies that the earnings function is misspecified, unless ability increases the marginal product of schooling. In fact, it requires that ability increase the marginal product of schooling on earnings rapidly enough to more than offset the rise in opportunity cost associated with higher ability up to the optimal level of schooling investment.

Hause's second hypothesis concerns the effect of ability over time on earnings for a given level of educational attainment. Hause argues that there is no tendency for the coefficient on ability to attenuate with time; there may well be a tendency for it to increase, especially at high levels of education. Behind this hypothesis lies the idea of more able people being more effective than the less able in raising productivity through job experience; that is, measured ability and learning in the labor force are complements in producing earnings.

Hause tests his hypotheses by looking at four different data samples, but we shall report here only the results from the National Bureau of Economic Research–Thorndike sample because it is also used by Taubman & Wales. Hause seeks interaction effects by running separate, within-schooling-level regressions and also by looking at cross-product terms for the pooled sample. With this pooled sample, Hause regresses 1969 earnings on background variables, the AFQT test scores, years of schooling, and the product of the test scores and years of schooling. Despite multicollinearity among these variables, the coefficient on the interactions term appears positive and significant, which supports the hypothesis that measured ability and educational attainment have significant complementarity. Hause's coefficients imply that the difference in earnings of college graduates with one degree who differ by one standard deviation in IQ is about $800, while the corresponding difference for high school graduates is $250. It is interesting that when a pooled regression is run using the log of 1969 income, the interaction coefficient is again positive, although not highly statistically significant. Hause attributes this to the intercorrelation of these variables. When either the linear years or ability term is dropped from the regression, the remaining two coefficients are highly significant. Why this difference should occur between the linear and log forms of income is not completely clear. By comparing earnings functions using 1969 earnings and 1955 earnings, Hause reveals an increasing role played by ability over time. Hause also argues that the overstatement of rates of return to a college education compared with high school, due to an understatement of ability-related opportunity costs, does not appear to be a serious source of bias if ability data are unavailable. Burton Weisbrod (1972) mainly criticizes the Hause paper for omitting an account of the differences in motivations among individuals in the sample. Weisbrod also raises the question of whether the ability measure used is the proper one.

Paul Taubman & Terence Wales (1972) go somewhat further in analyzing the relationship between attainment of higher education, mental ability, and earnings. They estimate earnings functions for two points in the individual's life cycle 14 years apart, testing for interactions among ability, school quality, and years attended, also looking for biases in the coefficient on years of schooling when ability is omitted. Taubman & Wales allege that mathematical ability, not IQ, is as important as education in explaining the range of earnings: The bias, when ability is omitted, is about 30–35 percent at various education levels for mathematical ability and only 9 percent for other types of mental ability. They also explain the low bias due to omission of an ability measure revealed in the Griliches & Mason paper by the fact that the latter used an improper measure of ability. The variance in results may also be due to the fact that Taubman & Wales use a sample of higher ability, and there is a positive interaction between ability and years of schooling. If average educational attainment in the Taubman & Wales sample is higher, we would expect the impact of ability to be higher as well as the bias from omitting ability to be greater. Finally, a detailed study of the other control variables (for example, socioeconomic background) used in the earnings functions in each paper would probably reveal other interactions and intercorrelations that would explain the direction of difference revealed by omitting ability.

To allow for nonlinear effects of ability, Taubman & Wales divide the variable into fifths, which they acknowledge may be closer to population tenths. They find that in 1955 those in the top fifth earned about 9 percent more, and those in the bottom fifth 8 percent less, than the average, while in 1969 the corresponding figures were 15 percent and minus 10 percent. Thus, over time, income of those in the top fifth has risen faster than the income of those on the lower end of the ability scale. For those in the middle fifths, the growth rate has been about the same as that of the average high school graduate in the sample.

Interestingly, Taubman & Wales find practically no evidence of any difference in the effect of ability at various education levels in 1955, although they do find some evidence in 1969 that those in the fourth, and to some extent fifth, ability groups who had graduate training received more income from ability than those at lower educational levels. However, ability is an important determinant of earnings even for high school graduates. They argue that Hause's findings of an interaction between ability and education is attributable to his selection of a restrictive functional form.

Taubman & Wales take a brief look at the effects of quality of schooling using a subjective academic rating known as the Gourman Index: At the "some college" and "BA" levels only, the highest quality fifth affects earnings significantly; for graduates, this is true for the top two undergraduate school fifths and the top graduate school fifth. Differences in income at a given educational level attributable to college quality effects appear to be very large.

Taubman & Wales also estimate the social rates of educational benefits. The most striking aspect of their results is the general decrease in the rates of return with increases in education, which hold even with adjustments for large, nonpecuniary rewards to elementary and secondary school teachers who are concentrated in the BA, some graduate, and Master's categories. Compared with high school graduates with the same abilities and background, the social rates of return realized in their sample (before deflation) are 14, 10, 7, 8, and 4 percent for two years of college only, an undergraduate degree, some graduate work, a Master's degree, and PhD. Rates of return calculated without standardizing for ability and background are generally about 20 percent higher.

So far the discussion has centered around research that tends to demonstrate that education increases incomes more or less. Why education performs this function has, nevertheless, been left unanswered. Finis Welch (1970) argues that in an era of rapidly changing technology, the more educated are more willing to innovate and to take risks. More simply, if a new type of tractor is invented, we cannot expect it to be used by an illiterate farmer who cannot read the operating instructions, whereas an educated farmer would more easily be able to adopt the new technology. This explanation, however, accounts for greater productivity of farmers or other individuals with some, versus no, education but does less to explain the productivity of general (liberal arts) higher education. Alternatives to the general argument claim that education produces additions to an individual's cognitive or effective skills that result in higher incomes.

A number of people have asserted that a primary educational role is to serve as a credential, particularly in highly paid managerial and professional occupations. As Taubman & Wales (1972) put it:

> To demonstrate that education is being used to screen people out of high-paying occupations, we must show that some people with low education are not in the occupation in which their marginal product and earnings are highest, but that highly educated people are allocated properly. If education is used to screen people, then the extra earnings a person receives from education are due both to the skills produced by schooling and to the income redistribution effect resulting from supply limitations. . . . There are several possible . . . [reasons why firms use education as a screening device] including snobbery and a mistaken belief in the true importance of education.

Taubman & Wales devise an ingenious test for the screening argument. By estimating the predicted occupational distributions by education levels (given ability and other attributes) and comparing that to the actual one, they find that people with less education are disproportionately underrepresented in high-paying occupations.

A number of other recent studies have supported the screening argument. Ivar Berg (1971) has done a series of tests that he argues confirm the screening argument as well. Berg observes that although the change in skill requirements between 1940 and 1965 for a large number of jobs was rather small, the educational requirements to be hired rose dramatically. There seems to be little relationship between changes in educational level and changes in output per worker. Thus, it appears that educational requirements have risen much more than skill requirements in a large number of occupations.

Screening may be consistent with profit-maximizing behavior, not merely the result of the (mistaken) belief that those with a degree are more productive. If successful performance in certain jobs depends upon an individual's possessing a set of skills identifiable only by expensive tests, firms might require a college degree if they believe that college graduates *on the average* (or are more likely to) have the desired skills. Thus, to save on hiring costs and mistakes on the job, firms use information on educational attainment, available at near-zero cost, as a preliminary screening device. The case for screening may be due either to market failure arising from lack of knowledge or to the high cost of obtaining knowledge. Of course, it might be profitable to some firms to acquire the testing mechanisms and properly ascertain the best people for certain jobs. They would then avoid the costs associated with screening by an indirect measure of productivity, namely, the college degree.

The screening argument says that employers are willing to pay more for more-educated rather than less-educated employees, even though their productivity differences do not warrant the extra pay or indeed extra occupational rank. In one way or another, these arguments rely on assertions of market imperfections. Why, then, don't some employers move into the breach and hire less-educated, but equally skilled, workers, at lower salaries and make greater profits? Perhaps the productivity is being improperly measured: The extra value of the more highly educated employees might not be recognizable as differences in physical output but might be present nevertheless; perhaps more-educated people generate "goodwill."

While economists have investigated the contribution of education, ability, and school quality to income, and even what makes education productive, sociologists have asked quite similar questions, concentrating more on the effects of background variables. Much of the work under the general supervision of Otis Dudley Duncan at the University of Michigan, William Sewell at the University of Wisconsin, and James Coleman at Johns Hopkins has attempted to explain differences in occupational status by well-conceived measures of family background (socioeconomic status), individual ability, and years of schooling. Apparently the correlation between occupational status and income is very high. According to Blau and Duncan (1967, p. 120):

> The multiple regression of percent "excellent" or "good" prestige ratings on the education and income measures was calculated. The multiple correlation, with the 45 occupations as units of observation, came out as .91, implying that five-sixths of the variation in aggregate prestige ratings was taken into account by the combination of the two socioeconomic variables.

There is a reference to the classic work of Blau and Duncan in the first sentence of each of the three papers that I cite explaining occupational status. The Blau and Duncan model begins with two variables describing the early stratification position of each person—his father's educational and occupational attainment status. It then moves to two behavioral variables—the education level of the individual and the prestige level of his first job. The dependent variable is the person's occupational prestige position somewhat later. The model accounts for about 26 percent of the variance in educational attainment, 33 percent of the variance in first job, and 42 percent of the variance in 1962 level of occupational attainment.

In two papers William H. Sewell and several (different) associates (1969, 1970) extend the original Blau and Duncan framework to apply social psychological concepts to the explanation of variation in levels of educational and occupational attainment. In particular, they add to the model measures of mental ability as well as measures of the influence of others on the individuals studied. Figure 1 presents the most likely of the causal linkages in the Sewell model. In it straight, solid lines stand for causal lines that are to be theoretically expected; dotted lines show possible, but theoretically debatable, causal lines; and curved lines represent unanalyzed correlations among variables that cannot be assigned causal priority in the present data. A more refined version of this diagram is presented in Sewell (1970) but, in general, the values of the coefficients are approximately as hypothesized in Figure 1.

Significant others' influence (SOI) is of central importance: SOI has direct effects on the level of educational and occupational aspirations, as well as educational attainment. In turn, each aspiration variable appears to have substantial effects on its respective attainment variable. Socioeconomic status affects SOI directly and measured ability affects it indirectly through an effect on the youth's academic performance. The variables used account for 34 percent of the variance in the level of occupational attainment and 50 percent of the variance in the levels of educational attainment. These R^2 are higher than those obtained in economists' earnings function estimates: Although we cannot account

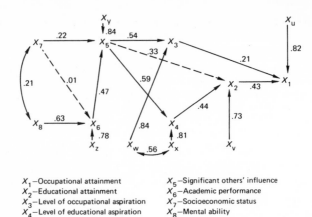

X_1—Occupational attainment X_5—Significant others' influence
X_2—Educational attainment X_6—Academic performance
X_3—Level of occupational aspiration X_7—Socioeconomic status
X_4—Level of educational aspiration X_8—Mental ability

Fig. 1. Path coefficients of antecedents of educational and occupational attainment levels. (From Sewell *et al.*, 1969, p. 85.) Reprinted by permission.

for occupational and educational attainment by a prescribed group of variables, translation of occupational status and education into dollars is a more uncertain procedure. Luck and other random events have a lot more to do with income earned than with education achieved or even occupation entered. Also, the background variables are better specified in the sociological studies.

It is interesting to note that if SOI is an important factor in occupational and educational attainment, external agents might intervene to change educational and occupational attainment levels. Clearly, SOI is a variable amenable to manipulation. The results also seem to indicate that aspirations are in fact performing mediation functions in transmitting anterior factors into subsequent behavior.

The Sewell data (1969) began with a survey of high school seniors in Wisconsin in 1957 but included only those who responded to a follow-up questionnaire in 1964, who were male, and whose fathers were farmers in 1957. This left under 1,000 cases. The standard question of how representative this sample is can be raised, but probably this should not worry us too much. This research was revised somewhat (Sewell *et al.*, 1970), using the more complete Wisconsin sample. The first study enters education as a variable, indicating whether the respondent had attended college. The second study uses a four-way classification—no post–high school education, vocational school, college attendance, and college graduation. The main difference in the second study is that for the revised model, educational attainment has a greater effect on occupational attainment, while the level of occupational aspirations has slightly less influence on occupational attainment. Of course this is probably due to the more precise measure of educational attainment; certainly a more refined education variable would have had even more power.

The two Sewell papers add significantly to the knowledge regarding the role of variables that mediate between such predetermined variables as social-class origins and measured ability and such outcome variables as educational and occupational status attainments. However, other variables contribute only moderately to occupational attainment, which suggests that additional research is needed to find other influences on occupational status. Perhaps factors tied to the person's marital status might help. These have proved significant in the economists' earnings functions.

The second paper confirms the critical role of SOI in the status attainment process, but also points out effects of academic performance on aspirational and attainment variables not mediated by SOI. The later research also looks at the model, broken down by type of residence, and demonstrates that this has been found appropriate for young men from a variety of urban and rural residential backgrounds. However, the model's adequacy for very large cities needs to be established. Finally, it should be noted that no women and only a very small number of blacks are included in this sample.

The work by Coleman, Blum, & Sorensen (1971) attempts to explore the relationship between the status of the first full-time occupation held by a male and his occupation 10 years later. They focus on intervening labor-force experience as well as on events in other realms of the individual's life, in particular, at differences in black and white occupational changes.

Regressions to explain first-job status show several things. First, for both blacks and whites, the respondents' educational attainment far outweighs all else. Second, education is more effective for job status for whites than for blacks. The increment of occupational status associated with a unit increase in educational attainment is almost twice as great for whites as for blacks. Thus, blacks suffer educationally in two ways: Their level of educational attainment is lower; and a unit increase in educational attainment shows less than half the benefits in occupational status it brings for whites. Coleman *et al.* acknowledge that the quality of education available to the two groups has been quite different. Most of the effect of parental background takes place through educational attainment, rather than apart from it. However, for both blacks and whites, the occupational status of the father shows some independent effect. The authors also attribute some of the differences between blacks and whites to discrimination; in this case, race is used as a screening device rather than (or in addition to) the use of college graduation, as alleged by Taubman and Wales and by Berg.

In their analysis, the authors find a correlation of .506 for whites and .395 for blacks between first-job status and status of job held 10 years later. Interestingly, a striking number of variables have a larger zero-order correlation to second job for whites and a smaller one for blacks. Family background, represented by father's occupational status, is still quite important for job growth for whites but much less so for blacks. The major effects are from first-job status and educational attainment, with the latter much more powerful.

The evidence that the effects of certain characteristics persist or become even stronger 10 years after entering the labor force is consistent with the human capital theory of income determination (Mincer, 1970). All factors bearing on an individual's potential for income or occupational status do not come into play as soon as that individual enters the labor force. Many people forego occupational status or income when accepting a first job, particularly in order to obtain further training on the job. If the more qualified individuals forego this income status, then it is only after a number of years, when returns—not only to the factors possessed when entering the labor force but also to on-the-job training—take effect, that the true differentials in occupational status or income will be realized.

Coleman *et al.* examine factors intervening between status of the first job and of the later job; additional educational activity constitutes the most important of these. For whites, occupational activities are second, while for blacks it is the events in the marital and family sphere. This greater importance of the marital sphere is suggested by two results: the strong relationship of first-job status to wife's education; and the greater contribution to explained variance by a set of marital and family variables. Intervening events seem to have a greater effect in terms of occupational status for blacks than for whites, although background factors show greater efficacy for whites. The dominance of educational attainment in influencing occupational status does not preclude the possibility that parental background exercises a major indirect effect through its effects on the educational level. However, its direct effects are not great.

In assessing the differential impact of education levels and other background characteristics, it is possible to determine the proportion of the overall difference in initial status level due to different levels of background resources and that due to different efficacy of resources in establishing occupational status. Results indicate that 58 percent of the observed status difference between blacks and whites is due to differences in the levels of background resources brought to the labor market, and

32.5 percent is due to differences in the efficacy of these resources in producing high occupational status. The analysis of later-job status shows that, whereas the initial status difference between the two groups was 5.59 status units, it has widened to 10.95 units by the end of 10 years. Approximately half of the difference in status change is due to the differences in the levels of resources and status-bearing activities. About half the difference in latter-job status is unexplained, either by different levels or by different efficacy of those resources measured. Perhaps on-the-job investment might be helpful to consider here.

Otis Dudley Duncan (1969) helped direct sociologists to the use of income as the dependent variable when he asked, in 1968, whether black–white income differences were due to inheritance of poverty or inheritance of race. He estimated different path and regression coefficients for blacks and whites, concluding that the Negro had a double handicap. First, the Negro typically begins the life cycle with characteristics that would be a disadvantage to anyone, white or Negro—specifically, low levels of parental socioeconomic status. Second, achievements at subsequent stages of the life cycle cannot be capitalized on as readily. This is consistent with the Coleman results above. Duncan observes that the black–white income gap was $3,790, of which family background differentials account for just one quarter, $940. The disadvantage to Negroes of having a large number of siblings provides a handicap that, if eliminated, would increase income by $70 per annum. Furthermore, the educational gap accounts for $520 of the $3,790 difference actually observed, less than one seventh. Of course, this measures education in number of years rather than in terms of some quality-adjusted unit. All these variables account for 12.0 of the 23.8-point occupational gap, attributing roughly half of it to educational differences, family size, and family background. The remaining 11.8 points are not otherwise explained by the model, and Duncan labels the amount "occupational discrimination." This converts to $830 or one fifth of the total dollar gap. Occupational discrimination is due to the fact that Negroes as well educated as whites and originating in families of comparable size and socioeconomic level do not have access to employment of equal occupational status. However, a difference of $1,430 remains between Negro and white incomes. This cannot be attributed to differential occupational levels, differential educational attainment, differences in family size, or socioeconomic status thereof. Duncan calls it "income discrimination," and he concludes that inheritance of poverty is less important than discrimination per se. Duncan does not worry about incorporating school-quality variables because, he argues, they would be related to years of education attained.

Duncan also claims that about one quarter of the gap in mental ability scores is attributable to Negro–white differences in family socioeconomic level and number of children. The remaining three quarters of the gap must be derived from other factors that can, perhaps, be summed up as differential mental development. Although the introduction of mental ability into the model allows us to account almost fully for the educational gap, the same is not true with regard to occupation and earnings. Thus, Duncan concludes that discrimination still explains a large part of black–white income differentials.

Samuel Bowles (1972) recently argued that the relatively small explanatory power of socioeconomic background is due to improper measurement. Moreover, he questions studies that seem to show that extra schooling exerts a major effect upon earnings or occupational status independent of the social-class background of the individual. Bowles points out that the misspecification of socioeconomic status is due to the omission of parental income or wealth; the usual measures of occupational status come from father's occupational status and father's education.

Bowles's study [using the same data as Blau & Duncan (1967), from a U.S. Census Survey] reveals that family background measures explain 52 percent of the variance of years of schooling obtained by the respondent. Also, years of schooling attained appears to significantly determine earnings of the members of his sample. This partial relationship of schooling to income, with socioeconomic background controlled, is less than 60 percent as large as the gross return indicated by the simple relationship between the two variables. Bowles thus concludes that much of the apparent economic return to schooling is, in fact, a return to socioeconomic background. Moreover, the variance of earnings explained by social background variables alone is only slightly less than that explained by these variables along with educational attainment of the respondent. Apparently, years of schooling attained exerts a comparatively minor influence on earnings, independent of social background.

The Bowles results are unusual primarily because of his different measure of socioeconomic status. However, there is clearly a high correlation between the traditional measures of socioeconomic status—namely, the father's educational attainment and occupational status—and family wealth. Moreover, the R^2 obtained by Bowles is not much greater than that obtained in the traditional earnings functions in which occupational status and educational attainment of the father are used.

Becker (1972) acknowledges that family background is one of the most difficult variables to measure, since it is based on student recall of earlier parental conditions. However, properly measured family background may increase *or* decrease the power of other variables. Becker feels that Bowles has overstated the effect of background compared to own education by referring to the addition to R^2 when education is added after family background. Sociologists have argued that this is a legitimate test, since background did occur *before* schooling. Bowles ignores effects of postschool investment and, in particular, its positive correlation with years of formal schooling.

Becker also points out that a major effect of family background comes through a mother's preschool and other nonschool investments in her children. Mother's education probably is more important than father's in influencing productivity of children. Also, a wealthy home facilitates financing of foregone earnings and other school costs.

Robert Hauser *et al.* (1971) have recently attempted to relate socioeconomic background and the earnings of high school graduates, using the Wisconsin sample noted above. Occupational status now has an intermediate position. Consistent with the human capital theory and the results from the Coleman study, Hauser observes an increasing stabilization of earnings capacity with respect both to social background and to one's own educational and occupational achievements with increasing labor-force experience. The authors find that the effect of education on income is reduced by 19 percent when ability is entered as an additional explanatory variable. This is more in line with the conclusion of Taubman & Wales than that of Griliches & Mason. Hauser *et al.* compare their results with those using other data sets and find the interpretation of the education, occupational status, and earnings relationship is quite similar. They also test and confirm the validity of their assumption of a linear model.

It will be worthwhile at this point to summarize the results of the most complete model used in Hauser *et al.*'s study:

> Each socioeconomic background variable (related to the mother and to the father) has a modest direct effect on ability while ability has a large effect on educational attainment. The direct effects of each background variable on educational attainment are essentially equal in size and about as large as their effects on ability. Educational attainment has a very large direct effect on occupational status, which is also directly influenced by father's occupational status and by ability. That is, students with equal educational credentials are slightly better off in the job market if they are unusually bright or if their fathers had unusually good jobs. However, mother's and father's educational attainments and incomes have no influence on one's occupational achievement beyond their influence on ability and educational attainment. Finally, in the determination of earnings, ability and educational attainment have modest and roughly equal effects while the effects of occupational status and parental income, also roughly equal in size, are about twice as large as those of ability and educational attainment.

The authors emphasize the effect of parental income on earnings of young men: It is as large as the effect of their achieved occupational status. Their important finding of direct social inheritance of earnings capacity is consistent with the finding from the Bowles study. The family confers a modest economic advantage or disadvantage, independent of ability, educational attainment, or occupational achievement.

Father's education is apparently an important determinant of a child's schooling. However, the use of income as the final dependent variable in the path analysis has revealed the greater power of parents' income as a direct determinant of child's income. Recent work has elucidated the proper roles of various aspects of family socioeconomic background.

In summary, we might assert that many economists and sociologists have sought answers to the same question: How can we explain later-life success (and differences in success) by education, individual ability, and background considerations? Perhaps sociologists have worried more about the exact nature and specification of the background factors while economists have investigated the proper role to be attributed to investments in human capital as represented by formal schooling. In general, they have attempted to unravel the interrelationships between the three sets of important variables. Throughout this review, it has been obvious that investment in schooling has generally been measured by years completed, though occasionally there is a reference to the fact that different returns to different amounts of schooling might rest on quality of schooling. A few studies attempting to calculate educational quality have used student change evident immediately on leaving college as output measures. One further extension of this kind of analysis is the introduction of precise measures of school quality into the earnings relationship. This will be discussed later in "The Definition and Impact of School Quality" (pp. 77–102).

REFERENCES

Ashenfelter, O., & Mooney, J. D. Graduate education, ability and earnings. *The Review of Economics and Statistics*, 1968, 50(1): 78–86.

Astin, A. W. Undergraduate achievement and institutional "excellence." *Science*, 1968, 161: 661–668.

Becker, G. S. *Human capital, a theoretical and empirical analysis, with special reference to education*. New York: National Bureau of Economic Research, 1964 (General Series, No. 80).

Becker, G. S. Comment on S. Bowles, Schooling and inequality from generation to generation, *Journal of Political Economy*, 1972, 80(3, Pt. 2): S252–S255.

Berg, I. *Education and jobs: The great training robbery*. Boston: Beacon Press, 1971.

Berls, R. H. An exploration of the determinants of effectiveness in higher education. *The economics and financing of higher education in the United States*. Submitted to the Joint Economic Committee, U.S. Congress. 91st Congress, 1st session, 1969.

Blau, P. M., & Duncan, O. D. *The American occupational structure.* New York: Wiley, 1967.

Bowles, S. Schooling and inequality from generation to generation. *Journal of Political Economy,* 1972, 80(3, Pt. 2): S219–251.

Bridgman, D. S. Success in college and business. *The Personnel Journal,* 1930, 9(1): 1–19.

Centra, J. A., & Rock, D. College environments and student academic achievement. *American Education Research Journal,* 1971, 8(4): 623–634.

Coleman, J. S., Blum, Z. D., & Sørensen, A. B. *Occupational status changes for whites and blacks during the first ten years of occupational experience.* (Rev. ed.) Baltimore: The Johns Hopkins University Center for Social Organization of Schools, Report No. 76, October 1971.

Daniere, A., & Mechling, J. Direct marginal productivity of college education in relation to college aptitude of students and production costs of institutions. *The Journal of Human Resources,* 1970, 5(1): 51–70.

Duncan, O. D. Inheritance of poverty or inheritance of race? In D. P. Moynihan (Ed.), *On understanding poverty: Perspectives from the social sciences.* New York: Basic Books, 1969.

Griliches, Z., & Mason, W. M. Education, income and ability. *Journal of Political Economy,* 1972, 80(3, Pt. 2): S74–S103.

Hansen, W. L., Weisbrod, B. A., & Scanlon, W. J. Schooling and earnings of low achievers. *American Economics Review,* 1970, 60: 409–418.

Hanushek, E. A. *Education and race—An analysis of the educational production process.* Lexington, Mass.: Heath Lexington, 1972.

Hause, J. C. Earnings profile: Ability and schooling. *Journal of Political Economy,* 1972, 80(3, Pt. 2): S108–S138.

Hauser, R. M., Lutterman, K. G., & Sewell, W. H. Socioeconomic background and the earnings of high school graduates. Paper presented at the meeting of the American Sociological Association, Denver, August 1971.

Heist, P. *et al.* Personality and scholarship. *Science,* 10 February 1961, 133(3450): 362–367.

Hines, F., Tweeten, L., & Redfern, M. Social and private rates of return to investment in schooling by race-sex groups and regions. *The Journal of Human Resources,* 1970, 5(3): 318–340.

Hunt, S. J. Income determinants for college graduates and the return to educational investment. *Yale Economic Essays,* 1963, 3(2): 305–357.

Mincer, J. The distribution of labor incomes: A survey with special reference to the human capital approach. *Journal of Economic Literature,* 1970, 8: 1–26.

Morgan, J. N., & David, M. H. Education and income. *Quarterly Journal of Economics,* 1963, 77(3): 423–437.

Page, E. B. Seeking a measure of general educational advancement: The bentee. *Journal of Educational Measurement,* 1972, 9(1): 33–43.

Reed, R. H., & Miller, H. P. Some determinants of the variation in earnings for college men. *The Journal of Human Resources,* 1970, 5: 177–190.

Rogers, D. C. *Private rates of return to education in the United States: A case study.* New Haven: Yale University Press, 1967.

Schultz, T. W. *The economic value of education.* New York: Columbia University Press, 1963.

Sewell, W. H., Haller, A. O., & Ohlendorf, G. O. The educational and early occupational status achievement process: Replication and revision. *American Sociological Review,* 1970, 35: 1014–1027.

Sewell, W. H., Haller, A. O., & Portes, A. The educational and early occupational attainment process. *American Sociological Review,* 1969, 34: 82–92.

Taubman, P. J. Comment on Z. Griliches & W. M. Mason, Education, income and ability. *Journal of Political Economy,* 1972, 80(3, Pt. 2): S104–S107.

Taubman, P. J., & Wales, T. Earnings: Higher education, mental ability and screening. Unpublished manuscript, University of Pennsylvania, 1972.

Weisbrod, B. A. Comment on J. C. Hause, Earnings profile: Ability and schooling. *Journal of Political Economy,* 1972, 80(3, Pt. 2): S139–S141.

Weisbrod, B. A., & Karpoff, P. Monetary returns to college education, student ability, and college quality. *The Review of Economics and Statistics,* 1968, 50(4): 491–497.

Welch, F. Education in production. *Journal of Political Economy,* 1970, 78(1): S35–S59.

Welch, F. Black–white differences in returns to schooling. Unpublished manuscript, National Bureau of Economic Research, 1972.

Wolfle, D., & Smith, J. G. The occupational value of education for superior high-school graduates. *Journal of Higher Education,* 1956, 27(4): 201–212, 232.

DOES COLLEGE MAKE A PERSON HEALTHY AND WISE?

A Social–Psychiatric Overview of Research in Higher Education

Anne Ellison and Bennett Simon

Introduction

This review of the literature on what college is supposed to do for students includes our own comments about our sense of what the research does show, what it purports to show, and areas that have not been sufficiently emphasized. We are not writing from the vantage point of investigators who have labored for many years in the vineyards of educational research but rather as neophytes. What we have read is, in large part, by way of background and preparation for a particular small-scale research endeavor at MIT—a project on students who chose an experimental curriculum. We have drawn heavily on sources and digests that are widely available, such as Feldman & Newcomb's *The Impact of College on Students* (1969), as well as the results of research done by others at MIT over the past 10 or so years. All of this is a slightly roundabout way of saying that we are not presenting a definitive "review of the literature" but rather a view of what people coming to this literature from the outside might encounter.

We will describe in some detail a particular framework of development

and maturation that seems to inform much of the research on what
happens to people who go through college. This framework is made
most explicit in works such as Chickering's *Education and Identity*
(1969) but seems to us to be the prevailing paradigm in research on
college. The paradigm is a kind of distillate and composite of notions
drawn from several interrelated and overlapping sources:

1. Eric Erikson (on the steps in late-adolescent development), as
   well as several other psychoanalytic writers
2. Carl Rogers, with the themes of "self-actualization"
3. Personality theories and studies closely associated with the work
   of Henry Murray
4. Those who developed the concept of *The Authoritarian Personality*
   and the F-scale
5. Twentieth-century statements (such as are to be found in many
   college catalogues) as to the values of a liberal arts education,
   values that have a long history in our culture—for example, So-
   crates' "The unexamined life is not worth living"

A particular test instrument, the Omnibus Personality Inventory (OPI)
(Heist & Yonge, 1968), is the embodiment of these notions and has
been extensively used in the research we are summarizing.

It should be noted, too, that the most intensive work using (and
refining) this model (and to some extent this particular test instrument)
is associated with schools such as Vassar, Harvard, Princeton, Berkeley,
MIT, Haverford, and some smaller innovative schools such as Goddard
College. While we are in general impressed with the overall import
of the studies that have utilized this model, we do wish to point out
certain possible shortcomings, biases, and built-in value statements. These
all may limit what kinds of changes in personal development an investigator can discover and accordingly place some constraints on the value
of this research for large-scale policy recommendations.

Another general consideration that will appear throughout this review
is exemplified in Feldman & Newcomb's section "Problems in Adjusting
for Student Inputs When Explaining Student Outcomes" (1969, pp.
359–364). It is an issue that has occupied a number of serious workers
in this area. Astin (1968) and others, from the perspective of predicting
outcome, have attempted to tease apart the influence of precollege characteristics of students from the influences of college characteristics.
Needless to say, this task has proven extremely difficult. Even if we
turn to studies that attempt to control for initial input characteristics
by using matched groups of college attenders versus nonattenders, there
is a serious methodological difficulty: Some crucial undetected variables

that affect personality change in college may be the same variables that determine whether or not the student will attend college. This general problem imposes a sort of "ceiling" on what inferences can be drawn about the value of college, particularly when it comes to planning policy changes.

Background Characteristics of College Attenders

Much of what is summarized in this section, by way of factual finding, is drawn from the study by Trent & Medsker (1968) of 10,000 students who graduated from high school in 1959 and were followed for the next four years. The work comprises, as far as we can determine, the only major study that compares large numbers of students who went to college with others who did not and, at the same time, goes beyond surface description. We will also address the issues—with several illustrative examples of research on family background and child-rearing behavior—as to how far back in the life of the individual one can go to understand the determinants of what makes people go to college.

Of the Trent & Medsker study group of 10,000, 40 percent entered college, and 60 percent did not. The two major variables determining choice to attend were: (a) academic ability and achievement (as measured by College Board scores) and (b) socioeconomic status. Socioeconomic status appears more important: Large numbers (for example, 40 percent) of the highest two fifths on ability scales did not attend college; these nonattenders were primarily from lower socioeconomic status groups. From the high socioeconomic status level, 60 percent of the lowest two fifths in ability went to college. From the low socioeconomic status level, only 40 percent of the two fifths with highest ability went to college.

Another example of the action of these two variables can be seen in a 1957 study summarized by Feldman & Newcomb (1969) on the relative percentages of men and women attending college. The lower the socioeconomic status, the smaller is the percentage of women (relative to the percentage of men) who will attend college. As ability levels increase, the percentage of both women and men attending increase, but the increase is proportionally greater for men. [More recent data (Andre Daniere, "Economics of Education: The Changing Scene," pp. 365–379), however, indicate that there has been a dramatic increase in the numbers and percentages of students from lower socioeconomic classes attending college, as well as a marked increase in the numbers (and percentages) of women from all socioeconomic classes. How stable these changes will be, particularly in the face of some economic adversity, remains to be seen.]

Overall, the data point to the interrelation of socioeconomic status and of parental educational levels, of how both are associated with an atmosphere of encouragement and support for higher education. Mother's education level, as in a number of other studies, seems particularly important and holds equal importance as a factor with father's occupation. Holding father's occupation constant, the mother's attendance at college is an important determinant of the child's going to college.* Other important findings, consistent with the importance of socioeconomic status and parental education show:

1. For attenders (compared to nonattenders) a view of education as worthwhile in and of itself, apart from practical (vocational and monetary) gains;
2. Strong academic motivation—for example, a decision to go to college is made before entering high school.

There are differences between the college attenders and nonattenders on the personality inventory scales (principally, certain subscales of the Omnibus Personality Inventory) that purport to measure "personal autonomy" and nonauthoritarian disposition. However, these differences are not striking, even at the outset. The two groups, however, diverge considerably on these scales after four years of college with the non-college group remaining static in their scores and the college group showing substantial increases.

Trent & Medsker examined the background characteristics of the subgroup that showed the most dramatic positive gains on the personality tests. Most of these were college attenders, but some were not (the "Exceptional Change Group"). Three factors (based on questionnaires) distinguish this group: (a) parents' education level; (b) students' level of academic "aptitude" (College Board Scores); and (c) liberality of religious orientation in the home.

Interviews with students bring out a clearer notion of what is entailed in these questionnaire findings. These show a general home atmosphere of autonomy for individual members and excitement about and interest in sharing enriching intellectual experiences. Exceptional changes are strongly associated with choosing to attend college and with persisting through four years of college, but there are some important deviations from this pattern. Though socioeconomic level is important and is highly correlated with the motivational aspects of going to college, to some extent motivational factors have a life of their own. Thus, in a later

* This is consonant, for example, with a report by Kagan & Moss (1962) that mother's *education level* correlates more highly than the mother's IQ with the child's IQ.

study by Trent (1970), it is found that if socioeconomic status is held constant, those who drop out of college for "financial reasons" often do not utilize available financial resources such as loans. Their peers who stay in school take the trouble to investigate and to follow through on procuring loans. Similarly, lower socioeconomic status students who choose college seem to utilize teachers and guidance counselors more than do the nonattenders.

These last considerations agree with what we know of individual students who have come from lower social and economic backgrounds, been reasonably bright, but outstanding in the degree to which they have plugged away, persisted, and gotten a good education. It is important to know more about these people, their inner resources, their family background, and their interactions with potentially helpful people, such as teachers and advisors, in their life. One case, sketched below, is presented in detail by Stanley King (in press).

A young man lived in a small town in a northern Plains state. Both parents (his father had emigrated from Eastern Europe and become a farmer and small retailer) died during his early adolescence. The boy did not shine academically but was a star baseball player. He had, in addition, a family of older brothers and sisters who gave him much love and support both before and after the deaths of the parents. A businessman in the town, a Harvard alumnus, thought the boy had a good deal of personal spark and academic potential. Eventually this businessman (and others) paid his way to a year at private boarding school and continued to encourage him, morally and financially, to go to Harvard. The further details of the case are instructive, including the boy's path through college. A combination of happenstance and the young man's personal (and apparently personable) traits helped him get a rich educational opportunity and effectively utilize his talents.

On a larger scale, the Trent & Medsker study of "exceptional changes" shows that by going to college, the emotionally rich get richer. Those with family backgrounds most characterized by autonomy, liberality, and flexibility of thinking change more often, and to a greater extent, than those with more impoverished family backgrounds.

The question of what, or what kind of, college students choose is an important one. Trent & Medsker's work, as well as other studies, suggest that the same factors that tend to discriminate between college attendance and nonattendance also discriminate between those who go to more "prestigious" (or academically superior) schools and those who choose less prestigious schools. Higher socioeconomic class, in concert with higher parental levels of education, is associated with a student's higher educational aspirations (and his achieving them). Numerous other "decisions" about education tend to conform to the same pattern, for example, the decision to concentrate in an intellectually more prestigious field or one more practically oriented, or to go to graduate school or not. In our own studies of the characteristics of students who choose an experimental program compared to students who express interest but choose the regular curriculum, we have come across similar findings: some differences in socioeconomic class and marked differences in parental education, particularly a higher level of mother's education in the group choosing the experimental program.

After four years, the general level of dissatisfaction with their lives was very high for the nonattenders. A large percentage were unhappy in their vocational life, and many showed a continued lack of realism about vocational success. The jobs they wanted, for example, required *education,* and they seemed to ignore or minimize this fact. Probably the subgroup of nonattenders who showed the least degree of personality growth (and scored high on dissatisfaction) were the women who did not attend college, who married and had children within the four-year study period.

The issue of what goes on in the families of children who go to college, and who seem to profit from the experience, is a crucial and complex one. Two pieces of work that have come to our attention are important in that they illustrate the complexities of research in this area and at the same time utilize interesting and potentially fruitful methods of research.

The first is a study by Strodtbeck (1958) dating from the mid-1950s. He attempted to study the relationship between family characteristics and academic achievement in high school in two subgroups—Jews and Italians. An important part of the study was a home visit, with a family interview, plus a task that the family had to work out jointly during the course of the home visit. Father, mother, and son had to discuss and reconcile different answers that they gave (as individuals) on a questionnaire. The investigators focused on the *allocation of power* in the course of these discussions. What emerged was that the Jewish families were characterized by a greater willingness of the parents to share authority and that the Jewish children were by far greater achievers academically. The willingness to share power, to the extent that it appeared in the Italian families, was associated there, too, with higher academic achievement. Another important observation is that the value statements of the children in respect to questions about outlook on life (for example, "planning only makes a person unhappy since your plans hardly ever work out anyhow") correlated much more highly with the actual power relations in the family than they did with the stated values of the parents. If the father disagreed with that statement, but consistently overrode his son's opinions and decisions, the son was more likely to agree with the sentence. Though we have not consulted this literature in detail, there appears to be a body of work by McClelland and associates (1953) on the relation between child-rearing practices and later achievement motivation.

In this connection, a second study, by Kagan & Moss (1962), though not designed with any special educational research purpose, contains some rich and suggestive data. The work is a part of (and a summary of) a longitudinal study of some 70 children at the Fels Institute. The group was studied in detail by a variety of observations, interviews, and test measures from birth until midadolescence. There were detailed narrative summaries of the child at home, with parents, and at school. They were reexamined as young adults (in their twenties), and certain correlations appeared between earlier behavior trends and their adult investment in achievement recognition, particularly intellectuality.

Some of their conclusions are quite fascinating:

1. Achievement behavior (for both boys and girls) was rather stable behavior from childhood to adulthood (from age three up), but especially stable from six up. This is in contrast to patterns for passivity, dependency, and aggression, which were subject to many more changes and vicissitudes throughout the course of life.
2. Intellectual competence and general achievement behavior were highly correlated with parental education level.
3. Mastery behavior and persistence at age-appropriate tasks between zero and three years showed no relation to parental education level and no correlation to later achievement and intellectual behavior.
4. Behavior and school performance (as well as positive changes in IQ during the first few school years) were powerful predictors of adult intellectual behaviors and dispositions.
5. In particular, the IQ of boys at age 10 was a more reliable predictor than the IQ at age 6. The boys with more desire to master intellectual skills gained in IQ from 6 to 10. The same predictive difference did not occur for girls whose IQ's remained much more stable from 6 to 10. (The children were all of average or above-average IQ's.) This suggests that boys are subject to greater achievement pressures between 6 and 10 than are girls (though other hypotheses are possible too).
6. For boys, fear of bodily harm, childhood fearfulness, and dislike of athletics were positively correlated with high intellectual in-

volvement as adults. This relation did not obtain for girls. For girls, the traits of fearlessness, independence, and open competitiveness were correlated with adult intellectual achievement. The authors argue that the high-achieving boys and girls did not adopt their traditional sex-role attitudes and behaviors: "It may be that intense involvement in intellectual activity is facilitated by a weak identification with the traditional sex-role values of the majority peer group, (p. 145)."*

7. Other important correlates (or predictors) of achievement were the patterns of mother's treatment of the child. (This study in general had virtually no data on father's interaction with the child.) For boys, the pattern most likely to lead to involvement in intellectual achievement was early maternal overprotectiveness (from zero to 3 years), followed by encouragement and acceleration of mastery behaviors from 3 to 6 and 6 to 10. For girls, the pattern was different, with maternal "hostility" (though not of any extreme variety) during ages zero to 3 and acceleration of behavior during 3 to 6 and 6 to 10. In general these factors were not as weighty predictors as was parental educational level.

There were other behavioral concomitants of these patterns, which are of great interest but cannot be discussed here. These kinds of data ultimately need to be fitted together with a psychoanalytically oriented study of children with psychogenic learning difficulties. Thus, boys from 6 to 10 have many times more learning difficulties (for example, reading) than do girls. Their clinical descriptions seem to be consonant, oddly enough, with the picture (in Kagan & Moss) of the *intellectually achieving* boys. The overlap and the subtle factors that may lead, in one instance, to the mastery of castration anxiety through intellectuality, and, in the other, to the inhibition of intellectuality by castration anxiety, constitute an important area of investigation. (One study of boys with reading difficulties demonstrates a characteristic family constellation—a mother with greater interest in reading and intellectual matters than the father. The boy seems torn in his identifications.) A later study, also emanating from the Fels Institute (Crandall & Battle, 1970), carried this work much further and developed a much more detailed and refined kind of examination of the notion of "achievement." Particularly interesting is the distinction they drew between "academic achievement effort," i.e., the motivation to do well at school work, and "intellectual achieve-

---

* From a psychoanalytic perspective, the description of the boys could reflect an intense struggle with aggression and castration anxiety with the high achievers utilizing intellectual competence as a way of establishing their sense of male integrity.

ment effort," the motivation to learn, solve problems, and satisfy curiosity. Their operational definitions of these terms are quite complex, and the original work must be consulted. But, applying these criteria to the group of young adults, they found surprisingly little overlap between the groups characterized by being high (or low) on each of their parameters. Then they traced out (using methods somewhat similar to those of Kagan & Moss) the childhood antecedents of these two classes of motivation. On the whole, though the results are quite intricate and not reducible to a few formulas, the outcome did justify the original distinction. For example, boys who rated high on "academic achievement" were, as in the Kagan & Moss study, more prone to anxiety about rough and tumble, competitive sports. However, the opposite was true for the "intellectual effort" boy; he seemed to enjoy and flourish in such activities. Again, there were numerous developmental differences between boys and girls, although the "academic achievement" boys and girls resembled each other more than did the "intellectual achievement" boys and girls. The work of Crandall & Battle has the additional virtue of calling attention to the need to specify the varieties of *achievement* motivations in real life, although even their distinctions between intellectual and academic are inadequate. Again, these data are introduced here mainly to illustrate the nuances and subtleties that may underlie the motivational and skill factors later entering into the decision to go to college and the ability to profit from that decision. They also suggest the complexity of interplay among socioeconomic status, family styles, and individual motivation.

The Strodtbeck study (1958), the Kagan & Moss study (1962), and that of Crandall & Battle (1970) also raise the issue of where should one focus investigative efforts in the attempt to understand the development of academic motivation. Shall we begin with the Exodus from Egypt, the Flood, Genesis, or pre-Genesis? At what juncture in the life of the child are various interventions that may tip the balance most feasible, most productive, and most economical? Here, too, a potpourri of interventions—insuring adequate maternal nutrition and prenatal care, teaching the "new math," or enriching the kinds of counseling available in high school—are all potentially relevant and not incompatible with each other. But some are surely more relevant than others.

Changes Attributable to College Attendance

MEASUREMENT OF CHANGE

The measurement of change that takes place in college is not without methodological difficulties, as Feldman & Newcomb (1969) so ably point out. Individual changes are often lost when data are presented in the form of group means, obscuring the fact that individual diversity in change exists. Aside from the statistical problems of adjusting for inputs in the "before and after" designs frequently employed (since practical difficulties usually preclude experimental control), there is the problem of deciding what input variables to measure and control for. These have frequently been simply the variable being examined for change and the important variables of socioeconomic status and ability level. It seems reasonable, however, that subtle background and motivational factors, as we stressed above, also interact with college environments to produce the changes that occur over the college years. Although obviously "not everything can be controlled for," there is enough diversity in the changes in characteristics of college students to suggest that a more detailed investigation of the interactions of personality, motivational, and background characteristics would yield worthwhile and useful information. For example, in Trent & Medsker's (1968) study of change in social maturity as measured by an OPI scale, college attenders show a substantially larger mean increase in social maturity than nonattenders. Yet on closer examination, a fairly large number of individuals attending college show a decrease in social maturity. Trent & Medsker had sufficiently rich background data and interview information available about the students to suggest many of the additional parameters correlated with the decrease. From these they were able to construct a modal portrait of the type of individual involved. But, in general, "close-up" information of this sort about important features of change is not available.

Another problem arises when individual changes—either in students within a given group or in subgroups (such as types of institution) within a larger group—are being studied. The unreliability of scores measuring change, whether simple difference scores or more sophisticated statistical measures, is notorious and has been discussed considerably in the statistical literature (Bereiter, 1963; Finnie, 1970). This immediately limits the validity of individual change scores and causes difficulty when one attempts to examine associated factors. It also could crop up as a difficulty in follow-up studies on the persistence of change in college students.

We are not suggesting that these well-known difficulties are cause for derogating the interest in studies of change that have been carried out. But it does seem that consideration of individual diversity (in extent and especially in direction) of change and the methodological and statistical problems involved are in themselves reasons for supplementing and validating such studies with other methods. These would include interviews, participant–observation in the anthropological style, home visits, and questionnaires designed to elicit information about the change *process*. Some additional reasons for such studies will be discussed later in this section.

CHANGE IN COLLEGE

Measured change during college has centered around such parameters as achievement, "intellectual disposition," values, attitudes, interpersonal skills, and "maturity." There is the necessity, of course, of translating these concepts into some operational measure. Although this has been done in different ways, our general impression is that a surprisingly small number of test instruments have been consistently used and reused to measure a particular dimension. The OPI, for example, has almost taken on a self-perpetuating "life of its own" in education research. There are advantages to using the same standardized, validated test instrument in a number of different studies: economy and cross comparability of studies. However, there may also be difficulties:

1. When little or no change in college in a given area is found, it is not really possible to determine whether this reflects absence of true change or the inadequacy of the measuring instrument as a means of investigating the area of concern.
2. Although many of the test instruments used have been standardized on a given population, the diversity (and increasing diversity) of the college population today calls into question whether test results are actually comparable across different groups (males/ females, minorities/nonminorities, different socioeconomic levels). It is not clear *a priori* that these tests are equally appropriate for these different groups in face validity, or in capturing relevant detectors of change for a particular group, or are even identical for different groups. B. Snyder and associates (1967), in a study of change on OPI scales in the MIT student population over a four-year period, felt it important to validate the meaning of the OPI scales for this rather narrow population, using data from interview studies of some of the respondents (Snyder, 1967; Hockman *et al.*, 1967).

Colleges and universities might certainly be expected to contribute significantly to intellectual change in attending students, although "intellectual change" clearly covers a broad spectrum—from acquisition of specific skills through cognitive styles to more nebulously defined changes in "intellectual orientation and disposition." Scales from the OPI have been frequently employed in these studies. One important and representative example is found in the Trent & Medsker analysis of college attenders and nonattenders, which showed consistent, statistically significant—but small—advantages in changes on the thinking introversion and complexity scales for the college attenders. College attenders also showed a greater increase in the estheticism scale. Reports of activities and interests (browsing in bookstores, concert attendance, reading) that would be likely to attend changes in intellectual disposition distinguished the groups, but not always to the extent expected by the investigators. Feldman & Newcomb report (1969) that in a study of self-reports of changes in college, students seldom voluntarily mentioned changes in intellectual orientation.

In general, then, the findings tend to support the expectation that college will produce intellectual changes, but the reported changes are rather small.

A study by Perry (1968) takes a very different approach to intellectual change in college. He used interviews and a questionnaire to examine stages in development from "absolutist" to "relativistic" thinking (a dimension that bears some overlap and resemblance to the intellectual aspects of parameters variously described as "autonomy" and "nonauthoritarianism"). The emphasis was not on the percentage of students who "scored higher" (indeed, none reached the "highest" stage of development hypothesized) but rather on the sequence of their progress that facilitated or impeded movement from one stage to another and various "escape" routes through which a student could temporize, retreat, or avoid further change. Further work that would attempt to replicate this type of study and extend it to other areas of concern might be particularly germane to issues of how to teach and the development of diverse curricula.

Another dimension of change is in the area referred to variously as "nonauthoritarianism," "liberalism," and "autonomy." The F-scale and scales of the OPI have been used frequently to measure changes on this trait (or constellation of traits). What actually is being measured, however, is somewhat difficult to define. The F-scale is well-known to be a complex measure of personality and cognitive styles and specific content of beliefs. Although other indices attempt to measure personality and cognitive styles independent of ideological content, it seems that it is difficult (if not impossible) to avoid measuring change in specific content of beliefs as well. For example, in redefining the OPI scales used in their study of MIT students, Hockman et al. (1967, p. 13) describe the *autonomy* scale partly as follows:

> The Autonomy scale presents a series of simplistic, conformist statements on politics, sex, family life, and morals. High scorers will reject the majority

of items on this scale. Low scorers on this scale appear to have an uncritical attitude toward traditional morality with overtones of acceptance of the ethic of hard work, determination and ambition. . . .

The *nonauthoritarianism* scale, used by Trent & Medsker (1968), is said to be a refinement of the F-scale, measuring "independence and freedom from authoritarianism and opinionated thinking," while the *social maturity* scale measures "different dimensions of autonomy, openness, flexibility, as well as some cultural interests."

As Feldman & Newcomb (1969) point out, it is on scales such as these, complex as they may be, that one finds the largest and most consistent changes with college attendance. The students in the Snyder study show larger changes on the autonomy scale than on any of the other OPI scales employed; moreover, this was the only OPI scale that suggested a unidirectional tendency to change when individual student's scores were analyzed. Trent & Medsker's study points out large changes for college attenders on both the nonauthoritarianism and the social maturity scales: On the nonauthoritarianism scale, college attenders increased their scores, while nonattenders actually decreased. On the social maturity scale, all persons studied increased, but college attenders increased their scores very much more than nonattenders.

In the same study, the degree of change on the scales showed very little relationship to type of college attended (as measured by a rather rough classification), once student input characteristics had been controlled for. Once *in* college, change seemed associated mainly with *persisting* in college attendance. Students who withdrew from college resembled the nonattenders more closely than the persisters.

The question has been raised as to whether change on such scales represents true development in personality traits or attitudes or whether it represents merely superficial change in "sophistication" and knowledge of "social desirability." More research clearly needs to be done on the meaning of such variation, its relationship to behavior, and on the process by which change takes place. Perry's work (1968) suggests that perhaps changes in "sophistication" and knowledge of "social desirability" of some test responses could be viewed, not as failure in "true" attitude change, but rather as a stage in the internalization of attitudes, through which some persons may pass and others not.

Some of the other changes that take place in college attenders include increased aesthetic interests, increased complexity of thinking, increased religious tolerance and decreased religiosity, decreased political naïveté, increased impulse expression (as measured by the impulse expression scale of the OPI), decreased stereotypy of sex-typed interests, and realistic setting of goals and aspirations. In general, the Trent &

Medsker study demonstrates that personality development is more likely to take place in college persisters, followed by withdrawals, then by employed youths (male and female nonattenders). Women who become homemakers immediately after leaving high school, who experience neither college nor employment in the four years after graduation, show the greatest constriction of personality development.

WITHDRAWALS FROM COLLEGE

It seems that large (and perhaps increasing) numbers of students choose not to continue their education in college, or at least in the college at which they began their studies. In the light of the general finding that college attenders do profit, the question arises as to why students drop out and what happens to them as a result.

In Trent & Medsker's study (1967), "drop-outs" from college generally show a constriction in personality development relative to college persisters; in background characteristics they resemble nonattenders more than persisters (for example, they come from less-privileged socioeconomic backgrounds). The future drop-outs, however, score slightly higher than the persisters on the complexity scale of the OPI, although the differences are not statistically significant. At the end of four years, the mean complexity score of the persisters increases and that of the withdrawals decreases, so that their relative positions are reversed.

This latter finding is interesting in light of studies of withdrawals in narrower segments of the college population. Snyder (1967) and Hockman et al. (1967) find that students scoring high as freshmen on the thinking introversion, impulse expression, and especially the complexity scale of the OPI are more likely to leave MIT before graduating than the low scorers. Chickering (1969) presents data countering the suggestion that this is a phenomenon restricted to "elitist" institutions. The same pattern is found in 13 small "project" colleges. These findings suggest that the "creative, complex, independent student leaves more frequently than his more conforming and controlled counterpart" (Chickering, 1969, p. 304). Most interesting, this effect is related to the student's position on the scales *relative* to the student body of the college in which he or she is enrolled. That is, within each college, the leavers score higher than the stayers, even though in absolute terms the entire student body might score low or high on the average. The relevant frame of reference seems to be the college attended.

If the most creative, complex individuals tend to withdraw from their college, what is their fate? Many undoubtedly do transfer to another institution or later return to their original institution. But we do not really know what happens to those who withdraw and do not return to college. There is a depressing hint in the Trent & Medsker data that, as a group, these people tend to lose ground relative to their college counterparts, but we do not know how this applies to individuals within the group, or how they fare with respect to their original college reference group.

A number of studies (King, 1970; King & Blaine, 1971) suggest that college drop-outs show a higher incidence of use of the college psychiatric service than non-drop-outs. This finding is difficult to interpret in the sense that it is not clear what is implied about the students' "mental health." Snyder and his associates (1967, p. 92) find that MIT students visiting the psychiatric service score higher as freshmen on certain OPI scales such as social maturity and anxiety. The anxiety scale, they feel, has to be interpreted partly in terms of willingness to admit an awareness of anxiety, as well as existence of manifest anxiety. They also find a different pattern in the timing of visits to the psychiatric clinic among students in different subjects, corresponding to "critical periods" in the student's career (for example, taking a course meant to weed out potential majors from nonmajors.) Physics students who visited the clinic were most likely to do so in the seventh semester, while for civil engineering it was the fifth. In other words, many of the visits corresponded in time to dissonances within the students' immediate academic environment. The OPI results suggest that many of the students visiting the clinic may be more in touch with their anxiety and "less willing to go along with the system."

An analogy from a study by Jerome Frank (1963) of the effectiveness of psychotherapy suggests a hypothesis about the difference between drop-outs and non-drop-outs. In the study, both patients in treatment and patients on a waiting list improved the more they expanded their use of outside helping resources (friends, clergymen), although this happened in the psychotherapy group to a far greater extent than it did in the waiting-list group. In other words, psychotherapy seemed to be effective insofar as it served as a catalyst for people to use effectively the resources (in this case, sources of help) in the environment about them. College may serve a similar function. On the student's part, the mere availability of the environment and models may be insufficient; he must be able (and willing) to *engage* the environment and to *use* the models. "Dropping out" may reflect a deficiency in this area. (Of course this may be a function of the student or of the fit between the student and the environment.)

It is interesting to note that in Perry's study (1968) of Harvard students (in which the dimension studied—"relativistic thinking"—is presumably highly encouraged by the environment, with many role models available), students who first conform rather passively to the external demands of the environment later show the greatest gain in autonomous relativistic thinking, while students who become alienated, in the sense of showing an earlier appearance of "autonomy," eventually show less development.

Trent & Medsker's study supports the notion that students who withdraw engage their environment (and especially helping resources within it) less than persisters do. They are less likely to seek counseling, financial and housing aid, vocational guidance, occupational placement, and faculty advice (although students in general make relatively little use of the resources). Bright withdrawals tend to use faculty advice rather than to go to the counseling service when they do seek help, while the opposite holds true for bright persisters.

THE "MODAL" MODEL OF COLLEGE CHANGE

Underlying the choice of study areas is a "modal" model of what ought to take place in college—a model that epitomizes the values of traditional liberal arts education. This model is exemplified in Chickering's *Education and Identity* (1969), which emphasizes the following areas:

1. Achieving competence (intellectual, physical and manual, social and interpersonal) and a sense of competence
2. Managing emotions, for example, learning appropriate expression and control especially of sexual and aggressive feelings, learning to perceive accurately the emotions of self and others
3. Becoming autonomous and emotionally independent, that is, shifting from reliance on others to self; developing instrumental independence, for example, learning to cope with problems by oneself; and recognizing and developing a mature interdependence with others
4. Establishing identity—"an inner sameness and continuity"—including an awareness of one's strengths and weaknesses, and clarification of sexual identification
5. Freeing interpersonal relationships, including developing a tolerance for a wide range of persons and responding to people in their own right rather than as stereotypes.
6. Clarifying purposes, including vocational plans, avocational and recreational interests, and general lifestyle considerations, and integration of various aspects of plans
7. Developing integrity and a personally valid set of beliefs; achievement of congruent behavior

This model clearly points to important facets of personality development and has engendered a number of important and interesting studies. However, the model shows certain shortcomings as *the* primary paradigm for education, and there are several areas where these shortcomings might be remedied.

First, there appears in general to be a "fit" between the model and the types of empirical change found in college students. Thus, social maturity, nonauthoritarianism, autonomy, complexity, etc., epitomize the values of the model. In addition, change on these dimensions has been found to be greatest in certain prestigious institutions, to which, in turn, investigators have devoted the most intensive study. Thus, there may be a built-in bias in the model.

Although many excellent studies have been carried out, it seems that even within the context of the model, a richer picture of the changes that take place could be obtained. It is clearly important to determine whether change takes place *in* college; the extensive use of the "before and after design" and questionnaires, however, frequently leaves the reader with the feeling that "nothing happens" in the period between. Studies of the process of change, whether through observation of behavior, interviews, participant observation, or experimental situations, may provide more information about the effective college variables and the way they interact with different kinds of students. In addition, referring again to Perry's study (1968), certain changes are more subtle and represent a "stage" in development that may not show up as change at the level of conceptualization represented in the questionnaire.

This approach would also be helpful in validating scales for different populations (for some groups, tests may not be appropriate at all and may miss entirely the changes that are taking place, even on the underlying dimension being studied), in "fleshing out" the rather sparse operational definitions of the model provided by the scales, and in allowing the investigator to uncover areas of change that were outside his original set of hypotheses (both within and outside the modal model).

The model itself has a rather melioristic tone. Based on concepts of "self-realization," "growth," and "adaptation," it tends to minimize areas of unpleasantness, stress, and crisis in development in college.

In terms of specific content areas, there seem to be striking omissions in the model. For example, both the model and an overview of recent literature (for example, Sanford, 1962; Chickering, 1969; Trent & Medsker, 1968; Feldman & Newcomb, 1969) omit almost entirely any reference to competition. The few references that exist are vague and innocuous, referring to "good competitors" in athletics and "preparing for a competitive society." What underlies this tendency to ignore a widespread fact of college life is not clear. Some indirect evidence of an effect of competition comes from a study reported by Feldman & Newcomb, which shows that academic self-esteem, the student's estimate of his or her ability, tends to be relatively low at more select institutions. (The pass/fail system of grading during the freshman year at MIT, for instance, was instituted partly to try to eliminate the shock to self-esteem when a thousand bright, achieving freshmen suddenly found themselves rated comparatively with their peers.) We wonder what cognitive dissonance students experience who have adopted the model as the appropriate one as they are confronted by the competitive race of their instructors for tenure and publication. (See Snyder, 1971.) The literature of the 1950s is franker, with its many references to need-achievement, and so on. Similarly, there are few references in the education literature to the traits related to persuasion and influence on other people, even though these have been studied in more detail by social psychologists. A notable example is Christie & Geis's *Studies in Machiavellianism* (1970).

The model is obviously a normative one; one may surmise that traits felt to be undesirable are omitted. There is a notable lack of study on the "less desirable" aspects of college life—no mention of cheating, for example, even though term-paper "mills" flourish to the extent that recently a Harvard dean decided to stop using term papers as a basis for grades. An exception is a study by Finnie (1970) of Harvard students. He examined a number of variables not usually studied: "Aggressive heterosexuality" (stealing other people's girls, ditching dates, etc.) showed a consistent decline over a four-year period, and militarism (a militaristic, as opposed to cooperative or idealistic, stance toward one's conduct in international affairs to avoid war) showed an increase over four years.

A strong value judgment is involved, however, if the development of such traits is judged to be an unnecessary or negative outcome of education. We do not know their value for the individual or for society. What is most surprising is the avoidance of reference to and study of even the most "cleaned-up" positive aspects of such traits—the ability to accept success, fairly won, or to persuade others to accept one's point of view. M. Horner's work (1969, 1970) suggests that many women (and some men as well), high in need-achievement, are handicapped by an inability to compete and win, resulting in their performing considerably below their ability level. A common problem in the psychotherapy of college students with academic inhibitions is making the student conscious of the full extent of his rivalrous and competitive feelings.

In summary, the model both seems to omit certain features of the coarser reality of the college experience, while perhaps implying negative value judgments about traits whose actual values are mixed, or uncertain. The empirical study of such changes in college and concomitant features of the college environment have been sold short.

Finally, we would like to draw attention to one more feature of educational research that has been carried out within the framework of the model: Factors or trends that have culminated in rather dramatic changes in the aims and activities of segments (at least) of the college population have been missed. Amid the studies of development and maturation, the rise of student activism (and sometimes violence), the drug scene, the development of the counter culture—the emphasis on Eastern philosophy, meditation, etc.—seem to be unexplained and unexpected occurrences. In our studies of students, we have come across examples of behavior that do not fit very readily into the modal model: a conversion to fundamentalist increased religiosity, associated with dramatic changes in the direction of maturity; or fervent interest in the "objectivist" philosophy of Ayn Rand and "new rightist" politics (Simon & Ellison, 1972).

Impact of Different Colleges

All of the major trends described in the preceding section that are associated with college attendance are more strongly associated with some types of schools than others. To state the contrast in bold terms, changes in the OPI scales for maturity, nonauthoritarianism, and complexity of thinking are of a much larger magnitude at an academically superior, small, liberal arts college with relatively permissive administration and flexible curriculum than at a church-affiliated, explicitly religious, vocationally oriented, administratively strict and rigid school, with fixed curriculum.

It appears that students entering these two extreme types of school already show considerable difference in their OPI scores. In general, the larger the initial scores, the greater the change from freshman to senior years. This kind of comparison naturally leads to the quest for more precise definition of what it is in each school that influences the magnitude and direction of the change.

The implications of this kind of study have been explored and elaborated by Chickering (1969). His discussion heavily emphasizes the attitudes and values that characterize each school. One can, as Astin (1968) has done, pay much more detailed attention to the explicit activities and behaviors that constitute the student's day-to-day environment. His classificatory schemes (based on factor analyses of student reports of their own activities) afford the opportunity for rich and varied studies relating college characteristics to the changes in the students. Astin's analyses, combined with observations that attempt to capture something of the atmosphere of the school, can yield a vivid picture of what forces make for student growth or lack of growth.

In this context, we wish to emphasize the enormous importance of actual observation, and of participant observation, of the day-to-day school environment. At MIT, the work of Snyder, Kahne, and Parlett in this area is of considerable interest. For example, one of the investigators sat in on a freshman physics recital section for a semester (10 students and 1 instructor). He was generally appalled by the small amount of discussion among the members of the group. It was particularly striking that, for six months, the instructor—a graduate student—never called the students by name and vice versa; the students did not know if the instructor was "Mr.," "Doctor," or "Joe," and the instructor did not know whether to call the students by their first or last name—and no one asked (Kahne, 1967).

Such an observation says, for one thing, that size alone does not make for impersonality, nor smallness for intimacy. Rather, a confluence of forces (involving, for example, undue sensitivity to academic rank) can make for a dehumanizing experience in the classroom.

Conversely, observations of this sort may document and explain important and useful changes that take place in students who attend less prestigious institutions. In the first place, the usual practice of presenting questionnaire and change scores in the form of group means per college tends to obscure, as Feldman & Newcomb (1969) have pointed out, the considerable overlap among institutions in terms of initial scores of entering students and amount and direction of change. If the diversity of individual change is great (and it seems to be), there is probably considerable overlap between the amount of gain in personality development shown in more and less prestigious institutions.

Secondly, there is some reason to believe that "modal-model"-induced research (especially high reliance on OPI tests) may be missing change that does take place at some less prestigious institutions. It may be that such tests are simply less appropriate measures of the dimensions of interest for some student populations. Or it may be that the model neglects or deemphasizes certain dimensions of change (for example, training for a specific vocation) that take place at such institutions.

In addition, the sheer *availability* of some of the less prestigious institutions may determine part of their impact. As Feldman & Newcomb point out, students of lower-status backgrounds are more likely than students of higher-status backgrounds to focus on costs, location, and practical considerations in choosing a college. In homes in which continuing education is not discussed or encouraged, and where there is little knowledge of the prestigious institutions, the existence of a nearby, low-cost institution may be a factor in a student's motivation to attend college. [Proximity was found in Trent & Medsker's study (1968) to be an important determinant of college selection for most students.]

Another interesting point is relevant here. In most of the studies of the impact of different colleges, the absolute level of student input and college characteristics is related to student outcome. However, for several important variables, there is evidence that scores *relative* to the norm for each particular institution are effective in producing particular outcomes. There are, in general, large casualty rates for students scoring high on certain OPI scales, but as Chickering (1969) reports, this holds true not merely for prestigious institutions, whose student populations have high OPI scores, but also for less prestigious institutions whose mean OPI scores are considerably lower. In each, the individuals scoring high *relative* to their institution are more likely to leave, whatever their absolute score. Feldman & Newcomb report that students' estimates of their scholastic ability and academic self-esteem seem to be negatively related to selectivity of institutions and intelligence of the student body. Other studies (also reported by Feldman & Newcomb) suggest that relative standing in one's class is more predictive of type of future career than is an interuniversity comparison of intellectual ability.

Persistence of Change

The question of the persistence of the changes that take place during college is the most crucial; yet it is the one for which we have the least satisfactory answers. In large measure, the difficulty of obtaining meaningful information is tied up with all the problems of doing longitudinal studies. There are few that reexamine the same subjects 10, 20, or 30 years out of college. Studying the persistence of change in college students requires persistence of *unchanging* interests and dedication of the investigators over the years—an unusual occurrence. Or else, the investigator must train several generations of graduate students to carry on his work. Perhaps the most difficult job is to select those variables the research is to follow. One must build this selection into the design of the original research and expect that 30 years later it will still be meaningful and interesting (either to the same or to future investigators).

There are comparable problems of longevity and persistence of interest on the part of the subjects of the study. There is the issue of volunteer effects and the possibility, if not the likelihood, that those continuing to participate represent a group with a more positive and satisfying experience, both in college and since graduation, who have felt a loyalty both to the school and the values it represented. One investigation (which entailed interviewing, psychological tests, and repeated questionnaires over an eight-year follow-up) had roughly an 85 percent return on any one item mailed out to the group and an even higher overall persistence in the project as a whole. Rossett et al. (1966) comment: "Involvement in this study was a group phenomenon, anchored in their loyalty to the dean of admissions, one of the investigators."

Newcomb et al.'s 25-year follow-up study (1967) of political attitudes in Bennington students (discussed in detail below) also had a relatively high percentage of participation in its various tests (94 percent of those alumnae with known addresses). Much in their report indicates a high degree of *cohesiveness* among the graduates over the years and loyalty to the college. There was, in addition, a correlation between the number of years spent in the college and the percentage of questionnaires returned. This is the one study that documents an enormous degree of stability in the changes wrought by college.

The studies summarized in our two main sources (Freedman, 1962; Feldman & Newcomb, 1969) do not yield any simple or consistent conclusions. A few salient findings and conclusions and some of our own reflections about this problem are summarized below.

We know of no studies that assess longitudinally the factual knowledge—either general knowledge level, or retest of specific content studied in college—of college graduates. Our highly subjective estimate is that the half-life of most factual knowledge and course-specific skills is of the order of several months (perhaps even several days, if acquired entirely by cramming), unless the knowledge was more or less directly utilized in the postcollege work career. Does the lack of study in this area indicate some "agreement"—among both researchers and alumni— that the factual knowledge studied is simply not important? In one study of alumni actual course content was not rated high on questionnaire scales of "what was most important to you in college." On the other hand, Sanford (1962, p. 849) suggests that a large percentage of graduates, while pleased they had gone to college, were dissatisfied with the curriculum they had chosen. (We do not know the details of why they were dissatisfied.) Because so much energy is devoted in college to ingesting (and doubtfully digesting) large chunks of knowledge, this tacit dismissal of its long-term importance should be aired and acknowledged by faculty and administrators.

We wish to distinguish two separate aspects of thinking that might be expected to undergo change in college. "Cognitive style" refers to the kind of thinking assumed to be involved in various tests that demand the subject organize ambiguous perceptual or cognitive material. Some examples are Witkins' field independent/field dependent dichotomy, people who respond more physiognomically than geometrically to visual stimuli, and perceptual "levellers" versus "sharpeners" (see Rossett *et al.*, 1966, 1972, on predicting engineers' choice of work). These are probably rather stable traits of the person, affecting both the conflictual and conflict-free spheres of operation. They are well established by late adolescence and are probably not susceptible to much change. (They are also probably useful predictors of future occupational preferences.) "Complexity of thinking," on the other hand, covers tolerance for ambiguity in thinking, pleasure in tackling complicated thought problems, and ability to see shades of gray (see the preceding section). As far as we can tell, there is no firm available data in this area. Our guess is that these changes do persist, though the social support of others who "think complexly" is quite important.

Insofar as "values" can be divorced from ideological content, several studies suggest a general association between being a college graduate and being more tolerant of diversity, more willing to allow for variety and flexibility in society as a whole, and more supporting of civil liberties. We suspect these changes are of fluctuating stability, especially in times of crisis. (During the McCarthy era, according to one report, opinion among college graduates moved toward the more restrictive, less tolerant, and the more fearful.) However, the evidence is difficult to interpret.

There is evidently a drift in political and social ideology through college towards more liberality and, to some extent, "left-wing" ideology. ("Radical" would hardly be an appropriate description of most graduates.) Here, too, it is difficult to make general statements about persistence. The study of Newcomb *et al.* (1967) of Bennington students, 25 years after college, demonstrates, in brief, the following:

1. An important shift in political ideology—from conservative or middle-of-the-road Republican to Roosevelt Democrat or some explicit left-wing ideology—took place for many of the girls between their freshman and senior years at Bennington. The changes were documented for girls in all fields of study in the college, whereas a study of men at Williams College showed comparable changes only for those in political science.
2. Twenty-five years later, most of these women continued to hold

to values, beliefs, voting behavior, and political activity commensurate with the values they held as seniors. Some women did change from their senior position, but more changed from conservative to liberal than from liberal to conservative. The Bennington alumnae resembled other Bennington alumnae more than they resembled their own sisters and sisters-in-law who had not attended Bennington.

3. These women did not, on the whole, maintain their ideas in a social vacuum but lived (and chose to live) in a social nexus that affirmed, supported, and rewarded their liberal political views. They married men with comparable beliefs (some of these men were brothers of other Bennington alumnae), maintained contact with other Bennington alumnae, their classmates, and with the college.

4. In attempting to compare the Bennington of the thirties with the Bennington of the sixties, the authors found a more heterogeneous student culture in the sixties with the existence of several "deviant" subgroups. One of these, "the collegiates," went against the mainstream of Bennington values—intellectuality, unconventionality, and liberal political values. They seemed more oriented towards social- and high-prestige marriages than the typical Bennington student. They lived with each other and generally supported each other in their common "deviancy." Though there is yet no long-term follow-up on these girls, it would be valuable to trace the fate of their values and their social relationships over a period of years.

Apropos of this last point, there has been very little study of the details of the position of the student within the college subcultures and the subsequent persistence of "college-induced" changes. Similarly, there is virtually no information correlating personal student characteristics during college with long-term results of the college experience. The one study that stands out in this area [part of the Mellon Foundation study of Vassar (Sanford, 1956)] divided students into five categories: social peer-group orientation (girls who were "socially," not academically, oriented); overachievers; underachievers with high family (that is, *future* family) orientation; high achievers; and seekers of identity. These subgroups had different fates over the years since graduation. "The family-oriented underachievers are most alert and alive intellectually twenty years after graduation. The overachievers, the better students in a formal scholastic sense, have stagnated intellectually" (Freedman, 1962, p. 883). Similarly, more detailed follow-ups are needed that examine the relationship between the diverse kinds of college experiences and the later life patterns of their alumni.

The evidence on the relationship between level of education and richness of fantasy life is moot (Singer, 1966, pp. 60–61):

> One might speculate that persons of limited education or lower socioeconomic status may be stimulated by television or movies to envision romantic fulfillment without, however, any awareness of the intermediate steps necessary for such goal attainments. In contrast, the middle-class youth whose life is often structured from an early age in terms of series of linked subgoals, may demonstrate a more realistic type of fantasy content. . . .

There is some evidence that lower-socioeconomic, poorly educated Negro youths show initially very high fantasy goals, which then seem to prove frustrating and form the basis for a bitterness and despair. In contrast, higher education may stimulate fantasy but provide a realistic sense of means–end relationships and afford the wherewithal to achieve these goals. Finally, there is the finding of Kinsey that education and socioeconomic class are associated with different patterns of sexual life: The more educated report more fantasy and more sexual foreplay as integral parts of their sexual enjoyment.

For all intents and purposes, there are no data directly bearing on the question, "Does a college education have any effect on 'mental health'?" However, three kinds of work have some relevance (or potential relevance) to this admittedly nebulous area.

First, there are now several long-term, follow-up studies of populations of college students who were followed from the perspective of mental health and the success of their adaptation and coping in later life (Cox, 1970; Vaillant, 1972). The original design of these studies did not include a noncollege control group nor a detailed study of the college experience. Also, these students were selected on the basis of their competence, health, and well-roundedness (in the eyes of the college staff). Review of these studies may provide some valuable suggestions for the design of subsequent long-term, follow-up studies of "college and mental health." Such studies should not focus on "Does college increase mental health?" but on understanding what it is that college provides, or fails to provide, that may facilitate or impede adequate coping with emotional distress.

Second, in general, lower socioeconomic status, particularly extreme poverty, is strongly associated with a higher incidence of the more severe and more crippling varieties of mental illness (major psychoses, serious psychosomatic disease, alcoholism, addiction, etc.). It would be of great value to understand the pathways by which rising socioeconomic status is related to new potential and new opportunities for coping with inner turmoil.

Third, Adorno *et al.* (1950), as part of their study of the authoritarian personality, investigated whether there is a correlation between diagnosis and severity of psychopathology and score on the F-scale. Their results indicate no such clear-cut correlation but rather one between score on the F-scale and "style" of psychopathology. Those who were less authoritarian were more verbal, more psychologically minded, and more interested in talking as a means of treatment. The more authoritarian tended to express their difficulties in somatic language and hypochondriachal form and seemed less attuned to verbal psychotherapy. One effect of college education evidently could be such a shift in "style" of psychopathology, though this has not been explicitly studied as such. Education also is associated with the social and economic means for getting more "sophisticated" forms of treatment (verbal psychotherapies) rather than somatic therapies, such as electric shock and reliance on drugs. It remains to be seen how much this picture alters as psychiatric treatment becomes more available to all sectors of the population.

Finally, we wish to point to other omissions in the area of "persistence" of change. There are, first of all, important aspects of personal and interpersonal behavior that have not been adequately or systematically studied. *A fortiori*, the persistence of these traits—courage; qualities of effective leadership and of fellowship; "Machiavellian" skills; competitive skills (in a "socially acceptable" sense) and cutthroat types of behavior; the capacity to exploit intellectual style and intellectual jargon to rationalize, to deceive, and be deceived; the capacity to relate to fellow citizens of very different economic, social, and educational backgrounds—cannot be studied. Second, to speak of "persistence of change," without specifying the various contexts in which people live and work, is patently absurd. It makes no more sense than to talk of the changes that take place in college without reference to the variety of colleges and the variety of subcultures within any one college. We have to devote much more attention to understanding the requirements, in terms of aptitudes and values, of the different work situations available to college graduates. Engineering, law, medicine, small business, big business, etc., all make very different demands, and within each of these areas there are many different kinds of activities. We must also see what possibilities these different work environments have for the individual or the small group to change the situation and conditions of their work. In this context, it would be important to follow and study the efforts of that small percentage of college graduates who are attempting to organize communes, both for living and working. Perhaps more naturalistic and participant–observer studies of school and work situations could enlarge our understanding of the interaction of individual and environment and, in turn, enlarge the boundaries of what are to be considered relevant behavioral variables. It might be especially fruitful to follow those individuals who do not go to college for four consecutive years but rather experience some mixture of work and college (drop-outs who return; people who have attended, or will attend, "open universities" and "universities without walls," etc.) and trace their paths of change. It is not clear that 18–22 is the ideal age for all individuals to obtain the maximum benefits from college and the maximum durability of the positive changes occurring in college. It is also important to obtain more detailed information, by means of longitudinal studies, of the careers of people who do *not* attend college. This is another part of the need to identify those features of work experience that can promote growth and can form the basis of recommendations for change.

Concluding Cautionary Comments

We have summarized our reading of the contemporary college educational research literature. Sobered by the difficulties of our own research efforts, we appreciate the enormousness of the task of making accurate and meaningful statements about the behavior of students, let alone the behavior of colleges. We are even more respectful of the chasm between research conclusions and recommendations for policy change. It is fair to say that policy changes in this field will always have to be made on the basis of incomplete and outdated information. If anything, we have made a plea for broadening the base of what should be considered relevant and important in assessing the outcome of college education. We realize that what we have discussed serves to complicate, rather than simplify, the task of predicting and planning seemingly desirable changes. If that conclusion is too depressing, let us remember that one of the major goals of a college education should be to increase our tolerance for the complexities and ambiguities of human beings as they are.

REFERENCES

Adorno, T. W., *et al. The authoritarian personality*. New York: Harper and Bros., 1950.

Astin, A. W. *The college environment*. Washington, D.C.: American Council on Education, 1968.

Bereiter, C. Some persisting dilemmas in the measurement of change. In C. W. Harris (Ed.), *Problems of measuring change*. Madison: University of Wisconsin Press, 1963.

Chickering, A. W. *Education and identity*. San Francisco: Jossey-Bass, 1969.

Christie, R., & Geis, F. L. *Studies in Machiavellianism*. New York: Academic Press, 1970.

Crandall, V. C., & Battle, E. S. The antecedents and adult correlates of academic and intellectual achievement effort. In J. P. Hill (Ed.), *Minnesota symposium on child psychology*, Vol. 4. Minneapolis: University of Minnesota Press, 1970.

Cox, R. C. *Youth into maturity*. New York: Mental Health Materials Center, 1970.

Feldman, K. A., & Newcomb, T. M. *The impact of college on students*. San Francisco: Jossey-Bass, 1969.

Finnie, B. The statistical assessment of personality change. In J. M. Whiteley & H. Z. Sprandel (Eds.), *The growth and development of college students*. Student Personnel Series, American College Personnel Association, 1970 (No. 12).

Frank, J. *Persuasion and healing, a comparative study of psychotherapy*. New York: Schocken Books, 1963.

Freedman, M. Studies of college alumnae. In N. Sanford (Ed.), *The American college*. New York: Wiley, 1962.

Heist, P., & Yonge, G. *Omnibus personality inventory manual*. Washington, D.C.: The Psychological Corporation, 1968.

Hockman, E., Kahne, M. J., & Partlett, M. Omnibus personality inventory: Appraisal and report of findings. Massachusetts Institute of Technology student adaptation study. Unpublished manuscript, Education Research Center, MIT, 1967.

Horner, M. S. Fail: Bright women. *Psychology Today*, 1969, 3(6): 36–38, 62.

Horner, M. S. The psychological significance of success in competitive achievement situations: A threat as well as a promise. Unpublished manuscript, Harvard University, 1970.

Kagan, J., & Moss, H. A. *Birth to maturity: A study in psychological development*. New York: Wiley, 1962.

Kahne, M. J. Psychiatric observer in the classroom. *Medical Trial Technique Quarterly*, 1967, 15: 81–98.

King, S. H. The clinical assessment of change. In J. M. Whiteley & H. Z. Sprandel (Eds.), *The growth and development of college students*. Student Personnel Series, American College Personnel Association, 1970 (No. 12).

King, S. H. *Personality change during college: Lives of Harvard men*. Cambridge: Harvard University Press, in press.

King, S. H., & Blaine, G. B. The psychiatry of young adults—Normal and abnormal. *Psychiatric Annals*, 1971, 1(3): 10–70.

McClelland, D., *et al. The achievement motive*. New York: Appleton-Century-Crofts, 1953.

Newcomb, T. M., *et al. Persistence and change: Bennington College and its students after twenty-five years*. New York: Wiley, 1967.

Perry, W. G. *Forms of intellectual and ethical development in the college years: A scheme*. New York: Holt, Rinehart & Winston, 1968.

Rossett, H. L., *et al.* Personality and cognitive characteristics of engineering students. *American Journal of Psychiatry*, 1966, 122: 1147–1152.

Rossett, H. L., *et al.* Ego organization and scientific careers. Unpublished manuscript, Department of Psychiatry, Boston University School of Medicine, 1972.

Sanford, N. (Ed.) Personality development during the college years. *The Journal of Social Issues*, 1956, 12 (Whole No. 4).

Sanford, N. *The American college*. New York: Wiley, 1962.

Simon, B., & Ellison, A. *An evaluation of the unified science program*. Part I: Initial characteristics of students. 1972. (Mimeo, available from B. Simon)

Singer, J. L. *Daydreaming*. New York: Random House, 1966.

Snyder, B. R. Massachusetts Institute of Technology student adaptation study. Unpublished manuscript, Education Research Center, MIT, 1967.

Snyder, B. R. *The hidden curriculum*. New York: Knopf, 1971.

Strodtbeck, F. L. Family interaction, values, and achievement. In D. McClelland *et al., Talent and society*. New York: Van Nostrand, 1958.

Trent, J. W. *The decision to go to college*. Los Angeles: Center for the Study of Evaluation, UCLA Graduate School of Education, 1970 (Report No. 64).

Trent, J. W., & Medsker, L. L. *Beyond high school*. San Francisco: Jossey-Bass, 1968.

Vaillant, G. E. The natural history of male psychological health. IV: The life cycle from 18–50. *Seminars in Psychiatry*, 1972, 4: in press.

TO WHAT EXTENT DO MONETARY RETURNS TO EDUCATION VARY WITH FAMILY BACKGROUND, MENTAL ABILITY, AND SCHOOL QUALITY?*

Dael Wolfle

Phi Beta Kappa, the Bureau of the Census, and a variety of other organizations and individuals have over many years made such pronouncements as "A college education is worth a quarter of a million dollars." The evidence for these claims is that college graduates as a group have higher earnings than nongraduates.

In the past dozen years, using more sophisticated methods of analysis, students of the economics of education have reported that the average college graduate derives a monetary return on the costs of his college education, including foregone earnings, of about 12 to 15 percent a year throughout his postcollege working life. Studies using data from 1939 and even earlier in the century down to quite recent years show some differences but no systematic decline in the earnings advantage of college graduates. For example, Census records indicate that the mean annual income of male college graduates was 170 percent of that of high school graduates in 1958 and 161 percent in 1968.

* This paper is not a comprehensive review of work on the economic returns to education. It cites representative, and preferably recent, work that has attempted to answer the questions posed in the title.

Popular accounts frequently overlook the fact that all of these state-ments are gross oversimplifications, but students of the economics of education know that the higher earnings of college graduates are only partly attributable to higher education as such, for a portion of the earnings difference should be credited to the higher average ability, the stronger motivation, the more favorable family background, and other factors that differentiate young people who graduate from college from their agemates whose education stops at a lower level.

Data from a number of studies make it clear that all, or nearly all, of the sociological, psychological, and economic factors that differentiate college graduates from nongraduates are positively correlated with one another. School grades are correlated with scores on tests of intelligence; both of these variables are correlated with the socioeconomic level of the students' families; and school and college grades—and probably earnings also—are correlated with motivation.

Theoretically, it is not impossible to measure these variables inde-pendently, compute their intercorrelations, and determine the extent to which each contributes to the higher earnings of college graduates. Practically, the empirical data for such an analysis are not available. Data have been available, however, to enable several workers to estimate the portion of the higher earnings of college graduates that should be attributed to the cluster of variables that includes ability, motivation, and family background, instead of to higher education itself.

Denison (1964), in an epochal analysis of the factors that contributed to the economic growth of the United States from 1909 to 1957, con-cludes that in addition to the classic variables of capital and labor one of the important contributors is a steadily rising average level of educa-tion. In a further analysis of this component of national growth, and on the basis of empirical data reported by Wolfle & Smith (1956), Deni-son concludes that about two thirds of the income differential between high school graduates and college graduates are associated with college education, and about one third with differences in ability, family status, and geographic region.

Becker (1964), using the same empirical data, concludes that adjusting for differences in ability and family background reduces the average rate of return on the costs of a college education from approximately 11 percent a year to approximately 9 percent a year.

Weisbrod & Karpoff (1968) analyze the earning histories of 7,000 male graduates of many American colleges and universities who had, in 1956, been employed by the American Telephone & Telegraph Com-pany for 3 to 50 years. These authors have no comparable data for high school graduates who had not gone to college; but on the basis of some reasonable assumption derived from their data, they conclude that about one fourth of the difference between the mean earnings of college graduates and the mean earnings of high school graduates in the United States results from differences in ability and other personal factors.

Hines *et al* (1970) find an unadjusted private rate of return on the costs of higher education of 16.2 percent a year. When they adjust income differences to take account of differences in ability, the rate of return drops to 13.2 percent a year, approximately 80 percent of the unadjusted rate of return.

Taubman & Wales (in press), on the basis of information at several later points in the lives of a group of World War II Air Force officers, conclude that the unadjusted rate of return on the costs of college and graduate education have to be reduced by about 16 percent to take account of differences in ability and family background.

In summary, this sampling of studies generally agrees that comparisons of the earnings of college graduates with the earnings of high school graduates overestimate the rate of return that should be attributed to higher education per se by 16 to 33 percent. It seems reasonable that if one compares the average earnings of male college graduates in the United States with the average earnings of males who graduate from high school but do not go on to college, three fourths (more or less) of the difference represent a real economic benefit of higher education. The rest of the obtained difference should be attributed to differences in ability, socioeconomic advantages, motivation, and closely related factors.

Ability versus Family Background

A substantial amount of evidence indicates that differences in ability and differences in family background carry about equal weight in determining which high school graduates go on to college. One of these variables sometimes appears to be more influential than the other, and in some studies the relative weights are reversed for men and women. In general, though, at the point of transition from high school to college, the two seem to be about equally influential. As students move through college, and as some of them continue through graduate and professional schools, the relative influence of family background diminishes. Thus, it is not surprising that differences in earnings among college graduates appear to be more closely related to ability than to parental socioeconomic status. The direct evidence on this point is not very strong, but there is some experimental support. Reed & Miller (1970) find that

after they take account of age, color, college quality, and field of specialization (they have no measures of ability), there is essentially no discernible influence of father's education or occupation on the earnings
of college graduates or of graduates in dentistry, law, or theology.

Taubman & Wales (in press) find that among a large group of World
War II Air Force officers, on whom data had initially been collected
by Thorndike & Hagen (1959), those whose fathers had progressed
at least as far as the ninth grade earned about $300 a year more in
1955 and about $1,200 a year more in 1969 than did those whose fathers
had not entered high school. Here, as in a biographical index that also
shows some relation to later earnings, the differences in background
factors probably reflect a mixture of environmental and genetic factors.

The Effects of College Quality

Shane Hunt (see Becker, 1964) reports that after adjustments for
some other factors, graduates of more expensive colleges and universities
earn about 50 percent more than graduates of less expensive institutions.
Weisbrod & Karpoff in their analysis of earnings of college graduates
employed by the American Telephone & Telegraph Company also find
earnings to be related to college quality. A cross comparison of rank
in graduating class of these men with estimates of the quality level
of the college from which each graduated is given in the Table 1. (The
index numbers show earnings of each subgroup in comparison with
the average of 100 for the total population studied.) Within any of the
four ability groupings, the relationship is clear: Graduates of better
colleges earn more. Similarly, among the graduates of colleges at any
level of quality, the brighter ones earn more. Significantly, there are
also differences in the variance of earnings associated with both student
ability and college quality. The differences in earnings is larger for stu-

TABLE 1. COMPARISON OF RANK IN CLASS WITH COLLEGE QUALITY

Rank in graduating class	College quality			
	Below average	Average	Above average	Best
Top 10 percent	102.8	103.0	111.6	118.7
Remainder of top third	97.6	99.4	103.9	113.0
Middle third	93.7	94.4	99.1	103.5
Bottom third	90.1	91.0	95.0	96.9

dents who finish toward the top of their class than for those toward the bottom, and the differences are larger in colleges of higher quality than in those of less distinction.

Daniere & Mechling (1970) find a similar relationship between student ability and college quality. They used instruction cost per student as their measure of college quality and verbal scores on the Scholastic Aptitude Test as measures of student ability. Discounted lifetime earnings varied regularly with differences in both ability and college quality. On the ability scale, the differences grew larger toward the top. For all students, regardless of college attended, the difference between the top 1.5 percent and the next 8.5 percent was nearly as great as the difference between the bottom quarter and the group between the seventieth and ninetieth percentiles. The relationship of lifetime earnings, in thousands of dollars, discounted to age 18 at 6 percent, is shown in Table 2.

Interactions

Uncontrolled, and quite unknown, in these relationships among student ability, college quality, and lifetime earnings is the role of motivation. Strength of motivation is probably positively correlated with grades and with quality of college attended. In some complex way motivation, perhaps, is influenced by home background; strength of motivation is probably also correlated with lifetime earnings. If a reliable and reasonably pure measure of strength of motivation had been included in the above analysis, one can only speculate as to how much smaller some of the apparent relationships would have been. For example, do graduates of superior colleges earn more because they had better instruction or because they are more ambitious?

Another kind of interaction, on which there is some evidence, is that

TABLE 2. RELATIONSHIP OF LIFETIME EARNINGS TO COLLEGE QUALITY AND STUDENT ABILITY (IN THOUSANDS OF DOLLARS)

Instruction cost level	Student ability				
	Bottom 25%	Next 45%	Next 20%	Next 8.5%	Top 1.5%
High	—	$170	$178	$196	$200
Medium	$145	150	158	181	188
Low	129	138	150	169	—

TABLE 3. EARNINGS ADVANTAGE OF COLLEGE
GRADUATES OVER HIGH SCHOOL ONLY
GRADUATES

	Ability level	
Educational level	Bottom 90%	Top 10%
Bachelor's degree	47	100
Master's degree	58	111

between level of ability and amount of education. In their reanalysis
of the Wolfle–Smith data, Taubman & Wales compare the earnings advantage of college graduates with high school graduates of equal intellectual ability—as measured in high school (Table 3). (The figures show
the percentage by which earnings of the college group exceed those
of the high school only group.) College graduation or an advanced
degree is clearly of greater financial advantage to a student in the top
10 percent of the range than to one of lesser ability. It pays to make
sure that the best students get to college.

Of related interest are the findings of Weisbrod & Karpoff (1968)
and Daniere & Mechling (1970) on the interaction between student
ability and college quality, as reported above, and the evidence from
Daniere & Mechling of interaction between ability and education in
accounting for lifetime earnings.

Nature of the Educational Effect

Taubman & Wales have gone further than other investigators in trying
to determine how higher education affects later earnings. They conclude
that much of the observed difference in earnings at different educational
levels is due to the use of college credentials as an employment screen.
One must graduate from medical school to be allowed to practice medicine. Law and dentistry are also under legal controls. Some of the other
better-paid professions—engineering, industrial sciences, or college
teaching, and the higher ranks of industrial and business management—
are not legally restricted to holders of degrees, but college graduation
is "expected." Either by law or custom, the more prestigious and financially rewarding positions are open to persons with baccalaureate and
higher degrees but are impossible or difficult of entry to persons without
degrees.

Nevertheless, a number of nongraduates have succeeded in entering some of these better-paying fields. When Taubman & Wales divide the groups for whom they have data into occupational categories and then analyze the influences of ability and amount of education within each occupational category, they find that ability differences are usually associated with earnings, but educational differences are not. Bright salesmen earn more than dumb salesmen, but college graduate salesmen earn no more than high school graduate salesmen of equal mental ability. Among both high school graduates and college graduates, earnings are correlated with ability. And at both educational levels the relationship is stronger in the higher, and generally more intellectually demanding, occupations; it grows weaker or disappears in fields toward the lower end of the occupational hierarchy.

Ashenfelter & Mooney (1968) have reported supporting findings from their analysis of the 1966 earnings of male Woodrow Wilson Fellows chosen in 1958, 1959, or 1960. In this highly selected group of young men, mathematical ability is positively related to earnings among natural scientists, among social scientists, and among humanists, even when the three groups are studied separately. (Other measures of ability show no significant relationships with earnings in this highly selected and intellectually rather homogeneous group.) Earnings are also related to the degrees earned, the specific fields of science or scholarship in which the men are working, and to whether they are employed at colleges or universities or outside of the educational sphere. There is no significant relationship with the number of years of graduate study.

The Behavior of Employers

Few people would quarrel with the requirement that a physician have a formal medical education or that a college or high school teacher be better educated than his students. For some professional fields, college or more advanced education is probably the most satisfactory and efficient means of attaining justifiable entrance requirements. In some other fields, although the case for a degree is not as clear, its possession is either a normal requirement—as for teaching in elementary schools—or is believed to be a useful indicator of employability.

The findings summarized above are consistent with two hypotheses (Taubman & Wales, in press) concerning the behavior of employers. First, when the market permits, as it does now and will continue to do, employers discriminate in favor of college graduates and against applicants without college degrees. Nongraduates who for one reason or another are able to crack the credentials barrier earn as much as college graduates of comparable ability. But nongraduates, including many of the bright ones, who are unable to get over the initial hurdle must settle for other types of positions in which earnings are typically lower.

Second, although employers are not very good at estimating the potential ability of prospective employees, and thus use the college degree as a screening device, they are able to judge with some effectiveness ability as demonstrated on the job. Thus, the relationship between ability as measured in school and earnings or progress on the job increases with experience. Weisbrod & Karpoff find that the top 10 percent of college graduates (in class rank) progress in salary more rapidly than others. Taubman & Wales also show the importance of ability as an indicator of earnings to increase with length of experience.

As larger numbers of college graduates become available, the temptation remains strong to give them preference in employment. A recent report (The Brookings Institution, 1970) concerning police officers is illuminating:

> The President's commission argues that a drastic reevaluation of the educational requirements for police officers is needed and recommends that the ultimate aim of all departments should be that personnel with general enforcement duties have baccalaureate degrees. The precise contribution of a college degree is unknown. The strongest argument in its favor may be that if the education of police recruits does not keep pace with the steady rise in the educational level of the population, recruits will have to be drawn increasingly from that part of the population that is least prepared to assume the responsibilities of modern law enforcement.

Summary

College graduates earn significantly more than high school graduates. When account is taken of differences in ability and other personal factors, the earnings differential between college graduates and high school graduates is reduced to about 75 or 80 percent of the uncorrected differential.

Earnings are correlated with intellectual ability as measured by standard intelligence or aptitude tests. This is true of college graduates, and although the evidence has not been cited, it is also true of high school graduates who do not go to college. The relationship between ability and earnings is closer at the upper end of the occupational hierarchy and increases with experience.

Among college graduates, those who graduate from superior or more prestigious institutions have higher earnings than those from lesser institutions. Although diminished, the advantage is still evident after correction for differences in ability.

There is a little evidence that, for any given level of education, earnings are higher for men who come from more-favored socioeconomic backgrounds than for those from less-favored homes. However, among college graduates, the differences associated with home background tend to disappear when account has been taken of individual ability, college attended, and occupation entered.

Some of the interactions among these and other variables are uncontrolled and unknown. Strength of motivation has not been adequately treated in any of the studies cited.

The earnings advantage of college graduates and holders of advanced and professional degrees over persons with less formal education is attributable to three factors:

1. Higher educational credentials that give admission to occupational fields that offer higher financial rewards
2. The higher average level of intellectual ability (and probably also the higher rank in some other personal characteristics) of persons who continue farther up the educational ladder
3. The specific or general applicability to job performance of the knowledge and skills developed in college or university

The relative importance of these three factors depends upon the professional or occupational field involved and to some extent also on the length of experience. No study has been sufficiently comprehensive to show the detailed relationships with precision.

REFERENCES

Ashenfelter, O., & Mooney, J. D. Graduate education, earnings, and ability. *Review of Economics and Statistics*, 1968, 50(1): 78–86.

Becker, G. S. *Human capital, a theoretical and empirical analysis, with special reference to education.* New York: National Bureau of Economic Research, 1964 (General Series, No. 80).

The Brookings Institution. *Brookings Bulletin*, 1970, 7(4): 2.

Daniere, A., & Mechling, J. Direct marginal productivity of college education in relation to college aptitude of students and production costs of institutions. *The Journal of Human Resources*, 1970, 5(1): 51–70.

Denison, E. F. Measuring the contribution of education (and the residual) to economic growth. In *The residual factor and economic growth.* Paris: Organisation for Economic Cooperation and Development, 1964.

Hines, F., Tweeten, L., & Redfern, M. Social and private rates of return to investment in schooling by race–sex groups and regions. *The Journal of Human Resources*, 1970, 5(3): 318–340.

Reed, R. H., & Miller, H. P. Some determinants of the variation in earnings for college men. *The Journal of Human Resources,* 1970, 5(2): 177–190.

Taubman, P. J., & Wales, T. *Education as an investment and as a screening device.* New York: National Bureau of Economic Research, in press.

Thorndike, R. L., & Hagen, E. *Ten thousand careers.* New York: Wiley, 1959.

Weisbrod, B. A., & Karpoff, P. Monetary returns to college education, student ability, and college quality. *Review of Economics and Statistics,* 1968, 50(4): 491–497.

Wolfle, D., & Smith, J. G. The occupational value of education for superior high school graduates. *Journal of Higher Education,* 1956, 27(4): 201–212, 232.

Part II

INCOME-RELATED EFFECTS ON THE EDUCATED

THE DEFINITION AND IMPACT OF COLLEGE QUALITY

Lewis C. Solmon

My work attempts to add a new dimension to earnings function analysis by hypothesizing those features of colleges that might yield financial payoffs to students in later life and then testing to see which of these traits actually do add most to the explanatory power of the traditional earnings function.

Two general types of college attributes can be isolated and measured (if imperfectly):

1. *Student Quality.* A student supposedly benefits more from college, and hence acquires more of whatever colleges give that enhances future earning power, when surrounded by high-quality fellow students. This has been called the peer effect. Intuitively, it seems that the opportunity to interact with intelligent and motivated peers should enrich the college experience. We have several measures of average student quality by schools: the average Scholastic Aptitude Test (SAT) scores of entering freshmen (Cass & Birnbaum, 1969),* and an index of intellectuality

---

* Of course an individual's IQ will be highly correlated with his SAT scores. However, here we are looking at the effect of *average* SAT's of *all* students at a college on an individual's subsequent income, controlling for the individual's IQ.

of students obtained by Alexander Astin (1965) through factor analysis. Another variable that has been developed by Astin (1965), an index of selectivity based upon the average SAT scores of entering freshmen, is also used as a dimension of quality.

2. *Instructional Quality.* Better faculty will allegedly instill in students traits beneficial in subsequent years. One measure of faculty quality is average faculty salary (American Association of University Professors, 1964). This assumes that higher-paid faculty have more experience (and higher rank), better teaching ability, more professional prestige from research or greater opportunities to earn elsewhere, all of these indicating greater productivity in their professorial roles.* Another factor is school expenditure for instruction, research, and library per full-time equivalent student: High-quality faculty should be attracted by expenditures beyond those on salaries alone. Also, holding these expenditures per faculty member constant, a larger expenditure per student implies a greater teacher/student ratio.† Thus, this measure is a test of the influence of teacher/student ratios as well. We hypothesize the first derivatives of both expenditures per faculty member and faculty per student with respect to quality are positive.‡ Unfortunately, data of this kind ignore differing definitions of "full-time faculty" at different colleges. Teaching loads range from one course to four or more per semester at different colleges, and these differences may alter teacher effectiveness. Other problems with this proxy for quality arise, since it allows for no nonpecuniary attractiveness of particular colleges for particular faculty members. Schools located in undesirable areas (urban ghettos with high crime rates or isolated rural areas with no cultural life) may be forced to pay high salaries for even mediocre-quality faculty. Schools with attractive surroundings (scenery, a few top scholars, cultural life, exceptionally good research and teaching equipment or plant) may be able to attract high-quality faculty for low salaries. Low salaries may be paid to top-quality faculty where opportunities for lucrative outside consulting jobs abound. Of course, students may or may not benefit from "good" faculty who are away consulting much of the time. In

---

* One might question the relationship between these traits and academic salaries and also which of these have more important effects on students' later incomes. However, data limitations enable us here to look only at the gross relationship between faculty salaries and student incomes.

† This is true if we assume contact hours per faculty member are constant:

$$\frac{\text{Exp.}}{\text{Stu.}} = \frac{(\text{Exp.})}{(\text{Fac.})} \times \frac{(\text{Fac.})}{(\text{Contact Hrs.})} \times \frac{(\text{Contact Hrs.})}{(\text{Student})}.$$

‡ Quality can be thought of as college attributes that increase learning, which, in turn, makes students able to earn larger incomes in later life.

any case, the hypothesis to test is that schools that pay large salaries to faculty members who meet relatively small groups of students are more beneficial to students' subsequent earning power than those schools that pay low salaries or have large classes.

A related quality measure refers to the total incomes or expenditures per student of the colleges: Schools that spend (or receive) larger amounts per enrollee provide a higher-quality education and an educational experience more beneficial in postschool years.

Finally, as an additional test of school quality we have a subjective measure made by Gourman (1967). These ratings propose to be a "consensus of reliable opinion and judgment obtained from many and various sources deemed to be dependable and accurate" (p. 11). The study evaluates individual departments as well as administration, faculty, student services, and other general areas such as library facilities. An average of all items is calculated, resulting in an overall Gourman Index between 200 and 800. The interpretation of these ratings depends upon the weights given to the various criteria; unfortunately, these weights are not published. However, the index is one of the few quantitative ratings of a large number of colleges.

There is a question of whether or not all the measures of quality are really standing for the same thing. Table 1 presents correlations between pairs of college attributes. In general, these exceed .5.

Table 2 presents regressions with individual colleges as units of observation. These enable us to consider the relationships between the nonmonetary quality measures and the expenditure data and school size. It is obvious that the nondollar quality measures are significantly related to expenditures as a whole, faculty salaries, and size of student body. Size is negatively related to average SAT scores and the Astin measures; that is, better peer-group influences apparently are found in smaller schools. Gourman ratings are positively influenced by size. Interestingly, we explain about 50 percent of the variance in the peer-group measures by our model, but 70 percent of the Gourman ratings are explained.

Empirical Estimates of Earnings Functions with Quality Variables

For those with 13 or more years of schooling, the following equation was estimated:

$$\ln Y_{69} = a + b \text{ YRS} + c \text{ EXP} + d \text{ EXPSQ} \\ + e \text{ IQ} + f Z \cdot Q_{\text{UG}} + g Q_{\text{GRAD}} + h_i V_i + u,$$

where $\ln Y_{69}$ is log of 1969 earnings, YRS is years of education, EXP is years of experience in the full-time labor force (years since first job),

TABLE 1. CORRELATIONS BETWEEN THE VARIOUS ATTRIBUTES OF COLLEGES (COLLEGES AS UNITS OF OBSERVATION)

	2[a]	3	4	5	6	7	8	9	10	11
1. Average faculty salary	.6295	.6540	.7460	.6870	.7364	.8016	.7746	.6141	.6530	.2535
2. SAT verbal		.9069	.5603	.5649	.6101	.5888	.5545	.6592	.7667	−.0978
3. SAT math			.6068	.6093	.6613	.6169	.5927	.7205	.7758	−.0888
4. Departmental research, instruction, and library expenditures				.8178	.9555	.7540	.7262	.6247	.6312	.0482
5. Basic income					.8413	.6738	.6390	.5977	.6193	.0211
6. Basic expenditures						.7127	.6764	.6576	.6759	−.0803
7. Gourman overall							.9827	.6674	.6976	.3084
8. Gourman academic								.6615	.6811	.3318
9. Astin intellectuality									.7399	.0114
10. Astin selectivity										.0182
11. 1960 enrollment										

[a] These numbers refer to the numbered attributes at the left of the table.

TABLE 2. REGRESSION RELATIONSHIPS AMONG QUALITY VARIABLES[a]

	SAT		Gourman		Astin	
	Verbal	Math	Overall	Academic	Intell.	Select.
Constant	339.9	355.1	94.9	97.5	28.1	31.0
Basic expenditures (per student)	.0149	.0232	.0491	.0495	.0055	.0045
	(2.4495)[b]	(3.7548)	(6.8916)	(6.1135)	(5.4403)	(5.2771)
Undergraduate enrollment	−.0039	−.0036	.0063	.0075	−.0001	−.0001
	(−4.0248)	(−3.6735)	(5.5849)	(5.8327)	(−.5674)	(.8106)
Average faculty salary	.0031	.0200	.0269	.0274	.0019	.0020
	(6.7456)	(6.4415)	(7.5304)	(6.7516)	(3.7439)	(4.7070)
Adj R^2	.4740	.5206	.7114	.6700	.4629	.5043
Mean qual.	540.8	563.7	442.5	454.4	54.01	56.02
S.D.	60.99	64.87	96.4	102.4	10.1	8.8
Coefficient on basic expenditures when used alone	.0474	.0547	.0876	.0882	.0085	.0075
Adj R^2	.3694	.4348	.5058	.4551	.4299	.4544
Coefficient on expenditures for library, research, and instruction when used alone	.0724	.0834	.1541	.1576	.0134	.0117
Adj R^2	.3109	.3654	.3665	.5253	.3875	.3958

[a] 226 schools with all data are the units of observation.
[b] t values are in parenthesis.

EXPSQ is the squared value of EXP to take account of the nonlinear influence of on-the-job experience on earnings, and IQ is a measure of the level of ability (presumably affected by a combination of genetics and environment). The quality measure used is that for the *last* college attended by the respondent. This particular form of the quality variable was selected, since it appeared in preliminary work that those who went to more than one college (for example, graduate school) had incomes affected primarily by the nature of their final college. Hence, $Z = 1$ if years of education was 13 to 16 inclusive and 0 otherwise; Q_{UG} and Q_{GRAD} are measures of undergraduate and graduate college quality, respectively, and V_i are several occupational dummies. These were particularly necessary, because teachers are traditionally paid less than other people with the same education and doctors receive more.

For some regressions, a *single* variable—quality of the last college—was devised as the Q_{UG} for those not going on, and Q_{GRAD} for those with more than four years of college. This enables calculation of a single average "income elasticity" of college quality and ignores different pay-offs to quality depending upon years. It is also somewhat less cumbersome to deal with than two separate variables, although quality coefficients do differ depending upon attainment.

The data used are the National Bureau of Economic Research–Thorndike sample (Thorndike & Hagen, 1959), which has been described in detail in several other places (Taubman & Wales, in press). The respondents were white, World War II veterans, all of whom took a battery of aptitude tests in 1942 to determine if they were qualified to be pilots.[*] To take the test, one had to have above average IQ and be in good health. Those willing were surveyed by Thorndike in 1955 and by NBER again in 1969. They provided much information on earnings history, socioeconomic situation, and educational experience, including names of colleges attended, as well as aptitude test scores.

A question of sample bias arises, since only those who attended schools where quality data are available are in the sample. To be sure, biases would exist if one particular quality of school refused information, and one might predict that schools of low quality would be reluctant to report. However, this is not generally true. Many schools grant college educations and degrees to high school graduates who are not qualified to enter schools generally considered to be high-quality institutions. It is in the interest of these low-quality schools to become known by less-

---

[*] The IQ variable used is a combination constructed by factor analysis of several of the AFQT tests and has a mean of .30 and a standard deviation of 1.86.

qualified college aspirants. On the other hand, a number of schools with "good reputations" may be reluctant to report statistics for fear of revealing quantitative evidence that their reputations are not fully justified. Thus, there appear to be reasons why both high- and low-quality schools would not report. Schools may have still other reasons: Some, for example, require SAT scores only from lower-quality applicants (those graduating in the bottom 75 percent of their high school classes, but not those in the top 25 percent, must report SAT). Some schools might not feel that their available data are relevant, as when most faculty members are only part-time employees of the college. Other schools might not want to take the time to compute the data desired. There is no reason why these nonreporters should fall into any particular quality group, and the evidence confirms this.*

A potentially more serious problem with the quality data is that most of the information on schools is for the post-1960 period, whereas the respondents attended around 1950. Unfortunately, earlier data on colleges are not available. We must assume, therefore, that the correlation of college quality is unchanged over time; this assumption is probably not too bad, particularly in a gross sense (good schools are still good, but the ranking of the good schools might vary somewhat). We can view the differences over time as a random measurement error.

The only data available over a reasonable period of time are those on average salary. Data for 36 schools were made available for the years 1939–40, 1953–54, 1959–60, and 1969–70.†

Several tests were performed and these revealed significant serial rank correlation. Analysis of variance revealed that the variation of rank across schools was significantly greater than the variance of rank of a school over time.‡

The quality measures for later periods are highly correlated with earnings of those who attended earlier. One is tempted to argue that if quality measures for the more relevant year were obtainable, these would reveal an even stronger relationship with earnings. However, the ques-

---

* The colleges remaining in our sample range from the very top to the very bottom of each of the quality measures. However, the 1,511 individuals left for our study appear to have somewhat higher incomes, years of schooling, and ability than the full sample with 13 or more years.

† These were obtained through the generous cooperation of Mrs. M. Eymonerie of the American Association of University Professors, Washington, D.C. The 36 schools were not identified specifically but represent a cross section of American colleges.

‡ The F ratio was 12.43 and the critical F for the given degrees of freedom for significance at the 1 percent level was 1.99.

tion of effects of college quality are too important to put aside on the grounds that current data are imperfect.*

Table 3 estimates earnings functions with different quality measures. Regardless of how quality is measured, the traits of one's school significantly affect log of subsequent earnings (that is, log of 1969 earnings). These are effects after controlling for the individual's IQ, years of education, and experience. The t-values on quality (10 measures) range from 3.744 to 6.049 with 1,506 degrees of freedom. Here we use a single variable—the quality of the last college attended (graduate or undergraduate where appropriate).

We should pause at this point to note that the coefficient on years of schooling is only slightly over .03 in all the earnings functions of Table 3. These coefficients should *not* be interpreted as the rate of return to years of education. According to the theory of human capital, the rate of return to years of schooling equals the coefficient on years, r, times $1/k$ where

$$k = \frac{\text{Actual opportunity cost plus direct costs}}{\text{Annualized opportunity costs}}.$$

Hence, the coefficient on years is the (private) rate of return only if k equals 1. If direct costs equal student earnings, exactly 100 percent of potential income would be invested in obtaining human capital, k would equal 1 and r would be the rate of return.

The sample contains people who went to college under the GI Bill of Rights. These students had no direct costs of schooling and received subsistence payments as well: We assume that, as students, our sample members received $100 per month plus tuition under the GI Bill (President's Commission on Veterans Payments, 1956).† From the 1950 Census we can deduce that a white high school graduate aged 25 to 29 earned $3,008 per year on average (Bureau of the Census, 1953). This was

---

* It has been suggested that if graduates from certain colleges earned high incomes for reasons unrelated to our quality measures, they might have *subsequently* donated large sums to their Alma Mater. This would have enabled colleges to then obtain high marks in our quality measures. In this case, high incomes would support high quality. Moreover, high current incomes might be due to current prestige of one's Alma Mater regardless of the quality during the time attended.

† The Servicemen's Readjustment Act, known as the GI Bill of Rights passed in the Seventy-Eighth Congress in 1944. It paid up to $500 per year tuition plus $50 per month with no dependents of $75 per month with one or more dependents. In 1945 the monthly payments with one or more dependents were raised to $90 and in 1948 were raised to $105 with one dependent and $120 with more than one dependent.

TABLE 3. EARNINGS FUNCTIONS WITH DIFFERENT ASPECTS OF COLLEGE QUALITY

	Gourman overall	Gourman academic	Average salary	SAT verbal	SAT math	Instructional, departmental research, & library expenses	Basic income	Basic expenditures	Astin intell.	Astin select.
Constant	1.722	1.720	1.512	1.340	1.264	1.859	1.847	2.036	1.517	1.403
	(9.970)	(9.939)	(8.366)	(6.781)	(6.256)	(11.00)	(10.87)	(11.78)	(8.359)	(7.233)
IQ	.03536	.03560	.03232	.03352	.03209	.03431	.03556	.03543	.03252	.03355
	(4.911)	(4.946)	(4.467)	(4.634)	(4.418)	(4.745)	(4.913)	(4.859)	(4.487)	(4.629)
Years of education	.03142	.03174	.03052	.03420	.03473	.03176	.03370	.02448	.03147	.03327
	(4.347)	(4.347)	(4.198)	(4.750)	(4.838)	(4.356)	(4.632)	(3.000)	(4.337)	(4.600)
Experience	.03523	.03573	.03927	.03441	.03454	.03667	.03430	.03657	.03649	.03479
	(2.630)	(2.665)	(2.935)	(2.571)	(2.584)	(2.736)	(2.554)	(2.716)	(2.729)	(2.598)
Experience²	-.0008265	-.0008403	-.0009354	-.0008216	-.0008233	-.0008651	-.0008042	-.0008622	-.0008708	-.0008167
	(-2.506)	(-2.547)	(-2.839)	(-2.495)	(-2.502)	(-2.622)	(-2.433)	(-2.601)	(-2.645)	(-2.478)
Quality	.0005812	.0005576	.0004822	.001189	.001259	.0001324	.00008250	.00004069	.008721	.01011
	(5.124)	(5.047)	(6.049)	(5.520)	(5.778)	(5.175)	(4.373)	(3.744)	(5.808)	(5.297)
R_3^2 [a]	.07632	.07584	.08251	.07885	.08060	.07663	.07199	.06887	.08080	.07740
R_4^2 [b]	.06020	.06020	.06020	.06020	.06020	.06020	.06020	.06020	.06020	.06020
Quality mean	519.664	538.447	10339.5	555.124	576.404	115.108	1877.32	2270.97	580.304	59.5592
Elasticity	.3020	.3002	.4985	.6600	.7256	.1524	.1548	.0924	.5060	.6021
ΔR^2 [c]	.01612	.01564	.02231	.01865	.02040	.01643	.01179	.00867	.02060	.01720

[a] R_3^2 is the R^2 with all five variables including quality.
[b] R_4^2 is the R^2 after the fourth step (only YRS, IQ, EXP, and EXPSQD).
[c] ΔR^2 is $(R_3^2 - R_4^2)$ and is the additional explanatory power provided by the quality variable.

assumed to be the foregone earnings of people in the sample. Thus, k equaled roughly .35106 and $1/k = 2.85.$*

In order to estimate rates of return to years in college, we should multiply the years coefficient by 2.85. The rates of return for members of our sample who were in school in the late 1940s appear to be roughly 9.7 percent. Gary Becker (1964) estimated the returns to a white male college graduate in 1949 to be 13 percent.† Present estimates are below those of others for several reasons. First, our sample includes only people who have at least some college education; our coefficients reflect the return to an extra year of college *not* the return to college training compared to the return to high school attendance. Moreover, there is a preponderance of teachers in our sample, and teachers have high education and relatively low annual earnings. Finally, an examination of the drop-outs in our sample indicates that they were usually pulled out of school by good earnings opportunities, not pushed out due to poor achievement.

Another reason for the apparent low payoff to extra "raw years" in school is that we have controlled for college quality. Probably those with more years also attended higher quality institutions.‡ Thus, part of the return to extra years is reflected in the returns to quality rather than returns to years. The coefficient on years rises to slightly over .04 when quality variables are omitted from the earnings function, and this would imply a rate of return to years, not controlling for quality, of about 12 percent. Of course, the ability variable also detracts from the coefficient on years, since there is a positive relationship between innate ability and educational attainment (Taubman & Wales, 1972).§

After establishing that quality, however measured, is important, the task of determining which aspect of quality is most important is more difficult. Table 3 shows that average faculty salary has the highest t-value, closely followed by the average SAT scores of entering freshmen and Astin's measures of intellectuality and selectivity. One might conclude that faculty quality and peer-group effects are the most important (in terms of subsequent earnings) features of college quality. The peer-

* Assuming a nine-month school year,

$$k = \frac{\frac{3}{4} \times 3008 \times 1200}{3008} = .35106.$$

† Becker acknowledges the crudeness of the estimate. Ours also is imperfect.

‡ The correlation between years and quality of the last school attended is about .25.

§ Taubman and Wales estimate an upward bias in the coefficient on years when IQ is omitted of about 30 percent.

group effects are in line with the conclusions of James Coleman (1966) in his study of lower levels of education.

Before adding the quality variable the R^2 in the earnings function was .0602. The addition of the average salary variable raises the R^2 by .0223 to .0825. Once again, the quality variables measuring student characteristics add the next largest amounts to R^2.*

The per student expenditure variable adds the least to R^2. This might be explained by the fact that it is deflated by the number of full-time equivalent students. Indeed, average faculty salary, a prime component of expenditure, is the most powerful measure of quality. Welch (1966) has argued that for state elementary and high school systems, size has a significant positive effect on earnings, that it is an important aspect of school quality as we define quality. If scale economies are a positive aspect of college quality, then the expenditure data deflated are actually a ratio of two factors, each a positive influence on earnings. If expenditures per student are high because expenditures are high, holding constant the size of college, we would expect a strong positive relationship with later earnings. On the other hand, if the variable is large because number of students is small, holding expenditures constant, we would expect a negative relationship between the ratio and income. In a large sample of schools, the expenditures per student probably vary for both reasons, and so the overall effect is blurred. Moreover, only part of each dollar spent finds its way into projects that make students more productive. (What value is there to earning ability of gardening expenses for the college greenery?) Of course, a happier student may learn more and, hence, earn more.

We can calculate an income elasticity of quality—the percentage change in income for a percentage change in quality. However, these elasticities (Table 3) cannot be used to compare impacts of quality. A 1 percent change in average SAT level is not comparable to a 1 percent change in average salary. If we could calculate the cost of a 1 percent change in each of the quality measures, only then could we see the returns to each.

Table 4 presents two specifications of the earnings equation that include more than one quality variable. In the first, it is evident that

---

* It has been suggested that the *average* college SAT variable might be a better proxy for the innate ability of the particular student than is the ability variable we use. The average SAT variable may be picking up ability traits of the individual not captured by our individual ability measure. If this were the case, the suggestion of a peer-group effect would be wrong. To really confirm the peer-group effect would require both individual and college SAT scores, but the former are lacking. It would also be useful to have variance of SAT by college, but this is not available.

TABLE 4. Earnings Functions with Several Quality Variables

Constant	1.332	1.300
	(6.761)	(5.665)
IQ	.03105	.03099
	(4.285)	(4.265)
Years of education	.03053	.03055
	(4.206)	(4.190)
Experience	.03781	.03766
	(2.827)	(2.310)
Experience^2	−.0009073	−.0009029
	(−2.756)	(−2.736)
Average salary	.00003392	.00003342
	(3.343)	(2.108)
SAT, verbal	.0006215	.0005807
	(2.272)	(1.848)
Instructional, departmental research,		−.00001069
and library expenditure		(−0.2147)
Astin selectivity		.001087
		(0.3269)
Gourman academic		.00001541
		(.07664)
R^2	.08564	.08573

average salary and SAT scores have separate and statistically significant influence on income. The second version shows that when additional types of quality measures are added, the importance of faculty and student effects still stands out, but the other variables add nothing extra statistically. Two separate and important aspects of quality can be identified, faculty quality and peer-group (student) effects.* The other variables to measure quality apparently relate to income only as proxies for these two effects.†

Results at Different Points on the Life Cycle

College quality, no matter how defined, does affect earnings 20 years after attending. However, does college have an increasing or decreasing effect on earnings over time? To answer this question, we estimated earnings functions that included two quality variables—undergraduate

* As stated earlier, the significance of the average SAT scores might be measuring the effects of students' own abilities not captured by IQ. However, there seems to be no reason why 1963 SAT, for example, would better represent ability than would the ability measures taken in the Air Force usually before college attendance.

† Of course, it might be that other aspects of quality are important but are omitted from our model or merely poorly measured.

college quality for those with 16 or fewer years of schooling, and quality of graduate school for those with 17 or more. This was done to explain log of 1969 income, log of 1955 income, and log of real income in the initial year of full-time employment.*

A positive correlation between Q_{UG} and Q_{GRAD} for those with more than 16 years of education implies the coefficient on graduate quality is higher than it would be if Q_{UG} were entered for those with more than 16 years. When this was done, the Q_{UG} variable was not significant for those with more than 16 years.

Three different quality measures are used: the Gourman Index, average faculty salary, and average level of SAT math score of entering freshmen.† The results appear in Table 5. The three 1969 regressions are comparable to Columns 1, 3, and 5 of Table 3, where the "quality last" variable is not separated by years of attainment. Also, in Table 5 four occupational dummies are inserted to account for exceptional income–schooling relationships: Pilots generally have high earnings considering their education. Teachers usually have much schooling and low incomes due to fewer hours and alleged nonpecuniary rewards. Doctors have high incomes, partially due to monopoly elements in their profession; however, the reason for high pay for lawyers is less clear. The average of coefficients on Q_{UG} and Q_{GRAD} is not much different than the comparable coefficients in Table 3.

Quality significantly influences 1955 earnings; however, no matter how quality is measured, the coefficients are smaller in 1955 than in 1969. It should be noted that in terms of significance of the quality variables (t-tests or addition to R^2), the 1969 and 1955 results are rather similar. IQ has roughly the same effects on earnings in both years, and for some reason the coefficient on experience is greater in 1955. Another difference is that the coefficient on years of education variable is smaller when using 1955 education, when respondents averaged about 6.6 years of experience. There is evidence that a positive relationship between years of education and investment in on-the-job training exists. It is likely that those with more schooling had foregone more earnings while investing on the job in the first few years of employment. However,

---

* Since starting year differed among individuals, the first-year incomes had to be adjusted to account for year-to-year price level changes.

† Individuals were eliminated unless all three appropriate quality measures were available for them. When the regression for Gourman was rerun *not* eliminating for absent SAT or salary data, the sample was larger, of slightly lower IQ, and had slightly lower average college quality. In that case, for all three years both the Q_{UG} and Q_{GRAD} had smaller (but significant) coefficients. This indicates a positive interaction between IQ and school quality.

TABLE 5. EARNINGS FUNCTIONS AT DIFFERENT TIMES IN THE LIFE CYCLE

	Gourman overall			Average faculty salary			SAT math		
	Real INIT	1955	1969	Real INIT	1955	1969	Real INIT	1955	1969
Constant	.7358 (3.722)	.8621 (4.638)	1.401 (6.267)	.6400 (2.980)	.6908 (3.532)	1.068 (4.525)	.6262 (2.670)	.5685 (2.719)	.9939 (3.989)
Years of education	.0452 (3.679)	.0306 (2.883)	.0487 (4.105)	.0459 (3.723)	.0324 (3.043)	.0516 (4.332)	.0458 (3.672)	.0333 (3.080)	.0537 (4.408)
IQ	−.0255 (−3.105)	.0274 (4.421)	.0300 (4.005)	−.0272 (−3.264)	.0250 (3.975)	.0257 (3.414)	−.0263 (−3.164)	.0264 (4.187)	.0279 (3.681)
Experience		.0536 (4.639)	.0338 (2.511)		.0535 (4.636)	.0383 (2.850)		.0518 (4.466)	.0318 (2.353)
Experience²		−.0023 (−4.062)	−.00076 (−2.308)		−.0023 (−4.128)	−.0009 (−2.675)		−.0022 (−3.885)	−.0007 (−2.189)
$Z \times Q_{UG}$ ($Z = 1$ if UG)	.00015 (1.074)	.00065 (6.195)	.00074 (5.949)	.00002 (1.638)	.00005 (6.362)	.00006 (7.045)	.0003 (1.216)	.0010 (5.353)	.0013 (5.626)
Q_{GRAD}	−.00009 (−.5931)	.00050 (4.450)	.00062 (4.818)	.000003 (.3127)	.00004 (5.272)	.0005 (6.192)	.00008 (.3032)	.0009 (4.600)	.0012 (4.977)
Pilot	.1420 (1.045)	.1866 (1.828)	.4111 (3.306)	.1394 (1.026)	.1859 (1.824)	.4060 (3.282)	.1435 (1.055)	.1947 (1.901)	.4244 (3.409)
Teacher	−.1744 (−2.548)	−.2787 (−5.209)	−.3168 (−4.420)	−.1767 (−2.585)	−.2859 (−5.349)	−.3206 (−4.491)	−.1735 (−2.535)	−.2790 (−5.192)	−.3030 (−4.213)
MD	.0735 (.3550)	.6446 (4.111)	.6488 (3.619)	.0837 (.4049)	.6301 (4.024)	.6436 (3.611)	.0842 (.4068)	.6521 (4.139)	.6373 (3.552)
Lawyer	−.1766 (−1.807)	.0167 (.2043)	.1759 (2.000)	−.1720 (−1.761)	.0171 (.2098)	.1802 (2.060)	−.1727 (−1.766)	−.0130 (−.1583)	.1532 (1.741)
R²	.0186	.1201	.1205	.0195	.1215	.1291	.0190	.1136	.1184
Observations	1397	1199	1394	1397	1199	1394	1397	1199	1394

after six years, returns to all human capital acquired appear, and differences in income by education are clouded. On the one hand, more earnings are foregone by the more highly educated as they obtain more training. On the other hand, this group begins to reap returns to their human capital. The less-educated group invests less in on-the-job training (less income is foregone), but their earnings are lower.

Table 5 also shows earnings functions explaining income in the initial year of employment (when experience for each respondent was zero). Years of education still has a significantly positive effect with coefficients of over .045, despite predicted lower income (due to on-the-job training) for the more educated.

The IQ variable now becomes significantly negative, perhaps indicating a tendency for those more able to invest in greater on-the-job training in initial years in the labor force. If this relationship is stronger than that between years of education and on-the-job training, it might explain why the coefficient on years remains significantly positive in the initial year earnings functions.

Schooling quality is *never* statistically significant in the initial year earnings functions for either those with 16 or fewer years or those with graduate training. It is apparent that the importance of college quality grows with experience in the labor force, perhaps because students in better colleges are more prepared to benefit from on-the-job training in their postschool lives.

Interactive Models

How does college quality affect different types of people in our sample? How does quality interact with other variables in our earnings equations? First, separate regressions similar to those presented in Table 3 (that is, including IQ, YRS, EXP, and EXPSQD along with last quality) were estimated for individuals in our sample with IQ's above the sample mean (700 observations) and below the mean (811 observations). To show how the effect of college quality differed according to the ability of those who attended, Table 6 presents the elasticities derived as the product of the coefficient on quality ($d \ln Y/dQ$) and the mean values of quality. According to the t-test, the impact of quality is significantly greater for the higher-ability subsample for all definitions of quality but one.* (For SAT math the elasticities were not significantly

---

* The t-test was $H_0 : B_H = B_L$, where B_H is the coefficient of quality for the high-ability half of the sample and B_L is the quality coefficient for the low-ability half.

TABLE 6. Income Elasticities of Quality[a]

| | Gourman | | Average salary | SAT | | Instruc-tional, de-partmental research, & library expenses | Basic income | Basic expendi-tures | Astin intell. | Astin select. |
	Overall	Academic		Verbal	Math					
All observations	.3020	.3002	.4985	.6600	.7256	.1524	.1548	.0924	.5060	.6021
High IQ	.3363	.3654	.5761	.7703	.6937	.1744	.2143	.1217	.5762	.6862
Low IQ	.2492	.2375	.4328	.5636	.7579	.1283	.0850	.0480	.4470	.5207
t^b	5.003	5.9337	3.3917	2.9093	.8230	5.6336	13.1944	8.8326	2.8618	2.5765

[a] Controlling for YRS, EXP, EXPSQD, and IQ.

[b] The tests show whether there are significant differences in the elasticities for the high and low IQ parts of the sample. Differences are significant where t-values exceed 2.0 (approximately). The sample was divided into those with IQ above the mean and those below the mean of the whole sample of 1,511.

TABLE 7. INCOME ELASTICITIES OF COLLEGE QUALITY BY IQ QUARTILES[a]

	Low IQ	2	3	High IQ
Coefficient on $Z \times Q_{UG}$	.00094	.00061	.00050	.00097
(*t*-value)	(3.674)	(2.794)	(1.922)	(5.041)
Mean Q_{UG}	476.5	490.6	503.5	528.0
Elasticity	.448	.299	.252	.512
Coefficient on Q_{GRAD}	.00045	.00026	.00028	.0011
(*t*-value)	(1.691)	(1.138)	(1.044)	(5.393)
Mean Q_{GRAD}	501.6	518.6	532.1	552.0
Elasticity	.226	.135	.149	.607
Observations	376	421	338	434

[a] The quality measure used is the Gourman Overall Index, since this was available for all schools. The coefficients are from an earnings function explaining ln of 1969 income by years of education, experience, experience squared, IQ, and dummies for teachers, MD's, lawyers, and pilots. Income elasticities of quality are the coefficients times the mean quality. $Z = 1$ if education ≤ 16 years and 0 otherwise.

different.) The regressions from which Table 6 is derived reveal that coefficients on IQ were generally smaller, and coefficients on years in school and experience generally larger, for the high-ability group. The model explains 9 to 10 percent of the variance in 1969 income for those with ability above the mean, but only 4 to 5 percent of the variance of income of the lower-ability group was explained.[*]

These results lead us to further separate the sample into ability quartiles. Table 7 presents the coefficients on quality (measured by the Gourman Index, since it was available for the largest number of schools), undergraduate quality for those with 16 or fewer years, and graduate quality for those who achieved more than 16 years of education. We must remember that there were 10 variables in the earnings function, although we only present the quality coefficients and the elasticities. For the lowest three ability quartiles, both the quality coefficients and the income elasticities of quality are larger for those who attend school 16 or fewer years than for those with graduate work. For the top ability quartile, quality means more for those who have graduate work. Also, the effect of quality appears greatest, no matter the number of years, for those in the highest-ability quartile. Next greatest impact of quality is on those in the lowest-ability quartile. The students in the middle

[*] When SAT and average salaries are put in together, their effects are both more significant (*t*-test) and larger (size of coefficient) for the high-IQ half of the sample.

two ability quarters saw their incomes least influenced by quality of college. We must conclude that the interaction between college quality and individual ability is nonlinear. Since those in the lowest IQ quartile probably attended the poorest-quality schools, this result tends to confirm that differences in college quality are most important for low-quality schools. These results are invariant to the particular measure of quality used and to the addition of several other background variables into the earnings function.

Tables 6 and 7 indicate that college quality does influence incomes of the more able students more than it influences other students. Columns 3 and 4 of Table 8 reveal only a weak linear interaction between quality (now measured as average SAT verbal and average faculty salary rather than by the Gourman Index) and IQ. This is to be expected because of the previous* indication of nonlinearity.

Table 8 also tests for several other types of linear interactions, comparable to those in Table 2 (where the R^2, when SAT verbal was the quality measure, was .07885 and, when quality was measured by average salary, was .0825). The negative coefficient on quality squared (SAT verbal) suggests a slight lessening of the impact of quality as the level of quality rises. Finally, the effect of the quality of the last school attended did not seem to be a linear function of the number of years attended (Columns 5 and 6). This is not surprising in light of the relative importance of quality to those who do and do not have graduate training as demonstrated in Table 7. The earnings functions' explanatory power is only slightly improved by the addition of the interaction term.†

* Here the interaction term is specified as the product of the two variables concerned. That is, if

$$\ln Y = a + b \text{ QUAL} + c \text{ (QUAL)} \times \text{(IQ)},$$

then

$$\frac{d \ln Y}{dQ} = b + c \text{ IQ},$$

which differs statistically from b if c is significantly different from zero. This is a specific type of interaction. The high correlation between QUAL and (QUAL) × (IQ) tends to cloud interpretation of results. A quality squared term tests whether the effect of quality depends on its *level*.

† Since both SAT verbal and average salary were significant when used together, their combined interactions were studied in a single regression. The coefficient on the product of the two quality variables was not different from zero, indicating that the relationship between either quality measure and income is independent of the level of the other quality measure. The coefficients on the squared quality terms and on each quality measure times years were not significant. However, the coefficient on the SAT × IQ variable was significant according to the t-test (positive), and the average salary × IQ coefficient was almost significant (negative).

TABLE 8. EARNINGS FUNCTIONS WITH ONE INTERACTION TERM

	SAT verbal (1)	Average salary (2)	SAT verbal (3)	Average salary (4)	SAT verbal (5)	Average salary (6)
Constant	.3754 (.4927)	1.587 (4.066)	1.390 (6.994)	1.527 (8.415)	1.850 (1.896)	1.023 (1.481)
IQ	.03417 (4.700)	.03256 (4.473)	−.05133 (−.8881)	−.004114 (−.1029)	.03395 (4.668)	.03234 (4.441)
Years of education	.03635 (5.078)	.03324 (4.605)	.03667 (5.125)	.03356 (4.649)	.006485 (.1090)	.06290 (1.550)
Experience	.03067 (2.306)	.03512 (2.640)	.03153 (2.368)	.03570 (2.682)	.03035 (2.279)	.03591 (2.692)
Experience^2	−.0007403 (−2.263)	−.0008400 (−2.567)	−.0007506 (−2.294)	−.0008512 (−2.600)	−.0007259 (−2.217)	−.0008590 (−2.617)
Quality	.004657 (1.770)	.00003413 (.5338)	−.001058 (4.788)	.00004472 (5.382)	.0002603 (.1504)	.0009465 (1.461)
Quality^2	−.000003083 (−1.343)	.0000000005805 (.2027)				
Quality × IQ			.0001517 (1.488)	.000003481 (.9324)		
Quality × yr					.00005415 (.5094)	−.000002889 (−.7416)
R^2	.08110	.08425	.08136	.08476	.08015	.08456

TABLE 9. Simple Earnings Functions for Subsamples Divided by Own Ability and School Quality

	Individual high IQ		Individual low IQ	
	High SAT (math) average student	Low SAT (math) average student	High SAT (math) average student	Low SAT (math) average student
Constant	.6447	.4154	2.726	1.105
	(1.402)	(.8258)	(5.402)	(2.785)
IQ	.0345	.0105	.0487	.0436
	(1.835)	(4.948)	(1.913)	(2.267)
Years of education	.0543	.0621	.0233	.0282
	(4.124)	(4.733)	(1.740)	(2.721)
Experience	.0534	.0300	−.0089	.0289
	(2.207)	(1.250)	(−.3646)	(1.427)
Experience^2	−.0010	−.00049	.0002	−.0007
	(−1.704)	(−.8318)	(.2782)	(−1.385)
Quality^a	.0012	.0020	−.00008	.0019
	(2.208)	(2.467)	(−.1231)	(3.112)
R^2	.0764	.0792	.0185	.0486
Observations	494	465	448	656
Mean IQ	1.96	1.74	−1.01	−1.15
Mean SAT (math)	633	539	620	529
$\dfrac{\% \Delta \text{ Income}}{\% \Delta \text{ Quality}}$	.7596	1.178	−.0495	1.0051

^{a} Measured by average SAT (math) scores of entering freshmen.

The earnings functions were then rerun to include three interactions simultaneously: quality and IQ, quality and years of education, and IQ and years. When this formulation was estimated for the whole sample, only weak interactions between quality and IQ (generally positive) and quality and years of education (generally negative) were found. The interaction between IQ and years was never significant. Of course, by now multicollinearity is becoming a problem.

However, when only those with IQ's above the sample mean were included, a significant interaction (negative) between IQ and years was revealed. The interactions with quality now appeared weaker than for the whole sample. The estimates using people below mean IQ do not show a significant IQ × years interaction, but the interaction between quality and years (negative) becomes stronger.

The results just discussed are not presented in a table here for brevity. For people with below-average IQ, quality of college attended is more important for earnings the fewer years of college attended. Also, for people with above-average ability, the relationship between IQ and income is stronger the fewer years of education obtained. One problem with these formulations is that the arguments in the interactive earnings function become highly correlated. The strong differences revealed when the simple earnings function is run for subsamples, compared to the results from the interactive model, lead us to stress the procedure of dividing up the sample and running regressions for subsets of observations.

Table 9 contains simple earnings functions for the sample divided not only into high- and low-IQ groups, but within these, into those who attended high- or low-quality colleges.* These regressions indicate that the impact of quality, as measured by average SAT math scores of entering freshmen, is greatest at poorer schools. The coefficient on quality is .002 in both quarters of the sample where quality is below average and .0012 for the high-quality, high-ability group. The income elasticities of quality follow the same pattern. Interestingly, for the low individual IQ, high average SAT group, the coefficient on quality is not significantly different from zero. The t-values on average SAT are highest for the low-school-quality groups as well.

These regressions indicate a higher return to years of education for the high-ability people, regardless of college quality. The only group where IQ seems to be less important than others in terms of later earnings is composed of high-ability people attending poor schools. Returns to experience are also higher for the high-ability group.

We also tested for interactions within each of these four parts of our sample. There were only a few significant interactions: a significant negative coefficient on the quality × years variable for the high-ability, low-quality group; and a strong positive interaction between quality and ability in the low-ability, high-quality group. The interaction terms add to the power of the model, but not a great deal: The earnings functions for people falling into each of the four categories look different; however, precise patterns by school quality and individual ability are not immediately visible.

Table 10 examines earnings functions for those with 16 or less years of schooling and those with 17 or more years separately. Columns 1

---

* There are four regressions:

1. Those with ability greater than sample mean attending schools with average math SAT of entering freshmen above the sample mean
2. Those with high ability going to below-average-quality colleges
3. Those with low ability going to above-average-quality colleges
4. Those with low ability in below-average-quality colleges

TABLE 10. SEPARATE EARNINGS FUNCTIONS FOR THOSE WITH UNDERGRADUATE TRAINING ONLY AND FOR THOSE WITH GRADUATE TRAINING (DEPENDENT VARIABLE LOG OF 1969 EARNINGS)

	SAT math		Average faculty salary		Gourman overall		Generally poorer students at poorer schools			
							Gourman overall		Expenditures: research & library	
	UG	GRAD	UG	GRAD	UG	GRAD	UG	GRAD	UG	GRAD
Constant	.9672	1.142	1.063	1.157	1.334	1.412	1.414	.6265	1.520	1.009
	(3.463)	(1.733)	(4.019)	(1.852)	(5.347)	(2.278)	(8.650)	(1.842)	(9.539)	(3.027)
Years of education	.0602	.0349	.0602	.0410	.0594	.0378	.0593	.0827	.0602	.0804
	(4.292)	(1.289)	(4.299)	(1.551)	(4.226)	(1.417)	(6.390)	(5.818)	(6.512)	(5.639)
IQ	.0227	.0397	.0215	.0376	.0249	.0414	.0243	.0299	.0246	.0331
	(2.497)	(2.854)	(2.367)	(2.800)	(2.755)	(3.112)	(4.035)	(3.828)	(4.108)	(4.229)
Experience	.0281	.0328	.0353	.0247	.0307	.0185	.0178	.0066	.0189	.0097
	(1.861)	(.8828)	(2.327)	(.6847)	(2.028)	(.5054)	(1.794)	(.3346)	(1.909)	(.4888)
Experience²	-.0006	-.0006	-.0008	-.0005	-.0007	-.0003	-.0003	.0002	-.0004	.00006
	(-1.757)	(-.6518)	(-2.197)	(-.4916)	(-1.883)	(-.2578)	(-1.352)	(.2935)	(-1.468)	(.1094)
Q_UG	.0012	.0002	.00005	-.0000008	.0006	.0002	.0006	.0004	.0002	.00003
	(4.476)	(.4338)	(4.891)	(-.0505)	(4.170)	(.7166)	(5.415)	(2.979)	(5.780)	(1.014)
Q_GRAD		.0012		.00007		.0009		.0007		.0002
		(2.610)		(5.042)		(4.247)		(5.357)		(5.531)
Pilot	.4336	.2743	.4137	.2894	.4236	.1116	.4946	.4140	.4949	.5067
	(3.278)	(.6075)	(3.135)	(.6599)	(3.200)	(.2502)	(4.934)	(1.435)	(4.940)	(1.748)
Teacher	-.3311	-.2781	-.3423	-.2907	-.3254	-.2791	-.3115	-.2938	-.3172	-.3030
	(-1.713)	(-3.789)	(-1.775)	(-4.087)	(-1.680)	(-3.877)	(-2.818)	(-8.471)	(-2.873)	(-8.712)
MD		.6930		.7056		.7407		.6258		.5951
		(4.020)		(4.232)		(4.372)		(6.173)		(5.849)
Lawyer		.1967		.2281		.2270		.2238		.2253
		(2.039)		(2.446)		(2.401)		(4.362)		(4.378)
R²	.0760	.2317	.0793	.2750	.0737	.2604	.0730	.3119	.0746	.3037
Observations	1074	320	1074	320	1074	320	2241	856	2241	856

through 6 contain only respondents who had data for all three quality measures—SAT, average faculty salary, and Gourman Index—for their undergraduate schools and for their graduate school if they attended. Columns 7 through 10 contain a larger sample, omitting only those without Gourman and expenditure data. The larger sample had a lower mean IQ and lower average quality (Gourman) schools. In only one case (Gourman—larger sample) was undergraduate quality statistically significant for those who went on to graduate school. In almost all cases impact of last quality was greater (or equal) for those with more years; clearly, effects of quality are greater for this group if effects of undergraduate and graduate quality are combined. These results are at odds with some presented earlier, where the impact of quality was greater for those with 16 or fewer years, except for those in the highest-ability quartile. However, here we are no longer constraining the coefficients on other variables to be the same, since we estimate different functions by years of schooling. Also, those with 17 or more years surely were of the highest ability, and so the interaction between IQ and quality is evident again.

Conclusion

Astin (1971) has said that "the available evidence suggests that for students there is little or no intellectual 'value added' from attending a highly selective college" (pp. 633–634). However, our research demonstrates that high income in later life, an important goal of higher education, is powerfully affected by several dimensions of college quality.

Two distinct dimensions of college quality have been identified: peer-group effects, measured by average SAT scores of entering freshmen at a college, and faculty quality, measured by average faculty salary. College quality has increasing impacts on earnings over time; that is, the income elasticity of quality is not statistically significant in the initial year of employment and is greater after 20 years than after 7 years, although both of the latter are significant.

College quality appears to have a greater impact on incomes for high-ability students than for low-ability students, when comparing earnings functions estimated separately for the top and bottom halves of the sample by IQ. Also, the multiplicative interaction terms for quality and IQ were positive and almost statistically significant. When earnings functions were estimated for the sample divided into IQ quartiles, the coefficient on college quality rose steadily between the second lowest IQ quartile and the highest; however, the lowest quartile was affected by quality almost as much as the highest. This can also mean quality differences matter more for those in poor-quality colleges (usually attended by those with low IQ).

When divided into IQ quartiles, the sample revealed that the coefficient of undergraduate quality was greater for those with 16 or fewer years of education than was the coefficient on graduate quality for those who went on in all quartiles, except the highest IQ where the relative size of coefficients is reversed. For graduates, undergraduate quality is omitted, so the coefficient on graduate quality is biased upwards. However, when the sample is divided according to those with more than 16 years and those with no more than one degree, it appears that the former reveal greater impacts of quality, including both graduate and undergraduate. This result is probably due to the higher ability of those with more than 16 years of schooling. Sample size limitations precluded more detailed subdivision of the sample.

Data on the Gourman Index were available for more schools than were data on average SAT scores and average faculty salary. For comparison, the sample usually studied was the subset of people for whom all three relevant measures were available. As a check, the earnings functions were rerun for the larger sample that had Gourman only. This larger group was of somewhat lower mean ability (and had a lower average Gourman Index). The quality variables were still significant and revealed the same patterns, but the coefficients were *smaller*, once again revealing a positive interaction between ability and quality.

There is some weak evidence that differences in quality are more significant at low-quality schools than at better institutions. There also seems to be a negative relationship between college quality and years of education in terms of future earning power, except for those at the top of the ability distribution. Two general observations can be made: First, individual ability complements college quality; and second, additional years in school are substitutes for college quality.

Several limitations of these conclusions must be acknowledged. Only people in the upper half of the national ability distribution are included. However, if interactions between IQ and college quality are evident in the narrower IQ range, they should be even stronger with a more general sample. Secondly, no blacks are included. One of the implications of the "peer-group" effect is an advocacy of "busing," which usually has involved an explicit attempt to alter racial compositions of schools. The results found here should not be generalized to the black–white case, although the results in Coleman *et al.* (1966) and elsewhere look at both races and find similar effects of peers.

Finally, most of the work has not controlled for a number of important elements in the earnings process. When we attempted to do so, the results pertaining to quality were not changed, except the coefficients were smaller. Family background was either not considered or measured by a three-way (high, medium, low) ranking of father's occupation. Karabel & Astin (1972) have recently argued that socioeconomic status is postively correlated with college quality. Moreover, Hauser *et al.* (1971) and Bowles (1972) have indicated that father's income should be used to measure status. If these points are correct, then our coefficients on quality are biased upwards, standing for *both* college attributes and family background.

However, the studies of income that stress socioeconomic background do not ask the same questions about interactions. Thus, it is impossible to say whether the conclusions should be altered. Obviously, there should be more interaction among researchers of different focus, all of whom are seeking answers to essentially the same question—What causes different people to earn different amounts of money?

REFERENCES

American Association of University Professors. The economic status of the profession, 1963–64. *AAUP Bulletin.* 1964: 139–184.

Astin, A. W. *Who goes where to college.* Chicago: Science Research Associates, 1965.

Astin, A. W. Open admission and programs for the disadvantaged. *Journal of Higher Education,* 1971, 42: 629–647.

Becker, G. S. *Human capital, a theoretical and empirical analysis, with special reference to education.* New York: National Bureau of Economic Research, 1964 (General Series, No. 80).

Bowles, S. Schooling and inequality from generation to generation. *Journal of Political Economy,* 1972, 80(3, Pt. 2): S219–S251.

Bureau of the Census, U.S. Department of Commerce. U.S. census of population, 1950. *Education,* Special Report PE-5B. Washington, D.C.: U.S. Government Printing Office, 1953.

Cass, J., & Birnbaum, M. *Comparative guide of American colleges.* New York: Harper and Row, 1969.

Coleman, J. S. *et al. Equality of educational opportunity.* U.S. Department of Health, Education, and Welfare. Washington, D.C.: U.S. Government Printing Office, 1966.

Gourman, J. *The Gourman report.* Phoenix: The Continuing Education Institute, 1967.

Hauser, R. M., Lutterman, K. G., & Sewell, W. H. Socioeconomic background and the earnings of high school graduates. Paper presented at the meeting of the American Sociological Association, Denver, August 1971.

Karabel, J., & Astin, A. W. Social class, academic ability, and college "quality." Unpublished manuscript, Office of Research, American Council on Education, June 1972.

President's Commission on Veterans Payments. *The historical development of veterans benefits in the U.S.* Washington, D.C.: U.S. Government Printing Office, 1956.

Taubman, P. J., & Wales, T. Earnings: Higher education, mental ability and screening. Unpublished manuscript, University of Pennsylvania, 1972.

Taubman, P. J., & Wales, T. *Education as an investment and as a screening device.* New York: National Bureau of Economic Research, in press.

Thorndike, R. L., & Hagen, E. *Ten thousand careers.* New York: Wiley, 1959.

Welch, F. Measurement of the quality of schooling. *American Economic Review,* 1966, 56: 379–392.

DISCUSSION

ROBERT M. HAUSER: The "high" correlation between occupational status and income that Solmon reports ("The Definition and Impact of College Quality," pp. 77–102) (.91) refers to a population of occupation titles, not persons. Among U.S. males, it is more like .50, the correlation ratio of income on occupation. This implies the possibility—which is realized—of some autonomy in the behavior of occupation and earnings as dependent variables (Hauser et al., 1971).

Solmon's reference to Sewell's sample of Wisconsin high school seniors of 1957 is misleading where he says it includes fewer than 1,000 cases, including only those with farm fathers and including no women. While we have indeed dealt with subsamples like those Solmon describes, the full sample includes 9,007 respondents—male and female—to a follow-up seven years after high school—representing a seven-year response rate of over 87 percent. There is also a separate file of all persons in the top tenth in ability. We have Social Security earnings (for males only) as well as attitudinal, mental test, academic performance, social background, and follow-up data from such sources as the high schools, state testing service, and state tax department.

Solmon, like Anne Ellison and Bennett Simon ("Does College Make a Person Healthy and Wise?," pp. 35–63), refers to an alleged dominance of maternal achievement, aspiration, and encouragement in the determination of a son's social achievements. In our analyses of the full Wisconsin cohort we have found no support for this thesis. Neither maternal education, nor presence in the labor force, nor earnings has effects as large as achievements of the father (Sewell & Shah, 1968; Sewell, 1971; Hauser et al., 1971; Hauser, 1972).

When I first began to read the work of economists in the area of returns to education, I was puzzled by the fact that economists typically avoid the use of occupation as a variable intervening between education and earnings, while sociologists typically divide earnings differentials into components between and within occupations. After a bit of thought I decided that the concept of "returns to education" refers to a reduced-form coefficient, *not* a structural coefficient. While one may wish to specify a complete structural model, which should include variables preceding and following educational attainment, only the former are pertinent in estimating total returns to education. The latter, of course, serve the function of interpretation.

In this context I was puzzled to hear Solmon's assertion at the conference that "In order to get a proper measure of the relationship between education and these goals that might be acquired as a result of characteristics obtained in school, we must control for those factors prior *and subsequent* to schooling that impinge upon the education–income (or job status) relationship." For example, in Solmon's paper this notion takes the form of the introduction of "dummy variables" in the earnings function for occupations known to have "atypical" education–earnings patterns. In so doing Solmon produces a hybrid model in which neither the returns to education nor the full structure are adequately displayed. For example, in the 1971 paper by Sewell, Lutterman, and myself to which Solmon refers, we find that the effect of educational attainment on earnings is reduced by 53 percent when we control the full range of occupational status. Surely, we should not wish to make any such adjustment in our estimate of returns to education but rather to observe that about half the return is due to the better jobs of the more educated and half to the better pay of those with more education in the same job.

As Solmon correctly points out, one of the chief interests of sociologists in this area has been to measure and specify the effects of background correctly, yet this possibility is *not* pursued in his analyses of the National Bureau of Economic Research–Thorndike data, and with results we are unable to assess. Specifically, my hypothesis is that the *additive* college effects Solmon finds are artifacts of his failure to specify those socioeconomic and social–psychological factors that affect college choice. Let me illustrate the pertinence of the effects of background. Among nonfarm Wisconsin boys out of school in 1964 the zero-order, education–earnings correlation overestimates by 24 percent the effect of education with ability controlled, and it overestimates by 53 percent the effect of education with ability and socioeconomic background controlled. Likewise, controlling socioeconomic background as well as ability increases the estimated bias in the zero-order, education–occupation relation from 10 to 16 percent.

I find myself untouched by the spirit of Solmon's interest in college quality. First, I am not sure the results replicate. In the Wisconsin data Alwin (1972) finds modest additive effects of colleges upon length of schooling (drop-out) and on earnings, but *not* occupations. He finds *no* interaction effects involving type of college attended, nor does he find any substantial or consistent pattern of effects of college characteristics upon education, occupation, or earnings in the early career. Of course, this does not foreclose the possibility that larger college effects on earnings will appear later. Second, in a paper that focuses on returns to *higher* education it is understandable that sociological research on effects of school quality at the secondary level would be a neglected topic. Yet work in this area, of which the Coleman Report (1966) represents a perhaps too visible superstructure, may be pertinent. Two observations come to mind: (a) School effects on achievement and aspirations are rather meager relative to those of other variables whose character we are able to specify (Sewell & Armer, 1966; Hauser, 1969, 1971). If the argument for an interest in college quality is the extent to which it represents the major axis of differentiation in post-high school education in an era when it is becoming universal, then it may be pertinent to ask why the same kind of differentiation among schools did *not* occur when high school was the modal level of attainment. (b) The chief methodological lesson of sociological work in this area has been that understanding of the schooling process is fatally obscured by a reliance on aggregate characteristics of schools to represent variables in that process (Hauser, 1970, 1971).

Finally, I would like to reemphasize the point of Taubman & Wales, reiterated by Solmon, that one's samples ought to represent populations of interest.

REFERENCES

Alwin, D. College effects on educational and socioeconomic achievement. Unpublished doctoral dissertation, University of Wisconsin, Madison, 1972.

Coleman, J. S. *et al. Equality of educational opportunity.* U.S. Department of Health, Education, and Welfare, Washington, D.C.: U.S. Government Printing Office, 1966.

Hauser, R. M. Schools and the stratification process. *American Journal of Sociology,* 1969, 74: 587–611.

Hauser, R. M. Context and consex: A cautionary tale. *American Journal of Sociology,* 1970, 75: 645–664.

Hauser, R. M. *Socioeconomic background and educational performance.* Rose Monograph Series. Washington, D.C.: American Sociological Association, 1971.

Hauser, R. M. Disaggregating a social–psychological model of educational attainment. *Social Science Research,* 1972, 1: 159–188.

Hauser, R. M., Lutterman, K. G., & Sewell, W. H. Socioeconomic background and the earnings of high school graduates. Paper presented at the meeting of the American Sociological Association, Denver, August 1971.

Sewell, W. H. Inequality of opportunity for higher education. *American Sociological Review,* 1971, 36: 793–813.

Sewell, W. H., & Armer, J. M. Neighborhood context and college plans. *American Sociological Review,* 1966, 31: 159–168.

Sewell, W. H., & Shah, V. P. Parents' education and children's educational aspirations and achievements. *American Sociological Review,* 1968, 33: 191–209.

ALEXANDER W. ASTIN: There is one thing to keep in mind with the use of the Ten Thousand Careers data in Lewis Solmon's study, "The Definition and Impact of College Quality" (pp. 77–102): His measures of ability and social background were obtained sometime prior to the actual matriculation of these students in college. It seems to follow, then, that there were considerable differential shifts in ability, and to some extent even social background, between the time these measures were obtained and the actual decision of the college to accept the applicant, or the decision of the prospective student to apply. It would also follow, it seems to me, that the GI's who had spuriously high scores would be less likely to matriculate into a highly selective institution than those who had legitimately high scores, not just in terms of errors of measurement but also in terms of real changes in ability. Thus, we may be seeing that the increment to later performance apparently found by Solmon may be partly a result of differential changes that took place prior to college entrance.

Concerning Ellison & Simon's study, "Does College Make a Person Healthy and Wise?" (pp. 35–63), many of the changes that have been observed in such esoteric measures as personality inventories are also supported by self-reported, but reasonably trustworthy, behavioral changes. Those occurring during the undergraduate years include an increase in smoking, drinking, drug use, and a decline in church attendance. Oversleeping and missing classes increases tremendously, and there is a dramatic decline in the percentage of students who pick a formal religion when asked—a great increase in the "nones." The same people who change religious preference also tend to show a decline in church attendance, so at least our data are internally consistent.

Finally, it must be stressed that we have said nothing about reasons for these changes or the direction of causation.

MEASUREMENT AND DETERMINANTS OF THE OUTPUTS OF HIGHER EDUCATION

Alexander W. Astin

Measuring Student Outputs in Higher Education*

Any consideration of how best to measure the outputs of higher education necessarily requires that one clarify just what is meant by "outputs." I shall use a conceptualization of student outputs that has characterized recent longitudinal research on the impact of colleges on their students (Astin, 1970). While this view may be foreign to some readers, particularly to those whose backgrounds are in economics or related fields, I believe that it is useful in elucidating certain basic issues that might otherwise be overlooked.

THE SYSTEM OF HIGHER EDUCATION

Briefly, in this view, the process of higher education is regarded as comprising three conceptually distinct components: *student outputs, student inputs,* and the *college environment*. Student *outputs* refer to those aspects of the student's development that the college either influ-

---

* The first part of this paper has appeared in Lawrence, B., Weathersby, G., & Patterson, V. (Eds.), *Outputs of Higher Education: Their Identification, Measurement and Evaluation*. Boulder: Western Interstate Commission for Higher Education, 1970.

ences or attempts to influence. Although these outputs can be expressed at very high levels of abstraction (for example, "the ultimate happiness and well-being of the individual"), we shall limit our consideration of the problem to those relatively immediate outputs that can be operationalized. Specifically, then, student outputs would include measures of the student's achievements, knowledge, skills, values, attitudes, aspirations, interests, daily activities, and contributions to society. Other terms that are sometimes used to refer to student outputs are dependent variables, criterion variables, outcome variables, and educational objectives.

Student *inputs* are the talents, skills, aspirations, and other potentials for growth and learning that the new student brings with him to college. These inputs are, in a sense, the raw materials with which the institution has to work. Some inputs may be simply "pretests" on certain student outputs (scores on college admissions tests, for example), while others (sex and race, for example) may be relatively static personal attributes. Inputs can affect the outputs either directly or through interaction with environmental variables. It should be pointed out that economists and others interested in systems analysis or management information systems typically use the term "input" in a much broader sense than the one proposed here. Usually, this broader use includes what I have termed environmental variables as well as student inputs. In assessing the outputs of higher educational institutions, however, it is useful, if not essential, to differentiate conceptually and operationally between measures of student inputs and measures of the college environment.

The *college environment* refers to any aspect of the higher educational institution that is capable of affecting student outputs. Broadly speaking, the term includes variables such as administrative policies and practices, curriculum, faculty, physical plant and facilities, teaching practices, peer associations, and other attributes of the college experience that might affect the student's development. These environmental variables can, presumably, be changed or manipulated through reallocation of resources.

The relationships among the three components of the model are shown schematically in Figure 1. Note that student outputs can be affected by both environmental variables (Arrow B) and student input variables (Arrow C). Moreover, as Arrow A indicates, college environments can be affected by the kinds of students who enroll. In addition to these "main" effects of environments and inputs on outputs, there may be *interaction* effects involving student inputs and college environments. As the diagram suggests, there are two types of interaction effects: those in which the effect of input on output is different in different college

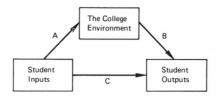

Fig. 1. The three components of the model.

environments (AC), and those in which the effect of the college environment is different for different types of students (AB).

The matter of assessing the outputs of higher education involves two
basic problems. The first is that of defining and measuring the relevant
output variables; this will be a major subject of this paper. The second,
closely related task is that of determining the *effects* of environmental
and student output variables. This latter problem, which involves primarily experimental design and statistical methodology, is dealt with
at length in another paper (Astin, 1970). Suffice it to say that no matter
how elegantly or appropriately the output variables are measured, no
management information system is of much use unless the *causal* connections between environmental variables and output variables are known.
In order to make trustworthy judgments about these causal relationships,
it is necessary first to conduct longitudinal studies that incorporate
data on student inputs, student outputs, and college environmental characteristics (Astin & Panos, 1970).

Conceptual Outputs and Output Measures

The measurement of any educational output ordinarily begins with
a statement about some aspect of the student's development that is
considered desirable or important. This verbal statement, or *conceptual
output,* originates in the value system of the person making the statement. The task in developing an appropriate *output measure* is to opera-
tionalize this conceptual output in some way (Astin, 1964). The process
of operationalizing typically involves collecting empirical data that are
judged to be relevant to the conceptual output. In some instances, the
raw data already takes the form of a "measure" (dropping out versus
staying in college, for example), whereas in others, the raw data must
be combined or manipulated in some way in order to derive the final
measure (answers to multiple-choice questions on an achievement test,
for example).

In attempting to "evaluate" an output measure, or set of measures,
one must keep in mind the distinction between conceptual outputs and

output measures. The appropriateness of any empirical measure can be judged only in terms of its apparent relevance to the conceptual output. In contrast, the conceptual criterion itself—being derived basically from value judgments—is not subject to the same sort of analysis.

Although we cannot differentiate operationally between the conceptual output and the output measure, the construct of *conceptual output* is important for at least two reasons. First, the relevance of any output measure and the rationale for its being selected are better understood if the conceptual stage is documented. Second, because the conceptual output often implies something more than the actual output measure, it may prove to be a valuable source either of future output measures or of improvements in existing ones.

SINGLE OR MULTIPLE MEASURES?

Any discussion of the measurement of educational outputs must give some attention to the question of using multiple measures versus a single "overall" measure of educational progress. Although a single output measure possesses certain obvious advantages because of its conceptual simplicity and computational convenience, it is unrealistic as well as misleading to reduce college impact to a single output measure. Therefore, in discussing the various problems associated with measuring student outputs, I have assumed that there are many outcomes, both planned and unplanned, that must be measured if an adequate and useful assessment of institutional impact is to be carried out. This assumption is based on a belief that even within a relatively homogeneous group of undergraduates, individuals can vary greatly in the importance they attach to any given educational outcome. Accordingly, this paper will not treat the problem of assigning relative weights to various alternative outcomes. Subjective weighting in terms of degree of "importance" requires value judgments that are more appropriately the province of the students, educators, planners, legislators, and others directly concerned. In other words, I have assumed that the conceptual and methodological problems associated with identifying and measuring relevant educational outcomes can be isolated from the more personal and value-laden problem of deciding what degree of importance should be attached to any particular outcome. The challenge to the researcher, then, is to make sure that his coverage of student outputs is broad enough to meet most of the major concerns of the various constituent groups.

Although it is important that any battery of output measures reflect the interests of as many persons as possible, an adequate assessment of the outcomes of the college experience cannot be limited solely to outputs that are either desired or intended. The unintended outputs or "side effects" of the college experience must be considered, too.

When we talk about side effects in medicine, they are usually regarded as undesirable; but the side effects of attending college may or may not be desirable, depending on the particular side effect and the value system of the individual immediately concerned. A new college curriculum, for example, may have its intended effects on the student's cognitive abilities, but it may also have unplanned-for effects on, say, the student's vocational and career plans. In short, as long as the possibility exists that a particular output measure is affected by the student's college experiences, that measure should not be rejected as "irrelevant" simply because it does not fit in with some *a priori* educational plan.

A SIMPLE TAXONOMY OF OUTPUT MEASURES

Because the number of possible output measures is very large, some sort of *taxonomy* of such measures is essential. Taxonomies are useful not only for classifying existing output measures but also for suggesting additional measures. As a beginning, I would propose that output measures be classified on the basis of three attributes: the type of outcome, the type of data, and the time span involved.

Type of Outcome

Behavioral scientists usually classify measures of human performance into two broad domains: cognitive (sometimes called "intellective") and noncognitive (sometimes called "affective"). Cognitive measures have to do with behavior that requires the use of high-order mental processes such as reasoning and logic. Of all the possible measures of performance that one might devise for evaluating student outputs, those involving cognitive learning and the development of cognitive skills are probably the most relevant to the educational objectives not only of students, but also of faculty, administrators, trustees, parents, and others concerned with higher education.

Noncognitive, or affective, measures have to do with the student's attitudes, values, self-concept, aspirations, and social and interpersonal relationships. Although the number of possible noncognitive outputs is very large, techniques for measuring such outputs are not as far advanced as are those for measuring cognitive outputs.

Type of Data

The second dimension of the taxonomy refers to the operations that are performed in order to obtain measurements of the cognitive or affective outputs under consideration. Again, two broad classes can be identified: *psychological* data relating to the internal states or "traits" of the individual and *behavioral* data relating to the observable activities of the individual. The measurement of psychological phenomena is usually indirect, in the sense that the investigator *infers* some underlying state within the individual from his responses to a standard set of test questions. Behavioral measures reflecting transactions between the person and his environment are usually of intrinsic interest. Since behavioral (as opposed to psychological) measures typically involve observing the individual in his environment, such measures might also be termed "sociological."

Any student output measure can be classified simultaneously by the type of outcome involved and by the type of data used, as shown in Table 1. Each cell provides examples of different types of outcome measures obtained using different types of data. The cell in the upper left of Table 1, for example, includes cognitive outcomes that are often measured in terms of the student's grade-point average or his performance on multiple-choice tests of ability and achievement. The undergraduate student's knowlege, basic skills, and critical thinking ability are often assessed by means of batteries such as the Graduate Record Examination (GRE). Achievement in specialized fields can be measured by means of the advanced tests on the GRE, and general achievement and intelligence by means of the GRE area and aptitude tests. One

TABLE 1. A TAXONOMY OF STUDENT OUTPUT MEASURES IN TERMS OF TYPE OF OUTCOME AND TYPE OF DATA

Type of data	Type of outcome	
	Cognitive	Affective
Psychological	Knowledge General intelligence Critical thinking ability Basic skills Special aptitudes Academic achievement	Self-concept Interests Values Attitudes Beliefs Drive for achievement Satisfaction with college

Behavioral	Level of educational attainment
	Vocational achievements:
	   level of responsibility, income,
	   awards of special recognition
		Choice of a major or career
		Avocations
		Mental health
		Citizenship
		Interpersonal relations

aspect of cognitive ability for which psychological measures are probably still not adequate is creative ability. Only a few exist (Taylor & Barron, 1963).

The upper right cell of Table 1 includes psychological measures of noncognitive or affective states: the student's ambition, motivation, self-concept, as well as his subjective feelings of satisfaction and well-being. Most of the research on college impact that has been conducted so far has been concerned with psychological measures of affective states. Thus, of the more than 1,000 studies of college impact recently reviewed by Feldman & Newcomb (1969), only a handful used measures of cognitive outcomes and, of these, virtually all used psychological rather than behavioral measures. This bias is, to some extent, probably a matter of logistical convenience. Psychological measures of affective state—attitudes, values, career plans, and the like—are simple and inexpensive to administer to undergraduates before, during, and after they attend college, whereas measures of cognitive outputs and measures of behavioral or sociological outputs ordinarily require considerable time and expense to administer.

The lower left cell in Table 1 gives examples of behavioral or sociological measures of cognitive outputs. Basically, this category refers to outputs that reflect the behavior of the student (or former student) in society and that ordinarily require cognitive skills. Presumably, these real-life achievements represent the behavioral manifestations of the cognitive traits listed in the cell above.

The fourth cell, located in the lower right quadrant of Table 1, includes sociological or behavioral features of the individual's development that reflect primarily affective states. Under "avocations," for example, one might include the amount of time spent by the person in various recreational pursuits. "Citizenship" might be manifested in the amount and quality of participation in community activities, the earning of special awards for service to the community, or, on the negative side, welfare or arrest records.

It should be pointed out that the two dimensions comprising Table 1 are really more continua than true dichotomies. For example, a person's earned income and job status (which would be subsumed under "vocational achievements" in the cognitive domain) may involve his noncognitive or personality traits.

With respect to the two types of data (psychological and behavioral) defining the two rows of Table 1, it is important to keep in mind that psychological measures are less likely to be regarded as socially relevant outputs than are the behavioral measures. Nevertheless, some psychological measures "acquire" behavioral significance as the result of empirical research. Measures of general intelligence and academic ability, for example, have acquired behavioral significance because longitudinal research has shown that persons with high scores on such measures are usually successful vocationally and socially (Terman & Oden, 1947; Nichols & Astin, 1966). The connection between psychological and behavioral measures in the affective domain, however, is much less well established. Perhaps the only instance in which psychological measures of affective outputs are known to bear more than a trivial relationship to subsequent behavioral phenomena is interest measurement. Measured vocational interests are closely associated with later career development and success over many years (Strong, 1955).

Time Span Covered by the Measure

The four cells shown in Table 1 could be extended into a third dimension to portray the temporal aspects of the output measurement being used. Although it is not often considered in discussions of educational outputs, time is a fundamental consideration. Is it more appropriate to measure the immediate outputs of the college experience—that is, those that take place after only a brief span of time—or the outputs that show the long-term effects of the college experience?

Most educational institutions are designed with the hope of producing long-term rather than short-term changes. The goals stated in college catalogs, for example, imply that the institution is primarily concerned with making an impact on the student that will last throughout his lifetime. The college, it would seem, tries to provide experiences that will assist the student in making the fullest possible use of his talents and in becoming an effective, responsible member of society. Presumably, such effects will, in turn, result in a more satisfying and rewarding life.

For many prospective college students, however, such long-term effects are too remote and too difficult to comprehend. These students are primarily interested in much more immediate goals—their actual experiences during the undergraduate college years—rather than in how these experiences will affect their later development. Educators frequently overlook the fact that the two, four, or eight years of college represent a sizable proportion of the student's total life span. To him, then, college experiences are important in and of themselves, not merely in what they will mean later on after the student leaves college.

It seems likely that psychological measures, particularly of cognitive outputs, are most relevant for the college years, whereas behavioral measures are more suitable for assessing both short- and long-term effects. The point to keep in mind is that the appropriateness of any output measure—whether it be cognitive or affective, whether it be derived from psychological or from behavioral data—is determined in part by the period of time spanned by the measure. Clearly, there are valid arguments for using both short-term and long-term measures.

The importance of timing in the development of output measures can be illustrated with a hypothetical example. Let us assume that a student from a small rural high school enrolls in a highly selective and academically competitive institution. His initial experiences result in a variety of relatively short-term or immediate outputs, both psychological and behavioral, both cognitive and affective. Affectively, the student feels anxious about possible academic failure, hostile and competitive toward fellow students, and proud of the institution. On the behavioral side, he devotes more time to study and less to social activities, and he becomes more intellectually aggressive toward his fellow students and his instructors, more inclined to argue with them. Such affective changes might be assessed by means of inventories or questionnaires administered at the time of matriculation and again after a few months in college. On the cognitive side, our hypothetical student becomes much more knowledgeable about certain subjects as a result of his increased devotion to study. Such knowledge would, presumably, be reflected in follow-up achievement testing. Behavioral manifestations of cognitive changes take the form of his being elected to honorary societies and receiving awards for special achievements (essays, authorship of publications, etc.).

The longer-range effects of attending the highly competitive institution can also be classified by type of outcome and by type of data used. To return to our hypothetical student, we find that in the affective domain his four years in the highly competitive institution have fairly long-lasting effects on his self-esteem, as well as on his feelings of competitiveness, anxiety, and inferiority. These psychological changes are also manifested behaviorally in the amount of time he devotes to his job and by the extent to which he competes with others on the job. Cognitive outcomes of attending the highly selective college are reflected in his successfully completing graduate school and, later, in his achieving a high-level position, a high salary, and special awards from his professional society for outstanding achievement.

It should be pointed out here that psychological measures of cognitive outputs, such as performance on standardized tests, are usually not obtained once a person leaves formal higher education. In fact, the person who holds a college degree normally does not have to take cognitive tests that are otherwise required by the military, industry, and the civil service. But there is no reason why cognitive testing could not be used at *any* time following college, given adequate resources and the subject's willingness to participate.

RELATIVE VERSUS ABSOLUTE MEASURES

Our discussion of Figure 1 has already suggested that the problem of defining educational outcomes is inextricably bound up with the methodology employed to secure the actual measure. Methodology involves not only the operations that are performed to gather the raw data but also the manipulations of the raw data by which the final "measure" is derived. In the field of achievement testing, for example, the common practice is to devise a list of multiple-choice test items; administer them to a sample of students; count the number of items answered correctly by each student; and then calculate a *derived* measure that is expressed in terms of a standard score, a percentile score, or some other relative value. That is, a person's final score reflects only how he has performed relative to others.

In achievement and aptitude testing, relative measures are used almost universally as measures of educational outcomes. But they present some potentially serious problems. Such measures indicate nothing about the student's *absolute* level of performance. They give no direct information as to how many items the student answered correctly, how difficult the items were, or what the student's test performance implies about his potential for performing well on the job, profiting from further education, and the like. More important, such relative measures offer no way of reflecting *changes* in the student's performance over a period of time. Thus, it is possible for a student's absolute (i.e., actual) performance or competence to improve considerably over a period of time, while his relative performance remains the same or even declines during the same period.

There are several explanations as to why specialists in educational measurement have a predilection for relative rather than absolute measures of performance. One argument for derived scores (particularly standard scores) is that they possess certain statistical properties that make them more suitable for some types of analyses. A more subtle explanation involves the meritocratic bias of the culture and, in particular, of the educational system. Derived scores, which are an indication of the person's relative ordering among his peers, provide a convenient means of identifying the most talented persons for purposes of recruitment into jobs, graduate and professional schools, and other areas where competition for a finite pool of talent is strong. Nevertheless, *for purposes of assessing the impact of any college on the student's development, derived or relative measures of student outputs appear to have very limited usefulness.*

There are several possible approaches to the problem of developing measures of absolute performance. If the measure is based on the types of multiple-choice items usually found in aptitude or achievement tests, perhaps the most straightforward approach is simply to record the number of items correctly answered. Change or growth in the student's development can thus be measured in terms of increases in the number or percentage of such items correctly answered. One useful elaboration of this approach is to develop expectancy tables that show the probability of various events (performing well on the job, for example) as a function of the number of items correctly answered. Change or growth can then be measured in terms of increases in these probabilities over time.

Another approach is to label particular points on the distribution of scores (whether they be raw or derived) in terms of the level of performance typical of that point. For example, if one were interested in using an output measure of general intellectual achievement, the lowest scores would indicate borderline literacy, and the highest scores would correspond to the level of intellectual achievement normally required of students pursuing PhD-level graduate education. The significance of particular scale points would be made even clearer if examples of actual items were used to show the most difficult types of items passed by the majority of people scoring at a particular point on the scale.

Absolute measures of performance probably provide the ideal basis for making educational objectives explicit. Let us assume, for example, that we have constructed a measure of cognitive performance that covers a wide range. This measure is represented by the distribution shown in Figure 2a (we have made the distribution "normal" in shape, but there is no necessary reason why the actual distribution of raw scores in the population could not assume some other shape). Two major cutting points on the score distribution have been identified: "borderline literacy," at the low end of the continuum, and "PhD-level performance," at the high end. Let us assume that the normal distribution shown in Figure 2a represents the scores of the total population of potential college-going students at the point of graduation from high school. Note that only a very small fraction of the population is performing at the PhD level at the time of entrance to college but that a substantial proportion is performing at or below borderline literacy. (The cross-hatched areas of the distribution above and below these two points are arbitrary; they have been drawn as shown simply for illustrative purposes). The desired educational output—goals of the higher educa-

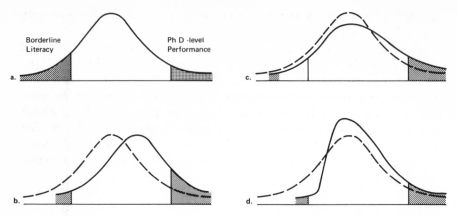

Fig. 2. Hypothetical distribution of intellectual ability in the population of entering
college students (a), and three possible outputs of the higher educational
system expressed in terms of changes in the shape of the distribution (b, c,
and d).

tional system, if you will—can be specified in terms of *changes in the
characteristics of the distribution.*

Although an almost infinite number of such changes might be desired,
Figures 2b, 2c, and 2d are examples of only three basic types of changes.
The solid lines in each of these three figures show the desired shape
of the distribution after four years of college (the student output);
the dotted line that is superimposed on each figure shows the distribution
at the point of matriculation (the student input). The first of these
hypothetical changes in the performance distribution (Figure 2b) involves an upward shift in the students' *mean* performance only. Note
that the entire distribution has simply shifted to the right and that
the shape or dispersion of people remains unchanged. One might refer
to this as a sort of "democratic" or "egalitarian" plan.

An alternative educational outcome is portrayed in Figure 2c. Here
the proportion of the students performing at or near the PhD level
has been substantially increased, while the scores of those at the lowest
parts of the distribution remain almost unchanged. This type of change,
which is concerned primarily with increasing the proportion of very-
high-performing students, might be characterized as an "elitist" plan,
in the sense that emphasis is placed on increasing the number of very
high performers; and there is relatively little concern with improving
performance at the lowest end of the continuum. This type of cognitive
objective has characterized much of American higher education in the
past.

A third alternative outcome, shown in Figure 2d, is concerned primarily with minimizing the proportion of low performers. Here the num-

ber of persons performing at or near borderline literacy is greatly reduced, but the number of performers at the high end of the distribution changes only slightly. Since it is concerned primarily with the eradication of illiteracy, this approach might be labeled as "remedial."

Many other changes in the distribution of scores are, of course, possible. My intention here is to emphasize that the specification of any educational output requires more than just the development of a measure such as "cognitive performance"; it requires as well the specification of what changes are desired in the distribution of the target population. Note that the desired change as specified in Figure 2b involves an alteration only in the students' *average* performance, whereas the changes shown in the last two distributions involve alterations in the *variation* of scores as well. The "elitist" approach results in an increase in score variation by stretching out the scores at the high end of the distribution; the "remedial" approach, on the other hand, results in a decrease in the dispersion of the scores because of major increments to the scores of the lowest-performing individuals.

Determining whether or not the desired changes in performance have taken place involves additional problems in measurement. It is not enough just to ascertain if the mean performance of all individuals has improved, or even if the variation (the standard deviation) has increased or decreased. (An increase in dispersion or standard deviation could result from a deterioration in the performance of the lowest-scoring individuals as well as from substantial gains in the scores of highest-performing individuals.) One method is to develop several dichotomous measures based on critical cutoff points in the distribution ("borderline literacy" and "PhD-level performance" represent just two such cutoff points). It might also be useful to study changes in the shape of the distribution as reflected in measures of skewness and kurtosis.

The input–environment–output model of student development in higher education (Figure 1) is designed primarily to aid the investigator in assessing the impact of different types of environments on relevant student outputs. Student input data are needed in order to measure changes in the student's development and to make statistical adjustments for the nonrandom distribution of students among institutions; environmental data are needed in order to identify those institutional attributes that affect the student outputs under investigation. Longitudinal studies involving these three types of data can yield information on the causal connections between environmental and student output variables. Such research information can, in turn, provide the basis for developing models of the higher educational system that can be used in planning.

Aside from the methodological problems involved in studying environmental effects on students, several considerations must be taken into account in designing or modifying environmental variables in order to produce changes in the distribution on some student output measure. First, the *target population* must be defined. Does the distribution shown in Figure 2a, for example, refer only to the college-going population, or does its include as well high school graduates who do not go on to college? Even if the target population is defined to include only those who will actually go to college, the investigator must be prepared to deal with temporal changes in the characteristics of this population. The number of available scholarships and loans may increase; recruitment activities may be intensified; and other changes may occur that affect students' decisions to go to college. In view of these possibilities, defining the population to include all *potential* college students* has the advantage of permitting the investigator to include recruitment practices and admissions policies among his array of environmental variables and thereby to estimate how various changes in these policies and practices would affect the distribution of the total population on the output measure.

Second, one must be aware that certain changes in a person's output performance may be *developmental* or *maturational* in nature. That is, no matter what sort of college experience a person has, and even if he never attends college, his cognitive abilities and other output performances will undergo change with time. Thus, if Figure 2a shows the output distribution in the population at one point in time, the distribution will probably be different at some subsequent point in time, even if none of the population attends college. For example, it seems likely that many persons at the low end of the distribution will show a substantial *decline* in cognitive performance after high school if they receive no further formal education. Clearly, one needs estimates of these expected changes in output among noncollege students in order to assess the potential impact of changes in recruitment or admissions policies.

Perhaps the biggest problem in using student output measures for educational modeling is posed by the existence of multiple output measures. The statistical problems in dealing simultaneously with several output measures greatly complicate the investigator's analytical task.†

---

* The population of "potential" students would include all those who could be persuaded to attend college under conditions of maximum incentive. Defining what constitutes "maximum incentive," given finite resources, is, of course, an important unsolved problem that merits a major research effort.

† Because they weight dependent (output) variables basically in terms of their *predictability* rather than their actual importance, statistical techniques such as canonical correlation and multiple discriminant analysis are probably inappropriate for dealing with multiple output measures; separate analyses for each output measure are probably more appropriate under these circumstances.

In addition, because persons differ so greatly in the importance that they attach to different outputs, what may be seen as an educational "side effect" by one person may represent the principal educational objective of another. Under these circumstances, the investigator's model must be able to accommodate several output measures simultaneously, so that any decision to manipulate environmental variables in order to produce changes in certain output variables can be made with a knowledge of how other output variables are likely to be affected.

I have attempted to deal with several problems related to developing measures of student outputs in higher education. The following are among my major points:

1. Student outputs can be understood if they are viewed in relation to the total higher educational system. Specifically, student outputs should be considered as part of a three-component model comprising student outputs, student inputs, and characteristics of the college environment. Educational planning requires a knowledge of how outputs are affected by environmental variables. Such effects, however, cannot be determined without information on student inputs.

2. Because of great variations in the values and objectives of different persons, any attempt to develop a single "overall" student output measure is unrealistic. Rather, the investigator must seek to develop a battery of measures that is sufficiently broad to satisfy the major concerns of a substantial number of students, educators, and planners. In addition, provision should be made to include measures of possible "side effects."

3. A preliminary taxonomy of student-output measures would include the following three dimensions: the type of outcome (cognitive versus affective), the type of data (psychological versus sociological), and the temporal aspects of the measure (short-term versus long-term). This taxonomic scheme should prove useful, both for classifying existing measures and for identifying gaps where additional measures are needed.

4. Although relative or derived measures are widely used in educational research, particularly in the measurement of cognitive outputs, such measures present serious conceptual problems that limit their value for modeling and planning. Whenever possible, the investigator should strive to develop absolute rather than relative measures of student outputs.

5. The use of output measures—whether relative or absolute—in educational modeling and planning requires that the desired popula-

tion changes, in the distribution of scores on each measure, be specified. In planning such changes, the investigator must consider changes in the *shape* of the performance distribution as well as changes in the mean and variance.

Higher Education Benefits Associated with Social Class, Ability, and College Quality

I would like to turn now to a discussion of some of my own work. The research program at the American Council on Education is currently involved in several studies of the relative importance of three factors: social background, ability, and college quality.

THEORETICAL INTERESTS

The Cooperative Institutional Research Program, which is now in its eighth year of operation, has two major purposes: to monitor changes in the higher educational system by means of data that are collected regularly on students, faculties, and college environments and to assess the comparative impact of different colleges on the development of the individual student. Each fall since 1966, about one in six of all freshmen entering colleges across the country has provided us with 150 items of information concerning his social background, high school achievements, and future plans and aspirations. Samples of these individual students are subsequently followed up at periodic intervals in order to monitor their educational development and to assess changes in their aspirations, plans, and values. The sample of participating institutions has been selected to permit us to generalize our findings to the entire population of institutions and students. Currently we have data on more than two million individual students and more than five hundred institutions.

Our measures of social background include information on the educational levels of both the student's parents, the income of the family, as well as racial and ethnic information. Data on the student's ability include grades obtained during high school and scores on college admissions tests provided by the college. We have employed several measures of college quality, but the most representative one appears to be the "selectivity" of the college, which we define as the average academic ability of the students who are admitted.

Like everyone else in this area of research, we have struggled with the problem of how to assess benefits. Although we have not yet followed our samples of entering freshmen long enough to obtain useful information on income or job satisfaction, we have obtained some data concerning shorter-term benefits such as cognitive achievement, persistence in college, and student satisfaction with the college. Student persistence is an especially useful and important measure, since many of the longer-term benefits of higher education are simply denied to those students who fail to complete their degrees.

One problem that plagues all who work in this area is that factors such as social background, ability, and college quality are far from independent. Although these intercorrelations create certain methodological problems for the researcher, they are also of interest in and of themselves. The relationship between social background and student ability has, of course, been a highly controversial topic that has been heavily researched and discussed. The correlations of school quality with student ability and social background, however, have only recently been a topic of much interest to researchers. Our data, for example, show clearly that social background and ability are both more highly related to college quality than they are to each other. Among entering college freshmen, for example, the scores on academic ability tests correlate only .29 with a composite socioeconomic status (SES) measure. College selectivity, on the other hand, correlates .65 and .36, respectively, with ability and SES (Karabel & Astin, 1972). The substantial relationship between ability and school quality, reflects, of course, the meritocratic nature of our admissions processes, where the most sought-after institutions (the ones that are perceived by prospective students as being of "high quality") use student ability as the primary criterion for admissions. These practices have created a kind of *de facto* track system in higher education, to which I will return in a minute.

In assessing the relative impact of these three factors on various measures of benefit, we have used a series of multivariate procedures (Astin, 1970). Basically, our approach to the problem of multicollinearity has been to compute "upper-bounds" and "lower-bounds" estimates of the possible contribution of the various independent variables.

A rational consideration of the nature of the variables involved can often help in resolving certain questions of collinearity. In the case of college quality and student ability, for example, one would be hard put to argue that ability or social background is caused by college quality, particularly if our measures of ability and background are obtained prior to the time the student is first exposed to the college environment. In the case of social background and student ability, however, the picture is not so clear. While sociologists have generally been inclined to argue that differences in student ability are *caused* wholly or in part by differences in social background and home environment, one could make a plausible case for causation in the other direction, or at least for some common mediating cause. The main reason for this ambiguity is our inability to pin down precisely the relative temporal ordering of occurrence of these two variables.

EMPIRICAL FINDINGS

Our first and possibly most controversial study so far was concerned with cognitive measure of benefit: the student's performance during his senior undergraduate year on the area tests of the Graduate Record Examinations (GRE) (Astin, 1968). Our principal goal in this study was to test the commonly held educational assumption that the student's cognitive development is enhanced by attending a "quality" institution.*
As it turned out, performance on the GRE was unrelated to college "quality," once student ability and social background were taken into account. Of course, if one totally ignores student background and ability and looks only at the zero-order coefficients, college "quality" shows a positive correlation with performance on the GRE. This means simply that many of the relatively bright students who attend highly selective institutions are still relatively bright four years later. College "quality" does *not*, however, appear to be related to student performance once initial ability and background are taken into account. These findings indicate that there is apparently no "value added" from attending a highly selective institution, at least with respect to cognitive performance as measured by the Graduate Record Examination.

Only one measure of social background appears to contribute in any way to GRE performance: Student ability, on the other hand, had by far the greatest contribution to later cognitive performance, even when the confounded variance involving college selectivity and ability was omitted. The average figures for upper- and lower-bounds contributions were 1 percent and 0 percent for social background, 13 percent and 4 percent for college "quality," and 47 percent and 37 percent for student ability. Although these data make it clear that college "quality" does not have its expected effects on cognitive development and that most of the predictable variance in cognitive performance is attributable to initial student ability, there is still nearly half of the total variance in GRE performance that remains unaccounted for in this particular analysis.

Turning now to academic achievement and persistence as two other measures of benefit, we find some highly interesting relationships. Student ability is by far the most important known determinant of academic

---

* Quotation marks are used here to emphasize the fact that we are referring to *perceived* quality (i.e., selectivity of admission), rather than to quality as defined by institutional effectiveness.

performance: Students of higher ability get better grades in college than do students of lower ability. College quality, on the other hand, has a *negative* effect on grades, so that a student of a given level of ability is likely to get poorer grades at a highly selective college than at an unselective one. This effect is, incidentally, masked by a *positive* zero-order relationship between college selectivity and grades; in other words, colleges of "high quality" award generally higher grades than do colleges of "low quality," but these differences are not as great as they should be considering the size of the differences in caliber of students who go to the different institutions.

To put this in quantitative terms, the chances that a given freshman will obtain a B average in an unselective college are about twice as good as they are in a highly selective college (Astin, 1971).

With respect to dropping out of college, however, we find that a given student is *less* likely to drop out if he attends a highly selective college. College "quality," in other words, has a positive effect on persistence in college. This effect is particularly puzzling, given the fact that the student gets somewhat lower grades at the highly selective college. Since poor grades are one frequent cause of leaving college, it would follow that students in the more selective institutions should have higher drop-out rates than students of comparable ability enrolled in the least selective institutions. But just the opposite occurs. In quantitative terms, the chances that a student of a given ability level will drop out of college after the freshman year are nearly three times greater at the least selective colleges than they are at the most selective colleges (Astin, 1971).

Of our three classes of variables, student ability, closely followed by college "quality," appears to be of greatest importance in determining who will complete college. Social-background variables run a poor third, although it is important to note here that the nature and type of the student's financial aid—as distinct from family economic circumstances as such—does seem to be a major factor in determining who will be able to complete college. Briefly, students who are able to secure scholarship or grant aid and students who are able to obtain support from their parents (regardless of ability or the parents' socioeconomic level) are most likely to complete college. One further qualification is needed here: In general, our ability to account for variance in college completion is meager; among our various benefit measures, this one yields the smallest correlations with antecedent variables.

The final outcome measure for which we have some preliminary results is student satisfaction with the college (as expressed four years after entering). Once again, we find a positive effect of college "quality":

Students who attend a highly selective college are more likely to report being satisfied with their undergraduate experiences than are comparable students who attend less selective colleges. Satisfaction has only very small, borderline relationships with measures of ability or social background.*

Our studies so far indicate that student ability and college quality are more important than social background in determining the benefits that will accrue to a particular student from higher education. The relative importance of ability and quality depend to some extent on the particular "benefit." College "quality" does not seem to have its expected effects on cognitive development, but it does have a positive effect on the student's ability to stay in college and on his satisfaction with college. Student ability, on the other hand, is a major determinant of later cognitive performance and of the student's chances of finishing college but only a very minor determinant of eventual satisfaction with college.

These facts make it clear that there are certain obvious benefits to be derived from attending a highly selective college. These benefits, however, do not apply only to the most able students—the few average or mediocre students who manage to get in the highly selective colleges also appear to show the same effects. Also, the effects are probably minor compared to the benefits that the student derives from college "quality" later in life. Regardless of what the student does or does not learn in the highly selective college, simply having a credential from that college probably yields certain significant benefits after graduation. It is well known, for example, that the graduate and professional schools and recruiters from business and industry often favor students from better-known institutions. Indeed, some federal agencies have in the past undertaken major recruiting efforts designed to attract a higher proportion of their prospective employees from the prestigious colleges.

The point is simply that *where* one goes to college may have important consequences for the individual's later career development. In our longer-term longitudinal studies for the future we hope to be able to put some quantitative estimates on these benefits, not only in terms of later income but also in terms of job satisfaction and other more personal benefits.

The apparent importance of college quality has led to a series of studies on factors that influence the type of college attended. Although student's ability is, I have already mentioned, the prime determinant of degree of selectivity of the college in which he enrolls, social back-

---

* Whether or not the student lives on campus is a far more important determinant of his eventual satisfaction with his undergraduate college than are his ability or social background.

ground is also an important independent determinant. A student of average ability is thus more likely to attend a "high quality" college if he is also from an affluent social background. Several of our current studies are attempting to look at these results in terms of their implications for the role of higher education in distributing privilege and in perpetuating the current system of social stratification.

REFERENCES

Astin, A. W. Criterion-centered research. *Educational and Psychological Measurement*, 1964, 24: 807–822.

Astin, A. W. Undergraduate achievement and institutional "excellence." *Science*, 1968, 161(3842): 661–668.

Astin, A. W. The methodology of research on college impact. *Sociology of Education*, 1970, 43(Pt. 1): 223–254; 43(Pt. 2): 437–450.

Astin, A. W. *Predicting academic performance in college*. New York: Free Press, 1971.

Astin, A. W., & Panos, R. J. The evaluation of educational programs. In R. L. Thorndike (Ed.), *Educational measurement*. Washington, D.C.: American Council on Education, 1970.

Feldman, K. A., & Newcomb, T. M. *The impact of college on students*. San Francisco: Jossey-Bass, 1969.

Karabel, J., & Astin, A. W. Social class, academic ability, and college quality. Unpublished manuscript, American Council on Education, 1972.

Nichols, R. C., & Astin, A. W. Progress of the merit scholar: An eight-year followup. *Personnel and Guidance Journal*, 1966: 673–681.

Strong, E. K. *Vocational interests 18 years after college*. Minneapolis: University of Minnesota Press, 1955.

Taylor, C. W., & Barron, F. *Scientific creativity: Its recognition and development*. New York: Wiley, 1963.

Terman, L. M., & Oden, M. H. *The gifted child grows up*. Stanford: Stanford University Press, 1947.

SOCIOECONOMIC BACKGROUND AND DIFFERENTIAL RETURNS TO EDUCATION*

Robert M. Hauser

Differential Returns to Education

I wish to report some data on *one* aspect of the question, "Are there differential returns to education by socioeconomic background?" I thought I might use this as an excuse to describe what—to some—are unfamiliar bodies of data (see Juster, 1972)—and also in the hope of shedding some light on a neglected topic.

Our analyses are based on data from Sewell's panel of Wisconsin high school graduates (Sewell *et al.*, 1969) and on data from the March 1962 Current Population Survey Supplement, "Occupational Changes in a Generation" (OCG). We have focused on the very narrow issue of differential returns to education by socioeconomic background. From our point of view this is not the only, nor even the most informative,

* Research reported herein was carried out with support from the National Science Foundation (GI-31604X), National Institutes of Health, U.S. Public Health Service (M-6275), and by the Social and Rehabilitation Service, U.S. Department of Health, Education, and Welfare (CRD-314). Computations were carried out at the University of Wisconsin, Madison Academic Computing Center and the Center for Demography and Ecology with the assistance of Harry P. Travis, Victor Jesudason, and Richard Wanner. William M. Mason and William H. Sewell contributed to my thinking on this topic.

way of interpreting the relations among socioeconomic background, schooling, and adult achievements. Rather than focusing on a single interaction in a single equation model, published analyses of these data have used linear, additive, structural equation models to render a recursive interpretation of processes linking background, schooling, and achievement (Blau & Duncan, 1967; O. D. Duncan, 1968a; Duncan et al., 1972; Sewell et al., 1969; Sewell et al., 1970; Hauser et al., 1971; Hauser, 1972; Sewell & Hauser, 1972).

Why should we think there are differential returns to education in the labor market to persons of differing social background? That is, why should persons of high-status origins obtain a greater increment in occupational prestige or earnings from each additional year of schooling than a person of humble origins? We might look for an answer in the functioning of schools or in the functioning of the labor market.

There could be differences in the quality of schooling between persons of disparate origin. For example, persons of lowly origin are less likely than those more favorably endowed to attend schools of reputedly high quality at the elementary, secondary, or tertiary level (Coleman et al., 1966; Wilson, 1959, 1963, 1967; Sewell & Armer, 1966; Hauser, 1969, 1971; Karabel & Astin, 1972). From all available evidence we are skeptical of the claim that school quality accounts for much variation in even so narrowly defined an output as academic achievement (Hauser, 1969, 1971), let alone postschooling, economic rewards. There are also well-known differentials in postsecondary areas of specialization by social origin, and there may be varying rates of return to investment in these alternative academic or vocational specialties. A related suggestion that applies with force mainly to intercohort comparisons of at least 30 years' duration, is that social origins—and especially race and farm origin—are related to the number of days in the school year. For example, mean school days attended per pupil in the United States rose from 99 to 160 between 1900 and 1960 (B. Duncan, 1968, p. 608). Finally, students with favorable social origins may have resources in the form of higher academic ability, more motivation, or greater social support by parents, teachers, and peers that permit them to profit more from the experience of schooling.

In the labor market the effects of reputational quality of schools on job placement and income, combined with the differential allocation of students to schools by origin, might yield greater returns to schooling for those with favorable origins. This seems a more plausible interpretation of measurable effects of school quality than any differences in what goes on in school.

The best-known source of differential returns to education is overt or covert discrimination in the job market (O. D. Duncan, 1968b; Thurow, 1969; Winsborough, 1972), which is generally believed to account for a large share of black–white income differences. It seems doubtful that a similar pattern of overt discrimination could be enacted against whites of lowly origins, once they had achieved a particular level of schooling. At the same time, both blacks and disadvantaged whites may gain less in the job market from any given increment in education because they lack social skills useful in job search or advancement, because they lack interpersonal connections and access to information about economic opportunities, or because they are in inferior geographic locations. Without pretending to have exhausted the theoretical possibilities, we turn to an examination of the data.

The March 1962 Current Population Survey (CPS), the large monthly household survey from which unemployment data are obtained, contained a supplementary questionnaire, "Occupational Changes in a Generation" (OCG), that was left with each sample male aged 20 to 64 in the civilian noninstitutional population. The supplement ascertained information about the socioeconomic standing and composition of the respondent's family of orientation and about his own first full-time civilian job after leaving school. Taken in conjunction with the March CPS data, the OCG supplement yielded the first definitive measurements of the intergenerational occupational mobility of men in the United States (Blau & Duncan, 1967). My colleague David L. Featherman and I have recently obtained the OCG person tape from the U.S. Bureau of the Census, and I have prepared a few tabulations that are relevant to the possibility of differential returns to education by socioeconomic background.

In Table 1 we present regressions of the status of first job on educational attainment within cells of a classification of men in the experienced civilian labor force by age and racial or socioeconomic background. The entries in each cell are the regression coefficients, and the numbers in parenthesis below them are approximate numbers of sample cases. Thus, for all men in the experienced civilian labor force aged 25 to 64 one year of education was worth about 3.2 points of occupational status in their first full-time civilian job after leaving school, and that estimate is based on about 15,540 sample cases. Given the CPS sample design, the standard errors of the regression coefficients are slightly larger than they would be under simple random sampling.

Educational attainment is coded in years of school completed, and it represents the entire range of schooling, not merely postsecondary schooling. Status of the first job is coded in the Duncan scale (Reiss, 1961). It is a weighted average of the educational attainment and income

TABLE 1. Regression of Status of First Occupation on Educational Attainment by Father's Occupational Status, Color, and Farm Background by Age: U.S. Men 25–64 Years Old in the Experienced
Civilian Labor Force, March 1962[a]

Color, father's occupation, and farm background	Age				
	25–64	25–34	35–44	45–54	55–64
All men	3.199	4.113	3.089	3.103	2.921
	(15,540)[b]	(4110)	(4630)	(4060)	(2730)
Black	.872	1.747	.656	.840	.378
	(1360)	(390)	(410)	(340)	(210)
Nonblack, farm	1.986	2.619	1.625	1.874	2.235
	(4170)	(800)	(1190)	(1200)	(980)
Nonblack, nonfarm. Father's occupational status:					
0–9	2.671	3.309	2.466	2.235	2.920
	(1350)	(350)	(400)	(390)	(220)
10–19	2.647	3.279	2.994	2.367	2.131
	(2420)	(710)	(720)	(610)	(370)
20–29	2.815	2.985	3.606	3.117	2.720
	(1090)	(320)	(330)	(280)	(160)
30–39	2.984	4.014	3.140	2.972	2.055
	(1450)	(420)	(440)	(360)	(240)
40–49	3.869	4.894	3.158	3.885	3.839
	(1110)	(370)	(310)	(260)	(160)
50–59	3.695	4.762	2.972	4.240	3.488
	(900)	(250)	(270)	(250)	(130)
60–69	4.480	5.478	4.800	3.618	3.295
	(800)	(250)	(270)	(180)	(110)
70–79	5.131	5.816	5.532	5.038	4.002
	(500)	(150)	(170)	(90)	(80)
80–96	4.317	6.185	4.578	5.210	2.882
	(370)	(110)	(100)	(90)	(60)

[a] Source: 1962 OCG Survey.
[b] Figures in parentheses are approximate numbers of sample cases on which regression coefficients are based.

of male occupational incumbents reported in the 1950 Census, validated
against prestige ratings of occupations obtained in a national survey.
Scale values range from 0 to 96; for the current occupations of men
mean status is about 45 with a standard deviation of about 25. Occupational prestige ratings have been shown to be largely invariant with
respect to method of measurement, the population of raters, and time
(Hodge et al., 1964, 1966; Treiman, in press). The classification
of men by background comprises 11 categories: blacks; nonblacks

of farm origin; and nonblacks of nonfarm origin, classified by 10-point intervals on the Duncan index for the occupation held by their father (or other head of household) at the time the respondent was 16 years old.

Looking at the results for men of all ages combined, we find a far lower occupational return to education among blacks (0.872) than in any other group, about a quarter of the rate for all men. This is consistent with virtually all other research on the topic, and it indicates that a simple upgrading of the black education distribution will not suffice to eradicate occupation differentials between blacks and whites. The return to education in the status of the first job is less for nonblacks of farm origin than for any other group of nonblacks, yet it is more than twice as large as the return for blacks. Among nonblack men of nonfarm origin we find a pattern of increasing occupational returns to education as we move from the sons of low-status fathers to sons of high-status fathers. The correlation between father's status and the occupational return to education is 0.93 over the nine categories of father's status, and the average increase in the slope is 0.031, that is, an average increase in the occupational return to education of a third of a point in occupational status of the first job for each 10-point increase of father's occupational status. This pattern of differential returns is replicated within each cohort, except the occupational returns to nonblacks of farm origin are greater than those to some nonblacks of nonfarm origin in the cohort aged 55–64, and the regression of occupational returns on father's status is not statistically significant in that cohort.

In short the data suggest that a year of education is worth more to the son of a rich man than to the son of a poor man in the status of his first job. Further, the social handicap imposed by rural upbringing or by being black is greater than that borne by even the lowliest non-black of urban origin. If this were really the case, it would give a rationale for men with unfavorable social origins to leave school earlier. However, some alternative explanations come readily to mind.

First, there is some evidence that ability interacts with educational attainment in the determination of earnings (Griliches, 1970; Hause, 1971, 1972); perhaps it also does so in the determination of occupational status. To the extent that father's occupational status is correlated with ability [$r = 0.212$ among male high school seniors in the Wisconsin panel (Hauser, 1972, p. 165)], and ability interacts with educational attainment, we cannot attribute the observed interactions to the effect of socioeconomic origins per se. This line of argument is tenuous enough so we are not inclined to give it much weight, but since we have no ability measure in this sample, we cannot dismiss it as a possibility.

Second, since father's occupational status affects length of schooling, mean educational attainment varies monotonically over the categories of father's occupational status. Thus, it is possible that the observed interactions represent nothing more than a curvilinear relationship between educational attainment and status of the first job, so the varying slopes are approximations to the several segments of a single curve relating occupational status to educational attainment. We are also dubious of this possibility because father's occupational status accounts for less than 20 percent of the variance in son's educational attainment, leaving men with a wide range of educational attainments within each category of father's occupational status.

A third possibility, which we are not prepared to dismiss out of hand, is that the observed interactions are an artifact of reporting errors in first occupation that are correlated with father's occupational status. Duncan et al. (1972, pp. 210–224) have noted that many men in the OCG sample reported ages at their first job that are manifestly inconsistent with their educational attainments. Assuming no systematic error in reports of schooling, they suggest that some men reported a job held during an interruption of schooling as their first full-time job after leaving school. The data tend to support this interpretation. For example, mean status of first occupations varies directly with age at first job within strata of educational attainment, so the occupational status of a college graduate reporting a first job at age 19 is closer to that of a high school graduate with a first job at age 19 than to that of a college graduate with a first job at a later age. Moreover, the social origins of men who reported inconsistently low ages at first job, relative to their eventual schooling, were poorer than those of men who entered the labor force later with the same schooling. Thus, we are suggesting that the lower returns to education of men with unfavorable origins may be based on disproportionate reports by them of low-status first jobs held before they completed their schooling.

Comparisons among the columns of Table 1 permit intercohort (historical) comparisons because the first job occurs at a more or less fixed point in the life cycle. In every background category we find larger coefficients for the youngest cohort (aged 25–34) than for the oldest cohort (aged 55–64), but the tendency is not consistent across all of the cohorts in several of the background categories. Thus, we find some tendency for the occupational value of education to have increased over time, but the pattern is not consistent enough to warrant a firm conclusion.

Rather than pursuing the analysis of first occupations, we shall take up other measures of social achievement whose temporal standing rela-

TABLE 2. REGRESSION OF STATUS OF 1962 OCCUPATION ON EDUCATIONAL ATTAIN-
    MENT BY FATHER'S OCCUPATIONAL STATUS, COLOR, AND FARM BACK-
    GROUND BY AGE: U.S. MEN 25–64 YEARS OLD IN THE EXPERIENCED
    CIVILIAN LABOR FORCE, MARCH 1962

Color, father's occupation, and farm background	Age				
	25–64	25–34	35–44	45–54	55–64
All men	4.187	5.145	4.490	4.025	3.662
Black	1.571	2.377	1.601	1.356	1.457
Nonblack, farm	2.988	3.394	3.270	3.037	2.836
Nonblack, nonfarm. Father's occupational status:					
0–9	3.675	4.526	4.260	3.289	2.958
10–19	4.020	4.749	4.440	3.845	3.577
20–29	4.247	5.194	5.448	3.930	3.728
30–39	4.087	5.372	4.908	3.906	2.775
40–49	4.318	5.529	4.600	3.765	3.267
50–59	4.254	5.337	4.350	4.082	3.518
60–69	4.308	5.340	4.057	4.206	3.288
70–79	4.475	5.770	4.590	4.752	3.889
80–96	4.714	6.450	4.389	5.101	3.236

[a] Source: 1962 OCG Survey.

tive to leaving school is not problematic. In Table 2 we present regressions of the status of 1962 occupations on educational attainment within
cells of the classification employed in Table 1. Again, we find occupational returns to education that are lower for nonblacks of farm origin
than for nonblacks of nonfarm origin and lower for blacks than for
any category of nonblacks. In general these observations hold for the
four cohorts as for the total sample. However, among nonblack, nonfarm
men the pattern of interactions with father's occupational status is
neither as strong nor as consistent as in the case of first occupations.
For men at all ages combined, the correlation between father's status
and the occupational return to education is .88, but the regression coefficient is only .009, which is less than a third of that calculated for
first jobs. Moreover, there are significant regressions of occupational
returns on father's occupational status in only two cohorts, those aged
25–34 and 45–54. Had we found a consistent pattern of smaller interactions as we moved from younger to older men, we could reconcile it
with the results of Table 1 on the argument that the advantages or
disadvantages imposed by one's origins tend to be dissipated over the
life cycle. This argument rests on a synthetic cohort interpretation of
the column headings in Table 2, where they are taken to represent

TABLE 3. Regression of 1961 Income (ln) on Educational Attainment by
    Father's Occupational Status, Color, and Farm Background by
    Age: U.S. Men 25–64 Years Old in the Experienced Civilian Labor
    Force, March 1962[a]

Color, father's occupation, and farm background	Age				
	25–64	25–34	35–44	45–54	55–64
All men	.08798	.08289	.09763	.09429	.09602
Black	.04642	.05112	.05572	.05738	.07299
Nonblack, farm	.07419	.08395	.07200	.07622	.07488
Nonblack, nonfarm. Father's occupational status:					
0–9	.07110	.06581	.07504	.03394	.15708
10–19	.06638	.05835	.08478	.06788	.07062
20–29	.08013	.01586	.13670	.11462	.07523
30–39	.04255	.04094	.05137	.05991	.05842
40–49	.05202	.07476	.04168	.03919	.07723
50–59	.06141	.00709	.07113	.08810	.09035
60–69	.09938	.10320	.09125	.10097	.10689
70–79	.04403	.03330	.08609	.05487	−.00889
80–96	.07108	.13949	−.00799	.11188	.08642

[a] Source: 1962 OCG Survey.

age, rather than period of birth or of entry into the labor force. However,
because the strength of the education by origin status interactions does
not vary monotonically across cohorts, the interpretation of that variation, if real, must be historical in character. Such an interpretation is not
obvious to me, but perhaps it will be to others. In any event, the findings
about effects of educational attainment on the status of 1962 occupations
do not indicate a clear or strong pattern of variation in returns to education by social background, except in regard to race and farm origins.

In Table 3 we present an array of regressions of 1961 income (ln)
on educational attainment. These may be of greater interest to economists than the preceding tabulations. For all men we find that the return
to an additional year of schooling is about 9 percent, an estimate that
is consistent with those found in the economic literature. We do not
find a clear or consistent pattern of interactions of socioeconomic background with the economic returns to education, not even with regard
to race and farm origin. In no cohort is there a significant regression
of the rate of return to education on the occupational status of the
fathers of nonblack men. Of course, the reader should bear in mind
that an absence of interactions under this specification (where income

is logged) implies a pattern of interactions when income is transformed back into dollars, provided there are differences in mean income between the social background groups. Since there are systematic differences in dollar income between the background categories net of educational attainment, a year of schooling is worth more in dollar income to a man with favorable social origins.

In Table 4 we present regressions of 1961 income on educational

TABLE 4. Regression of 1961 Income (ln) on Educational Attainment, Work Experience, and Square of Work Experience by Father's Occupational Status, Color, and Farm Background: U.S. Men 25–64 Years Old in the Experienced Civilian Labor Force, March 1962[a]

Color, father's occupation, and farm background	a	X_1[b]	X_2[c]	X_3[d]	R^2
All men	6.689	.0976	.03751	−.00058	.1096
		(.0035)[e]	(.00435)	(.00009)	
Black	6.636	.0631	.02229	−.00016	.0452
		(.0124)	(.01600)	(.00030)	
Nonblack, farm	6.919	.0769	.02929	−.00048	.0589
		(.0076)	(.00988)	(.00018)	
Nonblack, nonfarm. Father's occupational status:					
0–9	7.004	.0813	.02579	−.00035	.0821
		(.0115)	(.01393)	(.00025)	
10–19	7.175	.0707	.03313	−.00058	.0536
		(.0097)	(.01066)	(.00021)	
20–29	6.931	.0916	.03237	−.00046	.0852
		(.0140)	(.01501)	(.00028)	
30–39	7.299	.0490	.04875	−.00090	.0307
		(.0143)	(.01506)	(.00030)	
40–49	7.048	.0642	.04663	−.00071	.0599
		(.0138)	(.01455)	(.00030)	
50–59	7.131	.0716	.04835	−.00083	.1220
		(.0106)	(.01158)	(.00023)	
60–69	6.615	.1119	.04753	−.00076	.1376
		(.0150)	(.01550)	(.00032)	
70–79	7.198	.0626	.06033	−.00106	.0877
		(.0196)	(.01591)	(.00032)	
80–96	6.562	.0923	.05519	−.00083	.0545
		(.0394)	(.03454)	(.00078)	

[a] Source: 1962 OCG Survey.
[b] X_1 = educational attainment.
[c] X_2 = work experience.
[d] $X_3 = (X_2)^2$.
[e] Numbers in parenthesis are approximate standard errors.

attainment and work experience using a functional form suggested by Mincer (1970). Since educational attainment and work experience are negatively correlated, while each is a form of investment in human capital and leads directly to higher income, the effect of years of schooling and work experience are each understated unless both are entered in the equation for income. Further, since we expect the incentive to invest in on-the-job training to decrease as the number of future years in the labor force decreases, we enter a quadratic term in labor force experience, which we expect to take a negative sign when work experience is also in the equation. We define work experience as the difference between age in 1962 and age at first full-time civilian job, which may be in error in some cases for the reasons noted earlier. Since the results pertain to men of differing ages in 1962, rather than to a single cohort of men, the results are subject to error insofar as the true equations differ between cohorts.

As expected, the rates of return to schooling in Table 4 are higher in each subgroup than the corresponding entries in Table 3. Also, the shape of the income–experience curves has the expected form. The rate of return to schooling for blacks is lower than that of nonblacks of farm origin, and it is lower than the rate of return to education for all but one category of nonblacks of nonfarm origin. However, there is no apparent difference in the rates of return between those of farm and nonfarm origin, and there are no differences by father's occupational status among nonblacks of nonfarm origin.

The most interesting aspect of the results in Table 4 is the pattern of interactions of father's occupational status with the effects of work experience on income. Both the first- and second-order coefficients of work experience vary directly in absolute value with father's occupational status among nonblacks of nonfarm origin, and the coefficients are lower in absolute value for blacks than for nonblacks of farm or nonfarm origin. These findings are illustrated in Figure 1, where we show estimated experience–income profiles by social background. The horizontal axis represents work experience, and the vertical axis represents increments in current income (ln) over income at entry to the labor force. We have equated initial incomes, so the differences in estimated experience–income curves represent only the effects of differential returns to experience net of education. Clearly, the returns to work experience are greater for men with more favorable social origins, and their incomes approach peak levels more rapidly than do those of men with unfavorable circumstances of birth, even where the same level of schooling was achieved. The pattern of differences among social background groups in Figure 1 resembles the one that occurs among men

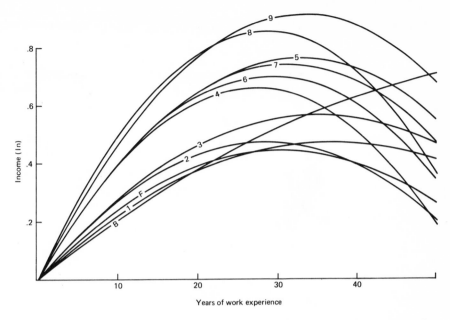

Fig. 1. Income–experience profiles by social background (with education controlled):
U.S. men in the experienced civilian labor force, March 1962. Subgroup
identification: B = black; F = nonblack, farm background; numbered categories refer to successive 10-point intervals on the Duncan scale for father's
occupation among nonfarm, nonblack men.

with differing levels of educational attainment, and this suggests there
is greater postschool investment in human capital by men with more
favorable circumstances of birth, irrespective of the level of education
attained (Mincer, 1970, pp. 8–14). It remains an open question whether
these effects of background are attributable to the confounding of socioeconomic background with ability (which we have not controlled here),
to other motivational or normative aspects of socioeconomic background,
or to some direct intervention of ascribed status characteristics in the
functioning of the occupational system.

We looked at one other set of data, Sewell's panel of Wisconsin high
school graduates of 1957, to see if there were a consistent pattern of
interactions between socioeconomic background and the effects of educational attainment on occupation and earnings. Some regression outputs
for one subsample of the Wisconsin panel are shown in Table 5. The
subsample consists of male high school graduates who were employed
in the civilian labor force and not in school in 1964 and who reported
nonzero Social Security earnings in 1967. Thus, the sample is restricted

TABLE 5. Regressions of 1964 Occupational Status and
1967 Earnings (ln) on Educational Attainment
by Farm Background and Father's Occupational
Status: Male Wisconsin High School Graduates of 1957 Employed in the Civilian Labor
Force and Not in School in 1964[a]

Farm background and father's occupation	Dependent variable		
	Status of 1964 job	Earnings (ln) in 1967	N
Total	9.098	.0360	2777
	(.215)[b]	(.0070)	
Farm	9.659	.0371	708
	(.480)	(.0204)	
Nonfarm. Father's occupational status:			
0–9	10.31	−.0263	353
	(.79)	(.0239)	
10–19	8.881	.0241	480
	(.546)	(.0182)	
20–29	9.795	.0329	206
	(.942)	(.0215)	
30–39	8.368	.0113	239
	(.681)	(.0171)	
40–49	7.642	.0482	376
	(.548)	(.0144)	
50–59	7.002	.0568	96
	(1.033)	(.0381)	
60–69	8.537	.0555	162
	(.725)	(.0190)	
70–79	6.814	.0277	81
	(1.123)	(.0226)	
80–96	7.714	−.0340	76
	(1.140)	(.0439)	

[a] Source: Sewell et al., 1969.

[b] Numbers in parentheses are standard errors.

as to age and geographic location, and the education distribution is
truncated at both the upper and lower ends relative to the distribution
for all men of about the same age. There are few blacks in the state
of Wisconsin, so no separate regression was calculated for them in Table
5, but the background categories are otherwise similar to those of the
earlier tables. Finally, our measure of remuneration is 1967 Social Security earnings, rather than income, adjusted for those with more than
the maximum of covered earnings and for multiple employment.

Looking down the columns of Table 5, we find no tendency for the occupational or remunerative returns to education to vary with socioeconomic origin. We have estimated other occupation and earnings functions for the groups in the table, but no systematic variation in the effect of education occurs. Taking into account our findings here and in the OCG sample as well, we conclude that there is no convincing evidence of differential occupational returns to education, except for effects of race and, to a lesser degree, of farm background. Except in the case of race, there are no systematic differences by background in monetary rates of return to education, although there very probably are such differences in dollar returns. We do find an interaction effect of father's occupational status, as well as race, with the returns to work experience in an equation for income: The experience–income profiles of men with higher-status backgrounds display a more rapid rise of incomes to (higher) peak levels. While this last point deserves further exploration, our findings are either negative or inconclusive with regard to interactions between socioeconomic background and education among white men with urban origins. In this major segment of the population the benefits of education appear to go to those who have it, regardless of their social origins.

Sources of Data

In taking this brief look at social differentials in returns to education we have referred to data from two sources, W. H. Sewell's panel of Wisconsin high school seniors and the 1962 CPS supplement, "Occupational Changes in a Generation." Since these and related bodies of data contain a wealth of information about the benefits of higher education and the social allocation of those benefits, we think a brief description of the data sets and prospective extensions of them would be worthwhile.

The sampling frame of the Wisconsin panel study is a survey of all high school seniors in the state that was carried out in 1957 under the direction of J. Kenneth Little (1958). Several years later the questionnaires were recovered by William H. Sewell, and he began the ongoing research program on the achievements of the Wisconsin cohort. The panel has two components. The first is a simple one third random sample (about 10,000 cases) of all males and females in the cohort, and the second consists of all persons (about 3,000 cases) in the top tenth in measured mental ability. The high school survey yielded basic social background data, including a home address and measures of the high school curriculum, educational plans, occupational aspirations, and perceived social supports for achievement.

These basic data have been supplemented from a number of sources. Measures of mental ability were obtained from the Wisconsin State Testing Services, which administered the Henmon–Nelson test to all high school juniors. Rank in high school class was obtained directly from the schools. Measures of parental occupation and of parental income during 1957–1960 were obtained from the State Department of Revenue, whose files are open to the public for legitimate research purposes. Social Security numbers for male students were also obtained from the state, and complete earnings records were merged with the remainder of the file. (We should note that files containing Social Security data are not directly accessible to us, and only the Social Security Administration is able to identify individual respondents with their earnings records.) Finally, in 1964 a mail survey ascertained data on the postsecondary education, military service, marital history, and occupations of members of the cohort, and an overall response rate of 87 percent was achieved. We have already referred to some of the analyses carried out with these data. Many of these are summarized by Sewell (1971) or by Sewell & Hauser (1972).

At the present time three extensions of the Wisconsin data file are under way or projected. First, we are updating our file of Social Security earnings data to include the years 1968 to 1971. Second, we are planning a mail and telephone follow-up of all members of the panel, in which we will update their educational, military, marital, and occupational histories and ascertain selected additional items on social background and post-secondary-school experiences. Thus, we will be able to write the history of the panel up to about age 35, and we will be able to look into some questions about which interest has grown since the inception of the study. Third, a similar survey of Wisconsin high school seniors was carried out in the spring of 1968, and we are presently considering a replication of the 1957 panel study in which a follow-up can be carried out in 1975. Provided a close replication can be achieved, the second panel will yield a wealth of data on temporal change in processes of socioeconomic achievement.

If the Wisconsin panel studies are valuable for providing detailed information about the social–psychological aspects of social mobility, the 1962 OCG has been equally important in providing base-line measurements of social mobility in the total U.S. population and in important subpopulations (Blau & Duncan, 1967; Duncan et al., 1972). In addition to variables from the March Current Population Survey, the OCG supplement contained relatively few items: nativity of parents, father's occupation and education, number of siblings and sibling position, stability of the family of origin, size of place of origin, first occupation after leaving school, and, if married, wife's number of siblings and wife's father's occupation. While the value of the 1962 OCG data for men has largely been realized, David L. Featherman and I have arranged for the Bureau of the Census to merge those data with the CPS records for the wives of married-spouse-present men in the sample. Thus we will be able to produce limited base-line measurements of social mobility for this large segment of the female population.

Because of the widespread public interest in the trend of opportunity in the United States and in related policy questions, Featherman and I are presently engaged in a replication and extension of the 1962 supplement, the national component of which will be carried out in conjunction with the March 1973 Current Population Survey (Featherman & Hauser, in press). The largest component of the new study will be a strict replication of the 1962 study, permitting exact trend measurements of opportunity and of factors affecting it for important components of the population. A second important facet of the study will be the oversampling of minority populations, blacks and persons of Spanish origin, and the inclusion of additional items in the supplement that will be relevant to the achievement of women. As resources permit, we will add some new items pertaining to the structure of the family of origin, nonregular schooling, military service, and the process of entry into the labor force. Mechanisms of assessing the quality of the data have been built into several parts of the study, including reinterviews and matches back to earlier Census returns for the fathers of current respondents. Finally, a parallel survey, to be carried out in Wisconsin, will permit us to ask some questions not feasible in a Census field operation and to measure a large number of social–psychological outcomes of the achievement process.

REFERENCES

Blau, P. M., & Duncan, O. D. *The American occupational structure.* New York: Wiley, 1967.

Coleman, J. S. *et al. Equality of educational opportunity.* U.S. Department of Health, Education, and Welfare. Washington, D.C.: U.S. Government Printing Office, 1966.

Duncan, B. Trends in output and distribution of schooling. In E. B. Sheldon & W. E. Moore (Eds.), *Indicators of social change,* pp. 601–674. New York: Russell Sage Foundation, 1968.

Duncan, O. D. Ability and achievement. *Eugenics Quarterly,* 1968a, 15: 1–11.

Duncan, O. D. Inheritance of poverty or inheritance of race? In D. P. Moynihan (Ed.), *On understanding poverty,* pp. 85–110. New York: Basic Books, 1968b.

Duncan, O. D., Featherman, D. L., & Duncan, B. *Socioeconomic background and achievement.* New York: Seminar Press, 1972.

Featherman, D. L., & Hauser, R. M. Design for a replicate study of social mobility in the U.S. In K. C. Land & S. Spilerman (Eds.), *Social indicator models*. New York: Russell Sage, in press.

Griliches, Z. Notes on the role of education in production functions and growth accounting. In W. L. Hansen (Eds.), *Education, income and human capital*, pp. 71–127. New York: National Bureau of Economic Research, 1970.

Hause, J. C. Ability and schooling as determinants of lifetime earnings or If you're so smart, why aren't you rich? *American Economics Review*, 1971, 61: 289–298.

Hause, J. C. Earnings profile: Ability and schooling. *Journal of Political Economy*, 1972, 80(3, Pt. 2): S108–S138.

Hauser, R. M. Schools and the stratification process. American Journal of Sociology, 1969, 74: 587–611.

Hauser, R. M. *Socioeconomic background and educational performance*. Rose Monograph Series. Washington, D.C.: American Sociological Association, 1971.

Hauser, R. M. Disaggregating a social–psychological model of educational attainment. *Social Science Research*, 1972, 1: 159–188.

Hauser, R. M., Lutterman, K. G., & Sewell, W. H. Socioeconomic background and the earnings of high school graduates. Paper presented at the meeting of the American Sociological Association, Denver, August 1971.

Hodge, R. W., Siegel, P. M., & Rossi, P. H. Occupational prestige in the U.S., 1925–1963. *American Journal of Sociology*, 1964, 70: 286–302.

Hodge, R. W., Treiman, D. J., & Rossi, P. H. A comparative study of occupational prestige. In R. Bendix & S. M. Lipset (Eds.), *Class, status and power*, pp. 309–321. New York: Free Press, 1966.

Juster, F. T. Microdata requirements and public policy designs. *Annals of Economic and Social Measurement*, 1972, 1: 7–16.

Karabel, J., & Astin, A. W. Social class, academic ability and college "quality." Washington, D.C.: Office of Research, American Council on Education, 1972. (Mimeo)

Little, J. K. *A statewide inquiry into decisions of youth about education beyond high school*. Madison: School of Education, The University of Wisconsin, 1958.

Mincer, J. The distribution of labor incomes: A survey with special reference to the human capital approach. *The Journal of Economic Literature*, 1970, 8: 1–26.

Reiss, A. J., Jr. *Occupations and social status*. New York: Free Press, 1961.

Sewell, W. H. Inequality of opportunity for higher education. *American Sociological Review*, 1971, 36: 793–813.

Sewell, W. H., & Armer, J. M. Neighborhood context and college plans. *American Sociological Review*, 1966, 31: 159–168.

Sewell, W. H., Haller, A. O., & Ohlendorf, G. W. The educational and early occupational status attainment process: Replication and revision. *American Sociological Review*, 1970, 35: 1014–1027.

Sewell, W. H., Haller, A. O., & Portes, A. The educational and early occupational attainment process. *American Sociological Review*, 1969, 34: 82–92.

Sewell, W. H., & Hauser, R. M. Causes and consequences of higher education: Models of the status attainment process. *American Journal of Agricultural Economics*, 1972, 54(5): 851–861.

Thurow, L. *Poverty and discrimination*. Studies in Social Economics. Washington, D.C.: The Brookings Institution, 1969.

Treiman, D. J. *Occupational prestige in comparative perspective*. New York: Seminar Press, in press.

Wilson, A. B. Residential segregation of social classes and aspirations of high school boys. *American Sociological Review*, 1959, 24: 836–845.

Wilson, A. B. Social stratification and academic achievement. In A. H. Passow (Ed.), Education in depressed areas, pp. 217–236. New York: Columbia University Press, 1963.

Wilson, A. B. Educational consequences of segregation in a California community. *Racial isolation in the public schools* (Vol. 2, Appendix C3). U.S. Commission on Civil Rights. Washington, D.C.: U.S. Government Printing Office, 1967.

Winsborough, H. H. Age, period, cohort and education effects on earnings by race. Paper presented at the Russell Sage Foundation Conference on Social Indicator Models, New York, June 1972.

NEW DIRECTIONS FOR RESEARCH

Carl Kaysen

The impulse to measure the economic benefits of higher education arose out of a quite different set of concerns from those that occupied the Conference on the Benefits of Higher Education or that occupy educational decision policy makers. It grew out of the difficulty economists had in explaining the growth of the national income in terms of their own intellectual constructs. They expected to show that we get richer and richer because more people work harder and for longer hours, save more, and invest it in more capital equipment. These greater inputs of labor and capital would then lead to more outputs. About 15 years ago there were two very important pieces of work—one by Denison (1964) and one by Solow (1957). They observed that measured additional inputs of labor and capital really had not accounted for much of the observed growth in total U.S. output in the last half century; there was something else. We've been chasing that something else ever since, and that chase has led to a basically wrong way of looking at the problem. Perhaps Solmon's studies, "Schooling and Subsequent Success" (pp. 13–34) and "The Definition and Impact of College Quality" (pp. 77–102), show us we are at the end of that road, or near enough to know that it is a dead end.

Historically, variables have been added into the output function to keep explaining a little more of the residual growth beyond that which

147

was accounted for by labor and capital. One of the first candidates was education. It is an old, established fact that people with more schooling earn more. But Denison attributed only two thirds of the difference in income to educational attainment. Since then economists have continued to add variables to explain the remaining difference, and now the only limit to the number of variables is how many regression coefficients one can get on a page.

I would suggest that we are really well past the limit of what can usefully be done on an aggregate basis. There is no such thing as a single labor market or mobility across all labor markets. There is not *enough* interplay among labor markets for the concept of an average return on years of educational attainment to mean much. There has been absolutely no specification of educational mechanisms in any of these models—for the very good reason that we do not know how to specify them. It is time now to pay attention to that.

Some speak as if years of educational attainment were the putty capital economists have been talking about for 15 years that can turn into anything we want it to be.

The theory of the capital market has limitations enough as an explanation of the observed behavior of firms, but there are a great many forces—including market competition and the fact that firms are managed by people paid to manage them, make money, and look around for new methods and products—that make this a fairly good model. Translated to the life of an individual, it is absurd. Our lives are not managed by people paid to produce economically rational results. Even if they were, our society is not structured to permit that kind of behavior: Doctors do not stop being doctors at age 40 because they suddenly discover there are more remunerative occupations; people who did not become doctors cannot very well learn how to at age 40 because in our educational and social institutions, one is allowed to make that decision once between the ages of about 18 and 23, and, give or take a few exceptions, can never make it any other time. Solmon called attention to, but shrugged off, the anomalies in the earnings behavior of teachers, pilots, lawyers, and doctors. Yet those are exactly what we should be examining. What the field needs is an analysis of careers, recruitment patterns, occupational income distributions, lifetime earnings, and time patterns of earnings. What we can usefully learn with aggregate studies, we have learned; the next step must be a little different.

Our implicit model of education and attainment is the model for professors, MD's, engineers, and perhaps lawyers. But that model is irrelevant for most people with higher education, who hold managerial posts in business, middle-level government posts, or nonpolitical civil service jobs. In academic life, a transferable capital of skills does accumulate. When Jacob Mincer reads an article on econometrics, he is making an investment he will turn into another article in *Econometrica*. And perhaps that model applies to other of the learned professions.* But the investment-in-education model applies much less readily to the business or civil service world, where stratified bureaucracies with formal job structures and internal promotion systems operate in a rather different way.

From the policy-making point of view, it is important to have microdata with a lot of qualitative understanding before discussing the underlying issues. What is involved in the process we are analyzing? Training? Rationing? Certification? Selection? Any reasonable man will suspect that the answer includes all of these things. What we want is not some aggregate beta coefficient but a deep understanding of different kinds of career training.

Recruitment in the status system is not open and competitive; it's nepotistic in a variety of complicated ways, and though it has become more open and more competitive in two generations, it still has a long way to go. I think Lloyd Reynolds once said that the way to understand the job market was to think, not of the capital, but of the marriage market. This is especially true if we are discussing career choices of higher-paid occupations; these tend to be made and not unmade.

Finally, it is important to remember another pair of bits of data—not correlation coefficients, just bits. In our society the highest-paid occupations—not occupations, activities—are in some of the popular arts, sports, and probably business speculation. A study was made of the risk-avoidance and risk-seeking behavior of college students versus Massachusetts national guardsmen. Apparently, in the higher education world we train people to be rational, to be risk avoiders, not to take a 10 to 1 chance on a 5 to 1 payoff. On the other hand, for the uneducated man, 5 to 1 is a good payoff. Perhaps, the people at the top of the income distribution are adversely selected by the higher educational process; certainly, a sample of successful plungers—oil men, cattle

---

* However, on-the-job training does not always have the kind of convexity we generally assume. On the contrary, in many higher-income jobs, better pay goes along with greater education. There is also some supply and demand pressure that can lead to the same results. Thus, for example, the big Wall Street firms once paid less for top first-year law graduates than smaller firms. This is no longer true, despite the fact that on-the-job training on Wall Street is more valuable. It consists of talking to a certain set of people and learning things that simply aren't taught at other types of law firms.

raisers, and stock buyers—won't necessarily have the highest levels of educational attainment. But these fables remind us how much vitally important detail we suppress by looking at aggregate data. We've had enough regression coefficients. Let's take a look at microdata and career and occupational histories.

REFERENCES

Denison, E. F. Measuring the contribution of education (and the residual) to economic growth. In *The residual factor and economic growth.* Paris: Organisation for Economic Cooperation and Development, 1964.

Solow, R. M. Technical change and the aggregate production function. *Review of Economics and Statistics,* 1957, 39(3): 312–320.

SCHOOLING, SCREENING, AND INCOME

*Barry R. Chiswick**

Introduction

I feel safe in saying that in the last few years there has been no conference on the relationship between education and income in which it has not been argued by someone that schooling really does not affect a worker's productivity. It is argued that schooling is a screening device used to sift out those who are to be rewarded handsomely by society from those who shall receive less, that it is the "sheepskin" rather than the education that is rewarded. These arguments have been presented in several forms. (See, for example, Arrow, 1971; Berg, 1971; Bowles, 1972; Cohen, 1972; Hapgood, 1971; Thurow, 1972; and Taubman & Wales, in press. For critiques of "screening" see Becker, 1972; Mincer, 1972.) I will attempt to outline the screening and sheepskin hypotheses and examine their implications. In addition, I will offer alternative explanations for the phenomena these hypotheses are supposed to explain.

The characteristics for which years of schooling serves as a proxy have been suggested to be family background (or "social class"), affective behavior, and ability. With respect to ability and affective behavior it is important to distinguish between schooling as a means of sorting

* I appreciate the comments received on an earlier draft from Jacob Mincer and Carmel Ullman.

by these traits and schooling as a means of changing these traits. The screening argument refers to sorting. If schooling changes affective behavior or measured ability, and these changes increase productivity, then schooling affects productivity.

Family Background

The "family background" variety of screening says that the children of wealthier parents have greater earnings because they come from the "right" families. There are two possible reasons for this: First, there may be a desire by society (or the powers that be) to maintain the social structure; second, there may be discrimination by employers who "like" employing children from wealthier families. Wealthier parents buy more schooling for their children because they know the "rules of the game"—that schooling is used as a screen—or because it is a consumer good with a positive income elasticity of demand.

The family-background screening hypothesis is consistent with some empirical findings. First, it agrees with the positive simple correlation between father's permanent income (measured by schooling, occupation, income, or "social class") and the child's schooling. Second, it corresponds to the observation that, holding child's schooling constant, there is a positive partial correlation between father's permanent income and the child's earnings. Third, it is consistent with the reduction in the effect on earnings of an additional year of schooling when father's permanent income is entered into the regression analysis.

These findings, however, also support another hypothesis. Clearly, schooling is only one form of human capital. In a complete analysis of the effects of human capital on earnings, nonschool as well as school investments must be considered. The quality of preschool and nonschooling investments during school years has yet to be measured. However, some evidence does exist that can shed light on the effects of preschool and concurrent-with-school investments. In a recent doctoral dissertation, Arleen Leibowitz (1972) found that mothers with higher levels of schooling decrease their labor-force participation more than do less-educated women when a child is born, and the decreased participation lasts longer. Using time-budget studies, Leibowitz also found that mothers with higher levels of schooling spend at least as much time in child care (including reading, talking, or playing with the children) as do less-educated mothers. If the time of educated mothers is more productive in child-care activities than the time of those with less schooling, a child whose mother has more schooling would acquire more units

of human capital before school and concurrent with schooling.* More
training of these kinds may increase the productivity of later investments
in training.

Suppose genetic differences in ability are inherited and those with
greater genetic ability find training more profitable and have higher
earnings, *ceteris paribus*. Then we would observe a positive correlation
between the father's wealth, the child's level of training, and the child's
subsequent earnings. In addition, greater parental wealth implies a lower
discount rate and greater ease in financing investments in the children's
schooling and postschool training.

If children from families with higher permanent income invest in
more total training after schooling starts and we stratify by years of
schooling, they necessarily have either larger investments per year of
labor market experience or have purchased a higher quality of schooling.
These effects are not captured by the explanatory variables years of
schooling or years of experience but would show up as a positive partial
effect of father's income on the child's earnings.

Thus, the findings that appear to support the view that years of schooling is a means of screening workers by parental background are also
consistent with the hypothesis that earnings are a function of human
capital, where human capital includes schooling and nonschooling investments. When there are two alternative hypotheses to explain the same
data, an implication that differentiates the hypotheses is needed.

Screening by family background suggests that father's education is
a more important variable for explaining child's earnings than is mother's
education. First, father's education is likely to be more highly correlated
with the family's permanent income and consumption than is mother's
education. Second, father's education or occupation is more likely to
be known by others and viewed as defining the family's status than
is the mother's. However, for the reasons given above, the human capital
model suggests that mother's education may be a more important determinant of child's earnings than the father's education.

The strength of the effect on child's income of mother's schooling
was shown a decade ago by Shane Hunt (1963). Hunt was interested
in the determinants of the earnings of male college graduates, and he
had data on the individual's schooling and the schooling of his mother
and father. The effect of the mother's schooling was positive and statistically significant, while that of the father was positive but had a lower
slope and was not significant. More recent data sources have confirmed

---

* A pair of studies by Robert Michael (1971, 1972) do in fact demonstrate
a positive effect of schooling on productivity in nonmarket activities. However,
he did not look explicitly at child care.

this finding (Ornstein, 1971).* Thus, the partial positive effect of father's schooling on the child's earnings disappears when mother's education is included in the analysis. This is consistent with the human capital model but would be difficult to reconcile with the screening hypothesis.

Screening and Competition

One of the major problems left unexplained by the screening argument is whether screening (on a basis other than productivity) could coexist with competition. The difference in the present value of the future earnings of a college graduate and a high school graduate is substantial.† In terms of the family-background argument, screening implies that firms would pay the large increments needed to obtain college-trained workers when high school graduates are readily available‡ and are equally efficient, but come from the "wrong" families. Is it possible to argue that, with our social attitudes toward productivity and profit, firms would be willing to sacrifice so much profit to engage in this form of discrimination?

The screening by ability or affective behavior argument indicates that schooling serves only to label youths but does not change these traits. Is it conceivable that the educational system is such an efficient (i.e., lower-cost) means of identifying people's characteristics that firms are willing to pay college graduates thousands of dollars more per year than high school graduates? It would seem that cheaper methods, such as tests and trial periods, could be developed.

Indeed, if all schooling does is *sort* people on the basis of family background, ability, or affective behavior there would be a strong incentive for specialized firms to develop to perform this service at a lower cost. That such firms have not arisen suggests that the "sorting effect" of schooling has a low market value.

Schooling and Postschool Training

It has been noted that older workers with less schooling are frequently paid higher wages than younger workers with more schooling. Some

---

* The data are from the Coleman–Rossi 1968 sample of white males 30–39 years of age.

† The direct plus opportunity costs of a college education most likely exceed $24,000 on the average. Since the rate of return on schooling exceeds the discount rate, the present value of the increment in earnings exceeds the cost of schooling.

‡ This assumes that occupational licensing, which by law requires a college degree, does not exist or, if it does exist, is not effective in reducing competition among schooling levels. For an analysis of occupational licensing see Rottenberg (1962).

believe that this means that schooling itself is not productive, but that reasoning is fallacious. Young workers make large investments in post-school training, and these investment costs show up in the data as lower net earnings. Older workers receive a return on their previous invest-ments in training and make smaller current investments. The latter have higher productivity (and wages) if the effect on productivity of their additional experience exceeds the effect on productivity of the greater schooling, minus the current investments made by younger workers. That on-the-job training is a productive investment does not in any way mean that schooling is not a productive investment.

Correlation of Schooling and Earnings

It is not clear whether the advocates of the screening hypothesis be-lieve that the "sort" is permanent or temporary. If it is permanent, once an earnings track is entered a person remains in it until retirement. This suggests that the correlation of schooling with earnings would be constant if we looked at individuals at different levels of experience. Suppose, however, the sorting effect is temporary: Schooling level deter-mines one's first job but thereafter the effect of screening deteriorates as firms learn whom to promote. This suggests that the positive cor-relation of schooling with earning would decline with experience.

The human capital model offers a different prediction of the change in the correlation of schooling with earnings as we look at groups with successively higher levels of experience (Mincer, 1972). The model pre-dicts that the positive correlation of observed earnings with schooling may at first either increase or decrease but after a few years will de-crease. It distinguishes between gross earnings (the earnings that would be received in a year if there were no investment in training that year) and observed earnings (gross earnings minus the opportunity costs of training). The correlation between gross earnings and schooling declines with experience because of the effects on current earnings of individual differences in investment in training in previous years. Data exist only for observed earnings that can be viewed as differing from gross earnings by a "measurement error" (current investments). Investments are larger in earlier years of experience. Thus, the observed correlation of earnings with schooling is a downward-biased estimate of the correlation for gross earnings, but the downward bias decreases with experience. There-fore, the correlation of observed earnings with schooling could rise dur-ing the early years of experience if the effect of the decline in the "measurement error" is stronger than the decline in the correlation using gross earnings. Once postschool investments become small relative to earnings, the "measurement error" problem disappears, and the correlation of observed earnings with schooling declines with experience.

Thus, we have three hypotheses and predictions as to how the correlation of schooling with earnings changes with higher levels of experience. The permanent screening hypothesis predicts no change, and the temporary screening hypothesis predicts a decline. The human capital model offers an ambiguous prediction for the early years of experience, but predicts a decline for later years. The empirical evidence supports the human capital model: The correlation of schooling with earnings rises with experience for the first 10 years and then declines.*

"Sheepskin Effect"

The higher observed rate of return from schooling for those who complete college and high school compared to "drop-outs" is sometimes offered as evidence that schooling doesn't matter very much, but that the diploma (sheepskin) does matter. It is not clear why firms would persist in paying graduates higher wages that do not reflect differences in productivity.

I believe there are two possible reasons why drop-outs might have lower rates of return. First, schooling may not be a divisible investment. The productivity of four years of college or high school may be more than four times greater than the productivity of the first year.

Second, the decision to be a drop-out is not random; it is presumably made on the basis of the expected pecuniary and nonpecuniary returns from schooling, compared to the costs of schooling. Some of those who

---

* The coefficients of determination (correlation coefficient squared) of schooling with earnings within experience groups (experience = age minus schooling minus six) for male workers employed year-round from the 1960 Census One in One Thousand sample are:

Years of experience	R^2	Years of experience	R^2
1–3	.25	22–24	.17
4–6	.27	25–27	.15
7–9	.30	28–30	.14
10–12	.30	31–33	.14
13–15	.25	34–36	.07
16–18	.20	37–39	.09
19–21	.18		

Source: Mincer, 1972, Pt. 2, p. 24.

Ornstein (1971) also finds a rise in the correlation coefficient during the first 10 years of experience.

start a level of schooling discover that they have less ability for converting schooling into human capital units than they had expected. This raises the cost of graduating or lowers the expected returns from being a graduate. Schooling is now viewed as a less profitable investment than had been anticipated and may even be unprofitable. Rather than continuing, the youth becomes a drop-out. Thus, drop-outs may have lower rates of return, not because they are drop-outs but rather because of some other characteristic, such as schooling ability, that is lower than previously believed. In this view, it is the discovery by the youth that schooling is not profitable for him (i.e., he expects a low rate of return) that results in his becoming a drop-out.*

In summary, the observation that drop-outs have lower rates of return than graduates may be reflecting the self-selection of drop-outs on the basis of the perceived profitability of schooling or a degree of "lumpiness" in investments in schooling. The higher return to graduates need not be due to the marketplace rewarding a diploma without regard for productivity.

Conclusion

This paper presents the screening hypothesis that schooling itself is not productive but that it sorts individuals by family background, affective behavior, or ability. The predictions of the screening-by-family-background hypothesis, which are supported by empirical evidence, are the positive correlation of schooling across generations and the positive partial correlation of child's earnings with parent's income. The human capital model, in which schooling is viewed as a productivity-augmenting investment, is also consistent with these observations. The screening-by-family-background argument predicts that father's education is more important than mother's education in affecting the child's earnings; the human capital model offers an opposite prediction. The data appear to support the human capital model.

The hypothesis that schooling's main function is screening by family background, affective behavior, or ability does not seem to be consistent with the persistent substantial wage differential by schooling level over the entire life cycle. Alternative methods of identifying these traits—tests or trial periods—would most certainly be less costly to the firm than the wage differential paid over many years to those with more schooling.

---

* For a high school drop-out, there need not have been a learning process that schooling is not profitable. He may have known this all along but was compelled by minimum schooling laws to attend school until a certain age. For evidence that those with low ability have lower than average rates of return from high school, see Chiswick (1972).

The screening hypothesis predicts that the correlation of schooling and earnings is either constant or declines with higher levels of experience. The human capital model, however, offers no prediction during early years of experience but thereafter predicts a decline. Empirical evidence is consistent with the human capital model.

The "sheepskin hypothesis" argues that the larger payoff from schooling received by graduates compared to drop-outs is not due to productivity differences. It is not clear why firms would persist in rewarding graduates solely for their diploma; productivity differences may be due to elements of lumpiness in schooling-acquired human capital. More important, drop-outs are self-selected, and presumably those who anticipate low rates of return from schooling are more likely to become drop-outs.

These conclusions suggest that the screening and sheepskin hypotheses *cannot* be viewed as major determinants of earnings in our economy.

REFERENCES

Arrow, K. Discrimination in labor markets. Department of Economics, Harvard University, October 1971. (Mimeo)

Becker, G. S. Comment on S. Bowles, Schooling and inequality from generation to generation. *Journal of Political Economy*, 1972, 80(3, Pt. 2): S252–S255.

Berg, I. *Education and jobs: The great training robbery*. Boston: Beacon Press, 1971.

Bowles, S. Schooling and inequality from generation to generation. *Journal of Political Economy*, 1972, 80(3, Pt. 2): S219–S251.

Chiswick, B. R. Comment on W. L. Hansen, B. Weisbrod, & W. Scanlon, Schooling and earnings of low achievers. *American Economic Review*, 62(4): 752–754.

Cohen, D. Does I.Q. matter? *Commentary*, 1972, 53(4): 51–59.

Hapgood, D. *Diplomaism*. New York: Brown, 1971.

Hunt, S. J. Income determinants for college graduates and the return to educational investment. *Yale Economic Essays*, 1963, 3(2): 305–357.

Leibowitz, A. Women's allocation of time to market and nonmarket activities: Differences by education. Unpublished doctoral dissertation, Columbia University, 1972.

Michael, R. Dimensions of household fertility: An economic analysis. *American Statistical Association Proceedings of the Social Statistics Section*. Washington, D.C.: American Statistical Association, 1971.

Michael, R. *The effect of education on efficiency in consumption*. New York: National Bureau of Economic Research, 1972 (Occasional Paper, No. 116).

Mincer, J. Schooling, experience and earnings. New York: National Bureau of Economic Research, 1972. (Mimeo)

Ornstein, M. Entry into the American labor force. Baltimore: Johns Hopkins University, 1971 (Report No. 113).

Rottenberg, S. Theory of occupational licensing. *Aspects of Labor Economics*. Princeton: Princeton University Press, 1962.

Taubman, P., & Wales, T. *Higher education as an investment and as a screening device*. New York: National Bureau of Economic Research, in press.

Thurow, L. Education and economic equality. *Public Interest*, 1972, 28: 66–81.

EFFECTS OF HIGHER EDUCATION

Outcomes, Values, or Benefits*

Ellis B. Page

The field of education has the hospitable quality that most people consider themselves knowledgeable about it, and most disciplines have something to contribute to it. Surely, those areas represented at the Conference on the Benefits of Higher Education (among them economics, biology, engineering, psychology, sociology) have their own epistemologies and articles of faith. Thus, the "benefit" of higher education may possibly be viewed by the economist as life income, by the sociologist as upward mobility for a lower class, by the engineer as a better environment, by the humanist as respect for cultural roots. And education may be the better for such variety of perspective.

Each one brings his biases, and I confess to mine: As an educational psychologist, I prefer to think of educational "outcome" as a change in the behaviors and abilities of individual students. Yet such individual outcomes are not yet benefits, for the word implies a favorable evaluation, which, in turn, implies the presence of evaluators.

If we hold to a loosely democratic view, we might hope that the

* This study is partially supported by a U.S. Office of Education Grant OEG-1-72-0004.

society at large will be the principal evaluator. This means that society may establish some list of valued traits with some relative evaluation of each. This also means that society constructs some system of measurement to appraise these traits in the outcome. Then the educational "benefit" becomes a vector product of these societal values multiplied by these individual or group measurements.

If this viewpoint is accepted, groups attempting to get a handle on "the benefits of higher education" face some problems of staggering size. Curiously, for as long as we have had opinions about educational values (some millennia) and for as long as we have had scaling systems for individual achievement (some decades), we have hardly touched on the problem of reconciliation. Educational values are typically described at the highest level, and psychological measures are typically described at the lowest level. There has been no commonly accepted technique for bridging the gap. Moreover, the two concerns have seldom inhabited the same framework: One person has worked with philosophical principles and quite another with behavioral objectives. These workers, differently guided and motivated, have seldom shared a common language.

Let us outline one approach to bridging from values to measures and back again to values. With some serious technical work, perhaps conferences held in the 1980s will not need to be as drifting and impotent, in a technical sense, as conferences of the 1970s.

A Hierarchy of Values

One commonly speaks of a "hierarchy" of values, implying that some are *higher* than others in the structure and that some *descend* or branch from others. Let us, therefore, adopt the hierarchy in the form of a *tree* of educational values. Tree structures are scientifically well understood from biology; they have certain valuable mathematical properties from probability theory; and they are thoroughly manipulatable in computer science.

For this tree, let us declare into existence a *basic* value in terms of which all others may be defined. In psychological measurement, such a declaration, although novel, makes some sense. We are used to subtests (such as *punctuation*) that are parts of larger tests (such as *composition*). Let us simply take the process further up the tree to its apex and declare a measure of *general educational benefit*. It is plausible to standardize such an index, so let us state that this measure will be expressed in terms of T-scores (with a mean of 50 and standard deviation of 10). Then let us call the measure a "benefit T-score" or, for short, "bentee" (Page, 1972b).

A *bentee* will commonly range from about 20 to 80 for individuals at a given educational stage. For any group, bentees may be averaged. And for programs, bentee gains may serve as criteria of *overall* educational gain.

But what values are incorporated into such a general measure? Different disciplines may have different perspectives. Values might be declared corresponding to expected income, occupational status, and similar measures. But the psychologist will probably feel most comfortable with individual measures related to traditional school objectives. For illustration, the following traits are proposed to be of high educational priority: *verbal, quantitative, natural sciences, social studies, arts, physical,* and *personality.* Each may be defined to cover an extensive area of human measurement, and together they may be regarded as describing the whole student (Page, 1972b, pp. 42–43). In Figure 1, we see the *bentee* as the top node of our tree and these seven areas as the seven branches that join to make the total bentee.

We recognize that each major category, such as verbal, may be subdivided into areas such as *speaking, literature, reading, grammar, writing, vocabulary,* and *foreign.* Once again, these may be defined to cover the major content usually associated with overall verbal ability. Literature may be subdivided into a number of fields, one of them *poetic analysis,* which in turn leads to *meter,* which in turn leads to *iambic pentameter.* In only five steps or "generations" of our tree, we have moved from highest value-space to a level very close to the specific *item* of measurement and to the specific *detail* of instructional content.

But this tree is not fixed in the numbers of nodes at any level, in the names of those nodes, nor in the various linkages. This is one, arbitrary tree; another might have quite a different content. The structure of the tree may itself be divided through various group or individual decision processes. That some such hierarchical structure must underlie educational value, however, seems almost beyond argument when considered for society as a whole.

Establishment of Values

The mathematics of the *bentee* has been explored elsewhere (Page, 1972b, in press) but may be briefly summarized here. At any level of the tree, for the division and weighting of the branches from any node, an appropriate set of judges may be defined. For the topmost branches,

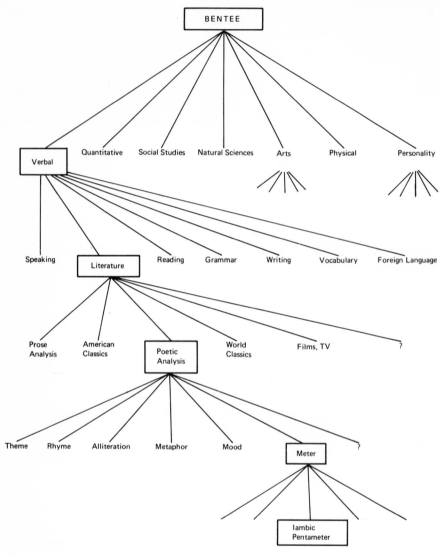

Fig. 1. The possible recursive feature of the bentee technique. As analysis moves from the general to the specific, a shift is made from societal to expert opinion and from value-space to test-space. From Page (in press). Reprinted by permission of *Educational and Psychological Measurement.*

perhaps the appropriate judges should be those reflecting the largest questions of social policy: whether groups of leaders, educators, parents, or citizens. A number of possible strategies are available, but one of the simplest has been called the *token* strategy and is represented by Figure 2.

Suppose that a judge, correctly identified, is given a set of definitions of measurement areas: verbal, quantitative, etc. The judge is then presented with seven boxes, corresponding to the names of the areas. He is also given 100 poker chips, all of equal value. He is requested to "spend" his chips according to his own set of values. If he believes that science accounts for half of the value, he will place 50 chips on *science*. Each chip, then, represents .01 of his total evaluation for the node at which he is working. If he is by chance the *only* judge of that level (as might occur in a particular culture, at a particular node), then his weighting would become the general evaluation. More common, however, would probably be a set of independent judgments chosen from a presumed population of such judgments, so that the values could be described, within ordinary statistical accuracy, as the values in that important, background population. The *average* number of tokens for a given value then becomes

$$v_i = \frac{1}{100J} \sum_{j=1}^{J} t_{ij}. \qquad (1)$$

Here v_i is the value of the ith branch; J is the number of judges; j represent the jth judge; and t_{ij} represents the number of tokens placed on the ith node by the jth judge. And v_i will of course have possible values from 0 to 1. If the value of this trait is established for a defined population of students, and student k is a member of that population, possessing

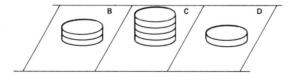

Fig. 2. The direct, or token, strategy for weighting subareas in importance. Each judge is given a stack of tokens and asked to "spend" them according to the importance or value of each topic. In this example, Judge J has awarded two to B, four to C, and one to D. For each judge the "value" of each topic is the number of tokens given, divided by the total N of tokens. From Page (in press). Reprinted by permission of *Educational and Psychological Measurement*.

measures m_{ik} for each v_i, then the *individual* bentee is defined as

$$\text{bentee}_k = T\left(\sum_{i=1}^{I} v_i m_{ik}\right), \qquad (2)$$

where i represents the ith branch, I is the number of branches in the node; v_i represents the value of the ith branch; and T represents a transformation of the sum to a T-score distribution.

At each node, an evaluation may be performed for the branches immediately below. Then the value of each branch follows the rules for a tree of independent probabilities, that is, a branch is valued as the *product* of the lineal branches above it. In still another way, such values are like those in a probability tree. Where a node-name occurs more than once (just as verse meter might be valued both in verbal and in arts), the values of the node name are summed across all such occurrences.

There are a number of remarkable advantages of such a tree. It is recursive, permitting a similar operation to be performed at each generation without fundamental shift of philosophy. It provides for a change of function of the judges as one moves down the tree: Earlier judges might be lay citizens, yet lower branches require experts in subject fields and in testing. It is flexible, providing for evaluation of part of the tree and an approximate allocation of value without evaluating in similar detail either the sibling branches or descendant branches. This is an important feature for the allocation of resources, for example, in developing early instructional and measurement programs for national systems of education.

It is also flexible in a number of other ways. Branch values may be reappraised regularly or as occasion warrants. Furthermore, the bentee *may be calculated according to the values for an individual or a specific group.* Equation (2), in other words, may be calculated with the replacement of v_i by v_{ik}. An individual's own bentee may be calculated a number of ways, one of them possibly representing his occupational goal. If student k seeks an engineering degree, it would be more plausible for him to have a high value on quantitative, than for a humanities major. Again, appropriate judges can redesign a pattern of values, and in some cases the student might be one such appropriate judge.

The word *bentee,* of course, is just as arbitrary and hollow as the word *dollar.* Each represents a medium of exchange, in terms of which values that are quantitatively distinct may be compared and traded off. The value of any object, in dollars or bentees, depends on what portion of one's capital one is willing to spend; neither the dollar nor the bentee will be considered by any philosopher to be a measure of all human value. Yet by a willingness to play a "dollar game," industrial managers have created objective functions of great utility in formal, powerful strategies (e.g., Wagner, 1969). But in order to employ optimization techniques from management science, a problem must have, among other characteristics, a primary focus on decision making and measurable values that unequivocally reflect the future well-being of the organization (Wagner, 1969, pp. 5–6). At no level have we enjoyed such values in education. It seems time to begin their design.

The Sources of Benefit

Assuming that we have, through some strategy, identified a measure of the benefits of higher education, where should we look for the sources of such measures? By definition, the benefits of education stem from the educational experience and not from the development that would occur without such experience. Yet, these are commonly confused: For example, the earnings of the average college man are sometimes contrasted with the earnings of the average noncollege man, and the difference is claimed as the "worth of a college education." This is, of course, nonsense and is so recognized by most serious students of the question: These averages represent different populations on almost every measurable dimension before any student attends his first freshman class.

Curiously enough, however, a related mistake is still more widespread and emerges repeatedly in certain discussions of higher education. This question concerns the desired "fairness" or "equality" of educational treatment. Various groups are compared (sex, race, and social class are currently the most frequent classifications) on the proportions accepted or succeeding in college. If group A has a larger proportion admitted, then group B is assumed to be a victim of "unequal" treatment. The unspoken assumption is that groups A and B would expectably do the same, if only the system of higher education or society at large did not impose handicaps. Seldom is any evidence provided for such an assumption; it appears to "go without saying." To challenge it is regarded as churlish, not to say unfashionable.

This question of fairness is intimately related to the question of benefits. One cannot sensibly calculate the benefits of various educational strategies unless one has come to grips with what constitutes such fairness, for one holds stubbornly and correctly to such a national principle. Astin recognizes this problem elsewhere (1971) and in the present volume ("Measurement and Determinants of the Outputs of Higher Education," pp. 107–127) when he poses certain competitive models of purpose in higher education (laissez faire, elitist, egalitarian, and remedial).

Atkinson (1972) outlines this problem in developing a theory of instruction. He postulates a variable $P_i(t)$ that represents the performance P, of student i, for time t. Time is limited, and each student's time t_i is a portion of the total time T (which may be here considered a general notation for the expenditure of limited resources). At any time t

$$P_i(t) = \alpha_i - \beta_i e^{-\gamma t}, \tag{3}$$

where α is the student's maximal level of achievement and $\alpha - \beta$ is his minimal level of achievement. The symbol γ is defined as a rate-of-progress measure, and e is as usually defined in growth functions.* Under such parameters, one student will gain more from a given investment of time than will another. The philosophical problem is posed, then, as to which optimization goal is to be preferred (p. 924):

(a) Maximize the mean value of P over the class of students.
(b) Minimize the variance of P over the class of students.
(c) Maximize the number of students who score at grade level at the end of the first year.
(d) Maximize the mean value of P satisfying the constraint that the resulting variance of P is less than or equal to the variance that would have been obtained if no CAI were administered.

These goals, though framed for a program of computer-assisted reading instruction, bear an interesting analogy to what constitutes fairness in the expectable benefits of higher education. Goal (a) may be said to reflect one view of the benefit to the total society as a functioning unit. The higher P is regarded as desirable, no matter where it resides. Goal (b) is egalitarian to an extreme; the aim is to narrow any difference among students. This might be accomplished by not instructing the able (or in an extreme case by actually handicapping the able) and spending time in proportion to the weakness of the students. Goal (c) aims at some minimum performance level for all, which would imply, again, a neglect of the able. And goal (d) would hold the *spread* constant (so that there is no more growth in range of performance) but within that limitation would maximize the benefit to society.

Given a class of first graders, not many would argue for the egalitarian model (b). Given a class of entering freshmen, not much responsible

* The reader is cautioned against a misprinted formula related to this one in Atkinson (1972, p. 924), acknowledged in private correspondence.

support would be discovered for such a model among the college faculty. In the case of the individual class, most would recognize that seeking equality of *achievement* in this way could only be done at the expense of equality of *opportunity*. Yet when we make judgments concerning identifiable *groups* within our society, this critical distinction seems to break down, at times with grotesque results.

An illustration was the admission policy of a prominent city college. On the one hand, it had very rich resources, and one might expect that it would be a capstone: The pay scale was high, and a number of able professors were recruited, sometimes from prestige institutions. On the other hand, its aim was partly to serve the youth of the inner city. Under the environmentalist ideology that dominated the founding of the college, differences among groups of students could only result from prior environmental deprivation.

Since student costs were to be minimal, and educational quality was to be high, applications were expected to soar beyond all capacity. Whom should the college admit? Test scores and prior educational experiences were by definition "racist," and one could therefore not simply admit those who could predictably do best at the college. The egalitarian ideology seemed to argue for choosing the *worst* applicants, those with least chance of success. Unable to resolve this dilemma, the college decided to pick a *random sample of applicants*. Needless to say, such selection led to a most unfavorable educational climate and collapse of public confidence in the decision makers.*

A thoughtful reconsideration of the problem of admissions, together with the problem of fairness, may lead us back to Equation (3). It appears that all of the three student variables, α, β, and γ, might be relevant, if they could be reasonably inferred from student data and from research in student accomplishment. One research strategy suggests itself: By concentrating on before-and-after achievement measures as criteria, we discover relationships between gain and student variables, between gain and environmental variables, and between student and environmental variables. From such analysis, assuming that we could optimize the environmental variables for each student, we calculate α as his maximal achievement estimate. We calculate β, then, as the maximal achievement minus his entering-college achievement, that is, as a measure of gap between present and potential. Then we calculate his γ as the rate of progress expected from each additional input of resources. Clearly, multivariate analysis is needed for estimating these parameters. In current research of college admissions and student

---

* Since the writer was a consultant for brief periods, the college is not identified. In any case, a number have somewhat similar early histories.

progress, some, but by no means all, portions of such analysis have been approached.

One benefit of such reconsideration could be a sharper definition of our objective functions. For example, the Atkinson model assumes that all of the students in the class have, indeed, a necessary place in the objective function. In college admissions, however, the question is whether to admit or exclude. And when one considers only the output of the individual college, then Atkinson's first objective (to maximize the mean value of P) might rather be to maximize the output of the college:

$$O_c = \sum_{i=1}^{N} x_i P_i(t), \quad \text{given that} \quad \sum_{i=1}^{N} x_i \leq X, \quad (4)$$

where O_c is defined as output for college c, $P_i(t)$ is defined as in Equation (3), and where x_i is either 1 or 0, depending on whether or not applicant i is admitted. And the constraint acknowledges that the number admitted may not exceed X, which is the college's determined admission capacity.

Since admission is a yes-no variable, however, in Equation (4) now $t = 1$, and the optimization becomes considerably simpler.

Suppose the college, however, seeks a "compensatory" model, in light of the society as a whole. Taking all of the applicants as the population of concern, the above college output model would not seem appropriate. Rather, the goal might become one that is not exactly the same as any of Atkinson's: to choose a class in such a way as to make the greatest *growth* during the years of study. If a student were judged to have already approached his maximal achievement, he would not be chosen, no matter how high his current achievement. On the other hand, an applicant with a large value of β and γ would be selected. It should be noted that this would not necessarily imply choosing students of present low performance. To the contrary, almost all research to date suggests that those who have gained a lead over their fellows in the past will *widen* the lead in the future. In other words, a truly compensatory selection might well end by choosing the same students who might be chosen under Equation (4): the brightest and "most promising." If this seems a contradiction, it may well be that we have not given any critical examination to the concept of such compensation. Surely, we should be careful that we do not, through faulty analysis, fall into an "egalitarian" model without recognizing what we are doing. And the possibility that we are doing so should indicate how urgent it is to research these student parameters.

To proceed with any such research, we must rely heavily on the use of standardized, objective tests; there is hardly any alternative. Yet objective tests are currently under attack by "compensatory" forces as being "culture-biased" in favor of some groups and against others.* The issue of "fairness" in higher education centers on the question of what cultural bias actually means, yet here again is a concept that is very poorly understood. The high heritability of a test is evidence against the presence of cultural bias, yet it is currently the most highly heritable tests (such as IQ) that are most often accused of such bias.† The question of hereditary aptitude, then, may affect the utility of measures of student parameters and deserves more attention than it usually receives.

Benefit and Heredity

In many of the essays of this volume, some attention is paid to "ability," commonly as measured in SAT or similar tests of aptitude. A fundamental realization about such scores is that they are highly heritable. This does not mean that heritability consists somehow of a father "passing his SAT score" to his son. Rather, it refers to heritability as statistically expressible, to the genetic component of any trait for which appropriate data are available. Thus, heritability can be calculated from a variety of formulas; one accepted form for "broad heritability" (that relevant to most policy considerations) may be:

$$H = \frac{r_{AB} - r_{CD}}{\rho_{AB} - \rho_{CD}}. \tag{5}$$

H refers to the broad heritability; r_{AB} refers to the correlation between pairs of some known consanguinity; r_{CD} refers to the correlation between pairs of some *lesser* degree of consanguinity; and ρ_{AB} and ρ_{CD} refer to the corresponding theoretical expectation of similarity, under purely genetic assumptions. AB pairs might correspond to identical twins together (ITT); and CD pairs might correspond to fraternal twins together (FTT). Some data calculated for IQ's, within a white Western population, might be:

$$H_{IQ} = \frac{r_{ITT} - r_{FTT}}{\rho_{ITT} - \rho_{FTT}}. \tag{6}$$

$$H_{IQ} = \frac{.94 - .54}{1.00 - .50} = \frac{.40}{.50} = .80,$$

* For a balanced consideration of claimed test bias, see Stanley (1971).

† A distinction must be made, of course, between heritability within a group and heritability between groups. This is a much-debated issue summarized in Jensen (1973) and has a large bearing on what constitutes culture bias and fairness.

implying that, for these data (Burt, 1958, Table 1), 80 percent of the variance in IQ is broadly genetic. Such measurement, though little understood, is near the heart of the current debates over nature and nurture and over the fairness of educational programs.

Those unfamiliar with such formulations should be warned that there is nothing permanent about such percentages. They reflect only the data of discoverable influence within a given population at a given time. In a society with less equality of opportunity, the environmental variance in IQ would expectably increase, resulting in a *lower* relative contribution of heredity. On the other hand, the fairer a society becomes in equalizing opportunity, the smaller will be the environmental contribution, and the larger will be the percentage of variation due to heredity. In this way, social classes may become increasingly separated by barriers of biology, though less hampered by barriers of social or educational bias of opportunity (Herrnstein, 1973).

IQ, of course, is not the only heritable trait of educational importance. To some extent, *any* trait that is measurable for consanguinity pairs, with some approximate control of environment, is going to yield such information. Most educationally useful traits are probably going to show heritabilities above zero.* That is, *some* of their variance will be attributable to genetic factors, for which not even the home environment, let alone the educational system, may be held responsible. Indeed, society may be held "responsible" for such hereditary influences only in the failure to acknowledge them or to adjust policy to their existence. Yet there is pressure in the academic world to prevent open consideration of hereditary factors (Page, 1972a). For a comprehensive discussion of these matters as they affect education, see Jensen (1973).

For scholars who seek an understanding of the benefits of higher education, there is a large responsibility for recognizing these genetic influences and their magnitude. Compared with these inequalities at birth, the variation from one college to another, one teacher to another, must assume a relatively subsidiary role. And all issues of fairness must be seen in terms of maximizing potential according to some realistic model of capacity to improve within finite resources of time and funding. It should be recognized, too, that the heritable nature of mental development implies that there may be substantial correlations between present

---

* For example, Stafford (1972) studies the hereditary components of mathematics behavior, and Klein & Cattell (1972) demonstrate the heritability of many "personality" traits. One remarkable work is by Bock & Kolakowski (in press), who trace almost half of the variance of "spatial visualization" to a single recessive, sex-linked gene.

status and rate of progress. This would argue for faster growth by the able and an increased variance in performance across the college years.*

Discussion

This paper has emphasized three major themes in the attempt to understand the benefits of higher education. The first is the need to develop some broadly accepted and summary measure of educational value and to relate such value to educational measurement by a series of plausible and technical steps. A "bentee" strategy is suggested as a thinking exercise toward such a system.

The second theme is the need to reconsider the problem of fairness or equality of opportunity in a much sophisticated way than commonly practiced. A comparison with a CAI model from instructional theory suggests that we have not paid systematic attention to those variables of most potential importance to decision making: the student's maximal development, his lag from that maximum, and his expectable rate of progress as a function of the allocated resource. Furthermore, society is still confronted with the choice of a correct objective function for any implemented solution. Each suggested optimization makes certain assumptions about one deep, and largely inarticulate, concern of society: whether it shall try to equalize *opportunity* or to equalize *achievement* itself.

Finally, the choice of such models may be partially dependent on our awareness of the sources of human difference. A common posture of the academic intellectual is to ignore our knowledge about the heritability of intelligence and of other important educational traits. The genetic component of our educational objectives may be the salient fact of the educational world, yet it remains one of the most neglected. It cannot, and should not, remain neglected much longer.

Taken together (and taken seriously), such themes could lead to an examination of higher education that would be radically different from the trapped concepts that often seem to have dominated us in the past.

REFERENCES

Astin, A. W. *Predicting academic performance in college.* New York: Free Press, 1971.
Atkinson, R. C. Ingredients for a theory of instruction. *American Psychologist,* 1972, 27(10): 921–931.

* "The first effect of teaching a methodology . . . is that of enhancing the capacities of the already capable, thus magnifying the difference in intelligence" (Dijkstra, 1972, p. 866).

Bock, R. D., & Kolakowski, D. Further evidence of sex-linked major-gene influence on human spatial visualizing ability. *American Journal of Human Genetics,* in press.

Burt, C. The inheritance of mental ability. *American Psychologist,* 1958, 13: 1–15.

Dijkstra, E. W. The humble programmer. 1972 Turing Award Lecture, *Communications of the ACM,* 1972, 15(10): 859–866.

Herrnstein, R. *I.Q.* Boston: Little, Brown, 1973.

Jensen, A. *Educability and group differences.* New York: Harper and Row, 1973.

Klein, T. W., & Cattell, R. B. Heritability of personality and ability measures obtained from the High School Personality Questionnaire and the Culture Fair Intelligence Scale. Paper presented at the Annual Meeting of the American Psychological Association, Honolulu, September 1972.

Page, E. B. Behavior and heredity. *American Psychologist,* 1972a, 27(7): 660–661.

Page, E. B. Seeking a measure of general educational advancement: The bentee. *Journal of Educational Measurement,* 1972b, 9(1): 33–43.

Page, E. B. "Top-down" trees of educational value. *Educational and Psychological Measurement,* in press.

Stafford, R. E. Hereditary and environmental components of quantitative reasoning. *Review of Educational Research,* 1972, 42(2): 183–201.

Stanley, J. Predicting college success of the educational disadvantaged. *Science,* 1971, 171(3972): 640–647.

Wagner, H. *Principles of operations research.* Englewood Cliffs: Prentice-Hall, 1969.

Part III

EFFECTS ON THE EDUCATED: EMERGING AREAS OF STUDY

THE EFFECTS OF COLLEGE ON INDIVIDUALS

*Three Life Studies**

Thomas J. Cottle

The Man Who Sought Education

We have spent a great deal of time together, Tom Jackson and I, speaking of a host of topics that matter to both of us. At least two or three times a month we have met and talked, sometimes for an hour or so, sometimes for an entire afternoon. In that time, we have told one another a great many things in a great many ways. Soon I shall go to the black community in Cincinnati where he was born and share a meal with his parents who presently await a visit with "one of their son's friends from college." Because they see little of Tom they will want to know everything about him: how he looks and feels, what he's thinking about, how his life at college is turning out. I will have much to tell them about this twenty-year-old college junior, with Tom's permission, particularly about school and the sorts of conflicts that such

* "The Man Who Sought Education" is a revised version of "The Dynamics of Institutional Change," reprinted from "Scientific Institutions of the Future,"—Prometheus Paperback, published by Acropolis Books, Ltd., Washington, D.C. 20009; copyright 1972 by THOR, Inc. A version of "Zero Man" originally appeared in *Change,* November 1972, 4:49–55. A version of "College at Middle Age" originally appeared in *Change,* Summer 1972, 4:47–53.

a young man experiences, for at one point these were some of the very questions I myself had wondered about.

"You know, man," Tom had said to me one day after school as we walked about the streets of downtown Boston, "school is a goddamn bore—one drag ass situation after another." We walked in a heavy way, our hands in our pockets, our heads hung down more with fatigue than anything else. "They haven't got anything over there that I really dig. Courses are a drag, you know. Got all these boring requirements. Gets me that in order to take one course in one department, you got to take about a million prerequisites. By the time you make it to that course you've learned everything anyway. Then the guy says, 'Well, we better go over some of the basics, 'cause some of you may not have had this before.' Then he looks over at the brothers and sisters in the class as though he were waving his nose right at us. Always got to be black folks who wouldn't understand. They look at us like we were a bunch of baboons."

I shook my head. It is the summer of 1971, and I am conversing with a young man who is generous enough to speak to me about his college experiences. We walk together in a night club and bar district of Boston called the combat zone. Neither of us comes here at night, although on several occasions Tom has taken me a short distance from here to the home of a girlfriend, who, in the dark hours of the week, walks the streets, a nineteen-year-old prostitute. He interrupts my thoughts and I wonder how much of what he has been saying I have lost.

"Sitting there like dumb baboons." He turned to me. "What *you* thinking about? Looking so sad you'd think someone just called *you* a baboon."

"I look sad?"

"Sure. You do."

"I was just thinking about your girlfriend."

"What were you thinking about her?"

"I don't know. About her life."

"Yeah? I'll bet you were thinking about all those men she packs away."

"In a way, I suppose I was."

"She's doing all right. She'll make out."

"I'm sure she will."

"Now wait a minute, man, you said we were going to talk about school. Right? So let's get off her. We're talking about *me*."

"Go ahead. We're in your class with all those prerequisites."

"That's it. I told you everything. Nothing else if you don't mind being treated as part of the earth's scum all the time." We walked on in silence.

"What's going on?" I asked.

"What are you thinking, Tom?" he asked. "About her again?"

"No. About you!"

"The thing is that a guy like myself can't make complaints. What the hell do I expect? Nothing different from what I got. You know they got their representatives from the students on all the committees now?"

"I know."

"So every day I hear what's going on. It's always the same thing. We got to have *special* programs, *remedial* groups, *tutoring* programs. They bring us here and turn us loose. They take us out of the shittiest high schools in America and tell us to sink or swim. So you know what I think?"

"Yeah. I think I do," I answered.

"What, then, smartass?"

"You think that you're as bright as any of the white kids in the school."

"You're fucking A, man." Tom Jackson stood up tall as we stopped in front of a record store and stared hard at me. "That's exactly what I think. That the black kids they got in that school can compete with anybody, and I don't mean only in football or track."

"I know. I know." We began to walk again.

"The committees are just as bad as the classrooms. You go into one class and there's two of us, then in the next one, maybe they got five. And you know goddamn well everybody's looking and everybody's counting. They got dudes on that faculty proud to tell their friends, 'I got black kids in my class.' They're so damned uptight about it. All they think about is that there's a black lit course going on the same time as their course and still they got a couple brothers siting in the middle somewhere. Makes me sick."

"Hold it a minute, Tom," I began. "I'm losing your point."

"Look, man," he started his explanation, "I don't want to be educated solely for the black business. This is a good school. You know that. I mean, you could agree to that?"

"Absolutely."

"Then why do I have to constantly be put in a situation where everything I do and am in education has to be colored over that way? You'll excuse the brilliant play on words," he grinned, "that comes into my head without me even planning it."

"I'm thinking about it."

"Screw, baby," he came back. "I'll tell you where it's at. I want to be educated in the old sense of the word. I mean, I want to read black literature like Cleaver and Malcolm X, but I want to read the classics as well. When I leave this place I want to go out into the world able to hack it among your kind, too."

"You mean the white world?" I suggested.

"No. There you go. You see. It's always got to be race. Even with you. Shit, man."

"I'm sorry." I said. "You mean intellectuals?"

"Of course that's what I mean. Don't go jiving me. You got more books and stuff in your office than all the people I know combined have read. You're an intellectual. You've read shit by black cats, white cats, all of 'em. That's what I want. I don't want anyone to corner me, label me a black this or a black that." He looked over at me and smiled. I tried to smile back. He knew exactly what was turning over inside of me. I had forgotten the hot day and the stifling feeling in the streets near the new City Hall. He was obliging me, giving of himself, but knowing full well the motivations behind my work, as well as the forces and constraints on our friendship.

"Take the Black Studies Program," he was resuming. "I did that whole thing on the basis of a sort of Cartesian method. You split the mind and politics in this case."

"You split what?" I inquired.

"You split your intellectual and political purposes and ideas. I haven't any interest beyond, you know, what most of us care about in terms of black sociology. I don't need any courses to teach me that stuff. You read. That's all. Anybody who reads doesn't need formal training in sociology and psychology, or history, for that matter. Most of the lectures and seminars in those fields are a waste."

"Plus which you've lived some of that history and sociology."

"That's the bullshit part, right there, man. You just put your finger right on it."

"Go on."

"It's the idea of a black experience that we push on you. What it's like to be black in a racist country. Black consciousness."

"And that stuff's not important to you?"

"Course it's important. It's *the* important thing. But what I'm trying to say is that sometimes I've been guilty of pushing politics when it was actually the intellectual stuff I believed in just as much. I pushed black studies for political *and* intellectual reasons. Okay? Social reasons too. We want to get black students into the goddamn school. But a black studies program can't be precious or selfish. Selfish is better. It can't be everybody pushing the same thing. If it is, it's going to be just another victim of racism."

"But I thought you said once that with the Black Studies Program college finally meant something."

"Sure, it was relevant and pure. But I'll tell you, there were some days sophomore year I was wondering what the white kids were reading and doing. It was the same feeling I used to have in high school, when we used to practice on a field near where the University of Cincinnati football team practiced. You couldn't always see them 'cause they'd put these canvas shades around the field."

"Secret practices."

"Right. Well, after a while, when I'd get through wondering what they were doing, I'd wonder in the bus coming home from practice what the regular students were doing. You know, what the classrooms looked like, and what books the students read." As we walked, he put his hand on my forearm. "You remember when you moved from junior high school to high school, and you had all these thoughts about not being able to pass and all?"

"Do I ever," I responded, suddenly caught up in recollections.

"That's the way I used to think about college. Only I used to think about sitting in all those libraries reading textbooks and philosophy. I never thought about reading only books by black writers. Now they got a bunch of students making a declaration that they're going to read nothing but black literature. For me that's no good. You read good shit, you read bad shit. You read to learn of black experiences, red experiences, white experiences. It's a waste, though, *just* reading about the black experience. Everybody has a black experience, so they put down a few words and some New York dude makes a lot of money publishing it. It's patronizing. It's part of the same old oppression. 'Here's the *real* Mississippi experience.' I'm the *real* Cincinnati experience. Then guys like you buy it and read it and assign it in all your courses. It's like everything else. There are gorgeous works; some aren't that well known, and then there are what's getting to be the old standbys. And then there's a lot of junk." Turning the corner we looked at one another. Sears Crescent, the new site of the Boston City Hall, the great brick-lined plazas and modern subway station lay just in front of us. A Dixieland band played at the bottom of the stairs leading into the giant City Hall. "You looked shocked, man," Tom was saying.

"I don't know. I'm not shocked, exactly. I don't know for sure, Tom, what I'm thinking." I was imagining seminars in black studies programs. I imagined black students angry with someone like me for being out of it, ignorant of the realities of their lives. "Yeah, man," I caught myself,

"I suppose I am a bit surprised. I'm begining not to get anything anymore that has to do with race."

"Don't cop out with me, man." His remark was made in anger and impatience. Always we would reach a point in our discussions when he would suddenly whip out a certain unequivocal tone. It made me believe that up to that point he was willing to go along with my ride. But then something would provoke him to regain a position of expert, of teacher, really, and he would have to settle the matter. At this instant it was the issue of race with which Tom Jackson had played loosely until I had thrown my retreating discomfort at him.

"Don't give me that shit, man," he said bitterly. "You know damn well how you better stand on the race issue. Don't say things like that; getting things confused that have to do with race," he muttered. "You get everything! If you don't get it, who's supposed to?"

"I didn't mean it that way."

"Sure you meant it," he persisted. "If not this way then what, say? What are you talking about, man? You talking in circles? When you tell me you don't get it anymore, you're starting up with the same motors these others cats start up with when they default."

"What do you mean default?" I asked.

"I mean give up on trying to discern what the hell the black man's trying to do! You default. Don't listen to all the jive. There's too much jive floating around universities. All that committee stuff and politics of yours is jive."

"Tom, you're being incoherent or something. I'm not getting what you're saying." Although he was trying hard to keep his fury in check, I felt as though a parent or minister were bawling me out.

"I'll lay it straight out for you. Don't shy away from the politics, man, especially from the racism. All that stuff's up front. You got that?" I nodded yes. "Now, all of that stuff means you got to read different sorts of books or, better still, read the same old books in a whole new way. Like we did that other time." I recalled the afternoon we sat together near the Charles River. Tom had brought three history books, widely assigned in colleges, all of which included outright racist passages written in elegant language. One of them had won a Pulitzer Prize. I had read portions of that particular one in college and had not once noticed the paragraphs he had prepared to show me. His copy was underlined, the columns strewn with comments and expletives. On one page, southern blacks were called, summarily, Sambo. In the margin, Tom had written: "Tom J., show to Tom C."

"What I want you to do is not be seduced by all the shit that's flying around colleges," he was saying. "There's a wrong kind of emphasis on the black experience. Christ, it's getting embarrassing going in the bookstores and seeing a row of books marked 'Novels,' and another row marked 'Poetry,' and then stack after stack marked 'Black Experience.' They're overcompensating so that those guys in New York can clean up. They'll drop it soon. You can see it happening already with the Women's Lib stuff. Pretty soon those bookstores will be filled with nothing but Women's Lib shit. You dig what I'm saying?"

"Absolutely."

"You're lying, man. You don't dig it 'cause it's too big for you. You got education figured out in the most straight way. I got to talk with you the same way sometimes I talk to my girl. You're like my two students."

"Don't give me all the crap," I said angrily. "What are you saying?"

"Now you're talking like a man."

In a way he was right. My growing impatience and anger with him were becoming, if not manly, then expressions as honest as any I had shown him that afternoon.

"My problem is very simple, doctor. I'm a black man. I always have been, I always will be. Now that ain't as stupid to say as it might sound at first hearing. Because the problem is that in their confusion and their guilt and their ignorance about my people, schools don't know how they're supposed to be, liberal or otherwise. Some of them think the way to act is just to avoid the fact that a bunch of people have black skin. So they spread that jive about all people being equal. Another group thinks that liberalism means going around setting up black program this and black program that, just as long as the school stays around 6, 7 percent. You might want to ask the question, how many hours a day a cat thinks about the fact he's black. Some days, man, that's all this school's got me thinking. They don't let me think about anything else but being black or coming from a ghetto. I go into the dorm and see black posters and black this and black that. I get tired of it, not 'cause I'm trying to avoid being black, but because the damn school is so white. It's so full of your kind, we got to keep putting up the symbols just to keep reminding ourselves that we shouldn't fall in and march with you."

"So the kids push you to it, too?"

"Yeah, my friends," he corrected me, "push me to it too. It's like drugs in a way. Every day, at some point, I got to do my black thing. Some days I feel it, other days I'd just as soon be left alone to read my books or do things. And *you* know which books."

I met Tom Jackson about a year and a half before in the lounge of his dormitory, where we spoke for only a few minutes. A strong, handsome young man, he carried two volumes of short stories, one by Jack London, the other by Ambrose Bierce. I recall making some remark like, "Are the books for a humanities course? Freshman English?" "No," he had smiled politely. "There are just for me." When we spoke that night, he put the volumes on a table next to him. From time to time he glanced at them, a watchman making his hourly check. "You look at those books," I had said, "as though someone were about to come and snatch them away." "Maybe that's what I'm feeling," he had said nodding his head. "Yeah. Maybe that's what I'm feeling." At the time I interpreted his words to mean, I've had so little in my life, I protect every bit that's now my own, even if it's only out on loan from a library. But this is not what he had in mind. What he had meant then and now again as we sat together by the rectangular pool adjoining the plaza, was his love for literature and especially for fictionalized accounts of American experiences. He had read all of Faulkner, London, and Eugene O'Neill. He had recently finished several books on the Sacco and Vanzetti trial, something we spoke about from time to time. When, in connection with these books, I mentioned the Chicago Conspiracy Trial he pushed my words away. Classical literature, Gibbon, Saint Augustine, Plato, interested him less, as did many contemporary white authors. Here he chose almost exclusively black writers. The novels, poems, and essays of Baldwin, Hughes, Du Bois, Malcolm X, Fanon, Cleaver, and Ellison occupied a special place in his brick and board college room bookshelf. *Black Rage* and Julius Lester's writings were there as well.

But it was the group of writers most of us unthinkingly label "the American writers" that especially moved him and increased his love for books. In the dormitory where he had lived in his first two years at college and now in the black students' off-campus house, one always found a few secondhand copies that he had purchased, or traded for, along with piles of volumes taken from the university library. Yellow charge slips from the library covered his desk, along with reminders of overdue books, fines, costs of books presumably lost. He had never lost a book, however, although returning them was painful. "It's like turning back a friend whose been kind to you," he told me one late afternoon in his room.

"Then don't ever return them to the library. They have enough money," I foolishly advised him, unable for some reason to tell him directly how lovely I found his sentiment.

Nonetheless, the books and the classes in which they were discussed remained white, a fact that hurt and confused him. Playing baseball together one day with a group of boys in a neighborhood lot not far from the university, Tom had told me of an incident that occurred in a literature class. In this class, the sort in which two lectures and a one-hour section meeting comprise the week's work, a young teacher had rerouted the context of a discussion of *The Red Badge of Courage* so that the feelings of slaves might be considered. "All the while the cat kept looking at me and this one sister in there as if to say, 'I'm making it relevant for you two.' Like, we got to get your shit in here too. It made me furious. Nothing about slaves in that book that matters. It's about courage, that book. That's the way I read it, man, that's the way it should have been talked about. I didn't have a thought in my head that day in class about making that book relevant for contemporary society. Nothing could have interested me less," Tom had said as we waited for our young infielders to get organized. "Sure, you want to bring it all down to Vietnam and these dudes backing out of the war, you can do that. But that's what we do in all our bull sessions. I don't need that from teachers. He'd been better off talking about southern history, about which I don't know a thing, except maybe for Jefferson Davis."

"So what did you do?" I had asked. Should I have told him how many times I had attempted something like that in one of my own classes? Had I not, in the past, tampered a trifle with the writings of Freud and R. D. Laing in a somewhat similar style.

"You want to know what I did?" Tom had asked me. "Don't quote me to anyone."

"Can I use it in a paper, if I write one" I had grinned at him.

"Sure. Freedom of the press. Always provide journalists with freedom of the press."

"What did you say?"

"I played good little black boy. I talked to the class about reactions to the goddamn Civil War by slaves. I threw around antebellum slogans. I talked about the social psychology of slave families and how people are forced to repress their anger. I didn't have the slightest knowledge of what I was saying, but all these people were looking at me, man, as though I were recreating the fucking scriptures for them. And this dude teaching the course—I guess he must have been a graduate student T.A., something like that—he's standing there looking at me as though I were the most eloquent sonofabitch in America. He's got this look on his face as he looks back and forth between me and this sister, who he probably thinks I'm putting away, that says: 'Oh God, how you and your people must have suffered.' And me, I'm quoting for this dude from Styron and Stanley Elkins and this one essay I read by Nathan Hare. I swear to God. You believe that? I'm quoting him from white writers I was reading for another course. How's that for bullshit? Now that's relevance for you all done up real pretty."

"That's an unbelievable story."

"You don't know the half of it. When I got through, the sister turns to me and says something like: 'Tom Jackson, you lying sellout. You quoted from William Styron.' And we just sat there laughing together. It was really something else, man. Nobody knew."

A brilliant light beat down on the red bricks of the plaza. Tom and I sprawled on benches near the small pond, our bodies shifting about every few minutes to relieve the pain caused by the hardness of the wooden slats. I often wonder, in these moments, as people glance at us, whether they might wonder about our conversation. What do they see when, on a weekday afternoon, two men loll about with seemingly nothing to do, apparently unemployed, and living as if there were no constraints imposed on them but a culture's sense of time? Usually, in reaction to these observers, I decide that what we are doing consti-tutes an enormous contribution to education and to social science. It is my own school without walls, I imagine, with each of us wanting his own special brand of credit.

"Well, so where are we?" I asked.

"I don't know, man. We were talking about my need to be black all the time in school."

"Right."

"What d'you mean, right?" he questioned me sleepily.

"I mean . . . C'mon. You know what I mean," I said.

"Here, let me tell you this. What scares me now is the pressure to keep pushing the black stuff, or the community stuff. There's going to be in trouble if they push this relevance thing too far. I mean it. There's going to be racist reaction to that too pretty soon. The fact is that lots of black students want to read good books. Just telling about one's experiences in the ghetto doesn't make a book good. As for myself, I don't need that kind of education right now. I want to be able to speak about literature and art and history and all the rest of that jazz, just like you do. You ought to know Julius Lester and Fanon or George Jackson, but I have to know Hemingway and Fitzgerald, white or black, and Faulkner, my old buddy Faulkner. Anyway, I don't want to be the only dude pushing his private experiences into the classroom. I don't want to have to play the role of professional black experience teller. And I sure don't want education to become just that kind of thing, otherwise I'm going to end up really second-class to the people who haven't had to bother with that stuff and just have time to read their books. Politics is always going to be important to me. I'll always be doing something somewhere, man. But I've had it up to here with this shit that I can't be a scholar 'cause there's no time to be doing that with the problems of the cities and all. Everybody's going around telling us we should be lawyers, get into the movement, grab all the power we can. We got these guys that talk to us about stocking up on ammunition for the revolution. . . ."

"Which of course is all you're thinking about," I said sarcastically.

"Yeah. That's all I got to do with my time is disassemble rifles from Nam and hide them in an attic somewhere ready to be assembled at a moment's notice. No, man. What I want to do right now is get me a nice big prestigious PhD degree like you have and settle into a room with lots of books and records."

"Better still," I suggested, "you need a position that will allow you to take out as many books from the library as you can."

"Indefinite loans. That's what I need, man. Indefinite loans. When I get all finished I can decide whether to become a revolutionary, or some sneaky quiet scholar."

"I like the sounds of it," I responded.

"Sure you do. You're just scared too many of us would start some revolution and wipe out all the libs like you."

"Well, there's some truth in that."

" 'Some truth?' Man, what the hell kind of jive you pulling on me?"

"That's scholar's talk."

Tom grunted. Opening his eyes to look at me, all he could do was shake is head. "Some kind of day," he muttered, turning on his back to face the sun. For a few moments we remained silent as the water below us swirled under the spout of a small fountain. I could hear the sounds of shoes on the bricks and of people talking. Without looking to see whether I was listening to him, he resumed.

"I want to be educated, man. It's no more complicated than that. This is what they should know in their committee meetings, especially when they write up those reports of theirs. And your articles, too. I don't know, really, that I felt this way in high school. Nah, I didn't. Christ, I chose Boston 'cause my cousin's here. Now it's different though, although the guys in the house don't always let me be. I'm not so sure they approve of me carrying all those books by honky whites. I mean white writers."

Barely opening one eye, he squinted an apologetic glance at me. I nodded begrudgingly.

"No, I'm sorry, white writers," he repeated. His tone was serious and honest. He closed his eyes again. "White writers. When we get together in the house I speak differently. It's hard to explain. There just are

times I'd like to get the black experience business to count in school
for something. Then I think, if the price I have to pay is to have some
student teach me in an all-black section meeting, I'm wasting someone's
money. There's nobody 18 or 20 knows as much as a 40-year-old dude
who's been studying that stuff all his life. So when the semester rolls
around I have to think. There ain't no one in that house can teach
me about lit. And there ain't too many faculty folks going to help me
much in the area of the black experience, or black history either. Christ,
you could just about count on one finger the blacks in the whole damn
school."

"I hope you mean one hand," I said.

"What did I say?" He looked at me quizzically.

"You said one finger."

"Maybe that's what I did mean." He squinted. "Yeah. You *could* count
'em on one finger. Your little one. What you guys call your pinkie.
Ain't that sweet! Pinkie."

"Sweet," I grumbled.

"It's the relevance and educational innovation crap that gets me. Even
some faculty doubt you if you want a traditional education. Especially
if you're black. You can float through so easily you hardly know you're
being educated. Even my girl said a couple weeks ago that it sure seemed
like my college was easier than her high school. Easier than mine too,
probably. I don't mind being used as a guinea pig, doing these sensitivity
experiences like we had in psych last spring. It's one thing if you know
what you're getting into. Even then we were all so defensive with everyone trying to analyze one another. Maybe that's unfair." Still lying on
his back, he threw his arm over his face so that his hand fell limply.
"There were some great sessions, though. You know, no bullshit sessions;
but so much of it was a complete waste.

"You know, man," he resumed as if in a reverie, "you professors are
becoming frightened. Lots of you are afraid just to teach what you
know. Everything's becoming a popularity trip. With the students too,
sometime. We're in it the same way. Everybody's so afraid to step on
one another, they're all doing things they don't even enjoy. Though
I got a professor in history now, he doesn't care what the hell's happening out in the world. Vietnam, peace demonstrations, he just keeps going.
He's not so great as a lecturer, but he's resolved he's going through
to the finish, and I'm going right with him. Only two of us in his class
but he's. . . ."

"Only two students?" I blurted out.

"Two blacks, dad. Two blacks." He wiggled the fingers of his limp
hand as though to admonish me. "No, there's about 40, 50 students,

I'd say, in there. And you know what? They come every day. His attendance is pretty all right for a mediocre class. But he knows what's going on. He just drones on, but he's some powerful intellect. There isn't any undergraduate, or graduate student for that matter, could teach that class that way."

Tom was suddenly silent. Feeling alone, my own thoughts turned, as they will, to romantic notions about education. I always visualize handsome college campuses with all sorts of people mingling about, rich and poor, young and old, black, brown, red, yellow, white. I imagine many languages being spoken and all kinds of costumes and styles. It's ludicrous, probably, what fills my mind, advertisements and slogans meant for the United Nations or National Brotherhood Week, but a part of me wants to believe in it.

Rolling over and propping himself up on one elbow as if he had just awakened, Tom Jackson peered at the Boston City Hall. Getting the building into focus seemed a great effort. "I wonder how many sticks of dynamite you'd need to fell that monster." Then, with a smile starting to form, he glanced at me. "What else you want to know about my education? Hey, how many articles you think you have from all this?"

I shook my head.

"Well, man, I've talked myself out. From now on the rest is classified."

"Which means?"

"You know I can't give you classified information. I'd get in trouble with my men."

"What do you mean your men?" My frustration was rising.

"My men, my men," he repeated quickly. "Folks going to start the revolution, man."

"And blow up the City Hall," I said with a blend of anger and sadness.

"Sure, why not," he laughed. "You couldn't have any reason to keep that ugly thing standing there, do you?"

"I'm lost. I can't keep up with you, Tom."

"There you go again, doing what I said you oughtn't to do; what I'm trying to teach you not to do. You guys are all so damned chicken scared. You're just so damned scared. You interview a bunch of cats and can't even tell when they're telling you serious things or jiving with you."

"That's for sure," I replied bitterly.

"How else we got to keep ourselves from becoming vulnerable to all that stuff you're pushing down our throats. We'll just have to keep kidding you along until the real happening comes."

How very exact his words were. Vulnerable was indeed what I had been feeling. Simple human vulnerability complicated again and again by impulses and then silence, or apparent complacency, as one maneuvers his priorities around and tries to figure out just who he wants to be every day of his life.

"Yeah, but I don't understand" I said. "One minute you're going on about how this history professor is admirable because he just keeps going on irrespective of what's happening in the world. You spoke about that positively just now and told me that you question the use of sensitivity groups, or whatever that was you did in psychology." We were sitting upright, and I sounded to myself like a child crying before a parent who had rescinded a promise.

"Sure I did," Tom replied. "What's your problem?"

"The problem, goddamit, is that I don't see what it is you're driving at."

"You're losing your cool, your therapy cool, man." He was grinning at me.

"Oh, screw you. This isn't therapy."

"Well then, you're losing that journalistic touch."

"You're making it tough. What the hell do you mean? Journalistic touch?"

"What do you want? Office Hours?" He yelled the words at me.

"No, of course I don't," I shouted back.

"Sure you do, man. You want office hours." He was on fire. "Ten minutes of nice, polite, white bullshit. You want to talk education, baby, you talk out here. In the streets. Where it's hot. And don't expect simple answers. Not when you talk to black folks. You may be a shrink, but you don't figure out people so easily. Maybe you can predict the ways of your white patients and all those students at 'Tech,' but I'm not going to let you or anyone else pin me down so that I become still another category for your mush-meal phony science. I ain't no case study."

"Tom, hold on. . . ."

"Hold on yourself, man. I opened myself up to you. I told you all about what it's like when you're trapped by politics and education. I gave you for free, man, for *free*, a look at the conflict that surrounds every goddamn course decision I have to make. This course or that one. This school or that one. This career or that one. For free! My fucking whore's more understanding than you are. I mean, she doesn't question the worlds I live in . . . or *charge* me for it. For you it's a gas, a turn-on of some sort, a jive that I make it with a whore chick or that I dig Jack London or Faulkner. You've been trying to analyze me now for one straight year, or whatever you call it. I'm sick of all that shit, man. What the hell you want from me? Simple answers? Everything easily categorized? Computerized? You sound like that sensitivity group leader we had. 'Seems to me,'" he mocked her, "'that the group is angry about. . . .' You should all go to hell with that phony racket of yours. You better learn about simultaneous expressions. You're fucking A right I can dig the politics and still want one of *your* educations. Just like you got, big fella. Just exactly like you got. The degree, the status, the bread. All of it, man. Just what you got. Only I ain't about to drop you into no slot so I can retrieve something when I need it. You ain't never going to understand me, man. You ain't never going to read me like you read a book. Next time some honky tells me to speak about slaves in English class, I'll spit in his face, man. Let's get out of here." He stood up and started walking away from me. "Are you a revolutionary or a scholar? the man wants to know. My ass," he was mumbling.

I was dumbfounded and hurt, and embarrassed. Several people had heard him. Obviously impressed, they had stopped to listen. Their presence encouraged him. I felt two inches high but overwhelmed by a desire to hump him from the back and flip him over on the pavement, something I cannot recall ever doing in my life to anyone. You better believe I'll write you up, I thought, bitterly. I'll get something out of this. Jesus Christ.

Then, from 20 feet away, like a mother who at last could reprimand her child no more, Tom Jackson turned around and beckoned me to join him. It was a gesture that said, all right, I'm done, let's go, we're back on even ground now. I threw my head forward and began to trudge after him as the small audience disbanded. "Jesus Christ," I said between my teeth but loudly enough for him to hear. "Jesus Christ."

He turned his head without breaking stride and with a huge and wonderful smile lighting up his face, he responded gleefully: "SUPERSTAR."

Zero Man—The Anatomy of Academic Failure

Jonathan Seagrin McCauley grew up in a home where excellence was a supreme ideal. He and his three sisters never witnessed anything that resembled weakness or inadequacy in their parents. Their father, Franklin Barnstable McCauley, an outstanding systems analyst and electrical engineer, recently assumed administrative control of a major corporation in the Southwest. Their mother, Audrey Shepard McCauley, was a graduate of Wellesley where she majored in art history. When she married and moved away from her native New England to Texas where her husband took his first job, it was only a matter of months before she became immersed in civic activities. Her knowledge and generous way of organizing groups interested in supporting the arts made her the logical choice to assume the assistant directorship of the city's museum as well as the position of chairwoman of the committee to plan a new civic center.

In school, all four McCauley children followed remarkably their parents' histories. Their grades at the private school they attended regularly put them near the top of their respective classes. Their interests were wide ranging, their talents for sports at times spectacular, particularly the youngest daughter. Jonathan's own precocious knowledge of science was not surprising, knowing his father's achievements. From early boyhood, he announced to everyone that he would become an engineer; there was no question about it. And by the time college applications were filed, it was evident there had been no change in his career plans. He studied the catalogues of America's prestigious universities and finally chose one known for its outstanding science and liberal arts programs. Everyone at his high school thought he should "shoot for the moon." Apply to all the best, many advised him after reviewing his fine grades and distinguished list of extracurricular activities. "Show them you have guts: Apply just to the one school you really want to attend," his uncle advised Thanksgiving day of the young man's senior year in high school. "Not a bad thought," his father added.

The girls did not approve of the idea. Like Jon, they had heard a myriad stories of college applicant casualties. This one had been a valedictorian, but Harvard *and* Yale *and* Columbia had rejected him, so he had to settle for a large out-of-state university with a moderate academic rating at best. And this other fellow had the grades and played tennis and his father gave a trillion dollars to Princeton or someplace, and still he couldn't get in. The oldest McCauley daughter confirmed the rumors. A sophomore at an eastern women's college, she authoritatively counseled her brother to apply everywhere "and make sure you have some fall-back places. Lots of kids are applying and lots of schools are filling up with minority students and hardship cases and all the rest, so don't take any chances. And also, don't buy this routine that if one place won't take you another one just like it won't either. I know a boy," she said, "who couldn't get into *one* school he applied to, except Princeton." "How about *that?*" the family responded, after hearing this news.

"Jonathan," his father said sternly, "your sister has spoken, and your way is planned out." Then, to his own brother he remarked, "Bill, you're outvoted. It sounds to me like Janie knows what the hell she's talking about."

Jon McCauley applied to six colleges using his own state university and one of its popular branches as "fall-back" schools. He was admitted to all six institutions, and quickly accepted the one which had been his first choice. His parents threw a small party for him, although he expressed embarrassment over this, his most illustrious accomplishment. During the summer he worked in the computer section of a large electronics firm specializing in communication projects for the space program, and, after a small vacation trip with two high school friends to the northern part of Texas, he headed off to school.

At the airport, there was a moment of pausing, as he would recall for me a year later. In the midst of his parents, two sisters, and his Uncle William, he suddenly felt alone. "Frightened and lonesome too," he said. "Everybody was there, waving and screaming and all that, and I was going through all the rituals I guess you're supposed to go through at times like that, when I began to see, of all things, my future going through my head. This may sound sort of strange to you," he continued, "although you being a psychologist and all probably have heard it a million times."

"Go on, Jon," I said. "Don't worry about what I've supposedly heard a million times."

"Well, I guess I didn't know where I was heading. I was all excited about coming up here to school, but that was really all. I really didn't know what I wanted to do. I mean, I said a whole lot of things about having a career and following my dad, stuff like that. Stuff you've heard a million times." He smiled. "But shit, man, I didn't have a plan in my head. I didn't have the slightest idea what I wanted to do. I just wanted to get into the school, and once that happened, I didn't have anything else to shoot for. Man, I'll tell you, at that airport I wanted more than anything else just to stay home. I was turning every which way inside. You know? You talk about not knowing where your head's at. That was me. I was the king of lost. You know what I wanted to do more than anything else?"

"Cry."

"No. Close though. I wanted to grab my mother and give her a big hug."

"So, why didn't you?"

"It ain't that easy." He looked away from me.

"I know." I had sounded too flip.

"Well, you're kind of right," he reassured me. "I wanted to. I wanted to be a little boy and have her take me home and feed me. Honest. Some college guy, eh? Some big man." I told him that many students feel as he did. "I know that. I can see it in their faces. Like, they'll give you all this jive about hating to go home for Christmas and Easter, but they go. Three, four days before the vacation's even started they're throwing their stuff together." He shook his head as though reacting in disbelief to something someone had just said. "Cutting out four days before they're supposed to get out, and going around telling everybody they got some chick waiting at home for them. It's a lot of shit. They miss their folks too. Miss their rooms and the food and just being home, probably. Hardest damn thing about this place, I suppose, is that it's this place."

"It's not home," I said.

"It's not home?" He laughed. "It's about as far from home as, I don't know what. As we are from heaven." He glanced questioningly at me. "How's that? You like that for a metaphor? From here to heaven?"

For a year and a half I saw him once or twice each month. I explained to him when we met that I was interested in observing and speaking with freshmen. I wanted to learn about their experiences. I threw clumsy words at him like adjustment, advisory systems, associations with new friends, but I did not have to sell him on the idea of periodic visits. So often in doing social science research, one finds that the work does not help the "subjects" of the research. The information one collects about another usually just helps the collector. It's as simple as that. He may get some ideas off his chest, as they say, but the investigator gets the article, or other coinage for his career. In this case, however, my defensiveness about the work seemed unnecessary. Jon was willing to meet with me. He had one question: "You ain't a shrink, are you? I mean, this project of yours isn't to see whether we're sick, is it?" I assured him that psychotherapy had nothing to do with it, and with that settled, he expressed his eagerness to speak with me. "I'll tell you anything you want to know about in terms of how I'm making out here. And speaking of making out, you don't by any chance have any girls in this project, do you?"

"I do," I replied, "but you ain't gonna see them. Get your own project started," I smiled.

"Thought I'd try. All right, so let's begin. Hey, what do I call you anyway?"

"Tom. What do I call *you?*" For such a simple question, I thought, he hesitated a long time. After waiting a while, I offered to call him Mr. McCauley if he preferred. I even gave a gratuitous little speech about how names mean a great deal to people. I had just reached the part where names matter too, because our parents give them to us, when glassy-eyed, he interrupted me.

"No. It's not titles. I was going to say that I wanted you to call me 'Mac' like everybody else did. Then I thought no, you're not one of the guys. I don't want you to be either. So Mac's out! Then I thought of J.S."

"Your initials. Like a business executive."

"Right. My sisters sometimes call me that. So does my Uncle William. My dad calls me Son, or Sonny most of the time, Jon when something's not going too well." He made a motion with his mouth. It was one of those statements that said I've just tried something daring and here's hoping it works out. "So you know what I've decided? Jesus. I sure am making a big deal over this name thing, aren't I?"

"You're one to talk," I interjected. "I carried an illegal name for 18 years."

"Oh yeah?" He seemed relieved. "What was the name?"

"My name is Joseph, but everyone always called me Tom. It stuck."

"Oh yeah? Joseph, eh? That's like Jon. Is that right?"

"What name did you pick, kind sir?"

"Johnnie," he blurted out. "It's what my mother calls me and you can go ahead and make anything you want out of that little tidbit. Goddamn psychologist types, anyway."

"I haven't said a word. Yet." I laughed, feigning self-protection.

"You will. Or you're thinking something anyway. Oedipus Rex, right?"

"And his brother Pie," is all I could think to say. He groaned. I apologized for it. To a great extent, however, he is right, and it is worth saying. So many students, intelligent, thoughtful, well read or just made sophisticated by the times, regularly find themselves encountering only two kinds of people. One group deals with very special and circumspect issues where emotions, feelings, play little or no role. The other group, in contrast, and I belong to it, seem so preoccupied with feelings and the "dynamics of interpersonal relationships" that learning, or just plain talking, sometimes seem almost out of the question. I exaggerate the students' predicament, of course, for there are teachers and fellow students who are more expansive, less analytical, gentle and compassionate. But the issue of psychological sophistication and what rubs off from psychotherapy is omnipresent, so that I am sometimes unable to discern whether students are feeling something inside that needs special protection, or whether their environment is either so impervious to their feelings or so overly attuned to them, that the students have to continually contrive protective devices that fit them all over again.

Johnnie McCauley and I, along with a group of eight other freshmen, became good friends. A couple of times each month we shared college experiences. They seemed particularly eager to tell me of certain events and occasionally insisted that I reminisce about my own college days. On one night, soon after first semester grades had been received, they encouraged me to divulge my own spotty history with grades. Naturally, I could now make light of my sophomore dive into academic probationary status.

"I wouldn't say I did bad, exactly," I told them, "but the deans thought they best examine reasons for my *passing* the few courses I did." The students enjoyed it. I was in fine form. What a great thing to talk about your stopovers in hell when everybody can now view you sitting squarely in heaven's most luxurious plaza.

"Probation to faculty," one of the boys remarked. "Not bad."

"Well," I began, "you gotta give the people in the records office a little action. You know how it is. One minute they're about ready to stuff a warning letter in an envelope and the next minute you're passing your courses again. Then the next semester you give 'em the old flunk routine, or you sorta open with two D-'s, an E and a C- . . . ."

"Two of a kind beats a full house," someone shouted out and we roared with laughter.

"I love it. Where were you all when I was going under?" I screamed to them trying to catch my breath in the hilarity of it all.

"In our cribs," Ellie Bettenhurst replied. That stopped us momentarily.

"You dirty dog," I said, pointing my finger at her. "You dirty, dirty dog." It was only then, as they began to laugh anew, that I caught Johnnie's face and saw trouble. He didn't want to speak about it in the group, which I understood, so we arranged to meet the next day, but leaving my office he mentioned that his grades had stunk. "Pro?" I wondered.

"No. But pretty close. We gotta talk, I think.

"I kind of did and kind of didn't do my best," he began the next afternoon, after we had sipped some tea. "If you know what I mean. I could get myself to work harder. I mean, I'm not worried about failing or anything like that."

"They don't want to fail people out of here, you know. I guarantee you that."

"Oh, I know. But, there's more to it than that. I mean, I know I didn't work that hard. I put a lot of stuff off 'til the end. Everybody does, but some of the guys can just pull it off better than some of us less fortunate ones. You know?"

"Hardly."

"Well, we are. You come to a place like this thinking, well, that, you know, that you're all right. You did well in high school and had all the activities, lots of friends. You know."

"You people are all right," I insisted. "If you could only . . ." But he interrupted me.

"Well, I know. I mean, we come here thinking we're the cat's ass, man, and they got thousands, millions of guys smarter than me. Millions. You take a look at my roommates sometime. I mean, they're quiet little farts, never say a word; they got girl friends here, they got all that stuff worked out. Boom, a little of this and that," he flipped his hand palm up then palm down several times, "and there they are on Dean's List."

"And there you are without a girl and heading for academic trouble."

"You got it. There I am. That's me."

"It doesn't necessarily mean anything. You'll work this term 'til it hurts. You wanna talk reality or fantasy? Fantasy says wish it were better, reality says work. Every day. Something every day."

"It's to easy for you, man. You made it."

"That's what you think, buddy."

"Well, like last night." I could see his reticence about reviving my joking summary of what in truth had been the most frightening and upsetting year of my life.

"I'm sorry about that, Johnnie. It was thoughtless. I got all caught up with it with the kids."

"No. It was fun. You were a fucking gas. They liked it. It made us feel good. Only, I got scared when I saw those grades. It was probably 'cause it was the first time."

"What'd you get?"

"Three C's and a D. I got the C's in lit, chem, and math. D in history."

"British, 1850 to the present?"

"Yeah. It's a fuckin' ball breaker for a dumb scientist." For long moments we just looked at one another. It seemed as though he was daring me to contradict him. Somehow he needed that image of himself, and access to the anger that image carried.

In retrospect, we agreed that this was the crucial insight. For his entire life he had worked out of the mold of the natural sciences and engineering. Feelings were always put aside and intellectual ambiguities degraded if not entirely discarded. History was comprised of facts essentially not intended for interpretation, he had argued with me time and time again during his freshman year. How certain historical facts connect is a matter of pure guess, something scientists will attempt but only as a last and ignominious resort. Literature and the social sciences, like the arts, were "girl stuff" he would just as soon have left to his mother and sisters. Science and engineering constituted the terrain of men, he declared.

Indeed, he was sanctimonious in his verbal excursions into science, at least in the early part of freshman year. By the end of that year, he expressed embarrassment over his "lack of education," his "illiteracy," as he called it, and his continuing inability to throw himself headlong into books. The so-called feminine quality about, well, my work was more easily resolved as he witnessed a man performing it, but the problem of motivating himself to undertake work in whatever courses he chose was severe. I suggested that he forget university requirements for the last semester of his freshman year and perhaps the first semester of his sophomore year as well, and concentrate only on those courses that tantalized him. "Don't worry about the end of all this," I advised. "Just take what you really want. Pick courses on any subject. Pick them on the basis of who teaches them, what time in the morning they meet, on their requirements. Now's the time to make life easy on yourself," I urged him on several occasions. "I've been there myself, man. I know. When I came back to school my third year, I took courses I really wanted to take. And you want to know something?" He nodded yes. "None of them, not a single one had anything to do with the premedical stuff I was supposed to be studying. I took comp. lit., race relations, anthropology, drama. The works? I had a ball."

"It work?"

"Yeah, for the dummy I thought I was, I did all right. I gave those envelope stuffers in the dean's office a twitch, you can be sure." As I recall, Johnnie appreciated my counseling. He smiled as if to congratulate me on my academic performance of more than a decade before, then he asked to borrow a university catalogue, while I impulsively wished that schools would abolish courses and grades.

"I'm going to have to pick some real easy ones next time. I just don't want to feel dumb any more. I mean, I don't *think* I'm dumb, but I must be. How the hell can you know around here with all these brains running around everywhere? Answer me that, Mr. Probation. Dr. Probation, I should say. How do you know what you know? The whole world thinks that if you're here you gotta be brilliant, at least. So how do you explain to them you're pretty God-awful common?"

"And to yourself, you'll excuse me sounding like a shrink?"

"And to your parents," he added. "Man." He blew out a long breath. "It'd sure be nice if I could get everything to stop for a while. Just slow down so I could figure things out a little bit. Here I got these bad grades, which incidentally, I'd just as soon nobody knew about, okay?"

"Of course." I sounded as authoritative as I could.

"Thanks. So I got 'em and I don't want people to know, except that my parents will have to find out sooner or later, I suppose. Gets me mad that I didn't work. I *never* did as bad as this. I swear to you. You see those grades, man? They're the worst! I maybe got the worst grades of everyone in this whole goddamn class. You believe that?" I couldn't answer him. "Jesus Christ," he was saying. "What a helluva way to start out here. Can you see me going home to all those people carrying a record like this?" He patted the breast pocket of his jacket suggesting that he was carrying his report card.

"They in there?" I inquired.

"You better believe it. I ain't leaving them around anywhere for people to see. I mean, I may be dumb, but I don't have to go around making sure everybody up here finds out about it. Jesus, you know what I was thinking coming over here just now? I was thinking about these three guys who applied here when we were seniors, you know?" He made it sound as if it were decades ago.

"Last year."

"Jesus. Last year. You're right. Seems like 85 years ago. You know that I've only been here six months? Six months! Holy God." He shook his head in amazement. "Anyway, before I get so old I can't talk, there were these guys, you know, who were applying. It got pretty competitive there for a while too. Especially right about March and April. Everybody was saying things behind people's backs, like this guy doesn't deserve it, or that guy is probably going to have his old man buy the school so his kid can make it. I wasn't a part of it actually. In a funny way, I mean, there was like this basic understanding that if there was one place open in the school, I should get it and the rest would have to sort of settle for that. Accept it, like."

"They respected you that much." Surely, I thought, this reminder would encourage him.

"Yeah, I guess they did. And now this." His voice dropped and he fingered his jacket pocket. "I got in, two others did too, and I guess two didn't. Three, I guess, didn't. So here we are with the big star who everybody thought deserved it the most about to be booted out."

"Doesn't happen so fast."

"Yeah, that's what I heard."

"Who were you talking to?"

"Pete Hamill. In the dorm? His brother flunked out two years ago."

"They let him back in?"

"Yeah. I guess so. But then again, he was a football player. I don't do anything like that of any importance to anyone around here, so maybe they won't be so generous with me."

Johnnie and I, along with the others, continued to meet regularly

during that first year. Johnnie picked his courses, more science, less
liberal arts, in an effort to shore up his grades. Two of his courses, chemistry and literature, were full-year obligations and hence no changes
could be made in those slots. No matter where our private conversations
would start, they would inevitably conclude with grades. Intellectual
content was hurriedly discussed, game playing replaced it. How to study,
setting up patterns of discipline, checking papers written in the course
over the last years, and inspecting previous examination questions preoccupied him. I asked him once, for example, what they were learning
one particular week in chemistry, straining to recall my own days in
the labs. He answered: "The formula for staying at college." That was
all he said.

"Arrows going in all directions and moles and mini-moles. Something
like that, right?" I pursued him hoping to lessen the anxiety of grading.

"Moles," he responded flatly, "are people like my roommates who
work all the time in the library, and who come out at midnight with
their fucking little heads filled with every single goddamn fact about
chemistry that there is to learn in that miserable nine-hundred-page
textbook. Everything! They know everything! And a mini-mole, as you
call it . . ."

"Milli-mole," I corrected myself.

"A mini-mole," he continued, ignoring my correction, "is a guy from
a rich family who's had everything in his life fall right into his lap
and never worked for a single goddamn thing ever, ever, ever, and
who can't get himself to study no matter what he does. I sit there,
man, picking my ears, my hair, my nose, my nails. I swear to God,
some night I'm gonna take my pants down and play with myself in
the middle of that place. I CAN'T WORK!" He yelled the words at
me. "And when I do, nothing happens. I worked like a dog, for me,
on the last midterm in 101. Every day for two and a half weeks and
here's what I get for it." He reached into the back pocket of his jeans
and handed me an examination booklet with his name and the course
title and number on it. The writing was small, impeccably neat. On
the right hand side of the page a column of figures was written, sometimes in colored pencil, sometimes in regular ball point ink. Clearly,
several section instructors had individually marked the various questions.
The final total came to 61. It was the only number circled. "61, Baby,"
Johnnie said nodding bitterly at the booklet. "Eight more and you win
the booby prize." Neither one of us said anything.

Whenever we met, I implored him to keep working, to have fun and
really get away "from the grind," but to keep hitting the books. Strange
how my advice always took on such a militaristic character. I was like
a second begging my fighter to keep at it, no matter what the pain

he might have been enduring, and believing almost dogmatically in the notion that one must start what one finishes. Still, in all fairness, he never once broached the option of quitting.

At the end of freshman year, Johnnie came to me with the news that he thought he had "hit his finals pretty hard." He seemed pleased with the way the year now appeared to be salvaged. I could see his standards being deflated, much in the manner of someone lowering a flag as the darkness fell. But he was resigned. "I ain't gonna make the big Dean's List," he reported toughly, yet with humor, "but I ain't gonna also be sent home on a blue slab."

"You sound like a prisoner getting out on good behavior," I commented as we walked back to his room together for the last time that year.

"Parole, baby. Just call it parole and don't get that word confused with *probation*." We laughed. "There's a helluva difference between those words, and you're looking at him."

"You're a good man, Mac," I said with pride.

"For a dummy," he mumbled.

"You're still pushing that crap?"

"Nah. Pulling your chain. I'm joking, man." He wasn't, of course, but this was not the appropriate time to resume our conversation on liberal education and what it might mean for one's self-image. His science aptitude had carried him through the year and for that he was thankful. Plenty of time remained to resolve the problems of what it meant to be intelligent, educated, even erudite. His interest, however, in the sciences was waning, or momentarily dulled, although this was not a function of the way his courses had been taught. On this point he was adamant.

"It's *me*, man," he had said in one way or another several times during the year. "If you're good you can catch on no matter how they present the material. If you're bad, they can stick it without you seeing it in your jello, and you still won't be able to swallow it. *You* know what I mean. I can make it in science. That's not all bad 'cause everyone, I think anyway, needs to feel really good at something. For me, that's studying science. At least it used to be science. I don't know anymore."

"Jon McCauley," I suddenly declared in the street on that early June day, "go home, get some home cooking, find your friends, have a good time. Run, jump, scream, swear, screw off, do something with boys, girls, spend money, save money. Forget this place. Play. You aren't a ghetto child. What can I say? Take advantage of it. Play. Then come back in September and tell me my advice stinks." He was surprised by my finale, but he gave me a shove that said he would abide by my prescription.

"Next year, you'll see, teach." He pointed his finger at me. "I might even take one of your easy courses. I've been thinking I might like to switch fields. Maybe do what you do."

"I gotta stay here this summer," I responded, wanting to say that he didn't *really* have to do what I do. But I was flattered.

"Yeah, I know about all that. But save a place, maybe in your seminar, okay?"

"I'll save two places." He looked at me quizzically before he understood.

"Oh, you know about Ellen, eh?"

"I get around."

"Nosy bastard. I'm coming out of this year smelling like a rose."

"You sure are. And I love it!"

"That's your favorite expression, isn't it?"

"One of them," I conceded.

"Yeah, well next year I'll be just in time for a nice sophomore slump."

"Get outta here," I barked at him. "Get out of my college. Get out of my town. Go home, college boy," I taunted him. He reached out his hand and I took it.

When the high's are high, I preached to myself on the way home, the low's are low. Come on blue books, be tough! B's. I'll settle for B's for him, the very B's I never got at the end of my freshman year.

Only one B in fact arrived. In late August I received a postcard from Johnnie with some casual greeting and a report that his final grades had amounted to three C's and a B-, in chemistry. "Too bad" were his final words. He signed it, "Sincerely, your dummy, Mac."

My heart fell as if the card had carried news of my own progress. Indeed, as I continue to have periodic dreams about course failures and incompletions, the postcard arrived as if sent from my own interior; that much did Jon McCauley's history touch my own. I did not write to him.

He telephoned me three weeks into the term. He had done a lot of thinking over the summer, he said. While his parents accepted his performance, uttering the right things about accommodation, adjustment, natural improvement, he was facing the year with trepidation. "Something tells me," he warned as we studied his schedule. He was moving heavily into the natural sciences. Some literature, very little social science. In fact, only three half-courses would take him away from his specialty of mathematics and chemistry.

"Sounds good to me," I remarked.

"Sounds *lousy*. I'm chicken. I can't do that other stuff. I'm narrow. So . . ."

Our meetings during the second year were less frequent. Two of our original group, having received excellent grades, had nonetheless taken leaves of absence from the school. This news shocked Johnnie. It was the first time he had seriously contemplated stepping out of the natural passage of school years. More perplexing to him was that competence should yield such a change of heart. "I can't understand why they'd leave. I mean, they were really smart. They worked. They were really good at all that stuff. I mean, they were really intelligent people. You and I would agree to that. Right?"

"They still are." My reply was inadequate. His entire background upheld the ideal marriage of success and steady continuity of effort. When you're good at something, he had been taught, you don't leave it; you build it up, make it even better, until you're the best; until you become the person that everyone, including your competitors, agrees is the single deserving person for entrance into America's finest colleges and careers. And my background dictated much the same thing.

Our infrequent meetings during the first semester of his sophomore year usually included his comments on the difficulties he was experiencing staying interested in his work. No course intrigued him that much. While some might have in the beginning, his interest lessened. He became involved with some political activities, but these too diminished in significance. And the same was true with friendships. There would be an initial period of excitement sparked by his meeting of a young man or woman, or even encountering an older faculty member, but then, after all sorts of pledges to himself and to me, the excitement dissipated. More exactly, it would be snuffed out by something. There was even a try at the college newspaper's open competition for membership. A competent photographer, Johnnie went on assignments for the editorial staff for three weeks, almost without rest. Physically exhausted at the end of that time, he was nonetheless exhilerated not so much by the fine work he had produced, but by the fact that he could stay at something as important for so long. The newspaper, however, rejected his candidacy. He did not inform me of this for two weeks but I found out.

"It's like I'm always telling you, man. They got guys around here that are out of their minds brilliant. My stuff was fine. I know that. But shit, they got guys ready for *Life*, if they could get a break. I thought my stuff was first rate, but it's shit next to theirs. It's my usual story. No sense boring you all over with it. It was a curse coming here. I had it made at home. I should have stayed. All I wanted was an acceptance to this place. I knew it at the time. Why the hell I have to come here? This place is for geniuses. Geniuses and minority groups." He saw me wince. "Aw well, you know what I mean. Those guys have it tough too. I don't see how they make it like they do. Man, if I'm having trouble, they must really be going under." His penitence changed to anger again and he pounded the arm of the chair. "But holy shit, I sure wasted a lot of valuable time in that goddamn darkroom. I'd been a helluva lot better off sitting at Eli's drinking, or playing the pinball machines somewhere."

"Yeah," I answered sarcastically. "Or pushing dope in the Square, huh?"

"Well then, suppose you tell me what *you'd* like me to do," he came back. "Why don't you just tell me. You got any more ideas about things for me to fail at? Wait 'til you see my grades. I'm going to need about 10 miracles to pass anything." He shook his head as if having to taste my words again. "So, what do you say, expert? What do I do? See a shrink, I suppose?"

"Maybe."

"Fuck no! No shrink, not at the health services. Not with those stories. I know all about those guys. They look in your head as though they were looking up your ass. I've heard about that horror show they run over there." He began an imitation of a counselor. His caricatured tone was gentle but obsequious. He used his hands delicately, like a dancer, to accentuate his characterization. "Well now, Mr. McCauley, what is it that we can do for you? Having trouble studying, are you? Well, you take these two little pills and see me again in nine weeks when I have my next free 11 minutes to spare, won't you? And please forgive me for keeping you waiting four months. I'm so famous, you understand, that the list to see me just extends from here to, well, shall we say, Texas. A little joke. That's the health service. That's what you get there."

"You been there?" I asked without smiling from his performance.

"I don't know."

"You have, haven't you?"

"Yeah, once," he replied softly.

"And it was bad."

"It was the worst! My folks thought maybe it was something I should try. It's the worst, man. I'd rather go to prison. It's easier to get in, at any rate."

"Maybe I could help somehow," I offered.

"Hell no! It's over." His reply was unequivocal. "The guy there was an asshole. All he knows is work hard and take pills. And hatred for my father. Talking to him was like, I don't know what. Cold motherfucker; *he* didn't even *have* a personality. He was about as slippery as a sneaker full of shit. I'd ask him a question and he'd just ask it right back. Like you do, sometimes, you know that?"

"Yes. I know that."

"Shrinks. You're a great help. Saviors for the younger generation." He couldn't have sounded more bitter and sardonic. "Gods, all of you. Gods dressed up in sport jackets. Ivy League gods. What you guys know about young people you couldn't shove up a bird's ass!"

We sat together for a while in silence; barely five minutes most probably, but it seemed like five hours, or two semesters. Every once in a while he would look up at the bookshelves or prints and messages that hung on the walls and shake his head from side to side in dismay and fury. Surely he was telling me, what possibly could you like about being associated with a university, and especially this one? What do you see in all these books, or in sitting at an IBM-looking desk reading and writing and going through computer printouts, and having to look nice all the time, and being responsible? Why do you do it? Why does anybody do it? Why does anybody want to lead their lives successfully, actively, the right way? The wrong way? Why lead a life at all?

When he rose to leave, muttering, "See ya," he appeared to weigh a million pounds. His leather jacket squeaked and his blue jeans, which made a brushing sound as he moved, clung to the tops of his socks. When he was seated, I saw him as myself, 10 years before, lost in this same school and not knowing where to go, what to do, and waiting for the very worst to happen. Now, in leaving, he resembled an immigrant youth who had just been refused entrance to America.

"You wanna stay?" I stood up as I called to him.

"You mean here now, or at school generally?" He threw me a hopeless look and left, closing the door quietly behind him.

At the end of the first semester, Johnnie's grades were a C, two D's and an E. He was placed on academic probation, "pro" as the students called it, and advised by letter and interview of the implications of his new and treacherous status. No extracurricular activities, no intramural sports, no leaving school until vacations officially commence. One more E or two more D's and the administration could expel him. "I'll do my best" is all he could say when finally we got around to meeting, one month into the spring semester. "I'll do what I can. No one can ask any more." Something like, "I'm sure that will be good enough," was all I said.

Our separation during the spring was caused in part by his embarrassment. It was terribly hard for him to meet with me while on probation. Even during those few brief visits our eyes rarely met. Probation for him was the last connection between us, broken wires of electricity. If he felt anything like I had, then he was spending countless energy making himself appear to the world as though everything were going along perfectly. For me, part of the shame of having done poorly is that a school singles you out. Knowing you have done poorly is one thing. Trying to keep this fact from others is something else. And then, trying to figure out just who probably knows and who probably doesn't and what they think of you and what you think of you is still a third thing.

"You going out for the newspaper again this term, Mac?" someone would surely inquire.

"No, man. This is my semester for books and girls."

"You ain't afraid to lose again, are ya? They say older guys, even our year, got a helluva lot better chance."

"No, I ain't afraid. Let the freshmen take over the paper."

"You wanna play B-ball then for the house?"

"No. Thanks. Books and girls, right?" Johnnie would answer, trying to shy away.

"Hey, you ain't on pro or something like that are you, man?"

"Pro? No. Why'd you think that?" And he would turn cold inside and feel his body's moisture; that is, if he reacted as I had.

About one month before the end of the term he entered my office unannounced. Fortunately I was alone, for had I been with someone he would have left. Our conversation that May afternoon jumped topics every four seconds. Everything I started he terminated, while his own thoughts were rarely sustained beyond two sentences, short sentences at that.

"Still got the same books on the same shelves," he said, looking around as he always did when that certain pain hurt his insides.

"Alas, same books, same prints, same me." He just shook his head. I recalled his previous wonderment about my fate. "I'm doing the best I can," I said for no apparent reason. "Ain't winning any awards, but I'm hanging in. How 'bout you?"

"Me?" he answered with a ludicrous air of surprise.

"Yeah, you, fella." I grinned at him and raised my head. "I know you came to tell me something, and you know I know."

"I'm leaving."

"Really? Where? When?"

"Leave of absence, I think."

"When?"

"End of the term."

"How you faring?"

"Fair. Faring fair." He smiled at the play on words.

"Faring fair," I repeated. "What's that mean?"

"Well," he let out a long breath, "it means I'll probably flunk the fuck out of here." Anger hung in his message, but at the same time, his eyes grew moist. "Yeah, I think so. I just never did hack this place, so why keep hitting your head against a stone wall. Right?"

"Well, I don't know."

"You ever take a leave?" he asked.

"No."

"Just stuck it out, eh?"

"Yeah. Not too well. Guys didn't take a lot of leaves then. It's better now," I offered.

"It may be. May be worse, too," he said. "I don't know. I live now, not then. So I don't know." One question came to my mind, but I did not ask it. Are you having thoughts of suicide?

What are schools doing to young people? What do health services do and professors and parents and classmates? And me, what had I contributed to this man's self-conception and obvious despair? I could not bring myself to ask about suicide. It might have been putting an idea in his head rather than verbalizing one already there. How many people had he told, for example, about the episode in the airport when he first left for college? Is there a connection between the inquiries of shrinks and those dispairingly called "soft scientists," and the questions mothers ask? How are things going? How are you feeling? Fathers ask about grades and course choices and the progress of career decisions. *In loco parentis!*

"I want to hear more about your plans," I said finally.

"That's all there are. You've just heard 'em."

"That's it? You're leaving, just like that?"

"You seem like you're angry with me, Tom. Don't you approve?" He sounded partly sarcastic, partly righteous.

"I'm taking the idea in."

"Bullshit. You disapprove."

"So do you."

"Don't hand me any shrink shit."

"Screw. You're quitting before you find out."

"Wouldn't you?"

"No. Yeah. I don't know. It's not me. It's you."

"Boo," he shot back.

"Boo nothing. What the hell you angry with *me* for?"

"I ain't angry. I'm just glad for once to see you being wrong."

"Where was I wrong? I mean, I'm wrong a lot, but where here?"

"You're never wrong, huh, big shot?" His voice was strong.

"I'm wrong a lot. I just said that. But where am I wrong now?"

"With ME!" he screamed at me. "With me! You thought I could make it and I CAN'T. I tried and I *can't!* So you're wrong. They're all wrong."

"I'm wrong," I tried, "because I *know* you're damn bright."

"Yeah. That's right."

"Because you don't really know what you want to study; because maybe you're afraid to get interested in humanities and social sciences, that's why I'm wrong?" I dared not say afraid to leave science and engineering.

"Yeah. that's why you're wrong."

"I don't buy it. Not for a minute. Not for one minute. Something's troubling you and you go ahead and make all these assessments about yourself that maybe do and maybe don't make any sense." He let me finish, but my mistake had already been made.

"Something's always got to be *troubling* me for you, doesn't it? It's always something in the *mind*." He stretched the word out as long as he could.

"No." I was backing off. "I didn't mean it that way. You know what I meant. C'mon."

"Yeah. I know what you meant." He sounded barely forgiving, barely ingenuous. "Here's a letter I wrote." The letter was to his parents. Very brief, it told of his decision to leave at the end of the year and try different things before he reentered the school, if the school permitted him reentrance. It said he wasn't exactly certain what he would be doing but that he was sure leaving was a good decision. He ended the letter by saying that he would call them and that he never had felt better in his life. He signed it, "your loving but I admit a little confused only son, Jon."

"Think it's all right?"

"Yeah. Fine."

"Don't be so down," he comforted me. "I ain't dying, just going out there in the big world to catch my breath for a second. I'm pretty sure I'll be coming back."

"But you're not positive?" I queried.

"Only thing I know positive is that we are all gonna die." For this one sentence he spoke in a dialect one associates with cowboys from the Southwest. He was grinning. "See ya, pardner."

Troubled and hurt by what I feared might be our last encounter, I called him the next day. There was no answer. It was over a week before I reached him. He was glad to hear from me and invited me to his room. In the end we met twice more, each time speaking about his plans. He seemed hopeful, but his mood was rimmed with failure and a sense of longing for something, or so I imagined.

My last visit in mid-June followed by minutes a phone call to him from the Dean's office. Some of his final grades were already computed, and it was evident that he had flunked out of school.

"Well, I did it." Johnnie met me in the courtyard of his residence house and we walked along the river near the college. "I did it, I guess. Top brass wants me in." He smiled as he spoke, his lips tightly shut as though his cheeks were being yanked back by invisible strings. I could feel my own teeth clenched tightly. With all my beliefs about how grades should long ago have been abolished, and my despair that they should so deeply affect students' very definitions of themselves, I could say nothing.

"It's like a funeral, isn't it?" he said.

"Yeah. Kind of. But I hope you aren't going to let this thing really shape what you think of yourself." He didn't have to tell me how weak I sounded. He just looked over at me and smiled. I felt his hand pat my shoulder.

"You never give up, do you?"

"You should only know," I responded wistfully.

"Don't," he commanded. "Stay with it. You got something going here. I haven't, maybe I will someday. I just gotta have time to figure it out. The difference between us, you see, is that way down you really know you're smart. You *know* it. Bad grades are way behind you. Ten years ago you might have had doubts. But not now. It's just like you were saying in the group last year. Remember? That stuff about screwing up the people in the Dean's office? Good one moment, bad the next?" I nodded yes. "I don't have any of that. You're messing around with your career but you kind of know where you're going. Me? I don't know anything other than that I had a tremendous high school record. After that it seems like time stops. I'm like an . . . one of those guys who can't remember anything. What do you call it?"

"Amnesiac."

"Right. I was thinking insomniac."

"That's a guy that can't . . ."

"I know," he interrupted, "can't sleep. I'm the amnesiac guy. The last two years? Nothing. Absolutely nothing. Zero, man." He shrugged his shoulders. "I *am* the zero man. Nothing good has gone into my head and stayed there. Sixteen half-courses and I couldn't give you a paragraph about all of 'em. Not a word. Man, I couldn't even tell you what I studied the last two weeks before finals. I swear to you. I don't know what the hell I was reading there." He poked his finger against his temple. "There's nothing up there, man. Not a damn thing but sawdust, and some high school chemistry."

"They used to say that when I was a kid."

"Me too." We looked down at the worn path bordering the river. "Do you know how much thinking about myself I gotta do now?" he began. "Do you have *any* idea? Do you know what going home is going to be like? Facing my father? Or my older sister? Walking around that town where my parents are such wheels, and people wondering why I'm not in school next September. This is really gonna be cute. You know who I just was thinking about? That kid who didn't get in here. I mentioned him once, didn't I?"

"Yes." I saw Johnnie studying the traffic, and squinting although it was not a particularly bright afternoon. He wore his brown leather jacket, although the weather was too warm for it. "School can really do it to you, you know that? You can tell yourself it doesn't matter, but it does. It's like I gotta tell myself that everything I was before I came here was real. That's the strange part. It's like having to put two halves of a puzzle together and wondering whether they're gonna fit."

"I think I know the feeling." We must have walked a half a mile before he spoke again.

"Hey, Tom, you wanna do me a favor?"

"Of course." I guessed that what he wanted of me was to write to his parents assuring them that he was a good person, or something of that nature.

"Let me write to you next year. You don't have to answer, but it would be a good thing kinda, just to know I could write."

"I'll answer. I'm not much of a correspondent, but I'll answer." Without stopping, we shook hands. Only after we had finished did we stop walking and inspect our location. Then he pushed his thumbs inside his wide brown belt and pursed his lips.

"Well sir, that's about all I have. I guess that's it for the moment, pardner. Guess I'll be moseying on."

College at Middle Age

"I love it. I'm young again. And alive. We're all alive. It's like I'm free and I'm never going to die. Let them go ahead and do whatever they want in New York, none of it's going to affect me. The city can float away; we'll wave to it if it floats by in the Sound. Anybody calls me or wants me, I just tell my wife to tell them that the old man can't be bothered. He's studying for his exams. Tell them he's busy being educated. Tell them that's what I'd say."

Elton Andrews and I were driving north on Massachusetts Route 3 toward Boston. The weather was cold and clear. The car's heater made a humming noise. Elton played with the radio dial, hunting for a station, then gave up and switched it off. Stretching his arms out straight, he pushed himself back against the seat and smiled. "I don't believe it still. 'Course your being here makes me think about it all over again, in the old way. I mean me, little old me, 46 years old and a junior in college. Damn good college too. Me, working for a degree. Somebody had told me I'd be driving here this morning, commuting to *college*, I'd have laughed in his face. Do you realize what I was doing four years ago?"

"Working in an insurance company," I answered seriously.

"Working in an . . . ? I was auditing *books*, my friend. I was auditing books. Columns of figures, that's all I saw all day long. Nine to five . . . three weeks vacation . . . Do you believe that?" He shook his head in mock disbelief. "I don't believe it even when I hear myself say it. I hated it. I mean I really hated it. Every damn figure, every column, the credit balance system, the place, the people. The works! I knew paper and pencils and books was my racket, but not those papers and not those books.

"Lookee here." He reached into a pocket of his suit jacket. "I still carry the pencils from the firm. They're like a reminder of where I was. Worse, where I might have ended up forever. Jesus. Can you beat it?" He stopped and looked at me. "All right. You ask the questions. I'm just rambling for you. Go ahead. Ask the schoolboy here whatever you want to know." He socked the steering wheel with his fists. I just shook my head, enchanted by the whole affair. What a superb man, and how different this scene was from my usual work with children in the poverty areas of Boston.

Elton Andrews, tall, slim, balding, was indeed a college junior in a large Boston area liberal arts school, a man of strength and a special brand of courage. He had worked almost 25 years with the same insurance agency, but every day he held in his head a vision of the college education he never received and wished that he might have his life over again. For years he and his wife Marjorie spoke of the necessity of college for their three children. He would insist that they attend college. How the parents had chosen to lead their lives would not serve as a model for the children growing up in a small New Jersey community minutes by car from the George Washington Bridge. If he had to, he would take additional jobs to accumulate funds for his children's education.

Then, as his first-born, Robert, undertook application to college, Elton became preoccupied with an idea. If his son could do it, why couldn't he? Waiting a year for the boy to be settled in a fine New York college, he arranged for the money and gathered his family about him on Thanksgiving night.

"I told them something like this: 'I've had an idea in my head almost 20 years now and I can't live with it inside any longer. You're the people who matter most to me and so you must hear it.' 'You gonna live on an island?' Robbie asked me. 'Close,' I told him. 'Very close. I'm going to try to get into college.' They were speechless. Didn't say a word. Four noisiest human beings on God's green earth and I had accidentally discovered a way to shut them all up. Speechless. So I asked them, 'Well, what do you think?' 'What? Where? Why? When? Now, at your age?' That's what they wanted to know. When? Where? Why? So I told them: 'As soon as I can; anywhere I can get in.' Why? That was the important one. 'Because,' this is almost exactly what I said, 'because I have a need to be educated. I read, you know that. I'm interested in good things, substantial things. I stay abreast of political issues, but I'm an amateur. I'm not a scholar. I'm not trained. I don't know certain things. I don't know how to *use* my mind.'" He pointed to his temple. "'There's no discipline. There's all the curiosity any professor could ever want from his students, but it's all helter skelter. I want to be educated. I always have, and I've decided to make the move.'"

More generally, this had been Elton's consistent attitude. While night courses, naturally, had been available to him, he had always believed that all college situations apart from full-time student status were second rate, less legitimate somehow, and surely not the ideal preparation for someone anticipating work on advanced degrees. He said little else about the subject, other than this. "There is a real way of doing it and that's the way I picked."

"Well, you can imagine the hassle. My daughter was only sorry that we had to move. My youngest son said I should wait for him. Robbie, bless him, thought I should apply to his school and we could room together. Nineteen years old and he was able to say that. That's something. Believe me, that's something." Elton's voice became quiet. "The big thing was Marjorie. But I'm blessed. What can I say? I'm blessed by God. She said it would mean her having to work and she was ready. I told her, put me through school—I still work a little on the side, of course—and I'll put you through when I'm done. And I've got news for you. She may go back too, what do you think of that? I just can't tell you. It's a new life. It means scraping a little here and there, but for the first time in my life I can honestly tell you I'm free, what the kids call liberated. I'm a liberated man. I'm back in school and I'm liberated. Strange, huh?"

"I love it," I responded. "I *love* it."

"You and me both!"

By late winter of his junior year, Elton Andrews was firmly committed to his academic work. From the beginning he pursued his goal of studying economics and political science, fields he believed to be consistent with his interests as well as his personal history. By his junior year he had completed such courses as money and banking, American political science since 1850, introductory economics and biology, modern European civilization, nineteenth- and twentieth-century French painting, a survey of Western literature, introductory philosophy, economic trends, a comparison of democracy and communism, political values and attitudes, basic composition, and others as well. He envisioned economics and political science as serious, if not masculine, disciplines that might humanize the real spheres of business and politics. A student pledged to read every page of every assignment, he had fulfilled his liberal arts requirements, saving the extensive notes he had taken for each course in neatly marked folders. His books were underlined in red, the inside covers filled with assignments and ideas written in his small and impeccable handwriting. He continued to audit as many courses as he enrolled in, modestly claiming that he had little else to do on campus. His course papers were well documented and thoroughly worked out, his examinations organized, easy to read, competently written. His earnest and level manner showed in all his work. Never did he seem rushed or frantic. Studying was his discipline, his joy, but his gratification was constrained by time. There was still a year and a half of college to complete and then, if accepted, several more years of graduate study.

At first, I saw him as being somewhat rigid in his work habits; he was overdoing it somehow. A gaiety about life was lacking, and the swing of moods that in a way constitute and reaffirm the life of many students was absent. It was all too controlled, and depersonalized. Often I felt an urge to tell him to loosen up. But eventually it was he who taught me how to perceive him. School was not a place for self-discovery, he said. If discovery was significant, he had already made his breakthrough when deciding to apply to college. Now it was work, depersonalized to be sure, in the style I had always imagined the Europeans approach education. Elton was never charged up by knowledge. Nor did any book or lecture diminish his need to keep learning. He could be infuriated by someone's perceptions or point of view, but quitting or making a temporary intellectual about-face never loomed as options for him. The intensity of feeling was present in the way he approached work, but the caprice of emotions and the sweeping range of temperament were, for the moment, invisible. "Look for any complicated answers you like," he told me once. "I'm happy reading and learning all that I can in the short time I have. You never finish, you know, you only stop. I just find that so much of the material is fascinating I hate to think I can't learn it all. I do very little of the recommended reading. I'll be curious to hear what you come up with about me, but I think you'll find that what makes me different is probably just my age."

We had reached the outskirts of Boston. Millions of questions filled my mind, but more than anything I was feeling anxious about attending school with him. For years I have been visiting classrooms in colleges and high schools, coming to know groups of students in different cities and rural areas as well. But now, strangely, I was nervous.

"You nervous, Elton?" I wondered aloud.

"Nervous? You mean about school?"

"Yeah. I'm nervous all of a sudden going out here with you."

"Yeah? Not me. I *was*. Oh my God, those first days. How many times I thought I was going to have to quit. Fact was I came home the second night, not the first night, the second night, and told her, 'That's it! I'm out!' They gave us reading lists, course outlines, everything. I couldn't do it. I just couldn't do it. I remember they sent us to this one campus bookstore, I didn't even know where to go to *ask* for what I needed. I'd never been in a college bookstore, you know, where they have books listed by course numbers. Jesus, it was mobbed. And dirty?" He was shaking his head.

"People look at you?"

"Nah. Nobody bothered. That wasn't it. It was all the work and finding your way around. This isn't any tiny place out here. It's big time. Takes me 20 minutes to get from one class to another. You'll see. I hope you got good shoes on. Spring comes, I think I'll go barefoot with the rest of 'em."

"Really get into it with the kids, huh?"

"Nah. Not really. We're attending the same classes but we're working different sides of the street. No doubt about that. You could almost say we're in different shools."

"Social life, you mean?"

"Sure. Totally. I've got very few friends. You know, you can see, I'm caught in between. Don't have very much to do with the kids, and of course I'm not in with the professors, although they do make a special effort in my behalf, I suppose. Most of the time, like at the beginning of a semester, they think I'm a visitor. When I tell them I'm just another junior, they look a little surprised. But they grin and say, welcome aboard." Elton smiled and looked at me. "It's like I tell you, it's absolutely crazy and wonderful at the same time. I've got no business being a college student, one year behind my own son, one year ahead of my daughter, who incidentally took a job to help *me* pay for books."

"That's really lovely."

"Lovely's not the word for it. I'm blessed. And I let her do it. This was her senior year in high school I'm talking about. I let her do it. Told her for her books there would always be money. Always money for books. You stop and think, for 20 years, 25 years," he corrected himself, "I invested nothing in books. Everything went into mortgages, the market, bills, expenses. I'll bet we didn't have a hundred books in our house. Now, I'm building a library. Not great, but it's going to be a very nice little collection. 'Course some nice American industries made it all possible and I'm very happy to thank them. But now it's books, not dividends and coupons."

The morning traffic increased as we turned onto the highway that winds around Boston's eastern edge. The university was still 15 minutes away. Elton fidgeted with the defroster, then turned his head quickly to make certain his brief case still lay on the back seat. It was a gesture he repeated several times.

"I do it too," I said.

"What's that?"

"Make sure my books and papers are there all the time."

"Oh God, I do it all the time." He smiled. "You become attached to those darn things. You underline a book, really read it carefully, you know, and it's like you're going to die if someone even looks at it. I don't know what this is. Never felt that way with library books. Some kid wants to borrow a book, I gotta make up a lie 'cause it would kill me to loan it out and maybe never see it again. I'm not all that crazy though. There's an enormous amount of stealing that goes on."

"Ripping off?" I interjected.

"That's the word. Not good. It's about the one thing they do that I think I'm 100 percent against. I don't like the stealing, particularly by kids who can afford to buy anything. There's a boy from your home town, Chicago, right?"

"Hmm."

"Comes to school in an M.G. Brand new. Obviously bought by his old man. Three thousand at least, if not a helluva lot more, goes into the book store and steals 8, 9, 10 dollars' worth of books, pads of paper, stuff like that." Elton hunched up his shoulders. "I don't get it. Guys in your profession must have an explanation for it. I suppose maybe they want something they can't have, or never got. Maybe they're starved for love. Who knows? I don't. Still, it's one thing I don't approve of."

"You talk to the kids about it?" I wondered what young people's response to this older colleague might be.

"My kids?"

"No, the students, I mean."

"No. Not really. I don't actually have that much to do with them. We talk a little between classes, things like that, waiting in line for something, but that's not really a way for us to get together."

"You feel self-conscious?"

"Wait a minute. Did I miss a turn here?" We peered out the window for familiar landmarks. "No, this is right. Let's see," Elton was continuing. "No, I don't feel self-conscious, I wouldn't say exactly. I don't feel like I *belong*, of course, because there's no status for a person my age. Most of the oldies come for evening sessions. Obviously. They have to work. It's a shame though, because college is really a day business. Have to be there day in, day out. You're not a part of it if you're there two, three evenings a week." He was looking out the window again. "Yeah, this is right. Just looked different there for a moment."

"Maybe 'cause spring's coming," I suggested.

"This your idea of spring?"

"Well, you know." We were both smiling.

"Brother, if this is spring, I'm going back to New York." He glanced at me. "Never! Let it stay like this. I'm staying here. It can snow all summer." We drove on.

"Say more about the age thing, Elton."

"Well, what can I tell you? You know as well as I, school belongs to the kids. It's really for them, and the few of us who haven't led our lives, or couldn't lead our lives, the way we were supposed to. You know. You go to college at the wrong time, you pay for it at some point. It could be worse . . ."

I reminded him of those who argue that higher education belongs to professors and not to students, not as a challenge exactly to his last response, but because his perspective was unique. Here was a man, after all, older than the majority of students and faculty, who brought a talent and a history that few academicians know much about. Moreover, while he pursued what some call an alternative life style, practically no one on the huge campus had ever inquired about his decision and the world from which he came. No doubt I identified with his affable man. At the same time I felt sorry for him. I imagined him alone, somehow disenfranchised. Clearly he was a representative of a peculiar minority group, a man very much on his own in a way that I had never seriously contemplated before meeting him. Clearly too, he was obliging me to face the biases toward older people attending college I never believed I maintained. Elton was answering my question:

"Oh, I'm sure you're right. The kids get very little attention. I was very surprised to see this. They're really forced to do everything by themselves. In this school, anyway. You see, it's all right for me. Professor gives me a reading list, I don't have to talk to him. Kids though, they need to talk. They gotta make contact. That's the whole thing. You know that. Young people need old people. Old people don't need young people in that way. Your own kids, that's something else. It kills me that I'm going to have two in college . . . See that? Right there?"

"What's that?" Instinctively I looked out the window.

"No," he laughed, watching me. "What I just said. See the way I kind of fall back and forth between being a father and a college boy? I didn't think in terms of *me* leaving the kids. Well, that's another issue altogether." He shrugged aside whatever he was thinking. "No, I think the students could do well to have more contact with the faculty than they do. Graduate students don't substitute for the real thing. Everyone knows it. Makes life tough for the graduate students too. But for me there's no problem. I'm just happy being there, listening, reading, taking notes, doing what I'm supposed to. I'll tell you something else. If they had a junior class made up of a thousand people like me, they'd never have a problem. They'd have a bunch of hard-working people just dedicated to being educated and earning their degrees. I'm serious."

"School would be pretty successful then, wouldn't it?" I was not totally certain I approved of his vision.

"It'd be boring as hell." Elton laughed out loud. "They oughta make a law you can't have more than 2, 3 percent old-timers. Kids give life to the school. I don't give it life. I do solid work, but you can see it in our seminars. Sure, there are all kinds of experiences that people like me bring. Being a father, having worked on the outside. The army. I make it sound like a prison."

"That's what some people call it," I interrupted him.

"God forbid. All prisons should be like where we're going now. No, but I bring these bits of experience to class and they accept it, although some of the professors feel they have to play down experiences of older people for some reason. I'm not so sure they think it's all that hot, but that isn't what school's all about anyway. You don't need school to exchange experiences. You want that you go to the student center or cafeteria. A classroom's something else. I'll tell you a difference between me and the kids. For me the classroom's sacred. It's as simple as that. I'm not a religious fanatic. Marjorie and I haven't been to church in . . . don't ask. But school's sacred to me. I don't mean the political stuff. Kids want to protest, bless them. They want to goof around, fine. But in the classroom, that's got to remain serious business. There I think you draw the line. That's where the play has to stop. That sound too severe? Huh? You've been studying education. Think that's too hard on my part?"

"Not at all. Really."

"Huh? Too severe?"

"No. I think it's right."

"I'm serious about this business. This has nothing to do with New York and the insurance racket. They don't have to know what I suffered through. No one needs to know that. That's another difference incidentally between me and the kids . . ."

"Namely . . ."

"Namely that when you get older, you don't have to advertise your experiences. People don't have to know *what* you did or *why* you did it. You get more closed in. Colleges could use a little bit more of that, I think. Don't get me wrong. They benefit by my being there. I set a kind of example. The only problem is that I don't spent time with the students so nobody follows me." He laughed.

I could never anticipate with Elton just when in a thought serious import fell away to allow for a burst of humor. His way of starting on one track and then derailing himself caused me to feel the pain that accompanied the liberation college granted him. School, naturally, is difficult for all people, but some have it a bit easier because the institution allows them their pain; the pain articulates with their experience so that those in control are made aware of it and perhaps even motivated to do something to help. But by their very presence, newcomers innaugurate hardships that institutions only later come to know. As sentimental as it seems, I saw Elton as a pioneer. He brought into the consciousness of his university the experience of adults, and he did it with pain, with a self-effacing humor, and with a curious necessity to denigrate his past, or at least hide it away, as if it were a child's toy, where others would not fall over it.

"Mr. Andrews, the older gentleman?" one of Elton's professors began. "He's fine. No trouble. Kind of fun actually seeing an older face out there in front of you when you lecture. I've spoken to him on a few occasions. I can't see that he's causing anyone any problems. I don't know that we could make a case for turning colleges over to people of his age, but a small amount livens up the class, I'm sure. It think it's good for the other students. There's a lot they can learn from him, not only their course work. Many things. But you know, as a teacher yourself, you have to grade these people, evaluate them as you would anyone else. They don't want us to bend over backwards to give them special attention, and I'm not about to communicate to him that merely because he's older he possesses special talents, or superior ability. I don't believe, moreover, that that's what he would want. Do you?"

"No," I replied, "I'm quite sure he doesn't."

One of the schools librarians, however, was more enthusiastic: "My day isn't complete," she said, "without seeing Mr. Andrews. He works hard, that man does. The others could learn from him. He sits and works. It's a very lovely sight. But what I like most of all about him is the respect he shows for books and for learning, for the whole university, I'd have to say. I don't see this in many students. Reading for them is just a job. For him it's much, much more."

What made our trip to school that morning and my other conversations with him over the last year so bittersweet, was the notion that society does not know how to treat a person in his mid-forties engaged in a role that seems "inappropriate." Absurdly, our tendency with people like Elton is to assume immaturity. We ask: What's he doing there? How can a man that old suddenly shift careers? What's he trying to prove? Hasn't he outgrown his adolescence? I admit to asking these questions of the situations in which I observed him. Though he never heard them, they were there. Despite good intentions, my first attraction to this man's life was based on the intriguing qualities of a newly un-earthed *"problem."* As much as I have argued for adults sharing the resources, indeed becoming the resources of higher education, Elton's story constantly stimulated in me thoughts about late adolescence, com-petition with one's children, and adults behaving as they are *supposed* to. Whether or not he sensed it, I felt out of place going to school with him. I was embarrassed and ashamed that I should feel this way.

On several occasions I provoked Elton, suggesting that he denied some of the hurts he incurred. He doubted this was true, but acknowl-edge the possibility of it. He reminded me that he was not a 20-year-old boy, but a man approaching 50, and that one's skin gets tougher and one's eyes, sadly, come to see less. He alleged that someone in my profession would probably understand his role in college better than he, but that I should remember that he was not attending school as a sociologist, but merely as a common student. His daughter Julie Ann supported this attitude of his:

"In a way," she said to me one evening, "I'm really glad you're doing a story on daddy, because he is special and other people should know just how special he is. He never complains about his work. He's never even admitted he's had second thoughts, although we can always tell when he's thinking that. But he's really modest. He's the most modest person I've ever met. I know how tough it must be for him. Robbie tells me what college is like. And daddy's in a school that is probably harder than ours. But I know that all this attention about a story embarrasses him. I wish he'd let you call us by our real names. But I s'pose I understand. I just think it's great."

This was not to overlook the incidents that especially troubled or amused Elton. Once, for example, at the beginning of a semester, a woman prevented him from registering, insisting that he was playing a trick. "We have no one of your age making full-time application to our courses," she advised him. He argued weakly with her at first, as if her allegation might be valid. By this time, a group of students had rallied around him pledging they would storm the registration table and kidnap the woman if she would not honor his registration packet. Finally, he lost his composure and demanded that he be allowed to speak to the dean with whom he had consulted when applying to the school.

"This was the one thing I didn't want to do," he told me. "I didn't want to invoke Clifton's name at all. My contact with the school was as a student. When I first enrolled they handed me an ID number. 52873 . . . 4 . . . 3 . . . something like that. I loved it I clutched it to my breast. The kids hollar about not wanting to be a number, you know. It's all a great affront to their identity. Me, I loved that number. Anonymous me. That's what I wanted."

It was for this same reason that he insisted that anything I might write would have to disguise him and his family. On several occasions he referred to the newspaper articles on "old-timers" going back to school as precisely the sort of patronizing notoriety he could not tolerate. "My definition of acceptance was to be lost in the crowd. I was in. No special treatment. I didn't ever want to see Clifton. When I talk to him it means special treatment, and that's what I wanted to avoid. The thing with the lady at registration was a test of whether I was really in or just someone on the sidelines. She capitulated. She found my records and from there on it went smoothly. You should have seen. The kids clapped."

Another experience that first year was a bit more disturbing and caused Elton to reflect on his new status and reasons for wanting to be a student. He had been walking through the campus one evening when a young woman stopped him. Mistaking him for her science teacher, she began apologizing for her low grades.

"I don't know what made me do it, but I just let her go ahead. I didn't have the heart to stop her. Within a matter of minutes, though, it was pretty evident that she was willing to make some kind of, what you might call a deal. A trade. Believe me, she was tempting. But of course, I . . . you know . . . That's all I would have needed. But I think that experience taught me something. It wasn't the sex. And it certainly wasn't the dishonesty. I told her right away that it was all a mistake. But what I learned was that I truly wanted to be a teacher, for the right reasons. I want to teach young people, help them with their problems too. It's a sorry state, though I'll admit a tempting one, when students have to prostitute themselves for grades. I'd like, if I could maybe, to change that. That girl allowed me to taste the part that teachers play in young people's lives. They respect them, some of the time. They matter. That's what I felt that night, and it was good. Better than sex. What do you think of that? Think I need a shrink?"

We laughed out loud together and I could not resist blurting out: "Yeah, I think you do."

Elton had two other experiences that stand out in my memory. In one, he had stayed late to study at the university library, something he was reluctant to do. He had resolved that college would not keep him from his family any longer than his job at the insurance company. It was almost midnight when he reached his car. Suddenly three young men came out of the darkness, grabbed him by the shoulders and upper arms, and threw him against the front of the car insisting that he confess to being a government agent. "CIA, FBI, where the hell you come from, grandpa?" they yelled at him. Bewildered and helpless, his pathetic attempts to deny their charges made them furious. They marched him to a nearby building where he asked them to telephone Dean Clifton. They refused. Instead, they called Marjorie, who cried and begged them to release him. Frightened, the two of them, Elton in the room, Marjorie on the phone, gave them the names of friends in Boston, New York, El Paso, Dayton, and Chicago who would assure them that Elton was not a government officer. They even suggested that they call Robbie at college, hoping they might be convinced by one of their contemporaries. After more than two hours they released him.

"They must have seen me at a protest meeting and found out I wasn't a professor. It's so ironic that you pick a meeting to attend just to show your classmates that you're taking an interest in what they're doing. I got into a discussion with some kids after government class, and they said I should come with them, so I went. These guys must have seen me. Maybe I should get a toupee or have my face lifted. Or maybe I should quit."

"But you wouldn't now," I said. As our friendship had grown and he had taken me into his confidence, I found myself unashamedly rooting for him. He *had* to succeed; nothing should cause him to even think about withdrawing from school. Older students, I reasoned after hearing the episode of the government agent, are not entitled to leaves of absence. They have had enough of them. But I was insensitive to the quiet fear that death and not inevitable human weaknesses can spoil a momentous commitment made later in life.

"Marjorie told me it was up to me. But you know, as terrifying as that night was, you have to keep asking yourself, what the hell is so courageous about this whole thing anyway? I mean, I'm not swimming the channel, or going to the moon. I'm not blockbusting. It's nothing, what I'm doing. I'm going to school and having a ball, working hard, so why should so much be made of it? What's so big about this? That's what I have to keep telling myself. It's really simple. I'm going to finish, and try to go to graduate school in political science. That's all. Nothing special about that. If they'd just leave me alone I could make it. Kids get all excited about politics; they worry that agents are all over the place, which they may be as far as I know, so they pick me out of a crowd and scare the hell out of me. Things like that happen. I didn't think they would on a college campus, but they happen." He was angry. "Thank God I can laugh about it now, but once I thought maybe I better go back to the safety of the New York streets and Central Park." He laughed and looked at me as if to make certain I had been comforted. I shook my head in disbelief. Always the serious tone was derailed by humor. And Marjorie supported me in this perception:

"Oh, I think he hides his fright. I can tell when things aren't going perfectly well. I suppose he told you that I may go back to school too?" I nodded yes. "Well, he comes first this time. I saw him working for 20 years at those jobs, he was a pitiful sight. He was very, very unhappy. There wasn't a whole lot of humor in our house then. Anyone who loved him could see that his life was giving him almost no gratifications. I knew what his plans for college were months before he told me. I just knew what was going on inside that head of his. So I told him finally, 'Do it. What are you waiting for?' He said he was thinking about part-time night school. I told him to do it the way he wants. He said, 'Full blast or no way at all.' I told him I'd stand behind him. Maybe even join him. Can you see us graduating together?" Again I nodded yes. "You can?" She laughed. "Well, then you have a better imagination than I do."

With one issue, however, Elton's seriousness was not easily derailed. Grades, and in particular the occasion of the first marking period, provided Elton an almost religious form of self-awareness and personal assessment. Despite his ideology and purpose, and despite the rhetoric he himself employed with me, the first marking period loomed as important as a parole board's decision in the life of a condemned man. During the last few weeks of the term he began losing weight. His sleeping and excretory habits were affected, and his anxiety made him irritable, indeed, irresponsible. I did not know Elton during that time, but his descriptions of those days touched me.

"I thought he might die," Marjorie confided. "I'd never seen him like that. Several nights there he just sat up in bed shaking, like he had a fever or something. The first time I really thought he was sick. I was going to call a doctor. El just sat there shaking all over. It was utterly pathetic. He wouldn't even let me touch him. He just sat up saying it was going to beat him. But he wasn't going to let it beat him. Can you imagine?"

"You know as well as I," Elton said to me, "when you make a decision like this—to go to school at middle age—it's not only the new thing you're taking on that makes you wonder about yourself. It's the decision itself. When somebody says, I wonder whether I made the right decision, they're not just thinking about what they've given up or what they're about to take on. It's the decision. For six months all I could think about was the decision. Even at the first registration I kept saying to myself: What are you doing here? Would you please tell me, what are *you*, of all people, doing in a nice place like this? You're supposed to be behind a desk counting figures, looking at the clock, getting up every three minutes to go to the water cooler, to stretch, look out the window, eat. Okay?

"About the first week in economics, general introduction course, he says, must have been about the fourth, fifth lecture, 'Your grade for the semester will be based on the following work: two midterms, a final pap . . .' That's when I really entered college. That's when I stopped thinking about any decision. That's when I stopped *auditing* classes. That's when it became the real thing. You're smiling?"

"I'm sorry, Elton," I said. "I was just thinking about the power of grades and what they do to people, and now here is your reaction. It gets me."

"That was some reaction all right. I went cold. I actually started to sweat. I wanted to get up and go to the bathroom. I mean it. I was terrified. You know, I looked around at those kids, they had their feet up on the backs of chairs, chewing gum, slumping in their seats, and they're all writing what he's saying in their notebooks."

"And yet they were freshmen too."

"Sure. Some of them. Most of them, I guess, in that class. But it's different for them. It's part of one story. Kindergarten, grade school, high school, college, it's all part of the same thing. Me, I got grade school, high school, electronics firm, army, insurance, marriage, children, more insurance, and *then* college. Anyway, I can't tell you how it frightened me. For the first time I took a look at myself and realized just how much I worried about failing. That's the single word that really, I mean, I'm really serious about this, that gets in my blood. You talk about kids with drugs, with sex, heroin, with what? Politics, communes, hippies. Nothing. Absolutely nothing. The word is failure. I tell you, I got out of that class, I had to walk miles to settle myself down. I even missed a humanities lecture because of it. I swear it. It consumed me. If I failed it meant my entire life was a failure; that the grade given to me by whoever grades us," unthinkingly he looked up at the ceiling, "was F. That's what got to me. You know, when you're young, in college, you can rebound. Kids can come back. They flunk one course, pass another. What do they care? They can always say I wasn't ready for college, which incidentally is what I hear all the time from people my own age who are trying to encourage me. 'I should do it now. I was too young.' "

"I think I said that same thing to you once myself."

"I think you did. Well, it may be true. But you can't fail at 35, 40, 45. You don't fail then. There's no room for it. No room in your life, no room in society. See, I can ward off all these people who look at me as if I were a middle-aged adolescent, expecting any minute I'm going to pull out a pack of marijuana or something, or be freaky. That stuff doesn't bother me. What bothers me is this business that, you know, he went back to college with his son, and he failed. He's not that smart. He couldn't do it. That's what hurts. So I had to work. Believe me, I worked. And don't think it's easy to be graded by people your age *and* younger who know a helluva lot less than you about many things.

"You know what Marjorie did when I got my grades? She cried. She cried."

"And you?"

"Me? I was in such a state of shock. Not for long though. I took out a bottle of bourbon and had a belt, and did we celebrate. And did my kids give it to me. How come, they wanted to know, I didn't get all A's? How do you like those devils? Not all A's. My own medicine they were giving me." I could see Elton reliving the relief and joy of that first marking period. He has never disclosed his grades, but his wife has, and they are high. He remains modest but proud, and every day I love the story of his life more and more. And so does his son Robbie, who wrote a letter to his father when the elder received his first grades:

> . . . Mom told me about your grades. You're great! Just like I taught you. Knew you could do it. Wish I could get myself to work as hard as you, but you know the younger generation. Hah hah. You should have come here, then we could have gone to class together. Maybe double on the weekends. What do you say? (Just kidding, Mom.) Dad—Do you know that you are eligible for varsity football? My roommate says if you haven't played before you can. Why don't you try? You could be the new Y. A. Tittle. I'll come watch you if you make the team. Like they say in the letters from college, I'll write soon. Send money for a new suit if there's any left over from your book collection. I'll be home in three weeks. Keep studying, Joe College. YEA!!!

We had reached the campus. Elton's manner was changing. I could see him becoming more serious, purposeful. Whereas during the drive he was essentially a colleague, sharing his perceptions about a particular aspect of higher education, he was now separating himself from me and preparing to enter this new world. At first I imagined he might act as a college boy showing his parents the campus for the first time. Instead, he was withdrawing from me. He seemed resolute if not shy, and I felt him glancing over at me when he believed I was not conscious of him. I was now more than a friend. I was a professor, a colleague of his teachers.

"You've been out here before, haven't you?" he inquired.

"Once or twice. That's all," I answered.

"It's a good place. They've been good to me."

"It's *your* school, Elton."

"Yeah. My school." He paused. "Not really though. It's my school when I'm home. Even when I'm riding in the car. But once I get here it's not mine anymore for some reason. Don't know exactly why."

" 'Cause it belongs to the kids?" I ventured.

"Yeah, I suppose." We walked along a path toward the classroom buildings, our bodies still warm from being inside the car. "Funny how education belongs to all people, to the entire culture probably, and schools, colleges especially, belong just to the kids. Maybe that's the way God intended it. I wouldn't know. Don't talk that much to Him." He smiled as he turned to me. "Maybe I should, except that I have a feeling that this is man's work, not God's. So if it's all right with you I'll just be thankful I'm walking here and not sitting in a New York office with my brain rotting. Whatever they think of me, freak, old-timer, CIA agent . . . remember? . . . a professor, an adolescent who never grew up, I know my brain's alive. They'll *never* know *that* in New

York. They'll never know what life a student carries in his mind. That's the excitement. It's not a rebirth exactly. Nor do I think I'm continuing something that never got finished the right way. I suppose it's not that complicated. I'm just going about my business, and for the first time I'm not thinking that much about regrets or about where I'll end up someday, although I hope it's in an office on a campus like this somewhere." He directed me to turn down a smaller path. "When the time comes, I think I'll be able to look at you eye to eye. Right now that's a little hard for me. You know what I mean?"

SOME LIMITATIONS OF TRADITIONAL RESEARCH ON THE BENEFITS OF HIGHER EDUCATION

The Case of Women

Michelle Patterson

The influence of ability, background, and formal education on schooling and subsequent success have been discussed at some length. Overall correlations of these variables with success tell us much, but about whom? Virtually every study discussed in this volume used as its subjects *males*—and in almost every case, *white* males. If we are really interested in the relationship between schooling and success, this approach may be locating the forest but missing the trees.

Perhaps it is time to consider another approach: Rather than seeking universal variables, we should specify for what population groups and under what conditions the effects discovered hold true. For example, Duncan (1969) and Coleman *et al.* (1971) point out that the best predictors of occupational status or income for white men are not the best predictors for black men; at least, they do not operate in the same way. Sewell *et al.* (1970) state that the educational and occupational status attainment process of women has been neglected in most previous research. They speculate that a recursive model for the educational attainment of women might not differ greatly from that for men; they suggest, however, that the occupational status attainment process of women is probably more complex. Nevertheless, very little hard research has been done. (Sewell's later work is discussed below.)

It is nice to know that male economists, as Lewis Solmon points out ("Schooling and Subsequent Success," pp. 13–34), recognize the externalities of education for women—that is, the social benefits derived from better-educated mothers produce even more successful sons and, presumably, even more efficient son-producing daughters. But, since women incur both private and public costs in attaining higher education, perhaps the time has come for society to internalize the costs of these social benefits and to explore the private returns to women from their own investments in education. We shall briefly summarize what is known about the educational attainment and salaries of women to suggest that the models specified elsewhere in this volume are likely to need revision in the case of women.

Although the sexes do not differ significantly in intelligence or academic ability, the educational attainment of women is considerably lower than that of men (Folger *et al.*, 1970). The proportion of women completing each degree after high school is smaller than the proportion of men, and the percentage of women declines with each higher degree. Women receive over 40 percent of the bachelor's degrees, about 33 percent of the master's, and only around 10 percent of the doctorates awarded. Sewell (1971) finds that the result of equalizing women's educational opportunities would be to increase by 28 percent the number of women who obtain some education beyond high school, by 52 percent the number who attend college, and by 68 percent the number who graduate from college.

Part of the difference in educational attainments of men and women is explained by socioeconomic status (SES). Ellison & Simon ("Does College Make a Person Healthy and Wise?" pp. 35–63) note the findings of Trent & Medsker (1968) that at the low-SES level, only 40 percent of the two fifths high school students of highest ability go to college, while 60 percent of the students from the bottom two fifths in ability from high-SES backgrounds continue their education. Feldman & Newcomb (1969) report that a 1957 study found that the lower the SES, the smaller the percentage of women (relative to men) who attend college. This was confirmed recently by Werts (1966). In a comparison of 76,015 boys and 51,710 girls, controlling for high school grade average and father's occupation, Werts finds that the college entrance rates of boys and girls of high SES are very similar, though among low-SES students, boys are much more likely to continue their education. Boys are also more likely than girls to continue among students with poor high school academic records. Moreover, Werts finds an interaction between the independent variables, suggesting that low grades are a greater deterrent to college attendance for low-SES girls than for high-SES girls.

This is not surprising in light of Kohn's (1959a, 1959b) studies showing that working-class and middle-class parents differ in their primary expectations vis-à-vis children of different sexes and in the degree to which they treat boys and girls differently. Gordon's (1969) analysis of Educational Opportunity Survey data demonstrates that the variable most strongly correlated with sex for ninth graders is the parental aspiration index. Boys are much more likely than girls to picture their parents as holding high educational expectations for them, although these same girls earn higher grades. The Werts, Kohn, and Gordon findings suggest that the effect of significant others' influence (SOI) documented by Sewell and his colleagues (1969, 1970), is important, although perhaps in a different way, for women as well as men.

Sewell's (1971) recent work confirms this conclusion. In comparing men and women, Sewell finds, not unexpectedly, that women's educational attainment is not as great as men's. More significantly, his recursive model discloses that women are most seriously disadvantaged relative to men in their level of teachers' and parents' encouragement and their own levels of educational aspirations. On the other hand, women have the advantage of achieving better high school grades and, in seeming contradiction to their lower educational aspirations, have somewhat higher occupational aspirations.

On the whole, Sewell's model tends to predict higher average educational attainment for women than they actually achieve. Since Sewell believes socialization and family effects are already manifest in women's levels of performance, SOI, and aspirations, all of which he measured during the high school years, he attempts to explain this discrepancy by pointing to effects immediately following high school and not included in his model.

It is possible that these measures of high school performance, SOI, and aspirations do not completely reflect the negative influences on women of socialization and family, especially during the high school years. Some years ago Coleman (1961) reported that the Chicago-area high school girls he studied were caught in a "double bind," wanting to perform well but also fearing that conspicuous achievement would cause them to lose popularity with boys. More recently, Horner, (1969, p. 38) has further refined this concept:

A bright woman is caught in a double bind. In testing and other achievement-oriented situations she worries not only about failure, but also about

success. If she fails, she is not living up to her own standards of performance;
if she succeeds she is not living up to societal expectations about the female
role. Men in our society do not experience this kind of ambivalence, because
they are not only permitted, but actively encouraged, to do well.

For women, then, the desire to achieve is often contaminated by the
motive to avoid success. Femininity and individual achievement are often
viewed as two desirable, but mutually exclusive, goals. "Whereas men
are unsexed by failure . . . women seem to be unsexed by success"
(Horner, 1971 p. 106).

What happens to those women who do pursue their education? Sophisticated research on income determinants comparable to that done
on white male samples has yet to be undertaken on female populations.
Still, studies are available that document the systematic practice of paying women less: Oppenheimer (1970) reports that the median income
of all women in the labor force is only about three fifths that of men.
Fuchs (1971) recently confirmed this finding. He suggests, however,
that this might be attributable to less experience, rather than employer
discrimination. In so doing, Fuchs demonstrates that, as he computes
it, the expected income of women is much less than that of men. Since
Fuchs' measure of expected income is based on the sex of the worker,
as well as other relevant factors, his data do not indicate to what extent
the women's lower expected income is attributable solely to their sex.

Research by Levitin et al. (1971) on a national sample of workers
in heterogeneous occupations avoids the pitfalls of Fuchs' study. Applying achievement variables equally to men and women, they find that
the average woman receives 71 percent less income than a man with
the same scores on achievement variables. They conclude that "the
legitimate achievement factors determining the allocation of income were
differentially applied to equally qualified men and women" (Levitin
et al., 1971, p. 252). In academia, Helen Astin's (1969) study of women
doctorates shows that the professional woman tends to make a lower
salary than her male counterpart, even when they are equal in educational attainment and experience in the labor force. My own research
(Patterson, 1971, in press) indicates that two of the reasons women
are paid less are (a) they are kept in lower-ranking positions, and
(b) in the professions at least, they are shunted off to the less prestigious
and less well-paying specialties. Even independent of field of specialization, employment setting, and academic rank, Bayer & Astin's (1968)
research on teaching scientists reveals that academic women earn less
money than men. A recent survey of the legal profession (White, 1967)
suggests that whatever their qualifications, women typically are paid
less than men.

The point of all of this is to demonstrate that we have not found the universal variables (family background, mental ability, and school quality) that predict future income and success for all groups in the population. Future research must specify for what groups, and under what conditions, the predictors isolated to date hold true. Most importantly, we need more work along the lines of Duncan's (1969) study to specify how much larger social forces, such as discrimination, enter into the equation and to identify their differential impact upon various segments of society. As Miller (1971, p. 63) states:

> The implicit model is one of detection, adding pieces together to gain a fuller picture, rather than one of locating the unique variable or variables which provide satisfying explanations. . . . [The absence of this alternative style] particularly mars [policy and] evaluation studies which tend to ignore the question of which subgroups are particularly helped or not helped by a particular intervention. Rather, the focus is on obtaining a "yes/no" verdict in regard to an intervention (read independent variable); the diagnostic issue of what is important to whom is usually left unresolved.

REFERENCES

Astin, H. S. *The woman doctorate in America.* New York: Russell Sage Foundation, 1969.

Bayer, A. E., & Astin, H. S. Sex differences in academic rank and salary among science doctorates in teaching. *The Journal of Human Resources,* 1968, 3(2): 191–200.

Coleman, J. S. *The adolescent society.* New York: Free Press, 1961.

Coleman, J. S., Blum, Z. D., & Sørensen, A. B. *Occupational status changes for whites and blacks during the first ten years of occupational experience* (Rev. ed.) Baltimore: The Johns Hopkins University Center for Social Organization of Schools, October 1971 (Report No. 76).

Duncan, O. D. Inheritance of poverty or inheritance of race? In D. P. Moynihan (Ed.), *On understanding poverty: Perspectives from the social sciences.* New York: Basic Books, 1969.

Feldman, K. A., & Newcomb, T. M. *The impact of college on students.* San Francisco: Jossey-Bass, 1969.

Folger, J. K. Astin, H. S., & Bayer, A. E. *Human resources and higher education.* New York: Russell Sage Foundation, 1970.

Fuchs, V. R. Differences in hourly earnings between men and women. *Monthly Labor Review,* 1971, 94(5): 9–15.

Gordon, C. Looking ahead: Self-conceptions, race and family factors as determinants of adolescent achievement orientations. Washington, D.C.: American Sociology Association, 1969.

Horner, M. S. Fail: Bright women. *Psychology Today,* 1969, 3(6): 36–38, 62.

Horner, M. S. Femininity and successful achievement: A basic inconsistency. In M. H. Garskof (Ed.), *Roles women play.* Belmont, Cal.: Brooks/Cole Publishing Co., 1971.

Kohn, M. L. Social class and parental values. *American Journal of Sociology,* 1959a, 64: 337–351.

Kohn, M. L. Social class and the exercise of parental authority. *American Sociological Review*, 1959b, 24: 352–366.

Levitin, T., Quinn, R. P., & Staines, G. L. Sex discrimination against the American working woman. *American Behavioral Scientist*, 1971, 15: 237-254.

Miller, S. M. The future of social mobility studies. *American Journal of Sociology*, 1971, 77(1): 62–65.

Oppenheimer, V. K. *The female labor force in the United States*. Berkeley: University of California, Institute of International Studies. Population Monograph Series, No. 5, 1970.

Patterson, M. Alice in Wonderland: A study of women faculty in graduate departments of sociology. *American Sociologist*, 1971, 6: 226–234.

Patterson, M. Sex and specialization in academe and the professions. In A. S. Rossi (Ed.), *Academic women on the move*. New York: Russell Sage Foundation, in press.

Sewell, W. H. Inequality of opportunity for higher education. *American Sociological Review*, 1971, 35: 793–809.

Sewell, W. H., Haller, A. O., & Ohlendorf, G. W. The educational and early occupational attainment process: Replication and revision. *American Sociological Review*, 1970, 35: 1014–1027.

Sewell, W. H., Haller, A. O., & Portes, A. The educational and early occupational attainment process. *American Sociological Review*, 1969, 34: 82–92.

Trent, J. W., & Medsker, L. L. *Beyond high school*. San Francisco: Jossey-Bass, 1968.

Werts, C. E. *Sex differences in college attendance*. Evanston, Ill.: National Merit Scholarship Corporation (Reports, Vol. 2, No. 6), 1966.

White, J. J. Women in law. *Michigan Law Review*, 1967, 65: 1051–1122.

PERSPECTIVES ON BLACK EDUCATION AND THE EDUCATION OF BLACKS

Charles V. Willie

Some frank talk is needed about college education for blacks and the meaning of their education for the majority and minority populations of this nation. Blacks in 1972, for example, continue to lag two years behind the white median of 12.2 years of schooling (Rosenthal, 1972, p. 53). However, it should be clearly stated that this lag has nothing to do with innate racial characteristics. Whites do not have superior capacities for learning compared with blacks, and blacks do not have inferior capacities for learning compared with whites. A recent Census report indicates that 12 percent of the nation's population over 25 years of age are college graduates. Among blacks, however, only 6 percent of the over-25-years-of-age adults are college graduates, as are 3.5 percent of the other minorities, such as Puerto Ricans, Chicanos, Orientals, and American Indians (otherwise known as Native Americans) (Bureau of the Census, 1971, p. 128).

Two reasons are suggested for asserting that no biological differences are connected with the differences in years of schooling between black and white populations in America. First, there probably are no pure races in the United States. We know that a considerable amount of interbreeding has occurred between black, white, and other racial populations since the early settlement of this land. The diversity of inherited characteristics exhibited by the people in any public gathering is ample evidence of the extensive cohabitation between all sorts and conditions of people over the years. As stated by Dobzhansky (1951, p. 18), "Race and species are populations which remain distinct only so long as some cause limits their interbreeding." Thus, any biological traits, including those associated with capacity to learn, that may have been unique to one racial population, now have been shared more or less with all populations in America, according to laws of heritability.

The second reason for doubting a biological connection between race and schooling exhibited by blacks compared with whites is the increasing evidence that blacks who have received educational opportunities have succeeded as well as failed in school. In some instances, their successes have exceeded those of whites, which would be impossible were their recorded current lower level of average achievement a function of heritability. A study of black students at white colleges conducted in New York State by a colleague and myself at Syracuse University revealed that blacks in general had a lower average for self-reported cumulative grades than whites but that black college seniors had a higher average than white seniors (Willie & McCord, 1972, p. 87). While it may be that the average for black seniors may have been elevated over that of white seniors due to a higher drop-out rate of low-achieving black students, the point to be made in terms of race and heritability is that some blacks have the capacity to achieve as well or better than whites. Indeed, it is highly probable that the differences seen among black and white populations with reference to schooling and other forms of achievement are functions of the "great plasticity and susceptibility [of the genotype] to environmental influences" (Dobzhansky, 1951, p. 23).

Probably the most fundamental fact about higher education and blacks is that it occurs in a racist environment. This is the experience for blacks and other racial minorities and certainly for the two thirds of black students now enrolled in predominantly white colleges (Willie & McCord, 1972). As pointed out by Andrew Brimmer (1971, p. 563), "Both the incentive for black students to attend college and the willingness of their families to pay a sizeable share of the cost remains strong." Yet, the question remains: How much is college education worth for blacks in terms of income, compared with the economic benefits of higher education for whites? The racist circumstances with which blacks have had to contend were described by Herman Miller with computations on 1959 income data. Based on these computations, he concluded (1964, p. 155) that "the average nonwhite with four years of college could expect to earn less over a lifetime than the white who did not go beyond the eighth grade." This finding, according to Miller (1964, p. 155), "support[s] the belief that much of the gap between the earnings of whites and [blacks] is due to factors other than differences in training or ability."

It is a fact that median income by schooling completed not only differs by race but tends to widen between the racial groups with increases in education. In 1968, for example, the difference in median income for whites and blacks (together with other nonwhites) who had graduated from elementary school, graduated from high school, or attended college ranged from $880 to $1,065 to $2,469; blacks and other nonwhites, of course, received less income than whites who had a comparable education (Miller, 1971, p. 170). These findings led Miller to state (1971, p. 167) that "there is some justification for the feeling by Puerto Ricans, Negroes and other minority groups that education does not do as much for them financially, as it does for others."

To be sure, there is a strong and positive relationship between income and schooling for blacks as well as whites. The median income for blacks and other nonwhites who attended college one or more years is $3,207 greater than the median for individuals in these populations who stopped their formal education after graduating from elementary school (Miller, 1971, p. 170). Nevertheless, these college-educated blacks and other nonwhite minorities still lagged nearly $2,500 behind whites of a similar education. This, then, is the racist context within which the motivation for higher education for blacks must be analyzed.

Notwithstanding gross discrimination, the inclination to get a college education remains strong among blacks—so much so that the 434,000 blacks enrolled in college in 1968 was an 85 percent increase over the 234,000 enrolled in college just four years earlier (Miller, 1971, p. 82). The study conducted by my colleague and myself indicated that black students in college came from families with modest financial resources. In the predominantly white colleges that we studied, median income of fathers of black students was only two thirds as large as that for fathers of white students. Moreover, 38 percent of the black students, compared with 54 percent of the white students, received parental support toward college expenses (Willie & McCord, 1971, pp. 78–81).

While a majority of the black students in our study (70 percent) looked upon college as a means to a secure future (Willie & McCord, 1972, p. 82) and believed that the opportunity system for graduate education was opening up, most felt that opportunities for employment in government or business were not as good today as they were five or more years ago. It was their guess in overwhelming numbers that job opportunities would be largely restricted to the traditional helping professions such as teaching and social work (Willie & McCord, 1972, p. 91).

The anticipation of racial discrimination in employment after graduation, together with knowledge of existing discrimination in income, notwithstanding the level of education one has achieved, seem not to have dampened the interest of young blacks in getting a college education. As mentioned earlier, there has been an 85 percent increase in their college enrollment over a four-year period. This fact means that young black people must be looking to college to fulfill goals that may include, but are not limited to, increased income. Because of this, I have been severely critical of whites who suggest that the proper function of formal education for blacks is to make them over in the image of whites. Although not referring to college-age blacks, Arthur Jensen (1969, p. 3) gives this impression when he states that "the remedy deemed logical for children who would do poorly in school is to boost their IQ's up to where they can perform like *the majority* . . ." (italics added).

Indeed, I pointed out in a lecture given at the 1972 International Conference of the Educational Testing Service, that "the poor and disadvantaged have some idea of their own about what they would like to get out of formal education." These might include such goals as, for example, learning how to endure, how to develop a positive concept of the self, how to gain a measure of control over one's environment, how to transcend difficulty, and how to effectively deal with danger (Willie, 1973). The moving autobiography of one of America's most distinguished educators who is black attests to my statement above. Benjamin Elijah Mays (1971, p. 60) had this to say of his college education at Bates in Maine:

> One of my dreams came true at Bates. Through competitive experience, I had finally dismissed from my mind for all times the myth of the inherent inferiority of all Negroes and the inherent superiority of all whites. . . . Bates College did not "emancipate" me; it did the far greater service of making it possible for me to emancipate myself, to accept with dignity my own worth as a free man.

This, then, is a unique function that a college education can perform for students of oppressed racial minority groups. It can provide an opportunity for these students to emancipate themselves, to develop a sense of their significance in society, and to accept with dignity their freedom, including its dual opportunity for self-affirmation and social obligation. College did all of these for Benjamin Mays, and several generations of black students have benefited from his knowledge, wisdom, leadership, and confidence that Bates College helped to develop. Benjamin Mays was president of Morehouse College in Atlanta, Georgia, for 27 years, including the period when Martin Luther King, Jr., attended that school.

Much of the controversy associated with the early development of Black Studies programs resulted from a misunderstanding of the unique functions of college for minority-group students that sometimes differ from the functions of college for majority-group students. Most faculties insisted that Black Studies ought to evolve similar to the way other subject matter fields evolved and should, more or less, fulfill the same academic goals. From our studies of black students at white colleges (Willie & McCord, 1972, p. 46)

> it is clear . . . that black students want Black Studies to fulfill a multitude of purposes. . . . It is proposed as a means of learning essential information, understanding of the history of one's people, promoting black identity and solidarity, providing relevant academic experiences, straightening out oneself, and charting goals for the future. Thus, the program is expected to deal with the present, as well as the past, and personal, as well as public concerns. It should convey a body of information, as well as induce a certain outlook on life or state of mind. It is fair to say that black students expect Black Studies to deal with both the prophetic and pragmatic.

At a period in the history of higher education when the integration of knowledge is being called for, Black Studies offers one vehicle for the achievement of such. Unfortunately, its detractors have not recognized this opportunity. Frequently innovations and new opportunities are missed when the majority believes the minority has little to contribute to society and should be remade in the image of the majority for maximum feasible participation in the society-at-large.

The black college is an example of an institution that has experimented with different ways of involving students in relevant community experiences. At a time when students throughout the nation are calling for relevancy in their academic programs, and institutions are experimenting with various community internship arrangements, black colleges could be most helpful in indicating how to provide a relevant education. Again, this national resource is overlooked because of the distorted prevailing view that black colleges are merely jerry-built imitations of the real thing—the real thing being the predominantly white, private, prestigious schools in the Northeast.

Of the 1960s, John A. Williams (1970, p. 37) has this to say about black college youth:

> The decade began with a rush. The activities seemed to be in the command of youth; it was the time of the sit-ins. Each escalation of the civil rights movement has a date and a place. The sit-ins commenced on February 1, 1960. The place was North Carolina A & T College in Greensboro. The students were directly influenced by the Montgomery bus boycott with its

nonviolent philosophy; its effectiveness persuaded the black youth that they, too, could successfully employ it.

William goes on to tell us that the basic aim of the sit-ins was "to spur [the nation] into action to abolish the system that insured the life of degradation for the majority of its nonwhite citizens." Following the sit-ins came the freedom riders, whose mission was to desegregate the interstate buses and accommodations in bus stations for interstate passengers. These, too, were led by black students. Two weeks of travel through the South led to beatings and humiliations. Williams tells us that more students from Fisk University and other black schools climbed aboard new buses every day to continue the movement (1970, pp. 48–49). These black students were getting educated all right. And the education they were receiving was relevant. They were helped and supported by their teachers in their efforts to change the world, in their efforts to make it just.

Providing an education that helps solve community problems is the task that many black colleges have been performing for a long time. In 1966 I returned to my Alma Mater, Morehouse College (a predominantly black, men's school), to give the Founder's Day banquet address. I tried to sum up this mission in these remarks.

> Thus far Morehouse has been on the side of the angels. It has respected the students' right to protest. The demonstrator has not been damned. Indeed, he has been exalted while the contemplative student also has been acclaimed. . . . Morehouse College has sons who can debate. Morehouse College has sons who can demonstrate. This is the breadth of its involvement in the community.

Then, I predicted that Morehouse College would move into the second century of its existence "strongly supporting all of its sons, including those who think and those who act." But more than that, I predicted Morehouse would strive to do two things—impart to the activists the benefits of reasoned thought and impart to the thinkers the methods and techniques of effective action. I saw Morehouse and other black colleges continuing to develop students who are ceaselessly active in public affairs (Willie, 1966, p. 9).

With methods and techniques of instruction such as those mentioned above, black colleges have educated their students to the realities of life and also have taught them how to endure hardship, transcend custom, and change society. This could be beneficial to whites, as well as blacks. Thus, the experience of black colleges is an important national resource, if other colleges and universities could humble themselves to learn from these schools.

The methods and techniques of teaching all sorts and conditions of students are particularly of value to other colleges today as the push for an open opportunity system for all young people at the college level increases. Black colleges have excelled in teaching students of disadvantaged circumstances. They have received many students other colleges would refuse and have helped these young people to become personally fulfilled, useful, and contributing members of society. Open enrollment, therefore, is a challenge that black colleges already have met. They now could assist other institutions of higher education in America to meet this challenge in an honorable way. The demand for postsecondary education is present. It remains to be seen if the existing colleges and universities can make an appropriate response.

In summary, differences do exist between black and white populations in number of years of schooling completed. However, these differences are probably due, not to biological characteristics but to unequal environmental experiences and, especially, to racist customs that limit opportunities for blacks and place them at a disadvantage. An example is the lower income that educated blacks receive compared with the income received by whites of similar or less education. Nevertheless, college education is positively related to increase in income for blacks as well as whites over what persons receive who have not as much formal schooling. The discrepancy between income for blacks and whites tends to widen for persons who have attended college compared with others. While blacks who attend college hope for a secure future, they know that racial discrimination continues to exist and could interfere with their maximizing returns from a college education. The number of blacks attending college has dramatically increased in recent years. Such an increase means that blacks probably believe that a college education will help them achieve more than just a higher income. Indeed, it appears that the education that blacks have obtained, particularly in black colleges, has taught them about the realities of life as well as how to change these realities. Black colleges met the challenge of open enrollment years ago and could be of assistance to other colleges as they struggle to deal with this new experience. Black colleges are an important national resource. They know how to serve all sorts and conditions of students. To borrow a phrase from Langston Hughes, black colleges are all caught up in "the sweet flypaper of life." They really know how to be relevant.

REFERENCES

Brimmer, A. The economic outlook and the future of the Negro college. *Daedalus*, 1971, 100: 539–572.

Bureau of the Census. *Statistical abstract of the United States.* Washington, D.C.: U.S. Government Printing Office, 1971.

Dobzhansky, T. *Genetics and the origin of species.* New York: Columbia University Press, 1951.

Jensen, A. How much can we boost IQ and scholastic achievement? *Environment, heredity, and intelligence.* Cambridge: Harvard Educational Review, 1969 (Reprint Series No. 2).

Mays, B. E. *Born to rebel.* New York: Charles Scribner's Sons, 1971.

Miller, H. P. *Rich man, poor man.* 1964. (Rev. ed.) New York: T. Y. Crowell, 1971.

Rosenthal, J. Census shows sharp rise in schooling. *New York Times,* December 8, 1972.

Williams, J. A. *The King God didn't save.* New York: Coward-McCann, 1970.

Willie, C. V. Into the second century: Problems of higher education of particular concern to Morehouse College. *Morehouse College Bulletin,* 1966, 35: 7–10.

Willie, C. V. A theoretical approach to racial and cultural differences. *Proceedings of the conference on testing problems.* New Jersey: Educational Testing Service, 1973.

Willie, C. V., & McCord, A. S. *Black students at white colleges.* New York: Praeger, 1972.

THE RESPONSIBILITY OF THE BLACK COLLEGE TO THE BLACK COMMUNITY

Then and Now*

Mack H. Jones

Black colleges have been roundly excoriated by diverse elements†
for defaulting on their responsibilities to the larger black community.
There are those who argue that black colleges have been too elitist
and have not given proper deference to the opinions and judgments
of the masses, while others have criticized them for failing to take the
initiative in giving these same masses sufficient guidance and leadership.
Some have inveighed against them for failing to approximate the role

* Reprinted by permission of *Daedalus*, Journal of the American Academy of
Arts and Sciences, Boston, Massachusetts, Summer 1971, *The Future of the Black
Colleges*.
† Critics, to cite a few, include such unlikely bedfellows as Nathan Hare (1967,
1968a, 1968b), an accomplished black sociologist and one of the leading intellectuals
in the black liberation struggle; Lionel Newsom (Commission on Higher Education
in the South, 1967), who is now president of a black college; William Carson
(1970), a white former marine colonel whose interest in guerrilla warfare and
counterinsurrectionary strategy led him to write a book on black students; Christopher
Jencks and David Riesman (1967), two white scholars with solid Establishment
credentials; and Bernard Harleston (1965), a black teacher at a white college.

attributed to major white colleges in American society as a whole, while others have vehemently denounced them for slavishly aping such institutions. These criticisms, along with myriad others repeatedly leveled at black colleges, obviously have some bases in fact. Black colleges have not completely fulfilled their responsibilities to the larger black community. However, much of the criticism suggests a profound misunderstanding of the relationship between institutions of higher learning and their sponsoring communities in general and an even more skewed perception of the place of black colleges in American society. Indeed, the critics themselves are often inconsistent, criticizing black colleges for not being "good" American colleges on the one hand and for not meeting their special responsibilities to the black community on the other.*

Such specious analysis is a function of the fact that much of the discussion of the role and responsibilities of black colleges rushes pell-mell toward evaluation before giving sufficient attention to the societal context within which they are obliged to function. Fundamental questions and their implications for the role performance of black colleges go begging—questions such as: Who decided that black colleges should be established and what purposes did they have in mind? How did these purposes affect the recruitment of faculty and administrative personnel, the composition of the student body, and the structure of curricula? And, in turn, how have all of these factors, singly and cumulatively, influenced the historical relationship between the black college and the larger black community? It is not so much that those writing about black colleges are unaware of the importance of these questions, for they are almost invariably alluded to in a prefatory manner. However, with the preface out of the way analysis usually proceeds with little or no deference being given to them. (To borrow a phrase from Malcolm X, such analysis makes the victim the criminal.)

The fact of the matter is that since their inception black colleges have had built-in antithetical goals and objectives. The white community, as is always the case with groups enjoying superordinate status in a society, has sought to maintain its position of dominance at the expense of blacks, while the latter have sought to achieve equal status,† and both have sought to use the black college as an instrument in their struggle. This assumption must be the focal point of any intelligent discussion of the success of the black college in meeting its responsibility

---

* The Jencks–Riesman (1967) and Harleston (1965) articles are replete with such inconsistencies. The careful reader will also notice similar ambivalencies in the Southern Regional Education Board publication (1967) and in Nathan Hare's analyses, though on a more limited scale.

† For further discussion see Jones (1972).

to the larger black community, and it is with this thought in mind that this essay will attempt to assess the past performance of traditionally black colleges and to suggest the nature of their contemporary responsiblities to their communities.

It is my contention that when black colleges were founded in the aftermath of emancipation their major responsibility was grounded in the conditions of the black community at the time. They were charged with developing a cadre of blacks who could challenge and overcome immediate threats to the survival of the black community while working simultaneously for equal status in American society. Contrary to popular sentiment, I contend that black colleges, collectively, met this responsibility. They were instrumental in developing among blacks in North America all of the skills necessary not only to survive but also to build a black nation as well. Since, however, the fulfillment of this responsibility has not brought about equality of status as black pioneers had expected, but rather a heightening of white oppression, black colleges are faced with new responsibilities to their communities. It is now their task to create a new political consciousness among blacks that will lead to a commonly shared ideological network or world view, which, in turn, will facilitate an understanding of the black predicament in an *international context*. Such an ideology would disabuse its holders of the many counterrevolutionary values that now impede the black struggle, define their friends and enemies, and order the priorities of the black diaspora in America. This task requires a radical restructuring of black colleges as we know them.*

The phrase "responsibility of the black college to the larger black community" should not be interpreted to mean two separate and distinct entities, even though much of the discussion about college–community relations suggests as much. The relationship is more of an organic one. The college, like myriad other institutions, is established by the community to perform certain functions deemed essential to its survival. The community, one must remember, is the sum total of the infinite patterns of goal-directed activities of its members acting both as individuals and as constituents of groups and institutions. Thus, the college is simply one of many specialized institutions having a number of community-defined functions, some primary, others secondary or even tertiary. The major responsibility of the college to the larger community, like all other community institutions, is to perform well those primary functions for which it was established. If it fails to perform adequately

---

* For one scholar's views on what a restructured black college would look like, see McWorter (1968).

its primary tasks, then its involvement in secondary and tertiary matters will likely be inconsequential or even counterproductive.

It is appropriate, then, to begin by asking what, in general, are the primary responsibilities of colleges to their communities? For what purposes are institutions of higher learning established? Essentially such institutions have always had as their primary purpose reinforcing the legitimacy of the prevailing regime as defined by those of power and wealth, predisposing subjects toward supportive behavior, and preparing students to assume productive positions in the community within the constraints imposed by the regime. That is the overriding purpose of higher education in every society—imparting to the students socially useful skills and sociopolitical consciousness that will lead them to choose to employ their acquired skills in a fashion consistent with the basic values of the regime. I am using the term regime to mean (Easton, 1964, p. 97):

> all of those arrangements that regulate the way in which demands put into the system are settled and the way in which decisions are put into effect. They are the so-called rules of the game, in the light of which actions by members of the system are legitimated and accepted by the bulk of the members as authoritative.

The forces determining the content of the regime, it is true, are not likely to be monolithic, but rather a mosaic reflecting the eternal struggle for dominance between and among competing interests. Nevertheless, there will be basic societal values, an ideological network, within whose constraints the behavior of its members will be expected to fall.

Institutions of higher learning, along with other socialization agents, are responsible for insuring that patterns of behavior dictated by the regime are accepted as legitimate. For example, the ideal product of the South African university system would accept the legitimacy of apartheid, and his Russian counterpart would show similar deference toward scientific socialism; the Tanzanian student would accept the behavior code implied in the Arusha Declaration, and the ideal American product would accept the constraints of capitalism grounded in white supremacy as legitimate.

In societies where sizable minorities exist in more or less separate and identifiable communities and are singled out for deferential and unequal treatment by the dominant element, educational institutions serving the former will be characterized by dual and conflicting purposes. The dominant community, in the absence of genuine pluralism, will use its superior power to influence the structure of these institutions such that they serve to reinforce the existing order, that is, their position of dominance at the expense of the minority community. The latter, on the other hand, will try to structure educational institutions serving them so that they are supportive of their struggle for liberation. These opposing forces may be referred to as the dirty worker* function at one pole and the liberation vehicle at the other.

In societies in which a group or groups are subjugated by others there exist a number of individuals and institutions who are hired or who hire themselves to administer, contain, and control the members of the group being dominated. These are the dirty workers; they earn their livelihood by keeping the subjugated in their place, as defined by the existing regime. Dirty workers who are recruited from both the oppressed and oppressor communities include, among others, policemen, real estate brokers, slumlords, social workers, rapacious neighborhood merchants, loan sharks, and, in some instances, teachers and clergymen. Dirty workers, consistent with the will of the dominant community, tend to perform their roles in a fashion that maintains the subordinate status of the oppressed community, though this is done not so much by centralized conspiratorial design as by a common perception of reality that dictates a network of normative assumptions about the nature and worth of minority group members and about the kind of treatment and respect to which they are entitled. Acceptance of these assumptions is reinforced by judicious manipulation of rewards and punishment by those elements with direct material interest in maintaining the status quo.

Liberation vehicle, of course, refers to institutions that accept as their primary function promoting and supporting those changes in the regime advocated by members of the oppressed community.

These conflicting purposes, as I have already asserted, are clearly evident in the history of black colleges in the United States, and herein lies much of the confusion and contradiction regarding their effectiveness in serving the larger black community. When black colleges were founded in the wake of the Civil War, the dirty worker syndrome was doubtless the dominant factor. To be sure, some of the founders and their philanthropic benefactors had benevolent intention,† and it would be uncharitable and historically inaccurate to suggest that they were engaged solely in Machiavellian techniques to maintain white dominance. Nevertheless, it cannot be gainsaid that the white community was more concerned with making blacks useful workers and consumers

---

* For further discussion of the dirty worker syndrome in black–white relations, see Jones (1970) and Joyce (1969).

† For a thorough history of black education, including the role of white benefactors, see Bullock (1967).

for American capitalism than it was with black liberation. Black colleges were structured not only to work within the constraints of American capitalism and racism but to reinforce their legitimacy as well.

Thus, efforts to assay the performance of black colleges in meeting their responsibilities to their community must take into account the salient conditions of the black community, the general goals toward which it tended, and the extent to which these goals challenged the dirty worker syndrome, for the effectiveness of black colleges in meeting their responsibilities depended upon the interplay of these factors. The conditions of the black community during the later decades of the nineteenth century when the first black colleges were founded were dire indeed. Blacks were largely illiterate, impoverished political subjects without political rights, whose claim to citizenship and, indeed, membership in the human family were questioned by the society in which they lived. The notion that they were inherently inferior and therefore uneducable was widely accepted. The responsibility of the black college was grounded in these abysmal conditions; it was charged with obviating them by serving as one of the primary vehicles for developing a cadre of black leaders in all walks of life who could move the community in its chosen direction. That direction, historical evidence suggests, was toward equal status within American society, although there was measurable support for the concept of an independent black society.

W. E. B. Du Bois (1942), in the light of these historical circumstances, reduced the responsibilities of the black college to the community to four basic missions. These missions, which may be utilized to assess their historical record, are:

1. Establishing the principle that higher education should be made available to blacks;
2. Defending the principle of racial equality by combatting national and international doctrines to the contrary;
3. Establishing freedom of Negro colleges to decide what they would teach and to whom it would be taught;
4. Promoting democracy and social power for black people by working for enfranchisement and gradual acquisition of political power.

On the other hand, elements from the white community moving from the dirty worker perspective had other objectives for the black college in mind. They stressed the acquisition of vocational skills at the expense of liberal education, and under their influence curricula were studiously structured to omit courses and activities that dealt realistically with the black predicament in America. The accommodationist philosophy of persons such as Booker T. Washington was warmly supported by the white community, while that of his rivals was condemned.* Every effort was made to insure that black students acquired a political consciousness that would lead them to accept their subordinate position in society. The social sciences and humanities celebrated Euro–American rather than African–Afro-American experiences. Indeed, it is reported that at one point Atlanta University, a school that leaned toward the liberation vehicle end of the continuum, was admonished to cut back on its efforts to reflect the African experience and to give more attention to "standard" European-oriented subjects (Professor Richard Barksdale, Dean of Arts and Sciences, personal communication). White opposition to black colleges as instruments for social equality was practically unanimous. In some cases, even whites teaching on black campuses demanded separate dining facilities.

Thus, one can see that the missions implied by Du Bois ran diametrically counter to the preferences of those sharing the dirty worker perspective. Recalling the inviolability of the old aphorism that the piper's patron has a disproportionate voice in tune selection, one can understand the dilemma of the colleges caught between these conflicting forces.

Nevertheless, by the mid-1950s black colleges, in spite of these constraints, had made considerable progress in satisfying the responsibilities enumerated by Du Bois. To be sure, many administrators accepted almost completely the role of dirty worker, and such administrators still exist in alarming numbers.† However, others refused to accept such a role and supported, in varying degrees, programs and policies implied in Du Bois' categories. For example, as early as 1887 Atlanta University publicly challenged dirty worker pressure (Bacote, 1969, pp. 86–102; Du Bois, 1942) and continued throughout the next several decades to support the struggle for equal rights. During the 1920s agitation on black campuses for equal rights continued (Brisbane, 1970). Similarly, the civil rights movement of the 1950s and 1960s was largely a product of the ferment on black campuses.

It is true, of course, that administrative authorities, most notably presidents, publicly opposed the involvement of their schools in the liberation struggle and expelled hundreds of black students and fired scores of faculty members for their civil rights activities.‡ However, to assess

* For a brief yet instructive discussion on this point, see Brisbane (1970, pp. 101–111).

† For a frank statement by one college president embracing his role as dirty worker, see the remarks attributed to the president of Mississippi Valley College in "Black Students Challenge the Order at Mississippi Valley State," New York Times, May 25, 1970.

‡ The author was twice so honored, being expelled as a student in 1960 and fired seven years later for his "civil rights" activities.

the efforts of the colleges solely on the disposition of their administrators is to make the mistake of saying that they, the administrators, are in fact the colleges. The college, to the contrary, is a composite of students, faculty, and administrators, with students the most important of the three. Thus, for example, in assessing the efficaciousness of, say, Southern University in Baton Rouge, the fact that students led the liberation movement there is more important than the fact that then President Felton Clark expelled 16 students for their involvement. Similarly, the contribution of Howard University lies in the fact that students struggled throughout the mid- and late 1960s to advance the cause of the black nation and not in the fact that the administration clung tenaciously to its role as dirty worker.

To say that black colleges have met the responsibilities entrusted to them at their inception is not to exonerate their contemporary successors from criticism, because the conditions under which African-Americans live have changed, the responsibilities of the colleges have changed commensurately, and black colleges have not moved to meet these new responsibilities. Instead they continue to operate according to the pre-scriptions of Du Bois' now obsolete missions. While it is impossible to say precisely when these new responsibilities evolved, it seems fair to say that by the mid-1950s the missions enumerated by Du Bois had been fulfilled, and it had become obvious that a new age had dawned.

At this juncture it is appropriate to ask exactly what happened to render obsolete the historical missions of black colleges and to usher in an era of new responsibilities. Essentially, as suggested earlier, it was the successful execution of a number of tasks implied in the earlier mission, the concomitant failure of these changes to bring about sub-stantive changes in the black predicament, the resulting heightened in-tensity of the black struggle, and the repressive response by the white nation. The new mission of the black college is grounded in the synthesis of these developments. Let us elaborate.

To begin, propositions that blacks are educable and that higher educa-tion should be made available to them have been firmly established, and doctrines of racial inferiority have been debunked (in spite of efforts to resurrect them). Impediments to the franchise and formal political participation also have been largely overcome. However, the realization of these objectives has not led to substantive changes in the lives of black people, *but rather it has demonstrated that their oppression is not an aberration in the system but an essential condition of the system itself, and that therefore accession to black demands for equal status requires radical restructuring of America's socioeconomic and political systems—a restructuring that makes demands both materially and psy-*

chologically on every American subject and that has profound implications for the role of the United States as the enforcer of European hegemony over colored peoples of the world. Both the black and white communities have begun to recognize these truths and to act accordingly. *These reactions constitute the new conditions under which the black community lives and structure the nature and content of the contemporary responsibilities of black colleges to their communities.*

The white community, both governments and individuals, has indicated that it lacks the will and resolve to restructure itself in a fashion consistent with black demands. A series of euphemisms have been coined to enshroud this development in respectability—white backlash, silent majority, reverse racism, middle American, forgotten American, and so on. In the context of black–white relations they all mean the same thing: Stop, nigger, you have gone far enough. You have become a threat to my superordinate position, and if you do not desist, I am prepared to visit severe punishment upon you, including the ultimate sanction, organized violence. As one black college president said, this climate is conducive to genocide (Jarrett, 1970). The blatant repression of black people by law enforcement agencies in places such as Chicago,° Augusta,† Orangeburg,‡ Jackson,§ Houston,|| and Detroit¶ are cases in point.

° Chicago police, according to a federal grand jury report, fired indiscriminately into quarters occupied by members of the Black Panther party killing two of the occupants. A *New York Times* editorial called it a police "shoot-in" rather than a shoot-out. See "Excerpts from Grand Jury's Report," *New York Times,* May 16, 1970; and editorial, *ibid.,* May 18, 1970.

† Police shot six unarmed black males in the back during racial disturbances in Augusta, Georgia. See "3 Augusta Victims Not Rioters?" *Atlanta Constitution,* May 18, 1970, p. 4B.

‡ Police wantonly fired into a crowd of fleeing black students on the campus of South Carolina State College in February 1967, killing 3 and injuring 27 others. Although 9 highway patrolmen were charged in the deaths, they were quickly acquitted by a jury of their peers after deliberating 90 minutes. See *New York Times,* May 28, 1968, p. 1.

§ Highway patrolmen fired indiscriminately into a crowd of black students on the Jackson State campus killing two and injuring numerous others.

|| In May 1967 Houston police fired hundreds of rounds into an occupied male dormitory before charging the building, arresting every male occupant and maliciously destroying the students' personal effects. For story and substantiating photographs, see *The Informer* (Houston, Texas), May 20, 1967; see also *New York Times,* May 18, 1967, and *Houston Post,* May 19, 1967.

¶ During racial disturbances in Detroit in May 1967, a group of black citizens were terrorized in a local motel before two were viciously slain by police authorities, who were, of course, acquitted. See "Was Justice Done in the Algiers Motel Incident?" *New York Times,* March 1, 1970, p. 10E.

The major responsibility of the black college to the larger black community in the face of these ominous developments is to interpret them to the black nation with a view to creating a universally accepted perception of the black predicament and providing a catalyst for serious discussion of the goals, both long and short term, of black people and of the most expeditious means for their realization. Of course, the colleges would continue to impart to their students specialized skills such as engineering, accounting, medicine, psychology, and so on. These skills would be imparted, however, in a different political context. Contrary to the apologists of "pure science," all knowledge is imparted in a political context, and in the United States that context is white nationalism.

How does the black college move to meet this responsiblity? It must begin by accepting the black predicament as the central concept around which everything else at the college revolves. As Du Bois argued as early as 1933 (p. 178), the Negro problem "has got to be" the center of the black college if it is to meet its responsibility to the black community. He went on (1933, p. 181):

> Starting with present conditions and using the facts and the knowledge of the present situation of American Negroes, the Negro university expands toward the possession and the conquest of all knowledge. It seeks from a beginning of the history of the Negro in America and in Africa to interpret all history; from a beginning of social development among Negro slaves and freedmen in America and Negro tribes and kingdoms in Africa, to understand the social development of all mankind in all ages. It seeks to teach modern science of matter and life from the surroundings and habits and aptitudes of American Negroes and thus lead up to understanding of life and matter in the universe.

To meet the conditions implied in Du Bois' exegesis present black colleges must radically restructure both curricular and extracurricular activities. Social sciences, humanities and the arts, and education curricula must be recast so that the beginning of all analysis is Africa and the problems of black people living in America; all other knowledge must be interpreted from that very beginning. For example, the history of African people would replace the course in Western civilization as the lodestar for historical analysis; political science courses would be concerned with acquiring and manipulating power to produce radical change, rather than with maintaining a stable commonwealth; similarly, sciences and technical subjects would be taught in a political context growing out of the problems of black people; extracurricular activities would be grounded in the experience of African people with their struggle against Euro–American exploitation being the focal point.

The products of colleges making such revisions would be radically different from present ones. Completely disabused of dirty worker inclinations, they would see clearly and understand fully the true position of blacks in American society and the prescriptive implications of that position for a normative assessment of international political movements. The incompatibility of their interest—liberation— and that of American capitalism grounded in white supremacy—exploitation—would be obvious. They would be impervious to the calls of that legion of diversionary pied pipers: black capitalism, soul power, Philadelphia Plans, poverty panaceas, and so forth. They would recognize them for what they are and act accordingly. From this new perspective a sustaining ideology would automatically flower, an ideology that would accentuate peoplehood among Africans throughout the diaspora. It would define both their allies and enemies, order their priorities, and etch in the contours of the future they envision for their progeny.

A number of black institutions have already begun to move in this direction: Malcolm X Liberation University located in Durham and Greensboro, North Carolina; The Center for Revolutionary Art and the Institute of the Black World, both based in Atlanta, Georgia; and the Center for African Education in Washington, D.C., are all moving from the perspective suggested in this paper. However, these organizations reach only a small number of black students. Black colleges, on the other hand, still train approximately one half of all blacks who enter college, including perhaps a majority of prospective primary and secondary school teachers who will serve the black community. The possibilities are enormous. Black colleges have the power to remake the political consciousness of the black student and ultimately of the black nation. That is their primary responsibility to the larger black community. If it is met, secondary responsibilities, such as working with community organizations, participating in community politics, providing staff assistance for community leaders, and so on, will take care of themselves. If the colleges do not meet their primary responsibility, their secondary involvement, as suggested earlier, will be of little consequence anyway.

REFERENCES

Bacote, C. *The story of Atlanta University*. Princeton: Princeton University Press, 1969.

Brisbane, R. H. *The black vanguard*. Valley Forge: Judson Press, 1970.

Bullock, H. A. *A history of Negro education in the South*. Cambridge: Harvard University Press, 1967.

Carson, W. *Promise or peril: The black college student in America*. New York: Norton, 1970.

Commission on Higher Education in the South. *The Negro and higher education in the South*. Atlanta: Southern Regional Education Board, 1967.

Du Bois, W. E. B. The Negro college. (1933). Reprinted in M. Weinberg (Ed.), *W. E. B. Du Bois: A reader*. New York: Harper and Row, 1970.

Du Bois, W. E. B. The cultural mission of Atlanta University. *Phylon* (1942), 3. Reprinted in M. Weinberg (Ed.), *W. E. B. Du Bois: A reader*. New York: Harper and Row, 1970.

Easton, D. The analysis political systems. In R. Macridis & B. Brown (Eds.), *Comparative politics*. Homewood, Ill.: Dorsey, 1964.

Hare, N. Behind the black college student revolt. *Ebony*, 1967, 22(August): 58–61.

Hare, N. Final reflections on a Negro college: A case study. *Negro Digest*, 1968a, 17 (March): 40–46.

Hare, N. Legacy of paternalism. *Saturday Review*, 1968b, 51(July 20): 44–45+.

Harleston, B. Higher education for the Negro. *Atlantic Monthly*, 1965, 216(November): 139–144.

Jarrett, T. Atlanta University position paper on race and violence in the United States. May 25, 1970. In *Atlanta Constitution*, May 26, 1970.

Jencks, C., & Riesman, D. The American Negro college. *Harvard Educational Review*, 1967, 37: 3–60.

Jones, M. H. The Kerner Commission: Errors and omissions. In P. Meranto (Ed.), *The Kerner Report revisited*. Urbana: University of Illinois Bulletin, June 1, 1970.

Jones, M. H. A frame of reference for black politics. In L. J. Henderson, Jr., (Ed.), *Black political life in the United States: A fist as the pendulum*. San Francisco: Chandler, 1972.

Joyce, F. Racism in the United States. In P. Long (Ed.), *The new left*. Boston: Porter Sergeant, 1969.

McWorter, G. The nature and needs of the black university. *Negro Digest*, 1968, 17(5): 4–13.

PROGRAMS AND PRACTICES FOR MINORITY
GROUP YOUTH IN HIGHER EDUCATION*

Edmund W. Gordon

In the past 10 years a great deal of publicity and attention has been given to efforts at offering expanded opportunities for higher education to members of minority groups or other disadvantaged populations. This recent movement, however, is not the first time that the attention of educators has been directed at this goal. There were some few black students in higher education even before the Civil War, and the postwar period of reconstruction included a concerted effort at making available postsecondary education for minority groups, especially blacks. As a result of the land-grant college movement and the work of certain religious groups and the Freedmen's Bureau, a number of new institutions were established, especially in the South, for the benefit of freed slaves.

These postwar colleges for the most part fell into two categories of orientation. Although most of the colleges made noble efforts to provide a thorough liberal arts education for their students, the growth and development of the institutions were made possible by the fact that they tended to be technical schools, most of them hardly comparable to the best academic high schools of the period. Preparing black students

* Reprinted, with permission, from *Barriers to Higher Education*, pp. 109–126, College Entrance Examination Board, New York, 1971.

for successful vocations was of necessity a chief concern, and this focus was encouraged also by the prevalent attitude in education that the emphasis should be on professional and technical preparation, that a liberal arts education was virtually useless amid the realities of everyday life.

A second influence on the nature of these institutions was the fact that many of them were founded by religious groups, and more had largely religious administrations and leadership—often white, and usually missionary-oriented. There were few colleges dominated by a black, intellectually oriented faculty and administration. The nature of these colleges remained largely the same throughout the late nineteenth and early twentieth centuries as more such institutions came into existence, many in the South and a few in such northern states as Ohio and Pennsylvania.

The situation began to change during the 1930s and 1940s with a rising interest in civil rights. During this time, black teachers in the public schools tended to accumulate more higher education credits than white teachers in order to make up for the salary differentials that were imposed by race. The result was a relatively large pool of blacks with postbaccalaureate training. Some of these blacks began to be attracted to the black colleges, and their presence, combined with the new concern for civil rights, created a different atmosphere on the campuses of these institutions.

A major development occurred during 1947 and 1948 with the establishment of the National Scholarship Service and Fund for Negro Students. Through this organization, some of the more prestigious white institutions joined in the search for talented black students who could be encouraged and assisted in the process of being admitted to better or higher-status institutions. Other black students found themselves doing postgraduate work in predominantly white universities as a result of the effort on the part of southern public institutions to avoid the most blatant violations of civil rights and still manage to exclude blacks from their universities; their solution was to grant tuition allowances to black students to take out of the state to other institutions where they were more welcome.

As increasing pressure was brought to bear on segregated state institutions, the response was an upgrading of black state colleges, with the creation of pseudograduate and professional schools. However, by 1950 the Supreme Court had ruled that the segregation of black students in publicly supported graduate schools was illegal, and following the 1954 public school desegregation decision, state institutions were legally on their way to being open to all regardless of race, although this principle has certainly not been implemented without opposition and violence.

The launching of the first Soviet space satellite, Sputnik I, in 1957, brought on a wave of concern for improving the national education system. The National Defense Education Act focused resources and interest on the discovery of talent and added governmental concern to that already being manifested by certain private institutions. Many more universities now began to view minority group, and especially black, communities as fruitful fields for recruiting academically promising students, and the number of black students in white institutions began to climb. As a result of this new interest, many of the traditionally black colleges were cut off from their supplies of top students. In addition, many institutions began to work toward the development of compensatory programs for their new populations of disadvantaged students. However, these colleges found themselves operating in a new area with no effective source of prior experience upon which to draw. Although the traditionally black institutions had had these kinds of concerns for years, they had been able to develop no special solutions; most had made curriculum adjustments, slowing the pace or lowering the quality of required achievement, and providing some remedial courses in the freshman year. For the most part, however, the quality of the efforts served to lend credence to the controversial criticisms of these institutions by Jencks & Riesman in the *Harvard Educational Review* (1967). There were some exceptions to this general situation, such as Morgan State College, in Baltimore, which concentrated on the development of test-taking sophistication, and Dillard University, in New Orleans, which gave attention to remedial education, reading, and language enrichment. Institutions such as Howard, Fisk, Spellman, Morehouse, and Talladega prided themselves on attracting top black students and faculty members and maintaining standards comparable to the other better institutions in the country.

However, whatever their accomplishments may have been in this area, there is little evidence that the black institutions were even consulted by the white colleges to investigate what they might have to offer. Most of the white institutions seem to have repeated the mistakes made by the black colleges earlier, especially in their assumption that traditional approaches to remedial education can provide an adequate compensatory effort. Nevertheless, the years from the late 1950s up to 1970 have been marked by increasing amounts of the same kind of effort and a rapid expansion of the movement to include more minority group and disadvantaged students in the higher education population. The drive seems to have peaked during the 1968–69 school year, when almost half of the nation's colleges and universities were making some effort to recruit and/or to provide special services for students from disadvantaged backgrounds.

Most of these colleges were using various combinations of several basic practices, some of which are designed primarily to help disadvantaged students enter college, with others used to help them succeed once they had been admitted. Many institutions have their own recruiting programs and offer substantial financial assistance for tuition and living expenses. Some offer special courses and programs prior to the freshman year to prepare students for admission. Counseling and tutoring services are made available, with personal counseling concentrating on facilitating the adjustment of the student to a new environment and academic counseling aimed at improving school skills and attitudes. Many colleges have tried special remedial courses and have offered a variety of programs to improve study skills. In some institutions special curriculum programs have been offered, and some programs provide for an extended period of time to complete degree requirements.

The rapid growth of the movement to open higher education to greater varieties of young people ran into a number of obstacles, however, which have shown themselves during the 1969–70 school year. One such problem is the very growth of the effort itself; as the number of these new students on the campuses has increased, college personnel have begun to realize that the success of educating them does not depend simply on good intentions. The complexities of the problem are being manifested in new forms every day. Many of the programs have been largely political responses to recently increased pressures from blacks and other minority groups for inclusion in all phases of the mainstream of life in the society. At this period, however, other pressures are competing insistently with the moral claims of disadvantaged groups. Money available for such innovative programs has decreased, or at least seems to be frozen at past levels; preoccupation with the war and the exploitation of the environment has occupied a good deal of the moral energy of those who might be expected to be concerned with the problem. It should be noted that some of those states that must remain particularly sensitive to the moods of their comparatively large minority populations have continued to make some progress in this direction; New York, for example, has been the scene of a good deal of effort toward devising an effective open enrollment policy for public institutions. However, the effort is tainted by the haste of political expediency, and its educational effectiveness is gravely in doubt. Even while similar political responses continue to be in evidence where they appear to be absolutely necessary, the frustrating effect of current economic priorities cannot be overestimated. Financial support for new and even many old programs and policies is simply drying up. Even if we succeed in recruiting the students and know what to do for them once they are in the colleges, if we cannot give them adequate financial support, our efforts will not stand a chance of success. And the cost of a successful effort, as we are beginning to see, will not be modest.

This brief background summary of efforts in the field to date is not intended to be encouraging. It can be seen that the more privileged, white institutions have not yet begun to contribute all that they may be expected to provide for the improvement of higher educational opportunity. One thing that should be emphasized is the fact that traditionally black institutions have made the major effort at compensatory education for minority groups over these past 100 years. Only very recently have white universities and community colleges undertaken a share in the task, and, even now, statistics on the distribution of students show that the older, black institutions still serve approximately 65 percent of black college students in four-year programs, 45 to 50 percent if the figures for two-year community college student populations are taken into account. There does appear to be some slight shift on the part of the white institutions from the mere discovery of talent toward the task of compensating for social and educational disadvantages, the *development* of talent. There seems to be a movement away from the traditional dependence on testing to greater emphasis on personal characteristics and previous pattern of social coping; from remedial education to heavier use of small-group and individual tutorials; from concern with the dispersal of students throughout the campus for the sake of integration to greater attention to minority student concern for group identification, interaction, and solidarity. There have even been some efforts toward a greater reflection of the background and ethnic identity of these new students in the curriculum and the administration of these institutions.

I say my summary is not intended to be encouraging; at this point I should be identifying those practices that have been particularly successful. Without intending to demean the considerable effort put into the many programs in the field, I am nevertheless forced to conclude that there are no generic patterns or practices that fit this description. I must note that some part of the problem may be the lack of effective evaluation efforts in the field; the closest thing to an important research work in the area has been the Clark & Plotkin (1963) follow-up of students aided by the National Scholarship Service and Fund for Negro Students, which revealed that most of the students included did successfully complete their college programs; the report made no effort to evaluate any of the educational programs or practices involved. I base most of my observations on the work of a team with which I have been involved, which has made a one-year study of programs in the area. From the results of this work it is possible to gain some impressions of the complex problems involved and even some hunches concerning the direction we should take in the future.

No aspect of the effort to include disadvantaged students in higher education has been without serious problems starting from the process of recruitment and admission. In an extension of the earlier concern with talent search practices, many institutions that have not yet served larger numbers of minority group students are simply adding those communities that do have large populations of minority group people to their recruitment circuit. Others use alumni to identify and encourage minority group students to apply. The use of the National Scholarship Service and Fund for Negro Students as a black student finding service has not been reduced in volume but has decreased in proportion. There is a growing competition among institutions for able minority students; potential recruits are wined and dined, as well as offered competitive scholarships, in a process of seduction comparable to the earlier efforts to grab off top athletes. The less prestigious or public institutions have been less concerned with traditional indices of potential and more concerned with having a large enough population of minority students to avoid accusations of racism and discrimination. All these efforts have reduced the number and quality of students available to attend those institutions that have traditionally served minority group students.

Once past the confusion of efforts and methods for obtaining a pool of disadvantaged students for the various institutions willing to accept them, one would expect that we would have a process by which the transition from high school to college could be facilitated. If an institution is determined to serve large numbers of disadvantaged and minority group young people, it must realize the futility of depending on standard testing procedures. But no institution seems to have viable alternative criteria to guide the admissions process. Most institutions claim to be concerned with the personal characteristics of students, yet our best device for ascertaining these characteristics is the personal interview and the comments of people who have known the student. With an insufficient analysis of our experience in using these criteria, we have no basis for making predictions in which we can place confidence. An alternative at the opposite extreme to selection on the basis of test scores is open admission in its many variations, a method that solves the problem by avoiding it but immediately confronts us with a variety of new problems related to placement and treatment, not to mention resources and facilities, problems for which I see no reasonable solution at hand or even on the horizon. Maybe the best that we can say is that institutions are at various stages of making up their minds about what kind of students they want and admitting them accordingly, and that there is as yet no really firm process for doing so. Most institutions seem to be superficially committed to developing heterogeneous populations as long as they are homogeneous enough to enable the institution to continue operating without significant change. Even in these institutions and systems that either have had or are moving toward open enrollment the innovation is deceptive, because even if a youngster is assured entrance into the system, he is not assured a higher education experience as it is traditionally conceived, although he may have a slightly enhanced opportunity to qualify for formal participation in this type of education. On the whole, however, we must conclude that the administrative processes of open admission, like those still prevalent in almost all higher education institutions, are still more influenced by considerations of meritocracy than those of democracy.

Since the development of academic competence is one of the common goals implicit to these efforts, one would expect that the greatest amount of activity and emphasis would be placed on changes in the collegiate curriculum that are designed to insure the success of this development for the new student population. However, it is in this area of curriculum development that it is most difficult to perceive meaningful innovation.

The developments in this area are anemic in relation to the magnitude of the problem. The most controversial and prominent change is in the area of ethnic studies, where many forces have resulted in a plethora of activities designed to append black, Puerto Rican, or chicano studies to the existing curriculum. Many of these have been hastily conceived and implemented and are likely to be a source of embarrassment to minority group students as well as to the institutions. A few institutions have responded with a general review of their curriculum content and practices with a view to revision and general improvement of the processes. These developments, of which the Thirteen College Project (Institute for Services to Education, 1969) is an example, have not been specific to the characteristics of needs of the minority group population but have focused on improved teaching in general. Where large numbers of students are involved, varieties of preparatory curriculum forms have been developed whereby this new population of students is held at bay or given special treatment until they qualify for admission to the regular program. Most institutions are moving away from earlier emphases on formal remedial courses toward the use of tutorials and independent study in attacks on specific problems. Probably the most subtle new emphasis is in the development of new degree programs that either reflect the special interests of many of these new students or represent somewhat less respectable routes to the academic credential. All of these developments, honestly or dishonestly conceived, have made some

changes in the academic opportunity structure for disadvantaged students. They have not, however, appreciably changed the quality of the
university's service to this population.

The problem that recurs in any discussion of the effort to provide
higher education for significant numbers of disadvantaged students is
the question of financial aid. The questions and pitfalls here may comprise the core problem in the area: In order to make an appreciable
increase in the number of minority group students, we will have to
see that they are sufficiently subsidized.

Earlier, scholarships, in the form of tuition grants and living stipends,
were available, although not always adequate. In addition, there was
the problem of the method of distribution of these funds to those to
whom they were granted; many minority group students came to feel
that the scholarship was little more than a new form of welfare, as
a result of the demeaning way in which the money was doled out to
them, with no effort to conceal the suspicion on the part of the institution
that these particular students probably lacked the discretion to handle
the money wisely. As the programs continue and expand, we not only
have the problem of maintaining and distributing the existing level of
support for individual students but also the problem of increasing support, since in most instances it is viewed by students as insufficient.
We must add to this the problem of a limited or even a shrinking
reservoir of money. Many of these programs were initially able to attract
support from external sources such as foundations because they were
regarded as particularly innovative; as they become institutionalized,
they must depend more heavily on the funds of the college. The utilization of institutional or public funds to support special programs is viewed
negatively by some segments of the population who see funds and resources used for this purpose as being competitive with or reductive
of resources available for the traditional populations served by these
institutions. I see no really novel solution to this problem as perceived
by those majority group members who have recently joined the upwardly
mobile population. Some people are suggesting the wide use of cooperative work–study programs, in which all students, and particularly economically disadvantaged ones, extend their period of study and divide
each school year between alternate sessions of study and remunerative
work. This model, most highly developed at Northeastern University
in Boston, shows promise so long as jobs can be found that pay well
enough to enable students to have sufficient funds to cover the alternate
periods of study.

However, we must realize that even in those instances where the
cost of higher education for the individual is modest or is completely

covered by financial assistance, the student must also consider the income loss to his economically deprived family as he is kept out of the labor market by his extended period of education. So long as the cost of higher education is viewed as a personal or private cost to be borne by the beneficiary and is not regarded as an investment by the society in the development of human potential, this problem will remain unsolved. Higher education as a societal investment must not only be free but must carry with it subsidies to meet the other responsibilities a potential student feels are his.

In addition to the problem of individual student support, however, there is the question of support for the special programs that may be involved. Here, it is important to realize that what is needed is not simply the bare minimum necessary to operate the program, but the amount necessary to give it parity of social status with other sections and departments of the university.

One of the most significant developments associated with the effort to democratize access to higher education has occurred most often without institutional sponsorship. For a long time many of us have suspected that there are noncognitive factors that are significantly associated with achievement in any sphere and particularly in higher education. Increasingly, it appears that those students who find in their college experiences islands of cultural, ethnic, or political identity and strength also find the college experience more acceptable and tend to show patterns of lower attrition. The emergence of the black cultural center, of patterns of residential assignment that maintain cultural solidarity in living arrangements, and of political and social action-oriented ethnic organizations are neither accidental nor incidental developments on the college scene. Even where they may have been political in origin they are perceived by many to serve a major pedagogical function. We have not been sufficiently sensitive to the social–psychological burden carried by the isolated minority group student who is constantly called upon to be the example, the representative, the interpreter of his culture, and the "house nigger" for his institution. We have given insufficient attention to the possible deleterious effects such pressures have on the total development of these young people. Our concern for integration has overridden a concern for the optimal development of the individual student, especially those from minority backgrounds. Fortunately, many institutions have responded positively to the message and have given support to this development. Others, frightened at the prospect of "black power" or similar bugaboos, have discouraged and resisted this development, probably unaware that their resistance served to strengthen such movements as well as to defeat the purposes of the special program.

It is not easy for an institution to react wisely to movements toward cultural nationalism. There are many pitfalls. While students from minority groups need to be able to identify with others of similar cultural background, at the same time there is need for them to be able to mingle with a variety of other students and to act within the larger group freely and significantly. The institution must do its part to maintain this delicate balance of social interaction; it must not respond to the demand for an opportunity for separatism with a system of enforced segregation. The problem is compounded by the fact that the greater and more voluble the demand for cultural nationalism, the harder it is to maintain the balance in the face of the majority group reaction to these efforts at independence. A somewhat simpler and more easily soluble problem is the availability of physical facilities for these efforts. The important need here is for the institution to be willing to provide facilities of obvious quality, comparable to those provided for other types of activities and in locations that clearly indicate that the group is as much a part of the university as any other. It may seem superfluous to make this point, but in too many schools, the hasty response to minority student pressure has been the provision of shabby facilities, as isolated as possible from the mainstream of student life. Such "other side of the tracks" treatment can only serve to further isolate and alienate the students it is so important to include.

The presence of a significant proportion of minority group adults in the teaching and administrative staffs of the university will also serve as a means of making the new kind of student feel more a part of the institution. As long as he can perceive only his difference from the staff and main student body of the college, the disadvantaged student will perceive it as an alien institution, and himself as part of an alien group, whose presence is merely tolerated. The presence of adults of his ethnic background will contribute to the student's sense that the college is his school, too, and that he has a stake in it. It should quickly be added that the efforts of these institutions to increase minority representation by quickly staffing ethnic studies programs or community centers with such personnel is not adequate to the need. Part of the problem is that these programs are already perceived as tangential. We need to have minority group faces in the chemistry laboratory, the history classroom, the psychology center. There must be a minority group presence of sufficient size and status to be regarded as a part of the main event and not as an exotic sideshow.

A great many of these problems derive from the origin of the programs we are discussing. Too often they have been spawned out of crisis situations, such as a political response to minority group pressures or as ways to fulfill the stipulations of special grants. Some institutions have begun such programs out of a desire to be up to date with what is currently fashionable in education; others undoubtedly have more genuine humanitarian concerns, for it must be conceded that the intellectual community has, at least, long had a tradition of liberal thought. No matter what the motivation, however, the majority of these programs have been poorly conceived and too hastily thrown together. Perhaps we should note as exceptions those institutions that began with the recruitment of a very few exceptionally talented minority group students and who persist in this limited practice, perhaps regarding it as the most they can do to fulfill any social responsibility they may have. These colleges are at least to be commended for caution, though their caution seems to overshadow concern for the real problem, since little in their efforts speaks specifically to the complex questions emerging in this field. Perhaps the best policy for those institutions that do feel a responsibility in the area is to conduct a searching examination of the real extent of their commitment, the kind of students they wish to serve, and the extent of their resources before proceeding to plan a program accordingly.

Once the institution has at least committed itself to the extent of establishing a special program, there are often problems of control and administration. Because the area is regarded as more political than other areas of academic concern, special project administrators and faculty may be deprived of the independence they need to work out a really effective program. The needs of these special students are too often subjugated to the political and public-relations needs of the institution as a whole.

The importance of a careful definition of the students to be served relates also to the kind of program and curriculum to be planned. A group of "disadvantaged" students may not necessarily be homogeneous simply by fact of disadvantagement. There may be many variations in the population from which students are to be drawn. Corresponding variations in the program may be needed to suit the special needs of students with different characteristics.

These areas of weakness certainly constitute a rather pessimistic picture, and this discouraging situation may be related to the essential nature of the problem at hand. For many years, higher education has served three functions: human intellectual development, professional skills development, and credentialing. In our concern for the democratization of access to higher education, the three have been greatly confused. Most of the concern for democratization has been with the credentialing function. But in response to the new pressures, many institutions have insisted that their major function is *not* credentialing but professional skills and intellectual development and that the credential cannot be separate from this.

An honest look at the history of higher education should reveal to all but the most biased that we have found ways in the past to admit and provide the collegiate credential to selected members of the population whose "qualifications"—or lack of them—have been not unlike those of the new populations we are considering, except that these former students have had some additional characteristic such as money, higher social status, strong political contacts, or athletic ability. Because of the efforts of the institutions involved, these kinds of students have received the baccalaureate degree, a necessary credential for admission to many of the more prestigious places in the societal mainstream. Many of these special cases function quite adequately, since, as Ivar Berg (1969) has pointed out, there is not necessarily a high positive relationship between the credential required for a particular career and the tasks that must be performed in that career.

Clearly, then, if we could separate out the credentialing function and universalize the opportunity for that, the problem would be simplified numerically. But we would still be faced with the problem of building intellectual and professional skills on an inadequate educational base. It is futile for the university to tackle this problem divorced from its roots in elementary and secondary education. Yet since the university *is* being called upon to provide high-level intellectual development for those students who are demanding more than a credential and who come with poor previous preparation, this very valid observation nonetheless does not relieve the university of responsibility for seeking a pedagogical solution. The educational habilitation of young adults with academically dysfunctional learning patterns is really the core of the problem. We have not yet reached that stage of pedagogical sophistication where the analysis of learning behaviors can lead to the design of formal learning experiences and the development of appropriate learning environments. These are the central aspects of the task at hand. The problem is not just a technical one. Another crucial consideration is the availability of human social interactions and opportunities for political expression that serve to motivate rather than frustrate. Solutions offered at this time do not address these aspects of the problem and will in all likelihood continue to fail for this reason. A possible reason for the failure to develop such solutions is that the problem has not been conceptualized in these ways. When these kinds of problems are brought together with the political economy of the disadvantaged individual's access to higher education, all but the most foolishly optimistic must realize that our *current* efforts are doomed to failure.

From these observations, it is possible to derive some general ideas concerning new directions for our efforts. It is clear that the question of financial resource support for students and programs is one of the most critical problems. If we do not have massive funds available for higher education and the tangential costs of income substitution for the families involved, we simply cannot talk seriously about higher education for large numbers of low-income young people. Even at the present level of commitment, many institutions are finding the effort too costly, because of the necessary special services and facilities. The current trend toward loans, while better than nothing, still does not provide an adequate answer. Many of the young people in the target populations still have to be sold on the idea of seeking a college education in the first place; they certainly can't be expected to be willing to go deeply into debt to obtain one. Given the current conservative political trend, probably the best strategy to follow is to seek broad state and federal support of institutions of higher education and students in general, without particular attention to financial need and ethnic background. If access to the institutions becomes easier for all, it will be easier for poor youngsters. When funds are available for individual assistance, they should be distributed as money to which the students are entitled, not as a dole; young people engaged in the effort to develop their talents more fully are contributing members of the labor force. Perhaps a monthly allowance would prove the best method of distribution, and the amount available should take into account obligations of family support.

A pragmatic strategy for the present political situation may be to appeal to the professed patriotism of the conservative majority by seeking expanded veterans' benefits; since minority group youth are particularly susceptible to the military draft, this move would tend to increase the higher education opportunity for one segment of the population.

All of these strategies are based on the obvious conclusion that fiscal problems currently operate to drastically limit efforts in the area and without their solution, other problems will not be soluble. However, although the financial problem is not to be solved without support at the highest levels, political realities and the moral responsibilities of higher education are such that ways must be found within the limits of current and modestly expanded budgets to begin rapid movement in this direction.

Unquestionably a problem of huge proportions is the amount of expanded facilities that will be required if we are to serve great numbers of new students who might not have been able to afford a postsecondary education previously. One solution may be to utilize community colleges to serve all students entering higher education and to transform all four-year colleges into senior colleges serving those students in their third and fourth years of post-high school study. In a sense, this proposal amounts to little more than a postponement of the problem, since it means simply extending the public secondary school education by two years and postponing the selection process; but by doing so, we could at least relieve senior colleges of the obligation to provide the first two years of this education, freeing some resources and facilities and allowing students an additional two years to make a decision concerning higher education. In the meantime, we would hope that more resources would be available for the building of more college facilities.

This suggestion is perhaps a too utopian solution in the sense that it certainly cannot be put into effect tomorrow. A more immediate approach should perhaps be simply to aim for a more equal distribution of talent and resources. If institutions are really determined to attack this problem, perhaps they should ask seriously why those colleges that supposedly offer the best education and reputedly have the best teaching talent should continue to serve only the supposedly best students. A better distribution of teaching talent and student quality would go far to equalize educational opportunity.

In addition, a work–study plan of operation can increase the number of students served immediately by any one institution in the sense that more students can be admitted to present facilities in any one year. This procedure could serve as a method of buying time for expansion as well as a method for providing support for indigent students.

The problem of college admissions procedures also suggests both long-term and short-term efforts at solution. These institutions are still interested in serving the intellectual development function and justifiably so, but we must also face the problem of democratizing the credentialing function. A decision that could be made within the individual institution is to devote half of its resources to the function of credentialing, with this half of its student body selected at random from an actively recruited, representative pool of high school graduates, and to concentrate intellectual development activities more particularly on the second half of the student body, selected after offering to potential applicants greater specificity as to the kind of student wanted; within this second group, a wider variety of characteristics might be sought, including membership in a minority group and more varied patterns of intellectual function.

This possible solution for individual colleges demonstrates that it is not necessary to move completely away from meritocratic considerations; it is possible to move both ways at once. If we were able to develop broader criteria for estimating excellence of potential, it might be possible to devise some sort of scheme whereby promising high school graduates could be assured admission to one of their top three choices of college to the extent that no more than 50 percent of available places are filled; after this point, the remaining 50 percent would be available to other students on a lottery basis, with some effort meanwhile being made to arrive at a method by which all students could enjoy some element of choice in their college assignment and be assured a high degree of quality in their educational treatment.

The rationale for this sort of compromise is the fact that there *is* a place in higher education for attention to the development of an intellectual elite, though the term may be distasteful to us; democratic values do not preclude the optimal development of available resources, and though this may not be an infallible plan for doing so, at least it provides that 50 percent of our educational facilities are devoted to the more democratic goal of credentialing for larger numbers of young people, while the other half of the facilities are used for the development of professional skills and intellectual excellence.

The problem of admissions cannot be divorced from the problem of educational planning and treatment. The principle of symmetry as advanced by James Coleman (1970), a member of the Commission on Tests, in a brief to the College Entrance Examination Board provides an appropriate conceptual frame for discussing the problem. Coleman argues that students, as well as universities, should have the benefit of rich information about each other in the mating process; the student should have as much information about the institution as the institution has about him. An extension of this principle involves the appropriate matching of the characteristics and needs of the student with the characteristics and resources of the institution. In order to serve both aspects of the principle of symmetry, data-gathering procedures associated with the admissions process must be revised. We need to have available for students making choices about institutions, as well as for administrators making choices about students, detailed information concerning commitments, strengths, weaknesses, and resources—information more detailed than that provided by commercial college guides or the typical college catalog. Even more important is the need for detailed and qualitative information descriptive of the intellectual and personal–social functioning of students—their strengths, weaknesses, and specific patterns of need to be met if their development is to be optimized.

In the area of curriculum design, there are at least three concerns that should be important influences in the drive to serve broader populations: (1) the utilization and modification of mental postures and learning patterns in inefficient or less-well-prepared young adult learners; (2) a problem faced in work with all students, the development of professional competence and expansion of intellectual development; and (3) the problem of sufficiently involving the student in the developmental task, the process of somehow bridging the gap between the student's perception of the institution as irrelevant to the concerns of his life so far, and the institution's own, sometimes overblown, notion of its own relevance for life as it is institutionally conceived.

Our earlier expressed concern with detailed, sophisticated qualitative information on the nature of the learning process in young adults who have not traditionally functioned well in academic settings could provide the data from which appropriate teaching–learning strategies can be developed. These strategies may range from shifts in the context and nature of the material to be mastered through the devising of alternate input systems for the acquisition of knowledge banks for those students who suffer from major deficits in information as well as impaired skills for acquiring it, to the design of elaborate instructional procedures that utilize sophisticated devices to monitor learner behavior in response to materials that are programmed to complement idiosyncratic patterns of affective–cognitive function.

To supplement activity at any one of these levels we will need to continue and expand what appears to be the relatively successful use of tutorials and individual work with students around their specific learning needs. Independent study centers have the advantage of not negatively identifying a student "in trouble," since they are also used for bright students who wish to supplement their regular school experience as well as for students working at a lower pace who require some kind of assistance.

As is the case in elementary and secondary schools, our focus on special populations calls attention to general inefficiencies in pedagogical practice for all students; higher education's responsibility for intellectual development requires constant work at improving curriculum. In this area, the Thirteen College Curriculum Program, directed specifically at the populations served by 13 predominantly black institutions, provides a useful model insofar as resources and time are set aside to allow college teachers to think about and work on improvement of collegiate instruction. Attention to curriculum development at the college levels is long overdue and is critical for disadvantaged students in particular, as well as being entirely appropriate to higher education in general.

I find it difficult to abandon my preoccupation with the development of strategies for directly attacking the problem of improvement of cognitive function, but I cannot be oblivious to the mounting evidence that fundamental changes in the character of cognitive function may

not be susceptible to direct attack, although derivative changes may
flow from work in the affective area, which Zigler (1963) argues is
more malleable than the cognitive. Hence, the third aspect of effort
at improvement in curriculum development is in this area we call motivation and task involvement. Here the problem is to make the relevance
of the essential aspects of the learning tasks of higher education more
apparent to the youngsters served. Information management, mastery
of knowledge, and intellectual competence and skills are not irrelevant
to real life in the society, but the society has moved to distort and
prostitute the purposes toward which these knowledges, skills, and com-
petencies are utilized. When the university becomes an accomplice in
this process of distortion, we are subverting the goals and objectives
that are fundamental to our purposes. When science is used to exploit
and victimize humanity instead of to help it, it is indeed hard to perceive
the relevance of the sciences. When economics is used to exploit,
colonize, and enslave, it becomes difficult to excite an honest student
about the study of this discipline. When I as a professor use my discipline to achieve my own personal ends and glory rather than to further
more general social goals, my students cannot be expected to respect
me or use me as a model. Many young people see in the university
a haven for the glorification of knowledge for knowledge's sake, rather
than a concern for knowledge for the service of humanity; a mecca
for the individual academic entrepreneur rather than a community for
scholars devoted to the facilitation of human development; an appendage
to the military–industrial complex committed to the continued subjuga-
tion of Third-World people. Such perceptions make difficult, if not impossible, their identification with these institutions.

When the university's resources for intellectual and professional development are made unacceptable to students because of the institution's
complicity with reactionary political or economic forces, the educational
relevance of conflicting views of the college becomes obvious. We may
win the battle of democratized access to higher education only to find
that those for whom the struggle was waged want no part of these
institutions to which we have opened the doors. As important as are
the problems of access, of even greater importance are the problems
of access to what. It is increasingly clear that the university must not
only protect the opportunity of students to express themselves through
social and political action, it must also become identified with the struggle to understand and guide the social and political development of
the society. The absence of either can interfere not only with the politico-
social development of our students, indeed, it can—by reducing or pre-
venting their involvement in the processes of higher education—preclude

their further intellectual development through the university. If the problems of the outside world make students unable to perceive the relevance of the academic disciplines, then the school must turn its attention to the outside world in order to relate these disciplines to the problems of that world and *make* itself more relevant; for we must realize that if our students perceive us as irrelevant, then we are irrelevant to their purposes. If we cannot foster and hand down our knowledge because students have no respect for us, then we have no useful function to serve for them. In this extremely critical time of social conflict and political resistance, we must see, as many of our students feel, that the university is one of the few hopes we have for fostering change; if the universities, havens of freedom and thought, choose to do nothing, they will be unattractive to increasingly large numbers of students. For many of those who continue to turn to the university and those of us faculty members who remain cloistered and insulated from the realities of a society desperately in need of intellectual and moral leadership, there is likely to be little that is alive, creative, and productive. It is well to remember that during the Nazi domination of Europe, many of the university faculties that were dominated by collaborators and the complacent became stultified and sterile; it was among those scholars who chose not to acquiesce but instead to go underground, to resist, and to help turn back the tide of social and political disaster that creative scholarship, and true relevance, flourished. The United States of America may not yet be on the way to fascism, despite the evidence that so many of our young people, and I, could easily cite, but they and our society need that the university move more actively to democratize access to its resources as well as to utilize its resources in the active defense and advancement of the democratic society.

REFERENCES

Berg, I. Rich man's qualifications for poor man's jobs: Are employers demanding too much education for the jobs they offer? *Trans-action*, 1969, 6: 45–50.

Clark, K. B., & Plotkin, L. *The Negro student at integrated colleges.* New York: National Scholarship Service and Fund for Negro Students, 1963.

Coleman, J. S. The principle of symmetry in college choice. In Commission on Tests, *Report of the commission on tests: II. Briefs.* New York: College Entrance Examination Board, 1970.

Institute for Services to Education. *Journey into discovery: The Thirteen College Curriculum Program.* Washington, D.C.: Institute for Services to Education, 1969.

Jencks, C., & Riesman, D. The American Negro college. *Harvard Educational Review,* 1967, 37: 3–60.

Zigler, E. Rigidity and social reinforcement effects in the performance of institutionalized and noninstitutionalized normal and retarded children. *Journal of Personality,* 1963, 31: 258–269.

Part IV

PUBLIC ASPECTS OF HIGHER EDUCATION

THE RATIONALE FOR FEDERAL SUPPORT FOR HIGHER EDUCATION

*Robert W. Hartman**

One of the ironies of recent years has been the concurrent development of a growing public budget for higher education and a widening chorus of people who can't see any reason at all for subsidizing it. The purpose of this paper is to summarize briefly the issues in the debate and discuss in some detail the more neglected aspects of the case.

The Case against Public Intervention

At its least subtle, the case against any form of public intervention can be made as follows:

- The only benefit of higher education is the enhanced earning power of the person who is trained.
- Those benefits accrue in the form of higher realized earnings after training, and students know this.
- Since scarce resources are used up in the training process, and since the benefits are known and will accrue to the students, there is no

* The views expressed herein should not be attributed to the trustees, officers or other staff members of The Brookings Institution.

reason not to charge full costs for the education and allow competitive markets to settle on the proper scope, extent of education, and distribution of its benefits.

No one believes in this argument exactly as stated, but it highlights some of the crucial assumptions and beliefs underlying opposition to government intervention.

THE "PROPER" ROLE OF GOVERNMENT

The first (and hidden) assumption of the above analysis is the presupposition that the government should take a passive role in the economy, unless specific reasons for intervention are adduced. More to the point, the antiintervention view derives from a belief that goods and services, including higher education, have no intrinsic merits beyond those that individuals, acting through free markets, would sustain. Government is simply a necessary evil that aids in the establishment of an environment in which such free choices can be expressed and individuals' utilities maximized. It is fair to say that almost all of modern welfare economics starts from this value position about the "proper" role of government.

There are, however, other views of the nature of the proper relation of the individual, economic goods, and the state that may lead to very different conclusions about government and higher education. These other views have found expression even in the United States.

First, there is the position that some goods are simply too important to leave their consumption to individual choice. The leadership of a democratic society may want to impose its preferences on the general public. When such goods are beneficial they are called "merit goods" (Musgrave, 1959, pp. 13–14) and when detrimental they are "illegal." (For example, in our society drugs and prostitution are goods and services whose consumption the nation does not allow to be regulated by consumer sovereignty.)

Second, economists are beginning to rediscover what political scientists and sociologists have long claimed: Society is (and should be) a collectivity possessing its own value orderings that are more than the sum of individual values. People may be willing in some cases to give up some freedoms to a government "which is charged to discover, articulate, and implement *social* priorities or collective wants" (Steiner, 1969, p. 27).

Third, although it is an accepted article of the conventional economic wisdom that redistribution of income is a legitimate concern of government, until recently economists have argued strongly that such redistribution can most efficiently be implemented through cash transfers (including a progressive tax system). Recently, however, several arguments have surfaced that suggest that redistribution through provision of *specific* goods and services may yield higher returns to society (and be more politically feasible). The argument is simply that the *donors* may not be indifferent between a cash transfer of $X and the provision of $X worth of a specific service (e.g., education) to the receiving group. If the donor group feels that it gets more utility from specific redistribution, society as a whole may be better off by adopting programs that redistribute goods and services rather than cash (Tobin, 1970).

The problem with these types of analyses is that they too easily fall into the trap of justifying every form of existing government program ("If we've got it, that proves that people prefer it that way.") What is needed is research specifically designed to elicit whether American society really does value higher education as something special, something deserving of nonmarket treatment, when all the alternatives are understood. Do people want special treatment (and are they willing to give up the resources through taxation) for just some types of education (freshman studies, law school)? For just some parts of the population (blacks, middle class)? Barring some better knowledge of the social welfare function with respect to education, it is a mistake to go either to the extreme of tacit acceptance of a passive role for government or to acceptance of what we have because it's there.

Market Imperfections

For purposes of argumentation, we accept the passive role of government and will explore reasons for intervention based on that view.

DISTRIBUTION OF INCOME AND SOCIAL MOBILITY

A laissez faire world may produce an income distribution that most regard as unfair. In that case a majority might accept government-supported social programs that promise to lead to a fairer distribution of income. "Free education" is often cited as one form of intervention that will operate to equalize incomes and thus make the distribution more fair. However, the theoretical case for equalizing incomes through increasing the amount of and equalizing access to education is not entirely unambiguous. Ignoring property income, education affects the distribution of income by changing the distribution of human capital. If the distribution of earnings can be divided up into a return on "raw labor" and a "return on human capital," the *dispersion* in earnings depends on the equality of distribution of each of these components, on the dispersion of returns in each category, on the relative importance of each in determining earnings, and on the interaction of education and such factors as native ability. As education becomes more equally distributed, opposing forces are created:

- Human capital becomes more equally distributed and this reduces variability in earnings among different people.
- Human capital, however, in which the dispersion of returns is greater than for raw labor, may become a more important determinant of income and this causes earning to become *more unequal* (Thurow, 1971, pp. 18–20).
- If education adds relatively more to the incomes of more able people, greater dispersion in income can be expected.

Thus, even the simple question of whether more education will cause the distribution of income to become less dispersed requires empirical evidence rather than *a priori* incantation. Such studies are in their infancy, and the findings are always confounded by the many other factors that affect income and are difficult to control for such things as "ability" and "motivation" (Becker, 1967; Chiswick & Mincer, 1972).

Changing the distribution of income may be a very large order for public policy to undertake; others have suggested that higher education's redistributive function may be more limited: to provide a ticket of entry to upward social mobility for children from poor or near-poor homes (Hartman, 1972; Mundel, 1971). As certification requirements for "really good" jobs in our society increasingly involve a college diploma, the chances for entry into such positions for students from cash-poor or nonsupportive homes depend on their enrollment in college. Given that their demand is likely to be less for college (they don't have sufficient role models to emulate; there are strong pressures to contribute earnings to the family as soon as possible), some public means of lowering the net price of college to such groups is necessary to encourage them to enroll.

Some empirical studies have shown that poor kids do respond to lowered prices (Hoenack, 1971; Educational Opportunity Grants Evaluation, 1971), but the statistical precision of such studies is not sufficient to allow public policy to fine-tune enrollment rates, by any means.

It is often argued by spokesmen for higher education that uniform low tuition is justified on the grounds of enhanced social mobility. But such a position has been criticized in part on the grounds that the tax system used to support low tuition takes away more from the lower-income groups than it yields them in enhanced mobility (Hansen & Weisbrod, 1969). The empirical validity of this position has been challenged (Pechman, 1970), and the outcome of this debate now seems to be twofold:

1. To know who really pays for the upward-mobility effects of higher education, one has to know which taxes would be reduced (and on whom their final burden would fall), if low-tuition policies were curtailed (Hansen & Weisbrod, 1971).
2. Mobility cannot be given a dollar price in any conventional way; one has to evaluate separately the mobility consequences and the tax consequences before netting one out against the other (Hartman, 1970, 1972).

Thus, in designing public programs for the encouragment of upward mobility, public funds should be targetted on those whose demand for higher education is likely to be low as a result of cultural or environmental circumstance. In the present state of knowledge, the clearest case can be made for families with low income, especially minorities. Research on the effectiveness of education for the upward mobility of such groups needs to be undertaken, using, wherever possible, longitudinal data, so that characteristics of real people can be studied, rather than devoting research resources to squeezing information out of aggregated cross-sectional data.

CAPITAL AND INSURANCE MARKET IMPERFECTIONS

In a society where slavery is prohibited, capital markets to support investment in education are necessarily limited. The free market in advanced societies provides capital for the businessman who wants to purchase a machine to enhance his firm's productivity or to the household that wishes to invest in a home. In each case the object of the investment can serve as collateral for the debt or as an asset behind the equity capital. The skills acquired by people in higher education cannot be so pledged to the providers of capital. The formation of human capital thus must overcome a special barrier—the failure of a capital market to develop to facilitate investment.

The importance of this barrier for public policy has been expressed in two different ways:

1. Some students see inequality of opportunity as arising from this source. Even if *demand* for higher education is equal for youngsters from all income classes (not unequal for lower classes, as argued above), the *supply* of funds for higher education would be unequal. Children from high-income families can benefit from their parents' ability to provide their own funds or to borrow

on their behalf, while students from low-income homes face much higher charges in the absence of a special market for human capital. Thus, equal opportunity can be served by the provision of a capital market that equalizes the supply curve of funds to all comers (Becker, 1967).

2. Forgetting equal opportunity and about who benefits or loses from the human capital market barrier, the efficient allocation of resources requires that marginal returns from all investment activities be equalized. Especially if one stresses the independence (of his family) of the college student, this implies that a capital market for all forms of human capital for all students be made equal to markets provided for physical capital, so that returns in the two sectors can be equalized (Zacharias *et al.*, 1967).

The public policy implications of these two views differ somewhat. In both cases, there is a case to be made for the government to intervene by acting as guarantor of educational loans; in this way, the government substitutes for the inability to repossess human capital. However, if one stresses the first view of capital market barriers—that it discriminates against poor families—a case can be made for limiting the governmentally aided loans to students from low-income families, perhaps through direct provision of such loans and/or regulation of eligibility (as in the National Defense Student Loan program). Under the second view, such limitations on eligibility are unwarranted: Anyone should be able to take advantage of the government *guarantee*. But in neither case is it necessary or justified for the government loans to be subsidized; interest rates should be left to the market once the government guarantee is in place. Similarly, there is no reason for the government to impose an artificially short repayment term designed to discourage borrowers (Hartman, 1971, Chapters 5 and 6).

Some rethinking of present educational loan policies is in order. We have to be clear about what goals are being served, whose needs are intended to be filled, whether control over beneficiaries is desirable, and what role below-market interest rates play. Present programs compromise on all these issues.

Risk to Borrowers

The federal government has gone a long way in providing more access to capital for higher education than would have existed without intervention. All the federally aided programs, however, (with the exception of a new program at Harvard University), are straight debt—the borrowers contract for fixed repayments after they leave school. Straight debt still does not quite put education investment on a par with physical capital. In the business sector, an investor can pool risks by spreading his funds over several firms; indeed, the corporation itself is a way for investors, with limited liability, to pool risks. Even in the household investment sector, a family can insure itself against certain types of risks (e.g., fire insurance on a home). Higher education, viewed as an investment, certainly gives rise to an *a priori* need for risk pooling: The variation in rates of return is enormous. In principle, therefore, a market for insurance against low payoffs from education makes sense, and we can expect underinvestment in higher education until such markets are provided (Hirshleifer, 1966, p. 275; Nerlove, 1972).

Risk to Lenders

There are essentially two ways to provide insurance against low payoffs from higher education. The most straightforward is to offer "policies" that would subsidize those whose future incomes are low by charging "premiums" to those whose returns from education are high. There are two major obstacles to private, profit-making insurance firms entering this business. First is the problem of *moral hazard:* The purchaser of the insurance can so regulate his activity (by not working hard and thus earning a low income) as to avoid paying the premium. Second, and a more severe roadblock, is the possibility of *adverse selection:* The group of people choosing to insure themselves will turn out to be preponderantly "losers," and high-earners will stay away from the program. Faced with this possible outcome, private insurance markets would tend to be selective, trying to limit policies to "good risks" or risk-rating students. (Yale University is bearing the risk of adverse selection in its Tuition Postponement Program—not the banks who are lending to Yale.)

The absence of a private market for low-income insurance parallels the pre-Medicare status of the aged population: Any older person could buy private health insurance—provided he didn't get sick. In that instance, the risks were socialized by the introduction of a public program. A similar case can be made for public provision for low-income insurance for higher education loans. Instead of charging premiums to borrowers, the government could absorb the risks of low returns from higher education out of general tax revenues (Rivlin *et al.*, 1969, pp. 65, 70). Harvard University has taken a small step in this direction by agreeing to repay the student loans of its borrowers whose lifetime earnings are low (Harvard, 1972). But a very few institutions have the wherewithal to make such a promise, and some have argued that low-income insurance is primarily a governmental function (Johnstone & Dresch, 1971).

Much more needs to be known about how large a deterrent to higher education is the absence of a private insurance market. Even given the need for insurance, there are different degrees of it that can be offered (Dresch & Goldberg, 1972). The case for government-sponsored experimentation is very strong.

EXTERNAL BENEFITS

Another market imperfection that may require government intervention in higher education is the presence of external (to the student) benefits. Under certain circumstances it can be shown that if higher education creates benefits (pecuniary or nonpecuniary) that society values, but that the individual student does not receive or values less than society, some subsidy to the student may be required to insure the socially optimum level of investment in higher education. The opposite is also possible—that higher education creates benefits for individuals that exceed the social gain—and in that case some form of tax on higher education would be needed for optimal investment levels to be realized.

Very little empirical evidence exists on external benefits. Economists who analyze public policy toward higher education have shown an increasing tendency to regard the absence of good, hard quantified data in this area as indirect evidence that no such benefits exist (Friedman, 1968). This may be more a reflection of the deficiencies in the economists' education or the narrowness of their perspective: Some things in this world cannot be quantified. Howard Bowen (1970) compared the external gains of higher education to love, a phenomenon known to exist but never measured. While it is easy to deride such a claim as "special interest pleading"—it is often just that—the derision hardly constitutes counterproof.

Changes in Values and Attitudes

The greatest difficulty in evaluating the external benefits of higher education arises in the area of the alleged changes in values and attitudes caused by higher education. Educators, especially humanists, see higher education's major role as aiding in the creation of more "cultured" people, in Matthew Arnold's (1867, p. 55) definition of the term ("increased sweetness, increased light, increased life, increased sympathy"). To the humanist, sweetness and light is what higher education is all about. And there is little question that many parts of a typical college curriculum ("the liberal arts") cannot be explained as serving any other purpose than such cultural enrichment.

Not only humanists or special pleaders for higher education place great emphasis on cultural payoffs to higher education: A recent survey of the 1950 graduating class of 74 different colleges asked respondents to indicate the areas in which they were "influenced or benefited" by college. Alumni response listed: critical thinking (73 percent said they were influenced "very much" or "quite a bit"); philosophy, culture, literary appreciation (62–63 percent); tolerance (56 percent); vocational training (42 percent). Students from 88 colleges, participating in the same survey, placed even greater emphasis on tolerance (80 percent) and on learning about other philosophies and cultures (69 percent) and even less emphasis on vocational training (40 percent) (UCLA Center for the Study of Evaluation, 1971).

Given that resources are used up in culture transmission, the questions for public policy are:

1. Is the signal heard? Do people really change their attitudes and values as a result of higher education?
2. Who benefits from such changed culture? Society in general? Is anybody hurt?
3. What is greater sweetness and light worth to the public at large?
4. Do we really need subsidies for greater culture, or is it a joint product of training that will be bought anyway? (See "The Need for Subsidies When Externalities Are Present," pp. 283–285.)

The Effects of the College Experience. Does college make a difference in the values and orientation of students? Research on this subject has recently been reviewed (Gurin, 1971; Berls, 1969; Feldman & Newcomb, 1969), and a brief summary will suffice here.

Students who matriculate and persist in higher education do come out as different people, and these differences continue in later life. But the data and research design of the studies do not permit one to feel very confident that these changes are produced by the college experience (as opposed to merely reflecting the socialization of students into changing values for all of society), nor to feel certain that the students in whom changes have been observed were not predisposed to such changes to begin with (that may be why they went to college in the first place, while their apparently "equal" contemporaries did not) (Gurin, 1971).

Given these caveats, highly educated students seem to show a greater openness, less prejudice, less tendency toward dogmatism; are more humanitarian and kind; and are somewhat less likely to believe that violence is necessary to produce change (Gurin, 1971, p. 28; Withey, 1971, p. 93) than others who did not attend college. Very little is known, however, about what aspects of the college experience produce these changes.

Is Attitude Change an Externality? If Jones "gets culture," what's in it for Smith? This is a key question in developing the argument for public support for higher education; it is not an easy question to answer. First, it may depend on who Jones is (was). If he suffered from the "lower-class" values and attitudes toward time and gratification as described by Banfield (1970), few would deny that Smith would benefit if Jones were to be transformed through higher education. (Smith would be willing, therefore, to pay part of Jones' educational bill.) But if Jones is merely changed in the sense that he now prefers Scotch to beer, foreign movies to bowling, opera to rock, the externalities depend on who Smith is! If he is a Scotch-drinking, movie and opera fan, he may benefit from the new Jones. If he is a migrant farmer, he couldn't care less (and wouldn't be willing to pay a nickel in taxes to support Jones' education).*

In short, there is no conclusive way to demonstrate whether such higher education attributes as attitude change benefit society as a whole or a few other educated people. Perhaps this can be demonstrated best by reporting a conversation between two university professors discussing just this subject:

> PROFESSOR A: What you are saying is that you would like to see more college graduates so that a larger part of the population will turn out to be like you. If you want that, "give to the college of your choice," but don't foist your tastes on the taxpayer. He's not sure he wants more of you.
>
> PROFESSOR B: Well put. When I went to college in the 1950s I was forced to read a 1946 essay by George Orwell. Two sentences in it ran as follows: "Thus political language has to consist largely of euphemism, question-begging and sheer cloudy vagueness. Defenceless villages are bombarded from the air, the inhabitants driven out into the countryside, the cattle machine-gunned, the huts set on fire with incendiary bullets: this is called *pacification*" (Orwell, 1946, p. 173). You are telling me that when I want more people to be exposed to such sentences in college, I do so only for selfish purposes? That the taxpayer has nothing to gain from a populace that listens to its political leaders through Orwell's ear? That I am selling a phony bill of goods? Nonsense.

It is hard for me to see how this debate can be resolved. But it is not trivial and the fact that no conclusions are reached on precisely who benefits from cultural externalities is not evidence that the claim is malarkey.

---

* It has been pointed out that attitude changes might result in Jones' voting for candidates who would be sympathetic to migrant farmers. The temptation is great to recall the story of the man who fed the horses so the birds could eat better. But it is conceivable that migrant farmers would be willing to subsidize Jones under these circumstances.

The Value of Cultural Externalities. Given that higher education induces higher cultural standards that are valued by the public at large, how much is it worth to them? This question is particularly difficult to resolve because "culture" has the character of a "pure public good": Once it is produced, "everyone" gets the benefit of it, and if I consume a little more of it, you don't have to consume a little less (Samuelson, 1954). Pure public goods cannot be traded in markets and priced, so we cannot get an objective measure of the marginal worth of the good. Thus, some other valuation procedure is required, in the same way that the value of national defense must be determined by nonmarket means. Although much work has gone into devising ideal voting procedures for valuing public goods (Johansen, 1965, Chapter 6), no feasible ideal has been discovered. In fact, when one takes into account the possibility that the current distribution of income (which may affect voter preferences) is not ideal, it may be impossible to define what the characteristics of an optimum would be (Aaron & McGuire, 1971).

In this country we leave these valuation decisions to the normal legislative process. That process can approach the ideal, whatever it may be, only if legislators are well informed as to what is happening with tax dollars and what the public thinks, and if the legislative process provides adequately for real choice to be exercised.

The federal government has a special role here in aiding colleges to modernize their budgeting and information systems (Newman *et al.*, 1971), strengthening the administrative capability of institutions (through such programs as the Higher Education Act, Title III, and especially Title V, part E) and rationalizing the federal budgetary process (for example, by providing for forward funding of student aid programs).

Other External Benefits

We have given first place in the discussion of externalities to attitude change and cultural enrichment because these are often slighted by quantitative researchers. Other external benefits that may be less important to alumni and students may be more amenable to quantitative analysis.*

Political Leadership. All of society benefits from the willingness of some people to exercise leadership roles in local, state, and national communities. There is plenty of evidence that college affects the willingness of people to play these roles (Withey, 1971, pp. 82–83). The social value of the increment in political leadership that we get from the last

* For a more comprehensive list of external benefits, see Bowen, 1971.

dollar of public subsidy to higher education is much more difficult to assess.

Learning at Home. There is some evidence that college-educated women may be better able to prepare their children for school. To the extent that society will bear the costs of public school education anyway, there is at least the possibility that subsidization of women college students may be a cheaper way to educate children than pouring resources into public schools to compensate for deficiencies in the home environment (Schultz, 1972). Research on this matter has yet to produce any conclusive evidence either way (Nerlove, 1972; Michael, 1972; Dugan, 1969).

Improving the Inflation–Unemployment Tradeoff. College-educated people enjoy unemployment rates well below the average (Manpower Report of the President, 1972). If their college training makes their labor market skills more adaptable (National Research Council, 1965), a case can be made that this should be considered an externality. While the individual benefits from a lower risk of unemployment, all of society benefits as well; the prospects for full employment without price inflation are enhanced whenever the labor force becomes more adaptable. Just as we support manpower retraining programs, the U.S. Employment Service, and antidiscrimination programs in labor and industry to shift the Phillips curve, so might we support higher education. To my knowledge, comparative studies of alternative methods of improving the inflation–unemployment tradeoff that analyze more support for higher education as a policy option have not yet been undertaken. Such a study would have to grapple with recent theoretical studies that deny that there is any long-term tradeoff between unemployment and inflation (Phelps, 1970; but see Tobin, 1972).

Interdependencies among Factors of Production. When Jones completes college, all the evidence seems to indicate that his wage rises. But the increment in his wage is not necessarily the full measure of the contribution of Jones' education to national productivity. Most studies of aggregate production functions show that the productivity of physical capital, for example, is enhanced when the labor force acquires more skills. This factor is often disregarded as being of second-order importance or as not unique to higher education investment. A recent study by Thurow estimates that "approximately 78 percent of the total gross returns [addition to GNP] to a 1 percent increase in the supply of educated labor will show up as increases in the returns to physical capital or as increases in the returns to uneducated labor"

(Thurow, 1971, p. 8). While this study cannot be regarded as definitive (no one has yet successfully estimated an aggregate production function that explicitly shows the returns to different categories of labor), it does suggest a fruitful field for further research and an important policy reminder. (Most existing studies of the returns from higher education *assume* that the observed average increases in wages of college-trained manpower accurately measures the marginal contribution to productivity. It may not.)

At the opposite pole from studies that claim wage differentials understate the productivity gains induced by higher education are those that claim earnings increases overstate the social economic benefit. One study (Taubman & Wales, in press) concludes that as much as half of the gain in earnings is attributable to a monopoly return to college-educated workers, not a real productivity gain. The monopoly return arises because college training is used by firms as a "screening device" to exclude less highly trained workers from high-paying occupations. If such workers were not excluded, they would drive down the wage of the high-paying occupations. Much more work could be done in pursuing the relation of job requirements and education.

Research. The case for public support of research is discussed at length elsewhere (Kaysen, 1969). The basic argument is that the production of new knowledge yields returns that cannot usually be captured by the person making the discovery. Thus, if society wishes to encourage new knowledge production it must support research directly.

In the field of educational research, an especially strong case can be made for federal support, even though the federal government is not the major source of funds to education in general. Educational services in this country are predominantly provided by not-for-profit organizations, in which the incentive to innovate is small. Moreover, the typical firm (decision unit) in the education industry is often too small to support a research program of any magnitude. Thus, research in general, and in education specifically, is universally recognized as an appropriate area for federal involvement. The federal budget shows the effects of this commitment (Special Analyses of the Budget of the U.S. Government, Fiscal Year 1973, 1972, Appendix R).

The Need for Subsidies When Externalities Are Present

The mere existence of external effects of higher education is not sufficient to make the case for public subsidies. First of all, higher education may produce large and valuable external benefits in the aggregate, but if the marginal external benefit is small, the case for subsidy is weak.

Second, to the extent that institutions would be willing to provide externality-producing activities and students would be willing to engage in such activities *without subsidy*, society can gain the externalities (get a "free ride") without intervention. Such a "free ride" would come about, for example, if (a) many students are now receiving a pure rent from higher education subsidies and would be willing to attend, persist, and take the same courses even if full costs were charged to them; and (b) institutions would offer the same package of courses in an environment where courses were priced at cost and sold to buyers. In this case, the externalities of higher education would be jointly produced with the private benefits, and society at large would lose nothing from abandoning subsidies.

The study of the effects of subsidies on the process of education is in a prenatal state. The recent financial difficulties of colleges offer some chance to observe what happens when funds are cut back, which may be indicative of how institutions would react to a fully market-oriented higher education world. The evidence seems to be that neither research nor the core of what most people would regard as a liberal arts education—the parts of the educational process that would seem most likely to produce externalities of the various types discussed above—is what institutions cut back on (Inner City Fund, no date). However, these short-run responses are dominated by budget exigencies and may not reflect long-run responses. In fact, some of the short-run responses—reducing teaching loads in the face of greater financial pressures—seem positively perverse (Cheit, 1971, pp. 83–90; Columbia Research Associates, 1971).

Only fragmentary evidence is available on how students would react to a withdrawal of subsidies. One interesting piece of evidence is the reported responses of Educational Opportunity Grant recipients in private universities to the question of what they would have done had they not received the subsidy. While a fairly small percentage would not have enrolled (24 percent), a very large number (51 percent) claim they would have attended other, presumably cheaper, schools (Educational Opportunity Grants Evaluation, 1971, p. 96). Cheaper institutions, by casual observation, tend to be more vocationally oriented and least supportive of the liberal arts.

While it is a near-certainty that some students would not change their educational behavior at all if subsidies were withdrawn, there is no evidence that this reaction would be, by any count, universal. And while many institutions may react in the short run to loss of outside support in seemingly educationally irrelevant ways, there is no evidence to support "business as usual" if large-scale, long-term withdrawals of third-party payments occurred. We do not know whether subsidies are necessary to support the externalities of higher education.

Sharing the Governmental Burden: The Federal Role

Most of the writing by economists in the public finance of higher education field has treated "the government" as one unit and drawn policy inferences for whatever particular level of government the study was addressed to. The federal nature of the support system has been all but ignored. In part this is due to the nonapplicability of orthodox economic theorizing to our present system of financing.

Orthodox public finance theory has two contributions to make to the question of what level of government should shoulder what burden:

1. *Spillovers.* If external benefits of higher education exist, and if the external gains can be divided geographically, the subsidies should be granted by the different governmental levels in proportion to the gains accruing in each geographic region (Break, 1967). Thus, if 1 unit of freshman studies for a white, low-income male in West Virginia yields 3 units of benefit to West Virginians and 7 units to non–West Virginians over and above the private gains, the state of West Virginia should contribute 30 percent of whatever subsidy is granted.

The nonrelevance of this analysis is due to our inability to measure external benefits, much less to identify their spatial incidence. (As indicated above, some people have compared the external benefits of higher education to "love." The correlate here is "Love, your magic spell is everywhere.") Some studies have attempted to measure external benefits of education by studying migration patterns of former students and observing their incomes and tax payments to establish whether the particular units of government are recouping their investment (Weisbrod, 1964). But where one lives has no necessary relation to the locus of the external benefits; one's income has no necessary relation to the external benefits one creates; and one's tax payments are irrelevant to rational government policy. (If governments tried to maximize the excess of tax receipts over subsidies, they would give preference to those with the highest marginal tax rates: the very rich!) Some analysts have used the very high mobility of people with graduate and professional training as an indicator of the need for federal subsidization of such studies, for example, in medical training (Fein & Weber, 1971). But these studies rarely (never, to my knowledge) demonstrate who enjoys the external benefits of such training, which would be necessary to make the analysis correspond to the theory.

2. *Redistribution.* It is simple to demonstrate that a variety of distor-

tions will be introduced into the economy when lesser (state or local) goverments undertake redistributive programs. If nothing else, such policies may cause the concentration of people of similar circumstances. (Welfare-eligibles move to New York City and others move out). Moreover, states with the greatest need for redistributive policies are least fiscally able to cope with the problem. (Among all states, Mississippi's government has the weakest fiscal capacity to grant aid to poor Mississippians.) Thus, redistributing income or redistributing access to higher education towards low-income groups should be a national responsibility, with the necessary aid being provided from Washington.

The trouble with this particular point is that we are not starting from scratch in financing higher education. If we were, it would be quite clear that a sensible structure for higher education financing would have the federal government emphasizing equalization programs with the states assigned such tasks as supplementary student aid (for high-cost states or institutions) and a major role as innovators or providers of lighthouse institutions. History has not worked out that way; the federal government cannot ignore the states' choice to directly provide higher education to the masses through low-charge public institutions. This has created a higher education market with private institutions put at an ever-growing disadvantage as their charges grow more rapidly than state-supported low tuition.

The federal government has been responsive to the growing difficulties in the private sector, as is shown in the overrepresentation of private institutions in the major Office of Education student-aid programs. Recent attempts to introduce a more rational, fairer, national student aid program were distorted by Congress, at least in part on the basis that it would not provide the differential aid required by the private sector. Similarly, the move toward giving special benefit to small institutions of higher education (predominantly private) in the institutional aid title of the 1972 higher education legislation was a reflection of the recognition of private education's needs (Hartman, 1972b). These compromises would make little sense in a rational policy world, but given the irrationality of state finance practices, such programs have considerable political appeal.

The analytical work in public policy required in this field is to uncover alternative ways by which the federal government can induce states to change their financing policies so that the joint action of state and federal policies attain the governments' objectives. On these grounds we need further analysis of whether the federal government should require states to put forth at least a minimum level of effort in support of higher education in order to benefit from federal programs (Carnegie

Commission on Higher Education, 1971), whether the federal government's matching of state scholarship support programs might be a more effective instrument (Education Amendments of 1972) or whether federal institutional aid programs can be designed to give incentives for state financial reform (Kirschling & Postweiler, 1971), etc.

The role of the federal government here is that of providing incentives for state governments to pursue better systems of support. Given the size of state support programs, such an emphasis may be more effective than federal programs that try directly to achieve governmental objectives. It also may not be. In any event, it is important not to ignore the existence and possible transformations of state support policies in assessing the federal role.

Other Institutional Justifications

The preceding discussion of federal incentives for state financial reform has brought this review out of the realm of the "optimal system" of federal support and into the fuzzier world of "second best." (Given some barrier to perfection, what is the best policy in a second-best world?) Two other cases where federal support may be justified because of institutional factors are in the areas of research and manpower.

RESEARCH

The section on externalities dealt with governmental support of research. The obvious way to support research is directly: The government should buy research services of people and firms who do research. In principle, such research support need have nothing to do with instruction or with educational institutions.

Suppose, however, that research and teaching are complementary activities, in the sense that a little more instructional activity produces a little *more* research, and vice versa. Some educators have claimed that such would be the case for a faculty member who was spending all his time doing one thing. For example, the full-time teacher might do better (equals "more") teaching were he to do some research. The research institute scribbler might do more effective research were he to spend some time teaching (Nerlove, 1972). If this were so, a government interested in investing in research (to insure that its externalities are realized) might find it advantageous to subsidize instruction in some instances. Moreover, institutions that are organized to take advantage of such complementarities (universities) become a proper object of governmental concern (Bowen, 1971).

To some extent the government recognizes complementarities by awarding indirect cost allowances on government research contracts that, in part, are actually used for support of instructional activities (Mundel, 1971). But it is not entirely clear that this is the best method to encourage complementarities to develop.

The whole area of the relationship between research and teaching and its implications for federal support is underresearched. So is the question of which institutional configuration results in the best research for the government dollar. (All universities? Teaching separate from research? Necessary size of a department for efficient research?) Until these questions are resolved, at least some weight should be given to the claims of complementarity and of the need to support the university-type institution.

MANPOWER

The American economy allocates college-trained manpower to occupations mainly through movements in relative wages. When shortages develop in a field, wages rise, and students respond to such changes by choosing major fields. The system works amazingly well (Freeman, 1971).

In two instances, however, the government may wish to intervene in the normal market process. First, sometimes there is reason to believe that (a) the market response would be very slow (for example, if the shortage field is a new one, and academic departments are not organized to train new entrants), and (b) the social cost of a slow adjustment process may be very high. Second, in some cases the government itself may be the major employer; it may be cheaper to train (or pay for the training of) people in the desired field than to change compensation rates and wait for the applicants to appear.

A large number of federal programs can potentially be justified on these grounds: all the fellowships in specific fields, training grants, and the like. A major difficulty with this class of programs is that no accountability system is built into them, and programs have a tendency to take on a life of their own, beyond any reasonable period of shortage.

Special manpower needs are a legitimate area for government intervention. But the primary system for allocating people to occupations should be the free labor market. Special manpower programs should be subjected to initial and continuing evaluation and comparison to market alternatives.

Evaluating the Case against Public Intervention

Standing against the long list of mainly theoretical reasons for public intervention is a long list of well-documented demonstrations that the private return on higher education is about equal to the private return on business investment in the United States. Without compelling demonstrations of the importance of the barriers, imperfections, and externalities outlined in this paper, many have argued that sound policy should involve a move toward withdrawal of public subsidies. (See Schultz, 1971, for a good summary of the evidence.)

But the empirical evidence on private returns is not quite as convincing as its producers would have us believe.

- Most of the studies use single-period, cross-section data: They base rate of return estimates on the earning experiences of different people at a point in time, while policy prescriptions demand that we know what would happen to a given cohort of people over time. Thus, cross-sectional analysis can be misleading. (See Taubman & Wales for one of the few longitudinal studies.)
- Earnings are much too narrow a definition of even private benefits. These should include at a minimum the nonpecuniary benefits of occupations that higher education allows one to enter and the consumption benefits of the college years themselves. In addition, the data need correction for the different amounts of leisure enjoyed by people of different educational attainments, as well as the more obvious ability–race–sex–region corrections. Although some of these corrections have been made in all studies, there is no body of data rich enough to permit all confounding variables to be controlled simultaneously.
- Empirical studies rarely make explicit the aggregate production function relationships that must be assumed (or can be inferred from the returns studies). Some investigators have expressed doubt that the education return studies are consistent with the aggregative studies (Thurow, 1972).

Conclusion

Policies cannot wait for all the returns to come in. Fortunately, there are good *a priori* reasons for and no empirical evidence against at least the following policy thrusts:

- Toward targeting existing subsidies at both federal and state levels on low-income students
- Toward encouraging research and innovation in higher education
- Toward building a healthier higher education industry by encouraging moves toward relative prices that reflect relative costs and by improving management

All of these goals can be pursued as the various claims for greater public intervention are sorted out, tested, experimented with, and studied. Answers to some of the questions may never be available to policy makers. But that does not mean that they should dismiss requests for support for lack of proof; it means they must learn to live with risk and uncertainty.

ACKNOWLEDGMENTS

This paper was originally prepared for the Office of Program Planning and Evaluation, U.S. Office of Education. It was intended to be, used as a background paper in response to questions about the rationale of the federal higher education budget posed by the Office of Management and Budget.

Helpful comments on an earlier draft of this paper were given by Henry Aaron, Robert Berls, Sal Corrallo, Bruce Johnstone, Robert Reischauer, and Paul Taubman.

REFERENCES

Aaron, H., & McGuire, M. *Public goods and income distribution*. Washington, D.C.: The Brookings Institution, 1971 (Reprint No. 202).

Arnold, M. Sweetness and light. In M. Arnold, *Four essays on life and letters*. New York: Appleton-Century-Crofts, 1947 (Originally published, 1867).

Banfield, E. *The unheavenly city*. Boston: Little Brown, 1970.

Becker, G. S. *Human capital and the personal distribution of income: An analytic approach*. Ann Arbor: University of Michigan Press, 1967.

Berls, R. H. An exploration of the determinants of effectiveness in higher education. *The economics and financing of higher education in the United States*. Submitted to the Joint Economic Committee, U.S. Congress. 91st Congress, 1st session, 1969.

Bowen, H. R. Speech given at a Conference on Higher Education sponsored by the American College Testing Program, Washington, D.C., February 1970.

Bowen, H. R. Finance and the aims of American higher education. In M. D. Orwig (Ed.), *Financing higher education: Alternatives for the federal government*. Iowa City: American College Testing Program, 1971.

Break, G. *Intergovernmental fiscal relations in the United States*. Washington, D.C.: The Brookings Institution, 1967.

Carnegie Commission on Higher Education. *The Capitol and the campus*. New York: McGraw-Hill, 1971.

Cheit, E. *The new depression in higher education*. New York: McGraw-Hill, 1971.

Chiswick, B. R., & Mincer, J. Time-series changes in personal income inequality in the United States from 1939, with projections to 1985. *Journal of Political Economy*, 1972, 80(3, Pt. 2): S34–S71.

Columbia Research Associates. *The cost of college*. Prepared for the Office of Program Planning and Evaluation, U.S. Office of Education. Cambridge, 1971.

Dresch, S. P., & Goldberg, R. D. Variable term loans for higher education—Analytics and empirics. *Annals of Economic and Social Measurement*, 1972, 1: 59–92.

Dugan, D. The impact of parental and educational investments upon student achievement. In J. Froomkin & D. Dugan (Eds.), *Inequality: Studies in elementary and secondary education*. Washington, D.C.: U.S. Office of Education, Office of Program Planning and Evaluation, 1969 (Planning Paper 69-2).

Education Amendments of 1972. P.L. 92-318.

Educational Opportunity Grants Evaluation. *The federal educational opportunity grants program: A status report, fiscal year 1970.* Prepared for the Office of Program Planning and Evaluation, U.S. Office of Education. New York: Bureau of Applied Social Research, 1971.

Fein, R., & Weber, G. *Financing medical education.* New York: McGraw-Hill. 1971.

Feldman, K. A., & Newcomb, T. M. *The impact of college on students.* San Francisco: Jossey-Bass, 1969.

Freeman, R. B. *The market for college-trained manpower: A study in the economics of career choice.* Cambridge: Harvard University Press, 1971.

Friedman, M. The higher schooling in America. *The Public Interest,* 1968, 3(11): 108–112.

Gurin, G. The impact of the college experience. In S. B. Withey (Ed.), *A degree and what else?* New York: McGraw-Hill, 1971.

Hansen, W. L., & Weisbrod, B. A. *Benefits, costs and finance of public higher education.* Chicago: Markham, 1969.

Hansen, W. L., & Weisbrod, B. A. On the distribution of costs and benefits of public higher education: Reply. *The Journal of Human Resources,* 1971, 6(3): 363–374.

Hartman, R. W. Comment on the Pechman–Hansen–Weisbrod controversy. *The Journal of Human Resources,* 1970, 5(4): 519–523.

Hartman, R. W. *Credit for college.* New York: McGraw-Hill, 1971.

Hartman, R. W. Equity implications of state tuition policy and student loans. *Journal of Political Economy,* 1972a, 80(3, Pt. 2): S142–S171.

Hartman, R. W. *Higher education subsidies: An analysis of selected programs in current legislation.* Washington, D.C.: The Brookings Institution, 1972b (Reprint No. 247).

Harvard University Press release, Jan. 28, 1972.

Hirshleifer, J. Investment decision under uncertainty: Applications of the state-preference approach. *Quarterly Journal of Economics,* 1966, 80(6): 252–277.

Hoenack, S. A. The efficient allocation of subsidies to college students. *The American Economic Review,* 1971, 61(3, Pt. 1): 302–311.

Inner City Fund. The effects of alternative federal operating subsidies on institutions of higher education: A preliminary report to the Assistant Secretary for Planning and Evaluation, U.S. Department of Health, Education, and Welfare. (Mimeo, no date)

Johansen, L. *Public economics.* Amsterdam: North-Holland, 1965.

Johnstone, D. B., & Dresch, S. P. *Income contingent loans for higher education.* New York: The Ford Foundation, 1971.

Kaysen, C. *The higher learning, the universities, and the public.* Princeton: Princeton University Press, 1969.

Kirschling, W., & Postweiler, R. *General institutional assistance: A scheme that depends on the educational efforts of the states and the attendance choice of students.* Boulder: Western Interstate Commission for Higher Education, 1971.

Michael, R. The role of education in production within the household. Submitted to the National Center for Educational Research and Development, Washington, D.C., 1972.

Mundel, D. S. Federal aid to higher education and the poor. Unpublished doctoral dissertation, MIT, 1971.

Musgrave, R. *The theory of public finance.* New York: McGraw-Hill, 1959.

National Research Council. *Profiles of PH.D.'s in the sciences, summary report on follow-up of doctorate cohorts 1935–60.* Washington, D.C.: National Academy of Sciences, 1965.

Nerlove, M. On tuition and the costs of higher education: Prolegomena to a conceptual framework. *Journal of Political Economy,* 1972, 80(3, Pt. 2): S178–S218.

Newman, F., *et al. Report on higher education.* Washington, D.C.: U.S. Department of Health, Education, and Welfare, 1971.

Orwell, G. Politics and the English language. In *A collection of essays by George Orwell.* New York: Doubleday (Anchor Books), 1954 (Originally published, 1946).

Pace, C. R., & Milne, M. College graduates: Highlights from a nationwide survey. *UCLA Evaluation Comment,* 1971, 3(2): 1–7.

Pechman, J. A. The distributional effects of public higher education in California. *The Journal of Human Resources,* 1970, 5(3): 361–370.

Phelps, E. (Ed.). *Microeconomic foundations of employment and inflation theory.* New York: Norton, 1970.

Rivlin, A., *et al. Toward a long-range plan for federal financial support for higher education.* Washington, D.C.: U.S. Department of Health, Education, and Welfare, 1969.

Samuelson, P. A. The pure theory of public expenditure. *The Review of Economics and Statistics,* 1954, 36(4): 387–389.

Schultz, T. W. *Investment in human capital: The role of education and of research.* New York: Free Press, 1971.

Schultz, T. W. Woman's new economic commandments. *Bulletin of the Atomic Scientists,* 1972, 28(2): 29–32.

Special analyses of the budget of the U.S. government, fiscal year 1973. Washington, D.C.: U.S. Government Printing Office, 1972.

Steiner, P. *Public expenditure budgeting.* Washington, D.C.: The Brookings Institution, 1969.

Taubman, P. J., & Wales, T. Education as an investment and a screening device. New York: National Bureau of Economic Research, in press.

Thurow, L. Measuring the economic benefits of education. Berkeley: Carnegie Commission on Higher Education, 1971. (Mimeo)

Tobin, J. On limiting the domain of inequality. *The Journal of Law and Economics,* 1970, 13(2): 263–278.

Tobin, J. Inflation and unemployment. *The American Economic Review,* 1972, 62(1): 1–18.

U.S. Department of Labor. *Manpower Report of the President.* Washington, D.C.: Government Printing Office, 1972.

Weisbrod, B. A. *External benefits of public education: An economic analysis.* Princeton: Princeton University Press, 1964.

Withey, S. B. Some effects on life-style. In S. B. Withey (Ed.), *A degree and what else?* New York: McGraw-Hill, 1971.

Zacharias, J. R., *et al.* The panel on educational innovation to the U.S. Commissioner of Education, the Director of the National Science Foundation, and the Office of Science and Technology, *The educational opportunity rank.* Washington, D.C.: U.S. Government Printing Office, 1967.

WHOSE EDUCATION SHOULD SOCIETY SUPPORT?

The Appropriate and Effective Bases for Social Support for and Intervention in Undergraduate Education*

David S. Mundel

The Role of Government in the Higher Education Sector of a Free Society

The proper role of governments in all societies is to provide programs and promote policies that maximize the social welfare of their constituents. Actions are taken to balance the results of individual decisions—by a bureau, a profit-making firm, a not-for-profit organization, a family, or an individual, each working for his own private welfare.

In some societies, the freedom of individuals to promote their own welfare is of little social value in comparison to the output or consumption of certain goods and services. In such cases, "proper" government policies would increase the production of these valued outputs but lower individual freedom. In other societies,† "proper" government policies

---

* This paper deals solely with undergraduate, postsecondary education. Although it is clear that undergraduate and graduate education interact through a diverse system of resource flows, these interactions are ignored.

† These "other" societies may even be societies at different stages of development. For example, many underdeveloped countries have limited individual freedoms in their efforts to stimulate economic and social development and have later removed or lessened these limitations after development has progressed.

are aimed at protecting individual freedoms—even at the expense of some decline in output. The American society values individual freedom highly and has an established free private exchange economy. Thus, the government's proper role is to insure the free operation of the exchange marketplaces and to establish them where exchange or transaction is *desired* by constituents but where traditional modes are either impractical or inappropriate if *freedom* (in a broad sense) is to be maintained.*

Government interventions, including those in higher education, should be based on the existence of (a) public goods and social benefits, (b) externalities, and (c) market imperfections. (Higher education possesses no "sacred attributes," although the religious proclamations of its advocates might, if taken at face value, lead one to think otherwise.) Various objectives are present within each of these rationales for federal aid to, or intervention in, higher education, which makes the development of an appropriate and effective higher education policy a complex and difficult problem.

In order to develop a basis for federal higher education policy, one must combine the following components:

1. A thorough analysis of the interaction of each federal program (and each set of programs) and behaviors within the higher education system
2. A comparative weighting (or valuation) system that measures the social value of each of the objectives
3. A thorough analysis of the impact of non–higher education policies on these same government objectives†

Developing the components themselves is beyond the scope of our current understanding of either government objectives or the impact of most government policies. The approach taken in this paper is to examine, in detail, the justifications for federal aid to higher education and attempt to develop an overall framework within which policy alternatives may be tested. These guidelines will outline an appropriate and effective pattern of undergraduate higher education subsidies among individuals from different economic backgrounds. A student's family economic position is crucial for two fundamental reasons: First, family income is a discriminator that governments have found relatively easy

---

* Included in these latter nonmarketable transactions are those by which government establishes and maintains a desired income distribution.

† For example, an important government objective served by higher education might be crime prevention, but in order to see if a higher education policy is justified for this purpose, one must compare it with alternative crime prevention policies or programs—e.g., street lighting.

to use. Second, family income appears to be a key attribute in locating students and potential students whose educations are most socially productive.

Government support or subsidy programs that treat different individuals differently have two bases, both resulting from the role of government in the maximization of social welfare: Some individuals may produce more of the benefits that are desired by the society at large. For example, public welfare programs support poor families rather than rich ones on the premise that changing the economic position of the former produces more social benefits than changes in the latter. Also, to efficiently stimulate the production of social benefits, government should avoid paying for public benefits that would have been produced in the absence of such payments. For example, government health programs subsidize, and thus increase, the care available to poor families as opposed to rich ones, not because the health of the poor is more socially beneficial than that of the rich, but because subsidizing the latter will simply cut their costs and not improve their health.

Analytically, this reasoning leads to two general guidelines for the evaluation of higher education policy alternatives (Mundel, 1971, pp. 96–97):

1. All else being equal,* the individuals whose education provides the larger marginal social welfare should receive the larger subsidies (or fractional price cuts) in order to maximize the social welfare resulting from the "aid to education" budget.
2. All else being equal, the individuals whose price elasticity for education is greater (i.e., whose amount of education is changed the most, given a price cut or subsidy) should receive higher rates of subsidy.†

This paper will deal solely with the first of these guidelines.‡

Whose Education Produces Which Socially Desired Outcomes?

Public Goods and Social Benefits

The categories of public goods and social benefits that may result from higher education and thus provide possible grounds for social sup-

---

* In this and subsequent contexts, "all else being equal" refers to the other criteria that affect the subsidy distribution guidelines.

† If different individuals pay different prices, this guideline is based on "price elasticity to price ratios," rather than on "price elasticity" alone (Mundel, 1971, pp. 222ff.).

‡ The second is dealt with extensively in Mundel (1971).

port include knowledge; economic growth; political, social, and economic system behaviors; geographic mobility; social and economic mobility; and intergenerational benefits.

The first two categories seem to have little, if anything, to do with the income level or socioeconomic status (SES) of the individual educated. The value of a particular piece of knowledge or the spillover economic growth benefits of a particular technological advance are not determined by the educated individual's family. The likelihood of a person's education resulting in creative activities that lead to these benefits may, however, be partially a function of his family, as well as the type of education acquired.* Some families may stress creative behaviors and risk taking in the upbringing of their children; others may encourage their children to perform strictly according to the rules and to avoid "rocking the boat." Hypothetically, one would assume that children brought up in the former, rather than the latter, mode would tend to be more creative and, when educated, to produce more of the public benefits resulting from knowledge and the resulting economic growth. There appears to be little hard information about the distribution of these family socialization styles among various family types.

This lack of data, however, does not strongly influence the development of support rules regarding undergraduate education: First, undergraduate education probably has considerably less impact on the type of benefits under consideration than graduate-level education. Therefore, interest in creativity benefits should lead to graduate-level support forms rather than to development of undergraduate mechanisms. Second, the predictability of eventual creativity is probably minimal; almost any conceivable subsidy instrument aimed at producing these benefits would be so blunt that its impact would, in all likelihood, be limited. A more effective set of policies would reward behaviors that create these benefits rather than subsidize training to develop persons who may be creative. Improving the patent process, supporting research and development efforts, and subsidizing creative artists are examples of policies that fall within this more desirable set.

A second source of national income–economic growth public benefits is probably more affected by undergraduate education. These result

---

* Although this is the first mention of type of education, it does not mean that all education is equally valued from the social welfare point of view. Little is known about the social benefits resulting from the education of different types of people, but even less is known about those resulting from various types or kinds of higher education. Wherever possible, an attempt will be made to develop a theoretical view of these later effects, but the reader should be readvised about the concentration on the differential treatment of different individuals within this analysis.

when the improvement of one productive input—labor, in the case of higher education—increases the productivity of other inputs—e.g., capital—within the economy. Although this relationship is relatively easy to conceptualize, making it specific enough to yield insights regarding higher education policy is somewhat more difficult. If education is a good measure of labor quality, and average labor quality is the determinant of productivity gains by other inputs, the increases in education would be equally valued regardless of who received them and at what level they were received. This would lead to the decision rule: If all else is equal, all individuals should receive the same subsidy per unit of education acquired. If, on the other hand, these external benefits decline as the level of education (or level of achievement, etc.) increases, the lower levels of education should be more highly subsidized. The reverse may also be true. Knowledge of these relationships might help develop rules for the subsidization of various levels of education, but they do not (by themselves) lead to social evaluations of education that depend on the family background of the student. If, however, the distribution of human capital* among college eligibiles is nonrandom with respect to family characteristics, the society may wish to use family background characteristics as subsidy criteria, even though they have little causal relationship to the desired social output.† For example, if the marginal social output decreases with increasing quality of labor, and college eligibles from low-income families tend to have less human capital, higher subsidies to lower-income youth (all else being equal) are justified. As the distribution of human capital among high school graduates became more random (compensatory elementary and secondary education programs are aimed at accomplishing this), the justification for this differential subsidy would decline. If this social or public output of human capital exhibits increasing marginal returns, then higher subsidies should go to higher-income youth.

The public benefits from the third category of higher education-changed behaviors—*political, social, and economic system behaviors*—are probably small and thus should not have a major impact on our choice of governmental higher education policies, though one reason for considering these impacts at the college and university level may exist: The increased complexity of a society demands more highly edu-

---

* Human capital can be considered to be that stock of attributes from which the flow of labor services results. The greater the stock, the larger the *potential* flow.

† Using a correlated attribute rather than the one that is the causal factor would make the policy instrument less than optimal, as some losses—due to misspecification—will occur. The higher the correlation, the lower these losses will be.

cated individuals to participate in public policy making. The electorate itself needs to be more educated—but probably not to the full college level. Interest groups within the electorate need even more highly educated spokesmen and leaders, for they provide important public benefits to the groups they represent. These benefits decline rapidly as more of the leaders or more of the interest group become educated. But in general, the smaller the number (or proportion?) of a group's members who are college educated, the larger the public benefit created by an additional graduate or enrollee. On these grounds, and the basis that college enrollment increases with income, higher education subsidies should vary inversely with income.

The fourth public benefit rationale for federal government intervention in higher education is the geographic mobility of educated individuals. If educated individuals produce localized public benefits but are highly mobile, it has been argued that local (or less than national) jurisdictions would tend to undersupport education. Thus if mobility increases with level of education, higher levels would tend to be undersupported to a higher degree than lower levels of education. If localized benefits also increase with education, the effect of this undersupport will be significant. On the whole, both of these hypotheses seem to be true. Numerous census studies have shown geographic mobility to increase with education, especially at higher levels of education. Most studies of local benefits (Hansen & Weisbrod, 1969; Lelong & Mann, 1968), especially at the state level, have looked, at least implicitly, at the tax yields resulting from college-educated individuals.* If local tax receipts are elastic with respect to income, and college education has high income rates-of-return, the undersupport caused by mobility will create significant losses. The most appropriate instrument for correcting these effects might be the federal establishment of an exchange marketplace through which payments flow from net importers of college-educated manpower to net exporters. If certain groups of graduates are the principal source of these benefits—e.g., teachers—this market might be established solely for these groups.† Without such a market, federal higher education support might be justified to bring about the properly increased level of college and university training.

Locally received benefits that vary either according to the student

* The argument regarding the appropriate definition of public benefits resulting from tax payments is outlined in Mundel, 1971, pp. 66–71.

† Although this "market" appears idealistic to most observers, a similar one actually exists in Great Britain. Several local education authorities operate teacher education institutions (both two-year and four-year schools), and the national government operates an exchange system in which local authorities contribute a set level of funds for each teacher they hire who was trained elsewhere. These contributions are allocated, in turn, among the authorities that trained the teachers.

who acquires the education or the type of education acquired justify differential subsidy amounts on social benefit grounds. Some observers have argued that local social benefits are proportional to an individual's income or ability. For example, if the marginal local social benefit of a college graduate is an increasing function of his ability, higher subsidies for higher-ability students may be justified.

Most studies of income changes have found income gains resulting from college to increase with ability, although the pattern is not as strong as the "ability liturgy" would have one believe.

Using 1949 Census data, Becker (1964) estimated the overall rate of return of a college education to be approximately 13 percent with approximately one quarter of this return (3 percent) based on the ability difference between college enrollees and nonenrollee high school graduates. If the returns among college students vary on the basis of ability in the same ratio as those between enrollees and nonenrollees, a differential subsidy on the order of 1:1.3 between upper- and lower-ability groups might be justified. If ability (or achievement) is highly correlated with family background, then differential subsidies of the same order of magnitude among students from different income families might be found if discrimination on the basis of ability were being attempted.

The fifth category of public benefits results from the social and economic mobility stimulated by higher education. Studies have shown that more education generally produces more income: Daniere & Mechling (1970) show high present value of college education to individuals from all ability groups; Becker's estimate of 13 percent rate of return is equally relevant here. A more thorough and recent study based on 1960 Census data, performed by Giora Hanoch (1965), shows the income effect of education—especially higher education—to be sizable. Depending on the other variables held constant, Hanoch finds the annual earning effect of completing college (i.e., 16 years of education) to be between $2,857 and $1,886 (1965, Table 1, pp. 24–25). (The latter estimate was calculated by holding occupation and industry fixed, which tends to ignore the labor market mobility that higher education enables.*)

The public benefits of income redistribution may not be simply a function of private income gains. If they were, public support for all private behaviors that produce income gains—e.g., personal investing in stocks and bonds or corporate acquisition of capital equipment—might be justified. Most public redistribution benefits arise from giving income—in kind or in money—to individuals and families who are, or, in the case of redistribution of income-producing wealth, would be,

---

* Thus, the Hanoch estimates of income gains are overcorrected or underestimates of the actual income effects.

poor. The public benefits are the welfare increases among taxpayers that result from the increases in income or income-related position of the recipients. In general, these benefits rise with the recipients' rising subsidized income (although the marginal benefits probably decrease) and decrease with increasing presubsidy income. In trying to evaluate redistributive benefits, higher education support programs can be considered to provide either subsidies to families whose children are enrolled in college or subsidies to individuals who are, themselves, enrolled.

Interpreting educational support as family subsidies requires either that public benefits result from changing the economic position of students' families or that the family be an important source of encouragement for student investment in public-benefit-producing education. If the latter is true, society, in its search to acquire these benefits, should create a system that rewards highly motivating families. Using change in economic position of students' families as the grounds for subsidization, subsidies should increase as family income decreases, if social benefits result predominantly from improving the position of the poor.

Some critics may argue that society is interested in improving the economic position of low-income families regardless of whether their children are enrolled in college. In that case, higher education subsidies ought not to be treated as family subsidies, and family income, by itself, should not be a basis for differential educational subsidies.*

If higher education support is considered a subsidy to individuals and is aimed at producing income-redistribution benefits, the recipients' presubsidy economic position must be examined. The relevant measure of this position is neither the current income of students who are not full-time participants in the labor market nor the incomes of high school graduates who did not go on to college; it is the expected income of subsidy recipients if they do not receive subsidies and do not enroll in college. Becker (1964) found that approximately one quarter of the 13 percent rate of return (about 3 percent) of college education could be attributed to student ability. Thus, in the absence of higher education, college graduates would tend to earn more than other high school gradu-

---

* A complication arises if government cannot be a perfect discriminator in the distribution of aid to students: Student subsidies create family income benefits for families who would have been willing to send their children to school in the absence of subsidies or who would be willing to pay more than the subsidy rules demand. Most feasible government policies will probably treat large classes of individuals similarly (e.g., all students from families with $4,000 annual incomes will receive a $1,000 grant), assuming perfect discrimination among students or their families is therefore clearly inadequate. Thus, family-income benefits must be considered for all policies, even if these are not the primary aim of the policy instruments.

TABLE 1. Estimated Expected Earnings for
College Graduates Had They Not
Attended College, 1969[a]

Age	Race and region	Expected "noncollege" earnings
27	Whites, North	$ 8,543
	Whites, South	7,456
	Nonwhites, North	5,783
	Nonwhites, South	3,643
37	Whites, North	12,091
	Whites, South	11,048
	Nonwhites, North	7,700
	Nonwhites, South	5,299
47	Whites, North	13,028
	Whites, South	11,932
	Nonwhites, North	7,828
	Nonwhites, South	5,339

[a] Source: Mundel, 1972.

ates. But without government subsidies, many potential students would still invest heavily in education. Thus, the income effect of the subsidies would tend to be less than the total difference between current college and high school graduate incomes. Table 1 shows an estimate for the "noncollege" earnings of 1959 college graduates calculated from Hanoch (1965).

If these estimates are accurate* and the public benefits of redistributing income decrease as recipient preredistribution income increases, there seems to be little justification for subsidizing higher education in order to produce these public benefits. The presubsidy incomes of almost all recipients would exceed virtually every commonly stated poverty line, even if no education were acquired, in the absence of subsidies. But Table 1 shows only average income levels, whereas the distribution of incomes of individuals within any of the age–race–region categories may include some incomes that fall below some "poverty lines." If the income distributions for each race–region group vary around the average values in the same way (i.e., equal standard deviations), the lower

* These income-earning data are average values and not the marginal value faced by the additional nonenrollees. It should be strongly noted that any major program or social event—e.g., a significant decline in the college-going rate—would change the income distribution and incomes of both college and noncollege educated workers. Thus, these estimates are somewhat less than accurate, although given the small likelihood of major events and the sizable gap between these estimates and most "poverty lines," the estimates are adequate for our interpretation.

the expected value, the higher the percentage of individuals of a particular group falling below a specified poverty line. Thus, the redistribution benefits would increase as one moves from subsidizing white, North; to white, South; to nonwhite, North; to nonwhite, South. This order would create a pattern of higher subsidies for lower-income students.

There may also be important distributional grounds for the support of higher education that do not specifically involve redistributions of income or income-producing wealth: If higher education stimulates greater social and economic mobility, and if public or external benefits result from this mobility, then social support for higher education may be justified. The second hypothesis, like most concerning nontechnical social benefits, is difficult to prove. The first is more easily "proven," but its correctness is still a subject of much debate.

Social and economic (or status) mobility has long been an important focus of commentary on American society. Some reviewers have called this claimed mobility the "great American myth"; others find ample evidence for Horatio Alger's climb to success. Whatever the case, the privately received benefits of upward mobility are relatively easy to conceptualize. Getting ahead and improving one's economic position confers large and important benefits on whoever does so. The publicly derived benefits (or costs) of mobility are more difficult to envision, let alone measure.

One source of these might simply be the existence of interdependent individual welfare functions. People may derive benefits from observing the mobility of others, for example. These benefits may also be negative. For example, if A's welfare position is a function of his economic position relative to that of B, B's upward mobility decreases A's relative position. Thus, the external benefits for A would be negative. In somewhat more concrete terms, the wealthy may experience losses if the children of the poor, as a result of education, can compete with their own offspring. It is difficult to specify the direction of impact of mobility on these individual welfare functions. Without any firm analytical basis, I would assume that upward mobility produces positive public benefits, and the level of these benefits varies inversely with the original position of the mobile individual's family.

Most studies of the American economy have found intergenerational mobility to be minimal.* In general, these studies support the hypotheses that both parental position and human capital combine to define an individual's social and economic position (Jackson & Crockett, Jr., 1964). Blau & Duncan's study, *The American Occupational Structure* (1967), is probably the most complete recent review of mobility. They find

---

* This observation, of course, is purely in the eyes of the beholder.

that college graduates are most likely to experience high upward mobility and the least likely to experience any downward status movement (p. 499). The data show that the proportion of men who experience some upward mobility increases steadily with education, while the proportion that is immobile (i.e., stable) declines steadily. Downward mobility does not, however, decline linearly with education. Men who have some, but not four, years of college are more likely to be downwardly mobile than those who either have less or more years of education. This pattern is important in the design of a mobility stimulation policy because a policy might encourage enrollments without causing greater numbers of individuals to complete four years of college. Based on Blau & Duncan, such a policy would create both a small increase in upward mobility and a large increase in downward mobility.

Critics of mobility studies have generally found the independent effects of education to be significantly less than those presented by Blau & Duncan. They argue correctly that parental position is an important factor in determining the amount and quality of education acquired by an individual; thus, the impact of education on mobility illustrated by them is an overestimate of the independent effects of education alone. They also argue that mobility studies have generally misspecified occupational status, which lead to overestimations of whatever mobility exists and of the impacts of education.

The effect of these criticisms on a mobility-stimulating higher eduction policy is complex. The finding that family position affects education, and thus that independent mobility effects of education are lower than observed, should cause one to switch resources from education to other mobility-creating efforts. The relative allocations within education—among education at levels and family types—may remain constant. If the strength of the critics' finding is so great as to show no influence of education on mobility, then supporting education on mobility grounds is clearly unjustifiable. In all likelihood, education (and increasingly higher education) is a necessary—although not sufficient—condition for upward mobility of youth from lower-income and lower-status backgrounds. If this mobility creates externally received benefits, and the remaining conditions that allow mobility are met (e.g., ending discriminatory labor market barriers), the education of these youth ought to be subsidized.

There are other public benefits. Wohlstetter & Coleman (1970, pp. 19–20) argue that

> The growth of the non-white middle class and of a class of high level managers, professionals, or entrepreneurs who make, say, $26,000 or more might be directly associated with the economic improvement of other non-whites—

through savings and investment, by helping to build information networks, and through key positions of influence that affect entry, promotion, and profit in higher-paying occupations.

Although directed only toward developing an upper class of non-whites, this same argument may hold for other economically disadvantaged groups. In general, the incremental public benefits resulting from educating a youth from a particular group would decrease (although remain positive) as more of the group became educated. On these grounds, public or group subsidies should decline as both group income and unsubsidized enrollment increases.

Public or external benefits may also result from stimulating mobility to deter socially costly behaviors—e.g., crime. As urbanization and access to information increase, individuals have a greater knowledge of the opportunities that surround them, and this increased awareness may make them more dissatisfied if a large share of the opportunities remain inaccessible. Some theorists view blocked goal attainment as a major cause of delinquency and criminal behaviors: Nearly all youth are exposed to and internalize the goals of educational attainment and resulting economic and social success, but some are less able to achieve these goals (Schaefer & Polk, 1967, p. 226). If this is a result of family or other conditions beyond the youth's influence, and if he is able to attribute the cause of some of these conditions to society at large—e.g., a black youth may correctly attribute part of his family's poverty to discriminatory practices by the white majority—it is easy to understand how his lack of educational opportunities might result in antisocial behavior. Furthermore, if high school is predominantly designed to prepare an individual for college, and college is thought to be unavailable, then high school becomes irrelevant. Publicly required participation in an irrelevant exercise may be a source of motivation toward delinquent behaviors (Schaefer & Polk, 1967, p. 232). The public policy maker must ask, "How significant are these goal attainment–delinquent mechanisms?" Table 2 shows the college plans and eventual college attendance of high school students by family income.

Society might wish to avoid crime and other socially costly behaviors resulting, in part, from a failure to achieve individually desired economic and social mobility by stimulating increased mobility. This might take the form of increasing attributes that allow mobility (e.g., education) or removing discriminatory barriers (racial- and class-oriented discrimination) that inhibit mobility. Mobility-oriented higher education policies would, on the basis of the above analysis of their benefits, give higher subsidies to individuals from lower-class—generally lower-income—family backgrounds.

TABLE 2. College Plans and College Attendance of High
School Seniors (October 1965)

Family income	Percent responding "yes" for planning college[a]	Percent having attended college by February 1967[b]	Percent of college goals unachieved
Under $3,000	46	17.2	63
$3,000–4,999	47	31.7	33
$5,000–7,499	58	36.8	37
$7,500 and over	71	56.8	20

[a] Unpublished tabulation by A. J. Jaffe & W. Adams of a Bureau of
Census Study, quoted in Froomkin, 1970, p. 20.

[b] Computed from Tables 3 and 8, *Current Population Reports*, 1969.

The fifth type of public benefits are intergenerational: the impact
of current education on future generations of "publics" and families
and the freedom of youth now. The impact on future generations is
twofold. First, current education buys an income distribution for future
publics. But, as argued earlier, the benefits of this type resulting from
higher education are probably slight. Second, current education influences future upward mobility by creating an infrastructure that benefits
future generations. As discussed above, these benefits would justify
higher subsidization of youth from lower-enrollment-rate (e.g., low-
income) groups.

The second and more important source of intergenerational benefits
concerns the protection of the freedom of youth. Parental support plays
an important role in higher education finance, and individuals growing
up in families who don't value education or whose income is limited
have restricted access to educational support. This limits their free choice
among colleges or between college and nonschool alternatives. Public
intervention may thus be justified, and this justification increases as the
limitation becomes more "crucial" to the individual's eventual condition.
On these grounds, intervention aimed at improving health or nutrition
would be highly valued, while that oriented to providing colored television sets would be less so. Support for education falls more nearly at
the former end of this spectrum. The resource constraints imposed on
students from lower-income families are graphically illustrated by the
amounts of parental support received (Table 3).

Additional factors may also influence the amount of family resources
available to potential college students. Holding income constant, larger
families would tend to have smaller available per student support levels
(Lansing *et al.*, 1959, p. 80).

TABLE 3. Net Parent Support of
College Students[a] (1966–67)

Family income	Average support
<$ 4,000	$ 349
$ 4,000– 6,000	610
$ 6,000– 8,000	664
$ 8,000– 10,000	719
$10,000– 15,000	895
$15,000– 20,000	1,167
$20,000– 25,000	1,531
$25,000– 30,000	1,696
>$30,000	1,740

[a] Social Security and tax expenditure subsidies are controlled. Source: Mundel & Zeckhauser, 1971.

In general, we observe that lower-income and larger-size families devote fewer financial resources to the college education of their children. This pattern of assistance is not the result of any decisions made by these children. Thus, shielding them from the influence of this pattern would increase their free, individual control over their futures. A higher education policy aimed at insuring or increasing this freedom would give subsidies declining with increasing family income and increasing with increasing family size.

Table 4 summarizes the public good and social benefits effects of subsidies to higher education.

EXTERNALITIES

The following categories of externalities or external effects are often noted as justifications for social policy for higher education:

1. Lower welfare and transfer program costs
2. Lower crime and crime prevention costs
3. Increased tax yields
4. External effects among students within the educational process itself

Most *welfare and transfer programs* are based on society's desire to raise the standard of living of families and individuals whose income is at the lower end of the income distribution. The costs of these programs can be lowered by either decreasing the number of these families and individuals whose incomes fall below "poverty line" for particular transfer programs or by decreasing the amounts of support received

TABLE 4. SUMMARY OF PUBLIC GOOD AND SOCIAL BENEFIT EFFECTS

Category of benefits	Strength of impact by undergraduate education	Recommended subsidy distribution (decision rules based on marginal social benefits)	Is family income actual (or correlated) factor?	Comments
Knowledge	slight	higher income higher subsidy	correlation with creativity	
Economic growth	slight	lower income higher subsidy	?	
Political, social, and economic system behaviors	slight +	lower income higher subsidy	correlation with low-enrollment rate	declines rapidly as enrollment increases
Geographic mobility	slight	higher income higher subsidy	correlation with ability	higher education support is blunt—improper instrument for this goal
Social and economic mobility				
Income redistribution	slight	lower income higher subsidy	yes (?)	income redistributed to moderate- and higher-income levels
Mobility redistribution	major	lower income higher subsidy	yes	probably most important effect
Intergenerational benefits				
Income effects	slight	lower income higher subsidy	yes	income redistributed to moderate- and higher-income levels
Protection effects	sizable	lower income higher subsidy	yes	capital availabilities might be al most as influential as subsidies

by eligibles by narrowing the gap between their incomes and the eligibility limits. Higher education adds significantly to the incomes of individuals who would have had above-poverty incomes without college or university education. Higher education does, however, have some slight impact on the incidence of poverty-level incomes.

Two factors must be carefully evaluated in order to develop subsidization guidelines in this respect. First, if the decrease in the probability of poverty of the college enrollee is matched by an increase in the probability that a nonenrollee will experience poverty, no cost saving can be achieved; the transfer payments will be simply redirected, because, on the margin, college-educated individuals simply fill positions in the labor market that would have been filled by nonenrollees ("labor market bumping"). Second, one must evaluate which individuals are more likely to experience poverty in the absence of higher education. If there are significant economic returns to ability, higher-ability individuals would be less likely to experience poverty than lower-ability ones, with both groups simply high school graduates. Thus, the higher education of lower-ability youth is more likely to yield reductions in transfer program costs, and their education should be more highly subsidized than that of higher-ability youth. Because of family wealth, economic returns of "style," and the inculcation of certain attitudes toward or tastes for work and earning a living, youths from higher-SES families may be less likely to experience later poverty than lower-SES students at equal, noncollege levels of education. If this is so, the higher education of poor youths should be more highly subsidized, assuming transfer program cost avoidance is the socially sought objective. On balance, these two factors and the minimum poverty-lessening effects of higher education—if "labor market bumping" does not occur—lead to a slight justification of higher education subsidization with greater subsidies going to lower-ability and lower-SES youths.

The *reduction of crime and the costs of crime prevention* is a second source of external effects. Crime data are notoriously bad, and the impact of education in general—to say nothing about a particular level of education—on criminal behaviors and the comparative impact of alternative prevention strategies is poorly understood. Little analytical thought, beyond that presented above in the discussion of social and economic mobility effects, can be added to the understanding of crime prevention goals through higher education support. In all likelihood, the efficiency of crime prevention through increased enrollment in higher education is so low compared with other strategies that justifying support for higher education on these grounds is inappropriate and incorrect.

The third and most frequently mentioned category of external effects is the *increased tax yields* (and the increased output of public goods and services they finance) resulting from the greater incomes of college-educated individuals. These effects are not as easy to specify, let alone measure, as most studies that concentrate on them would lead one to believe. They depend on the impact of higher education on the educated individual (Do his tax payments increase?); the impact of higher education on the labor market and thus the income distribution of the society as a whole (Do total tax payments increase?); and on the underlying philosophical basis of the tax system itself ("ability to pay" vs. "benefit" taxation).

Higher education undoubtedly increases an individual's income and thus the level of his income tax payments. An estimate of this effect can be derived by combining data on tax payments by income level (Gillespie, 1965, p. 135) with Hanoch's data on income changes resulting from higher education. This combination (Mundel, 1971, pp. 43–46) results in the following assessment of college-induced tax payment changes (Table 5).

Table 5 appears to be accurate, although the negative changes in tax payments that appear in the state and local taxes are somewhat disturbing. These may result from the distribution of taxpayers among state and local tax jurisdictions in Gillespie's 1960 sample. Although

TABLE 5. CHANGES IN TAX PAYMENTS DUE TO COLLEGE EDUCATION (1959) CORRECTED ESTIMATES

Age	Race and region	Changes in tax payments			
		Federal		State and local	Total taxes
		Individual income tax	Total		
27	Whites, North	$ 41.87	$ 18.24	−$ 11.34	$ 6.90
	Whites, South	17.07	48.30	102.66	150.96
	Nonwhites, North	2.81	14.08	7.64	21.72
	Nonwhites, South	20.26	74.05	33.36	107.41
37	Whites, North	257.71	86.99	− 120.98	− 33.99
	Whites, South	220.70	23.56	− 76.23	− 52.67
	Nonwhites, North	22.13	48.48	72.97	121.45
	Nonwhites, South	52.33	83.51	80.17	163.68
47	Whites, North	406.02	369.51	− 101.41	268.10
	Whites, South	314.38	119.24	− 124.71	5.47
	Nonwhites, North	4.17	11.11	22.66	33.77
	Nonwhites, South	28.86	29.31	− 7.92	21.39

no individual jursidiction's tax structure may be so regressive as to cause tax payments to decline as income increases, lower-income taxpayers may be located (on average) in jurisdictions with "higher taxes," while higher-income individuals are more likely to be found in jurisdictions with "lower taxes." Averaging the tax payments of income groups over all jurisdictions might thus show lower-income individuals paying higher absolute tax amounts, especially if state and local revenues in 1960 were used disproportionately to support services demanded by or related to the presence of low-income families (e.g., welfare, housing, etc.).

The overall rank of external-tax-benefit-producers (based on the federal tax system and little labor market bumping) from Table 5 (from large to small) is whites, North; whites, South; nonwhites, South; nonwhites, North. With slight interregional mobility, this pattern is also appropriate for educational subsidies, based on marginal social welfare effects alone. Given the regional and racial income differences, this subsidy pattern would tend to give higher subsidies to youths from higher-income families in 1959. However, if regional income differences are declining as the markets for college-educated labor become more national and the discriminatory practices influencing the incomes of college-educated nonwhites diminish in importance, the tax-producing subsidy pattern should become flatter or more equal over time. If, on the other hand, labor market bumping is an important result of government-stimulated, higher education enrollments, the tax effects of the policy are limited, and subsidization is unjustified.

The evaluation of public or external benefits is complicated by the following concerns when federal taxation is based on the "benefit approach":

1. The individual's altered tax payments are *not* external benefits, but, in actuality, private payments for privately received benefits that result from publicly supplied or supported goods and services.
2. The change in an individual's tax payment may *cause* external effects among other taxpayers, but the level of these effects may be larger than, equal to, or less than the change in the tax payments.

The complexity of the second concern severely limits any effort to design an appropriate subsidy format.

The remaining category of external effects are those that occur within the higher education process itself, rather than between educated individuals and the remainder of society. Generally higher-ability or higher-achievement students benefit their colleagues, both students who receive educational benefits and faculty members who are permitted to provide less education and receive more intellectual stimulation within academic institutions. Some schools use admissions criteria and variations in financial aid offers in order to generate an "externally productive" student body. Other institutions use strict continuation criteria (i.e., dismissal for poor performance) to assemble a desired set of students. Still other schools make no effort to assemble "productive" student bodies and rely almost entirely on faculty instruction to create desired educational outcomes.*

Each of the various restriction procedures benefits the individuals who enroll in those institutions and imposes costs or welfare losses on those who are denied admission. Potential students who would be willing to pay high prices for education at selective institutions but who fall below the admissions standards of such institutions are denied enrollment and thus prevented from acquiring what they feel to be desirable education. These restrictive policies may also impose costs on society at large, if the individuals whose educations would be most socially productive (on any of the public good or externality grounds discussed above) are denied entrance to institutions by the application of privately beneficial restriction policies. What should be the government policy response to these restrictive private policies?

Society may decide that colleges and universities are simply—like restaurants and theaters—places of public business and thus consumers cannot be denied (on other than price grounds) ability to acquire the services of these businesses. This decision follows those civil rights decisions that state the rights of blacks to be served even though their presence imposes "costs" on white proprietors and their white customers. This policy would redistribute benefits from those classes of students formerly acceptable to the restrictive institutions to those formerly rejected but desirous of enrolling. Alternatively, colleges and universities might be considered to be more like private country clubs; thus their discriminatory admissions processes would be considered legal. Pointing in the direction of the latter interpretation is the fact that students do not pay the entire cost of their education. Higher education is supported, in part, by private gifts and endowments under the control of institutions. Probably no policy would be adopted that limits the freedom of benefactors to choose to support the students whose education they find most valuable or to use endowment incomes to serve the objectives

* The majority of institutions in this latter set is probably made up of so-called open access, community or junior colleges, which are largely commuter institutions in which little interaction (at least in comparison to that found on residential campuses) occurs among students and for which high school graduation is the only admission criteria.

of past contributors. Schools that charge full costs are more likely to
be the objects of antidiscrimination policies.

If the restrictive entry policies of institutions are found to be legal,
their impact on society's efforts to achieve its goals must be carefully
considered. For example, the social and economic mobility goal might
be limited by the non-price-restrictive policies limiting the entry of
lower-achievement youth into more prestigious institutions. In an effort
to overcome this inhibition, society may wish to offer "bounties" to institutions that admit these "less productive" students, establishing a dual
price system: Less productive students would bring more revenues to
the institutions, while all students would still face a single institutional
price. Such a system of institutional supplements poses a number of
problems. First, a student's educational productivity is a function of
his position relative to that of the other students at a particular institution. Thus, an efficient bounty system would make the bounty variable
across institutions. Second, the nonprice rationing may influence the
enrollment possibilities of lower-achievement youth from all SES groups,
but only the limitations that influence particular segments of the population may cause social costs. Thus, the social bounties should only be
attached to these segments. Some efficiency losses would occur within
the program if the distribution of bounties could not follow these desired
discriminatory patterns.

MARKET IMPERFECTIONS

The three important market imperfections that affect higher education
are capital market imperfections, monopoly and oligopoly behaviors,
and the not-for-profit character of colleges and universities. Each of
these has important impacts on the operation of the higher education
system as a whole and is an appropriate guide for public or social
intervention.* Although these effects probably are experienced by all
students and potential students, they may be greater and more perverse
among specific segments of the population—particularly students from
poor and disadvantaged families.

The *imperfections in the capital market and the nonexistence of a
risk-insurance market* are likely to cause greater hardships among disadvantaged youths. Those from lower-income families are more limited
in their attempts to obtain financing for higher education than those
whose families have greater financial resources, if capital funds are lim-

---

* Although regulation and intervention are usually the appropriate mechanisms
for correcting market imperfections, the impact of imperfections on subsidy programs
and the possible amelioration of imperfections by subsidy programs should also
be considered.

ited and college enrollment requires sizable outlays from current cash resources. Given that a range of prices exists within the higher education system, we would expect (all else being equal) that youths with lower resource availabilities would enroll disproportionately in lower-priced colleges and universities. This expectation is confirmed by enrollment data.

The lack of an insurance or risk-exchange market or an income-contingent feature in existing loan programs also probably has a greater impact on students from disadvantaged backgrounds. If the latter must borrow more to attend college because no alternative resources are available, the riskiness of their investment is greater than that of youths who do not have to resort to mandatory repayment resources. Thus, the absence of an insurance market affects more the enrollment choices of youth from lower-income families. This is further compounded by other factors. High ability, high quality of elementary and secondary education, high family social status, and being white may all have positive effects on income. Individuals with these attributes may have higher postcollege incomes than those who do not, even though the net income effect of college itself for each group may be the same. If the marginal utility of income decreases with increasing income, individuals with higher expected postcollege incomes will experience less risk in borrowing than will those with lower expectations. Correlating noncollege income-producing factors with family income, youths from lower-income families would be more affected by the lack of risk insurance. Another factor is the student's relative lack of assets to serve as collateral for other types of loans. Even if no student loan market existed, it would be possible to borrow funds for college attendance if one possessed other assets—e.g., homes or automobiles—that could serve as loan collateral. Asset ownership declines significantly as income declines. Thus, youths from lower-income families are more reliant on the student loan market for capital funds and more subject to the detrimental impacts of market imperfections.

The *monopoly, oligopoly, and not-for-profit characteristics* of the higher education supply system may impose disproportionate losses on lower-income youths for several reasons. A demand for different forms or types of higher education than has been historically provided—e.g., ethnic studies—may be unfulfilled if a demand-responsive supply system does not exist. Second, although disadvantaged students may want to leave higher education with the same range of skills and attributes as their higher-income colleagues, their poor secondary-school experiences may inhibit their ability to benefit from current levels and styles of college instruction. If the supply side were responsive to demand, compensatory activities would be developed to upgrade those students who wish to enter these traditional programs. The correlation between high school achievement levels and family income is sizable enough to indicate that this nonresponsive supply is felt more strongly among lower-income students. A third factor may be the colleges' goal to maximize the quality of their graduates, rather than the net gains achieved by their students. An effective strategy for this end is to accept only the brightest students. But this will limit the enrollment and the resulting gains by lower-income youths who have lower measured abilities.

SUMMARY

This analysis has argued that the appropriate and effective bases for social support and intervention in a free market are public goods and social benefits, externalities, and market imperfections. An examination of each of these justifications has resulted in a recommendation that social policy concentrate its attention and resources on students from low- and moderate-income families. No effort was made to evaluate the behavioral effects on which policy should also be judged, although other analyses (Mundel, 1971, pp. 55 ff) that deal with this issue strengthen the recommendation for such a policy.

REFERENCES

Becker, G. S. *Human capital, a theoretical and empirical analysis, with special reference to education.* New York: National Bureau of Economic Research, 1964 (General Series, No. 80).

Blau, P. M., & Duncan, O. D. *The American occupational structure.* New York: Wiley, 1967.

Current Population Reports. Factors related to high school graduation and college attendance: 1967. Washington, D.C.: U.S. Bureau of the Census, July 11, 1969 (Series P-20, No. 185).

Daniere, A., & Mechling, J. Direct marginal productivity of college education in relation to college aptitude of students and production costs of institutions. *The Journal of Human Resources,* 1970, 5(1): 51–70.

Froomkin, J. *Aspirations, enrollments and resources.* Washington, D.C.: U.S. Government Printing Office, 1970. (OE-50058).

Gillespie, W. I. Effect of public expenditures on the distribution of income. In R. A. Musgrave (Ed.), *Essays in fiscal federalism.* Washington, D.C.: The Brookings Institution, 1965.

Hanoch, G. Personal earnings and investment in schooling. Unpublished doctoral dissertation, University of Chicago, 1965.

Hansen, W. L., & Weisbrod, B. A. *Benefits, costs and finance of public higher education.* Chicago: Markham, 1969.

Jackson, E. F., & Crockett, H. J., Jr. Occupational mobility in the United States: A point estimate and trend comparison. *American Sociological Review,* 1964, 29(1): 5–15.

Lansing, J. B., *et al. How people pay for college.* Ann Arbor: Survey Research Center, Institute for Social Research, The University of Michigan, 1960.

Lelong, D. C., & Mann. W. R. Systems analysis for institutional output decisions. In C. Fincher (Ed.), *Institutional research and academic outcomes.* Proceedings of the Eighth Annual Forum on Institutional Research. Athens, Georgia: Association for Institutional Research, 1968.

Mundel, D. S. Federal aid to higher education and the poor. Unpublished doctoral dissertation, Massachusetts Institute of Technology, 1971.

Mundel, D. S. Federal aid to higher education: An analysis of federal subsidies to undergraduate education. *The economics of federal subsidy programs.* Submitted to the Joint Economic Committee, U.S. Congress. 92d Congress, 2d session, 1972.

Mundel, D. S., & Zeckhauser, S. H. Who pays the higher education bill?—For which students? Unpublished manuscript, Committee on Student Economics, College Entrance Examination Board, May 1971.

Schaefer, W. E., & Polk, K. Delinquency and the schools. (Task Force Report, *Juvenile delinquency and youth crime,* President's Commission on Law Enforcement and Administration of Justice) Washington, D.C.: U.S. Government Printing Office, 1967.

Wohlstetter, A., & Coleman, S. *Race differences in income.* Santa Monica: The RAND Corporation, 1970. (R-578-OEO)

A SLIGHTLY DIFFERENT APPROACH

Kenneth E. Clark

It is obvious to everyone that our society benefits from the contributions of well-educated persons. Statements that our society depends on the continuous production of large numbers of technical and professional personnel go unchallenged. A high school drop-out is looked upon as a tragedy; the fact that some bright high school graduates do not continue on to college is deplored. We easily accept the proposition that a healthy segment of the lifetime earnings of a college graduate can be assigned to the increased capabilities he acquired by virtue of college attendance, even when his initial capacities are taken into account.

The preceding presentations in this volume have reminded us that the evidence to support our beliefs about the benefits of higher education is scanty, that the relationships we believe exist may not have the magnitude we expected or may be so subtle that we can discern them only with more sensitive analyses than we have used thus far.

While I, too, am disappointed to find the evidence scanty, I would argue that any change in the lifetime earnings accruing to an individual that is caused by his own college attendance, regardless of the size or the direction of the change, is of less interest to this study group than the effects of such education on the entire society. This is the issue we have dealt with as the matter of "externalities" was considered. Thus far, evidence about general societal effects has been viewed as

317

worth study only as a fallback position, in the event we should, with sadness, discover that direct benefits to individuals were not discernible.

I want to argue that the key issue in any study of the benefits of higher education is this class of factors called externalities. If it were the case that the only benefit of higher education were to increase the income of an individual who has improved his own capital value by investing in education, then the only effect on society is an increase in the cost of operating the society, nothing else. For the only thing that has occurred is an increased amount of money made available to one subset of the population by virtue of their greater education.

It thus seems critical to examine the effects produced by higher education other than the increase in income for the individual who attends. What are these effects? If there are none, then college attendance is merely an aspect of credentialism and has effects in terms of one variable only, namely, overall income. This appears, on the face of it, simplistic, foolish, and surely undesirable.

If one is to discover these other effects, it becomes necessary to study smaller aggregations of individuals in particular areas of higher education. In those smaller and more homogeneous groups it may be possible to discover something of the way in which change of income is related to something meaningful to the society. In the process of such study we need to examine the way in which a person finds a particular avenue for career development, or to discover the ways in which college-educated persons make a contribution to the total society, or to examine the way in which the overall quality of life is changed by virtue of a particular educational experience that an individual or a group has had. To study relationships only in gross aggregations, as we have thus far, guarantees that we will discover few effects of higher education.

The inference that one would draw about the nature of higher education in order for one to conclude that there are outcomes of the sort that have been hypothesized in earlier papers does not resemble the system of higher education that I have become acquainted with. Students are admitted to a college or university, spend four years on a campus, take perhaps a total of 30 to 40 courses, and receive a degree. Each one of those courses has less intellectual content and less activity on the part of the student than the Conference on the Benefits of Higher Education generated in three days. Faculty members learn a great deal by teaching a course. Students do not learn very much. After two years if you give students the same final examinations that they had taken at the end of the course, they usually do not remember enough of the details of the subject matter to pass the course. How much then is their benefit to an employer going to be increased by their sitting in any classroom, any lecture, or in any seminar? My answer is that it will be infinitely small, based on examining what actually occurs in such classrooms. If we now multiply the tiny residual benefit of attending each class by 200, as the number of class periods per semester, and then by eight for the number of semesters, the product is considerably larger but not, in my opinion, large enough to lead me to believe that an employer will be out eagerly seeking that particular individual.

Until some critical social experiment is completed, we must remain in doubt about the magnitude of the impact of four years of college experience on a student's worth to society. Almost every effect that we observe might actually be the effect of four years of increased age at the time of entry into the labor market. Another effect may be ascribed to the "credentials" aspect of higher education, in which a baccalaureate degree is required for entry into the professional schools of business, medicine, and law that provide access to careers guaranteed to have higher than average incomes. Part of the effect may be related to the increased acquaintance with the way the system works, acquired perhaps through the friendships with persons from widely varying backgrounds that develop during the four years of college experience.

One reason we emphasize the four-year experience is that we want to see colleges and universities subsidized. We believe in higher education. We want to see money come to higher education. In truth, however, we do not want it to come to support the likely increased income of our undergraduate students but rather to support the scholarly and research activities of our faculty and their students. What the faculty does is very important. They serve as the intellectual leaders of our society. They provide a group that challenges every commonly held belief. We hope that many students will follow the model that our faculties offer, become professors themselves, or play an important role in an intellectual community that will make some difference to our society. It therefore is very important to us that other persons go to colleges and universities. It improves my life and it improves yours.

No college or university is a single institution; it is many institutions, and it has a wide variety of effects on different students. Some students go to college for purposes that have nothing to do with income or their lifetime earnings. Their college experience may be very highly successful for them and may actually depress their income, if they, for example, elect high school teaching rather than business. There are others for whom monetary considerations are the important factor; they are strongly motivated upward. For many of them it will make a great difference whether they go to one college or another. For some the primary activity will be social; for others it will involve library or laboratory work. For still others, the opportunity to try out a variety of possible areas of intellectual endeavor will be the key thing. The variety of motivations and the variety of college influences makes it difficult to deal with the effects of higher education in the aggregate and forces upon us the necessity of studying the phenomena of effects of higher education on smaller subcultures within the domain.

On a slightly different point, I was struck in many of the papers given at the Conference on the Benefits of Higher Education the frequency with which the words "assuming motivation was constant" are used. It seems to me that this is an item that requires more attention than it has received. The question is: What does the college or university do to change motivation? Does it affect the character and quality of a person's life in any ways that will show up on any of a variety of indices? To collect such data we must conduct studies not only of campus subcultures but of various occupational and interest groups and subgroups within them, in terms of the levels of aspiration of the students we are studying and in terms of outcomes other than income. When we have completed such studies in a variety of colleges, then perhaps we can put them together and look at aggregated data with an improved chance of gaining insight into the nature of college effects.

Finally, I do not believe that we should concern ourselves with issues about innate versus acquired abilities as we deal with issues of this sort. Sometime or other we will learn the critical features associated with the heritability of certain abilities. What should engage us in our current endeavor is the *immodifiability* of human characteristics. What are the features of an individual that are not changed by attendance at institutions of higher education or by other societal influences? I believe that if higher education does anything, it will increase the likelihood for change and modification over a life span; we should include in our models for study some way of identifying the person for whom the college learning experience is the one that launched him on a lifetime of continual development and renewal. We should be able to accumulate such evidence, since each of us can provide objective, anecdotal material that is directly relevant. We only require a program of systematic collection and analysis that is appropriately designed.

ON MYTHICAL EFFECTS OF PUBLIC
SUBSIDIZATION OF HIGHER EDUCATION

Social Benefits and Regressive Income Redistribution

Richard B. Freeman

There is a widespread and growing notion among economists that public spending on higher education redistributes income from poor to wealthy individuals or families. Since income distribution is important in social welfare, the finding of "regressivity" has great policy significance and deserves critical attention. It is also widely believed that higher education confers special "social benefits" that cause social rates of return to exceed private rates. Since divergencies between social and private gains are an important justification for public subsidies, the nature and size of the social benefits merit careful examination. Is there a case against public subsidization of higher education in terms of regressive income distribution effects? If so, do the social benefits of higher education outweigh the cost of redistribution?

Hartman's and Mundel's studies ("The Rationale for Federal Support of Higher Education," pp. 271–292 and "Whose Education Should Society Support?", pp. 293–315) are primarily concerned with the second question, reviewing and evaluating the public goods, social benefits, and externality effects of college training.

321

Social Benefits

The Oral Tradition of Chicago, a cranky old man reputed to be an illegitimate descendent of Adam Smith, is rumored to have referred to social benefits as "the last refuge of . . . ." Which of the benefits discussed by Hartman and Mundel might pass muster before this tough-minded fellow?

1. *Capital Market Imperfections.* The benefit of correcting capital market imperfections, presumably by loan programs of various sorts, is certainly the most "ok" justification for governmental activity given by Hartman and Mundel. Income equality within cohorts and efficiency are likely to be enhanced by the improvement in borrowing possibilities. Loan programs should, however, be equally accessible for all forms of human capital investment to prevent allocative and distribution effects favoring college students as compared to noncollege youngsters. The two and a half million Americans attending private vocational schools deserve equal financing possibilities for their training (as under GI bills) in any loan system.

2. *Changes in Values and Attitudes.* Hartman's list of the benefits of changing attitudes and values is the most controversial social gain from higher education. The difficulties are twofold: First, the studies of changed attitudes do not have the proper scientific precision (holding fixed IQ, background of students) in their comparisons of students with control groups and generally relate to attitudes rather than behavior. In addition, the cross-section evidence (for example, that the college-educated vote more) is not immediately reconcilable with time series evidence on changes in "good citizenship." Second, there is a variety of historical cases that go against the better citizen proposition: Lewis Feuer's study (1968) of student movements showing totalitarian biases, as well as such groups as Weathermen, John Birch Society, etc., which have many college-trained members. Neither college students, graduates, nor professors were in the front line defending German or Italian democracies against Nazism or Fascism; trade unions were. Until the research findings reconcile these diverse cases and show, in fact, that the changed values and attitudes strengthen desirable social institutions or attitudes, it is difficult to take them seriously.

3. *Labor Market Allocation.* As set out by Hartman and Mundel, governmental intervention in education for the purpose, or with the effect, of improving the geographic (see Mundel, p. 298) or occupational (see Hartman, p. 288) allocation of manpower, or to subsidize research and increase knowledge are more easily defensible. However, there are difficulties of accountability in such programs and the danger that once

begun, they "take on a life of their own." More can be done here in
the form of benefit–cost analysis of scholarships and the like to pin
down the optimum form and size of subsidies.

4. *Social Mobility*. Both Mundel and Hartman regard the increased
opportunity for low-income children to attend college or attain high-level
jobs as a major benefit of public subsidies. Theoretically, the effect of
subsidies on the decision to go to college depends on the way in which
the price line between college and other goods is transformed. If subsidies are limited to a single type of higher education—the local four-
year state university, for instance—the price line may be sufficiently
kinked as to cause persons who would otherwise go to college to choose
other goods instead. With many types of subsidized schooling, however,
the usual substitution effect can be expected to cause increases in enrollments. The available data, while limited, suggest very low elasticities
of response to subsidies—on the order of .30: A 1 percent change in
tuition induces approximately .3 percent change in enrollments. Even
if *all* of the individuals brought into college by the subsidies were from
low-income backgrounds, the vast bulk of the subsidy would accrue
as "rent" to other students. Estimates contained in Freeman (1971)
suggest that 75 percent of a $1,500 subsidy to students is pure rent.
Hartman's calculations (1972) in the *Journal of Political Economy* tell
a similar story: In his model it takes $311 million in subsidies to increase
college attendance by 28 percent from a population of 100,000 prospective students, suggesting a $244 million (78.5 percent) rent, the bulk
of which accrues to upper-income families. This buys an increase in
the enrollment of persons with family incomes below $10,000 of 4.8
percentage points; the enrollment rate rises from 11.4 to 15.9 percent
of eligible students. While it is incumbent to present alternatives to
this method of increasing the proportion of low-income persons in college, the free-tuition mechanism seems to buy relatively little for a sub-
stantive cost of tax funds.

There are other difficulties with "mobility benefits" resulting from
direct public subsidies. Some "less able" persons will be induced into
college while their "true" rate of return is below that in alternatives.
This occurs to the extent that differential (produced or innate) ability
rather than opportunities is the prime deterrent to enrollment. The total
college population will be increased beyond the socially optimal level.
Subsidies also produce inequities within groups by rewarding those who
invest in college as opposed to other forms of human capital such as
vocational schooling and apprenticeship. The poor who are academically
gifted enjoy the mobility benefit; those who are not, do not. Subsidization
of the "intelligent" poor, while it need not produce Herrnstein's (1971)
meritocratic castes, has mobility disadvantages as well as advantages.

Other alleged social benefits appear in various places in the two papers: Some of these are clearly invalid in terms of economic (marginal) analyses (interdependencies among factors of production), but most sound plausible. In the absence of quantification, however, it is impossible to evaluate their potential significance or to determine whether they exceed or fall short of costs, on the margin. *The existence of (unmeasured) social benefits does not, after all, tell us anything about the direction in which expenditures should be changed.* With current subsidies, the marginal gains from the alleged benefits may be much below marginal costs, or much above. What Hartman and Mundel have done is simply enumerate potential benefits while what is needed is knowledge of marginal benefits.

In sum, though not the fault of the authors, who are limited by available studies, the listing of possibly valid, possibly mythical benefits rapidly becomes sterile. For persons who believe that such benefits are important—or that on the margin they justify current or additional expenditures—it is incumbent to provide *numerical* estimates of what they amount to. Even rough estimates, similar to Denison's (1964) source of growth calculations, would put the discussion on an entirely new and more fruitful plane.

Is Current Funding Regressive?

If the social benefits case for subsidizing higher education is weak, so, too, is the argument and evidence that subsidization redistributes income from the poor to the rich. The data, properly examined, simply do not support this conclusion.

Studies of the regressivity of public subsidization consist of two basic steps: analysis of the incidence of taxes, which show the poor paying a fairly sizable sum due to regressive–proportional state and local taxes; and analysis of the family income of average college students or of the proportion of students in college, by family income. The basic comparison is between the dollars contributed by the poor in taxes and the dollars received in benefits. Hansen & Weisbrod (1969) show that to the average person who sends his child to college, there is a gain in any given year from the subsidization scheme: Since the average parents of college students have above-average incomes, there is a transfer favoring those with students in college. Pechman (1970), however, has (correctly) pointed out that this methodology in no way resembles what we normally regard as transfers between income classes. Except for the highest brackets, his calculations show roughly similar payments and benefits by income class.

Accepting the basic framework of these studies—comparison of dollars paid in taxes ("attributable" to education)* with dollars received—the analyses can be improved in several fundamental ways. The studies have omitted important aspects of the problem that argue strongly against the regressivity finding: the payback of taxes over the life cycle by students; the lifetime taxes paid by parents; the effect of increased numbers of college graduates on salaries; the link between the subsidies and other governmental activity.

In the first place, the studies generally ignore the extra taxes paid by students as a result of higher college earnings. Even with very modest assumptions about (a) the number of students induced into college by low-tuition subsidies; (b) the extent to which earnings are affected by college training; (c) the incidence of the total U.S. tax system (assumed proportional), calculations indicate that the payback of subsidies in taxes is substantial. Some rough-and-ready estimates I made to see if students as a group were freeloaders on the nonstudent population show for 1965 substantial return on subsidized schooling, largely through the federal income tax. While much better estimates can be made, the order of the magnitudes involved show that, discounted at an interest rate of 6 percent, *there is very little net transfer between students and nonstudents.* The taxpayer who subsidizes schooling receives 25 or so percent of the future return in taxes. If there is little transfer between students and nonstudents, of course, there can be little regressivity to the subsidization mechanism.

Similarly, families who benefit from having subsidized education for a child have contributed taxes for education over their entire working life. A middle- or high-income parent of a single child certain to go to a subsidized college will pay far more in taxes attributable to education than the value of the subsidy. A $12,000–13,999 family, for example, would pay on the order of $2,500 in present value of taxes in California (at 6 percent) and receive about $1,800 in benefits. With two children the family does better in benefits from the subsidy. More detailed calculations for the United States, taking account of the number of children and probabilities of public college attendance by income class, show that there is *little net redistribution of income among families due to college subsidization,* assuming changed subsidies are accompanied by proportionate changes in taxes.

All else being equal, subsidization of higher education is expected

---

* Pechman's critique (1970) of the Hansen–Weisbrod computations for using all taxes rather than those attributable to education is clearly correct and obviously mars their study. While some use of *ad hoc* logic is needed to make the relevant attribution, not to do so is indefensible.

to increase the number of college graduates. This increase will, in turn, affect the entire economic system: reducing the cost of college manpower—and thereby the price of college labor intensive goods—and inducing changes in consumption choices. The ultimate effect on distribution of incomes of the initial subsidy is by no means clear: In a three-factor (capital, labor, skilled or college labor) model, elasticities of substitution, factor intensities, and differences in consumption baskets all affect the final incidence. Until shown otherwise, however, it seems reasonable to expect the initial decline in college graduate salaries to dominate and for distribution to move in favor of the poor. This impact of subsidization has been ignored in most calculations, leading to a potential overstatement of the advantage of subsidies to those most likely to take direct advantage of them. More generally, the general equilibrium model used by Harberger (1962) to analyze corporate profit tax effects and by Johnson (1971) to analyze union wage effects is clearly an appropriate tool for investigation of the college subsidy.

Finally, there is the difficult problem of whether it is analytically legitimate to examine the subsidy of college students separately from other parts of the U.S. expenditure–taxation system. Even if the wealthy were to benefit most from public subsidies, this may be an "acceptable price" for an overall system with quite different redistributive impacts. More money for colleges may be the "payoff" to the middle class for additional funding of welfare programs or compensatory education. The question, which requires much more theoretic and empirical work, as Hansen & Weisbrod have properly stressed (1969), concerns the *separability of one program from an overall package*. In most calculations [including Freeman (1971) on the payback by taxes], a change in the level of educational funding is assumed to lead to a proportionate tax change (or expenditure change with the same redistribution properties). But if the system were initially in equilibrium and political bargaining power unchanged, the reduction in college subsidies would have to be matched by an equivalent change favoring the groups benefiting from the subsidy. There is great need for a model of how states and the federal government determine the subsidization, its interrelation to other parts of the budget, and of the political–economic factors that would permit the enactment, and influence the effect, of alterations.

Research Findings and Policy

If the arguments of this comment are correct, there is as yet no serious case for subsidizing higher education to obtain social benefits. The evidence and analysis given by Hartman and Mundel provide virtually no check or guide as to how we can spend funds to obtain various social goods or how much we should spend. There is also, however, no reason to defer expenditures because of deleterious effects on income distribution, though, of course, other uses of tax money may give more equality in opportunity or income distribution than public higher education. Indeed, the evidence that most of public subsidy is rent to the high-income and high-ability students, as indicated by all studies, suggests that, *if feasible*, more direct methods of aiding the human capital formation of the poor would be desirable.

The allocative effects of subsidizing higher education and the bias in favor of persons choosing or having the ability to pursue this route of advancement deserve more attention. Like other subsidies or sales taxes, the subsidization of college by below-cost tuition misallocates resources (in the absence of compensitory unmeasured social benefits) towards the activity. While there are, to be sure, other programs designed to aid the poor who have no chance to go to college, the selecting out of some (relatively few) persons to receive subsidies, rather than others in the same income class, is no great step toward more equal income distribution.

To improve the contribution of research to policy in the area of subsidizing college education, further work is needed in five main areas:

1. Quantification of alleged social benefits
2. Analysis (using consumer surplus cost–benefit or the general equilibrium framework) of the allocative effects of subsidies
3. Investigation of the relative importance of differential (innate or "home-produced") abilities and differential opportunities in deterring youngsters from college
4. Development of alternative programs—possibly involving more than loans or loan guarantees—to improve social mobility
5. Analysis of the way in which the current subsidy scheme is linked to the overall tax-expenditure budget leading to a better understanding of the possibilities of change

REFERENCES

Denison, E. F. Measuring the contribution of education (and the residual) to economic growth. In *The residual factor and economic growth*. Paris: Organisation for Economic Cooperation and Development, 1964.

Feuer, L. *Conflict of generations*. New York: Basic Books, 1968.

Freeman, R. B. *The market for college-trained manpower: A study in the economics of career choice*. Cambridge: Harvard University Press, 1971.

Hansen, W. L., & Weisbrod, B. H. *Benefits, costs, and finance of public higher education*. Chicago: Markham, 1969.

Harberger, A. Incidence of corporation income tax. *Journal of Political Economy,* 1962, 70: 215–240.

Hartman, R. W. Equity implications of state tuition policy and student loans. *Journal of Political Economy,* 1972, 80(3, Pt. 2): S142–S171.

Herrnstein, R. L. I.Q. *Atlantic Monthly,* 1971, 228(3): 44–64.

Johnson, H. *Two-sector model of general equilibrium.* Chicago: Aldine, 1971.

Pechman, J. A. The distributional effects of public higher education in California. *The Journal of Human Resources,* 1970, 5(3): 361–370.

ON EXTERNAL BENEFITS AND WHO SHOULD
FOOT THE BILL

W. Lee Hansen

Both Robert Hartman and David Mundel ("The Rationale for Federal Support of Higher Education," pp. 271–292, and "Whose Education Should Society Support?", pp. 293–315) list a number of important reasons why governmental intervention in the financing of higher education is needed. These include capital market imperfections, external benefits, and something called "social benefits." I believe I understand what market imperfections are and how we might go about assessing their impact. Social benefits, at least as described, appear to represent an aggregation of individual benefits, and so I am uneasy about listing them as a separate reason. They might probably better be included in the second category of external benefits, that is, those benefits that do not accrue directly to the primary beneficiary. Even if we accept this reclassification, it is not clear that external benefits can bear the load placed on them by Hartman and Mundel, who require us to accept the existence of external benefits on faith. Unfortunately, they offer little in the way of evidence as to the nature and magnitude of external benefits.

At the moment there exists an interesting intellectual impasse concerning external benefits.* The predominant belief seems to be that signifi-

---

* Clearly "external effects" would be more appropriate; there are both external benefits and external costs of education.

cant external benefits do exist. In addition, there is probably substantial agreement that elementary education produces larger external benefits than does secondary education, that secondary education produces larger external benefits than undergraduate education, and that undergraduate education produces larger external benefits than graduate–professional education. These views are not, however, based on any careful review of evidence; they reflect prevailing, constantly reaffirmed, beliefs. Some people have questioned these assertions, arguing that the benefits produced at the college level are largely internal or private and that any external benefits are probably negligible in amount.

The impasse arises because spokesmen for higher education argue that it is up to the critics to show that external benefits do not exist. Critics, on the other hand, argue that nobody has ever demonstrated that externalities do, in fact, exist; hence, those who claim their existence should produce supporting evidence.

Some would argue that since we cannot estimate external benefits with any degree of exactitude, we should not try to measure them at all, or that to try to measure these benefits will lead to erroneous measures that may prove to be more harmful than beneficial. Nevertheless, if the issue of subsidies rests so heavily on the presence of externalities, we need a careful study and a well-defined research program to determine exactly what are the external benefits, their magnitude, and their distribution.

How should we proceed to investigate external benefits? First, we might use the format presented by Alexander Astin ("Measurement and Determinants of the Outputs of Higher Education," pp. 107–127) for classifying benefits: cognitive versus affective and attitudinal versus behavioral. Then we must seek out measures of these different effects. Eventually I would hope there could be agreement as to what effects would be considered appropriate for inclusion and how to measure them, both quantitatively and qualitatively. Second, we might expand Astin's classification scheme, subdividing it to show which effects, or how much of them, are internal effects accruing to individuals receiving more schooling and which are external effects redounding to others. This task will not be easy; some effects probably have both internal and external dimensions. Third, we must then undertake an evaluation to decide which of these various kinds of effects might be described as benefits and which might be described as costs, and to whom. This is no doubt the most ticklish part of the entire exercise. Different groups may have quite varying views on the subject, and, undoubtedly, it will be difficult to gain a consensus.

To carry out these tasks we will, first of all, have to focus on how these external benefits vary, depending upon the kind of educational experiences produced. A glance at what colleges do suggests that we distinguish among the three major functions—instruction, research, and public service, with a further breakdown between graduate and undergraduate instruction. If we then concentrate on the external benefits of undergraduate instruction, we might want to distinguish among effects produced at two-year schools, four-year schools, and universities. Not only do these institutions profess to accomplish different things, students also choose among them because they desire different kinds of experience.

At the same time we must broaden our study to include other types of higher education. Individuals prepare themselves for productive lives and careers in a variety of ways: proprietary school attendance, adult education courses, on-the-job training, and various informal means (books and other publications, television, radio, and so on). These activities are also likely to produce a variety of effects, some of which can be classified as internal and others as external. We must examine these as well if we are to have proper benchmarks against which to compare the effects produced by college attendance.

One further point must be made. What is the size of externalities produced by government-subsidized activities, contrasted to activities in the private sector? Typically, external benefits from publicly produced goods are larger than those from privately produced goods. However, sizable external benefits may result from numerous privately produced goods. Consider the clothing industry: Clothes are purchased by people to cover their bodies and to make themselves look attractive; thus, they provide internal benefits. At the same time, other individuals gain external benefits from these private expenditures, not only by seeing that people are well clothed but also by appreciating the attractiveness of the clothing worn by these people. Fortunately or unfortunately, there is no easy way for owners of clothing to internalize these external benefits by levying a charge against people who look at them and gain satisfaction from doing so. But the usual argument (as it is applied to higher education) is that subsidies should be provided to the clothing industry to insure that the optimal amount of clothing is produced. The point is that the external benefits from a good such as higher education may be positive, but whether they are relatively greater than the external benefits from a variety of privately produced goods is something that has not been much discussed.

No doubt some observers would dispute the usefulness, if not the feasibility, of the approach just outlined. They would argue that this elaborate type of accounting is not going to answer several important questions: If we provide additional subsidies, will the added external benefits warrant the payment of the subsidies? If we decrease the subsidies, will the external benefits decline? I would guess that we cannot usefully answer these questions until we work through the larger exercise proposed. An analogous study would be Denison's (1962) estimate of the sources of economic growth, in which he examined the average effects of various inputs on the rate of economic growth and estimated the expected marginal changes.

Let us now turn to distributional issues. To determine what levels of government should be doing what amount of subsidizing, we must first distinguish among state, local, and federal government. State and local governments pay virtually all of the costs of undergraduate instructional programs, whereas the federal government is heavily involved in research funding and only partly involved in the support of graduate education. Given this historically determined pattern of shared financing of higher education, we need some system for allocating the external benefits among these different taxing units. This is obviously no easy job but very possibly could be a part of the research agenda.

This leaves aside an even larger issue concerning the distribution of external benefits among population groups. To what extent do the external benefits of higher education flow to other groups with more or less education? Do they accrue to the college-educated group itself? If, indeed, the external benefits of college attendance are concentrated among the college-educated population, then what would seem to be an external benefit from the individual point of view becomes an internal benefit to this particular population group. In such cases it would be appropriate to think of these external benefits as really being internal and to let the whole matter drop. This implies that there should be no subsidization for external benefits flowing back to the population group itself and that people going to college should individually and as a group pay for these external benefits.

While it may be possible to get a better fix on the distribution of external benefits (and costs) by taxing unit and on the size distribution of external benefits among different population groups, there remains the nagging question of exactly who pays and who benefits from existing or proposed subsidy plans. Assume for a moment that higher education produces higher incomes for individuals and also national external benefits. The federal tax structure reaps a rich harvest from the additional incomes (internal benefits) accruing to individuals by taking an average of probably 25 percent of the additional income generated by more schooling in the form of income taxes. Hence, the nation gains substantial revenue as a consequence of the subsidies to higher education provided by state and local taxes. Of course, states also gain from the incremental income produced, but by much less, because of their generally lower tax rates; moreover, the pattern of net migration will also affect the amount of the gain. In any case, one can certainly question the equity of a system in which the federal government gains so much at the expense of state- and locally financed subsidies (not to mention the individual expenditures required to help generate this larger income). But if the external benefits of higher education are exceptionally large and national in character, one might want to argue that the federal government should be providing much more generous support. As it now stands, the federal government not only gets a large tax windfall , but "gains" the external benefits at virtually no cost to itself.

We can approach this in still another way by examining the size of subsidies received and taxes paid over some relevant time period, for example, one college student's lifetime. Calculations for both California and Wisconsin (Hansen & Weisbrod, 1969; Hansen, 1971) suggest that state subsidies are not fully repaid by individual beneficiaries of public higher education, even when, as in Wisconsin, the tax structure is quite progressive; on the other hand, the minuscule federal subsidies are, on average, far more than repaid. These findings, based upon the overall data, do not mean that some individuals may not repay much more or much less.

In conclusion, the Panel on the Benefits of Higher Education should allocate some resources to explore the scope, magnitude, and distribution of external benefits and give high priority to this area of research. While economists are comfortable and familiar with the external-benefit concept—though not too knowledgeable about the empirical dimensions of the benefits—such a study should involve the joint expertise of economists, sociologists, psychologists, and possibly people from other disciplines as well. For it appears that people from many disciplines discuss external benefits, though they often use different terms. The importance of this project hardly needs restating. Only by learning more about the variety and magnitude of the external benefits will we be able to judge the appropriate levels and distribution of public subsidies for higher education.

REFERENCES

Denison, E. F. *The sources of economic growth in the United States and the alternatives before us.* New York: Committee for Economic Development, 1962 (Supplementary Paper No. 13).

Hansen, W. L. Income distribution effects of higher education. *American Economic Review,* 1971, 60(2): 335–340.

Hansen, W. L., & Weisbrod, B. A. *Benefits, costs, and finance of public higher education.* Chicago: Markham, 1969.

BLINDERED ECONOMICS

*Higher Education and Public Policy**

Stephen P. Dresch

The papers by Robert Hartman ("The Rationale for Federal Support of Higher Education," pp. 271–292) and David Mundel ("Whose Education Should Society Support?", pp. 293–315) provide an excellent representation of the state of the art in the economics of public higher education policy. Just as introductory economics textbooks are identical up to the specific arrangement of chapters and the quality of presentation, these papers, authored by two competent economists working independently, are identical in such essential respects as the topics covered, the general prescriptions in each case, and the overall conclusions. Mundel examines public goods and social benefits (including social mobility and income redistribution), externalities, and market imperfections as these relate to higher education, concluding with the recommendation that "social policy concentrate its attention and resources on students from lower-

* These remarks represent a very halting and tentative effort to come to grips with a range of complex issues beyond the purview of most economic analyses in this area. As such, they should be viewed more as an opening salvo than as the presentation of a reasoned position. These comments have not undergone the full critical review accorded National Bureau of Economic Research studies and are therefore solely the responsibility of the author.

and moderate-income families." Hartman discusses social mobility and income distribution, capital and insurance market imperfections, and externalities (including social benefits), with the primary conclusion that public higher education policy should move "towards targeting existing subsidies at both the federal and state levels on low-income students."

Because such unanimity might suggest that the economics of higher education policy is highly developed, it is important to point out (a) that there actually has been very little development in this field, that is, these papers could have been written 10 or 20 years ago with no substantial loss in content; (b) that this body of analysis really consists of little more than some conditional statements that contribute only slightly to the design or evaluation of alternative higher education policies and programs; and (c) that the domain of analysis is severely constricted, dealing with issues that contemporary economics finds accessible rather than with the issues of real social significance in this area.

As with most blanket indictments this one is unfair. It suggests that Hartman's and Mundel's efforts were wasted, while in fact they serve a very important function. However, the function is primarily political rather than scientific: not to enhance our comprehension of the workings of the higher education sector and its relationship to other social processes and objectives but to provide a platform for a predetermined set of policy prescriptions with which most economists, of both Chicago and non-Chicago persuasions, would agree. When, as in this case, the limited recommendations we are able to make contrast so sharply with actual practice, there is a purpose in the repetition that is so obvious here. In this context, perhaps, we need even more effective repetition of the basic themes of these papers.

I would suggest, however, that for purposes of both policy relevance and further understanding of the system these papers (and the larger body of analysis they represent) contain two basic and related flaws. First, the questions they raise are almost invariably cast from the perspective of a *tabula rasa*. Rather than examining the implications of alternative modifications in present policy, they raise effectively universal questions about "appropriate" policy. That this is counterproductive can be seen from the futile debate over the regressivity of state systems of subsidized institutions of higher education. I would argue that such a question can never be satisfactorily answered and, furthermore, that, for policy purposes, an answer is unnecessary. The relevant questions arise out of the context of an existing situation and concern the effects of alternative modifications in the *status quo*. Recast in these terms, the questions will become meaningful, our understanding of and agreement on empirical reality will be increased, and, more importantly, the relevance of analysis to policy will be significantly enhanced.

To attempt to identify "the effects" of public policy is to invite futility in the context of a complex and interdependent system. A consideration of the consequences of alternative changes in the system at least raises questions that can be approached and answered, if only by successive approximation. Thus, we may not agree on the overall regressivity of state higher education policies or even be able to ask the question intelligently, but we can, I think, agree on the direction of change in the income distribution that will result from particular modifications in these policies. I would not suggest that these questions are easy; they are at least tractable.

Not only must the nature of the issues be changed; the range of policy consequences must be broadened. In particular, I would argue that one of the most important consequences of higher education policy has been in the dimension of the structure and content of the higher education sector, an area not even considered in the Hartman and Mundel papers. The failure to raise questions in this area is not unrelated to the way in which the issues of policy are cast; when the questions are "all or nothing," it is difficult to say anything sensible in this or any other dimension. However, when placed in the context of alternative policies, of substitutions between alternative instruments of subsidization, it becomes possible to assess the consequences of policy for the structure and the internal characteristics of the higher education sector.

To make this clear, consider the objections of Hartman and Mundel to the existing system of public, primarily state, support of higher education. The reliance on institutional support, with subsidization of students taking the form of significantly below-cost tuition to all students, is objected to on grounds of allocative inefficiency and adverse redistributive effect. By allocative inefficiency Hartman and Mundel mean the failure of students to accurately measure the opportunity costs of college attendance and, hence, the tendency for at least some classes of students to overconsume education. This I would characterize as *inefficiency in the narrow:* Given the nature of the product and of its financing, it is overproduced. I would guess, though, that relative to other types of inefficiency, in particular inefficiencies related to the nature of the product itself, narrow allocative inefficiency is probably rather trivial in the specific context of higher education.

Similarly, Hartman and Mundel raise the Hansen–Weisbrod (1969) issue of regressivity, with which—once recast in proper terms—I would agree. But here, too, the direct redistributive consequences may be trivial compared to the ways in which the higher education establishment, on the basis of public policy, acts to restrict the nature of the product and, as a result, restricts access to higher education in a very biased, nonrandom manner.

Thus, public policies serve not only to influence resource allocation and to alter the income distribution in the narrow, direct (usual) senses but also to influence the very nature of the higher education process. Specifically, one of the most important and pervasive consequences of public higher education policy has been the establishment, maintenance, and perpetuation of an educational system that is very closed to change, one that does not evolve in response to changing technologies and opportunities. Public policy, as firmly embodied in both direct, institutional support and indirectly in accreditation, system planning, etc., has effectively created a higher education cartel that is immune to pressures for change from a rapidly changing environment. Indeed, this may be one of the most deleterious consequences of the prevailing policy menu.

The cardinal characteristic of this set of programs is the resultant elimination of any effective demand side of the higher education market. Public policy has created an insulated, unresponsive system that is so highly subsidized that no alternatives are viable. Alternatives to the *status quo* are nonrational simply because all public support is channeled through the existing institutional configuration. Thus, efficiency in the broad sense—that is, as would be reflected in a dynamically changing range of educational alternatives—is thwarted because the major mechanism for such efficiency-enhancing change, the freedom of potential students to choose from a range of alternatives on the basis of relative benefits and costs, has been artificially emasculated by public policies that support (and reward) institutional rigidities.

As in many other situations, it is impossible to separate issues of efficiency from those of distribution. Just as the inefficiencies in, for example, the health-care-delivery system have more serious implications for the poor than for the wealthy, the same is true with higher education. The fact that institutional subsidization does nothing to meet the disproportionate costs of foregone earnings borne by students from low-income families has often been noted, but the really insidious effect may arise from the perpetuation of a system that imposes unnecessary earning losses. That is, alternative forms of postsecondary educational delivery, forms that would impose lesser earnings loss, have been foreclosed partially as a result of a public policy that simultaneously does nothing to mitigate the adverse effects of the higher costs to which it contributes.

A number of other adverse consequences follow from the institutional and educational homogeneity fostered by a public policy configuration that destroys effective demand influences. For example, the cultural prerequisites for entrance at almost any point into the higher education system act in concert with financial barriers to significantly reduce the representation of lower socioeconomic groups. The point is not that the cultural aspects of conventional higher education are inappropriate per se but that they permeate virtually an entire system that effectively monopolizes the human capital formation process.

Similarly, the often-noted technological stagnation in higher education, implying secularly increasing real costs, can be argued to be another result of this policy-induced insulation of the higher education sector. The lack of productivity growth that underlies this continuous relative increase in costs is often assumed to be inevitable: *Given the nature of the product,* the technological advances that operate elsewhere in the economy to reduce costs simply are not applicable to higher education.

But the nature of the product is given only because the sector is so immune to pressures for change. Economic history suggests that advances in technology often require radical structural changes, that the older forms of institutional organization are simply incompatible with the requirements of new technologies. One could argue that the lack of productivity growth in higher education is the result not of the inapplicability of new technologies but of the changes in institutional structure and in characteristics of the product that are required by the new technologies. These changes the higher education sector has been able to preclude as a result, at least partially, of a set of public policies that has created a closed and self-perpetuating institutional system.

The point of this discussion is simply that a public policy that has contributed to the emasculation of the demand side of the higher education market has broader negative consequences than usually ascribed. The issue of the proper amount of subsidization is not the crucial one. The most important issue concerns the instruments of subsidization, the means by which the subsidy is distributed, or, more generally, the direct and indirect effects of alternative policies on the system. Furthermore, the criteria for evaluation of any policy nexus must be broader than those usually employed. Neither efficiency nor distribution in the usual narrow sense is adequate, simply because they assume the structure of the sector and the nature of the product given and unchanged, and it is precisely in this dimension that alternative policies may exhibit the most significant differences.

In conclusion, I would agree with the Hartman–Mundel call for a shift from institutional to student support, not only for the reasons they give but for the potentially important consequences of such a direction of change for the overall form of the higher education system. A targetting of subsidies on low-income students would only serve to accent even more the effects in this dimension.

Thus, the ultimate policy scenario I would advocate would (a) re-establish an effective demand side in the higher education market by shifting from subsidization of institutions to subsidization of students, (b) concentrate these subsidies on lower-income students, and (c) accommodate the remaining financial needs of all students through an improved, unsubsidized capital market [on lines suggested by Hartman and as I have discussed elsewhere (Dresch & Goldberg, 1972)]. The crucial questions, as indicated by both Hartman and Mundel, concern the effects of these changes on resource allocation and income distribution. But the primary vehicle of these changes is more likely to be demand-induced changes in the structure, content, and diversity of higher education than redistributions and reallocations within a given institutional context. Until economic analysis is unblindered, however, and extended to include these broader dimensions of sectoral performance in relation to policy, the relevance of the analysis will be severely limited.

REFERENCES

Dresch, S. P., & Goldberg, R. D. Variable term loans for higher education—Analytics and empirics. *Annals of Economic and Social Measurement,* 1972, 1:59–92.
Hansen, W. L., & Weisbrod, B. A. *Benefits, costs, and finance of public higher education.* Chicago: Markham, 1969.

FINANCIAL SUPPORT OF HIGHER EDUCATION
SO THAT THE POOR MAY LEARN

Gerald M. Platt

From the start, I will make my conclusion explicit: I want to encourage additional federal spending for higher education, especially substantial expenditures for poor blacks and whites. I would also like to see higher education maintain its present diversity as a system of pluralistically related universities and colleges. These must simultaneously sustain their diffuse organization of disciplines and schools and *increase* this diversity with new and experimental schools, programs, cross-disciplinary approaches, and applied fields. The greater the diversity in higher education, the more varied the opportunities and contexts of learning for the student—and that is a good thing. Nevertheless, higher educational institutions are places of pure or applied learning, that is their primary purpose and goal.

It is obvious, therefore, that I agree with the conclusions of Robert Hartman ("The Rationale for Federal Support for Higher Education," pp. 271–292) and David Mundel ("Whose Education Should Society Support?", pp. 293–315) that more money should be spent on the lower classes to subsidize and thus increase their attendance in higher education. I do not believe, however, that the arguments or the evidence they muster are compelling. Further, and more important, the basis upon which they legitimate additional expenditures for the poor could have potentially destructive consequences for higher education and for the quality of the learning the poor will receive once they get into the universities and colleges.

Both papers emphasize "cost" and "benefits" to society primarily (although not exclusively) in economic terms for additional expenditures. Apparently in these days of dollars and cents stringencies, legislators must be convinced of the value of higher education in terms of capital investment and profitable returns. Only in this way are large financial investments in the poor demonstrated to be worthwhile.

It is possible, however, to come to Hartman's and Mundel's conclusion by a different route. One could begin to legitimate additional expenditures on the grounds of social justice, as expressed in the formula, "equality of access to higher education without regard for ability to pay." We know, for example, that of recent high school graduates, 78 percent of the upper-middle class go on to college, while less than 15 percent from lower-class backgrounds pursue this same path (Spady, 1967; Jencks & Riesman, 1968, p. 103).* Given this disparity, which must be partly attributable to the ability to pay, the availability of funds would make it easier for the poor to afford college. Additional federal funds for higher education would lower the barrier of financial constraints and raise lower-class college attendance to a middle-class level.

Mundel's definition of the function of government suggests this line of reasoning. He writes (p. 293–294):

> . . . "proper" government policies are aimed at protecting individual freedoms—even at the expense of some decline in output. The American society values individual freedom highly and has an established free private exchange economy. Thus, the government's proper role is to insure the free operation of the exchange marketplaces and to establish them where exchange or transaction is *desired* by constituents but where traditional modes are either impractical or inappropriate if *freedom* (in a broad sense) is to be maintained.

Mundel confuses (perhaps intentionally) the concept of freedom with that of social justice, though I agree that in American society *one* of the functions of government is to assure some fair distribution of societal resources. Yet, Mundel and Hartman eschew moral reasoning and instead stress upgrading skills and abilities for occupational performance through college participation. Improved capacities among the poor, they suggest, will bring more returns to society in the forms of upward mobility, higher salaries, and, in turn, more tax revenue and a generally larger proportion of the national population with better work skills. What legis-

---

* It might also be noted that 51.7 percent of the upper-middle-class students, as opposed to only 6.5 percent of lower-class youths, graduate from college.

lator could turn his back on such promised profit for tax dollar investment?

Legislators are most satisfied when they can account for in precise terms the effects of spending public funds. Mobility, salaries, and taxes are easily accountable; they are what statisticians refer to as parametric, or ordinal and cardinal scales. Using these indices, it is easier to ascertain how much the mean or the median income of the poor has risen or that the tax coffers have increased by X percent over last year as a function of Y percent increases in higher educational expenditures.

It is understandable why Mundel and Hartman attempt to justify additional federal outlay in terms of the more measurable consequences of college participation. But both recognize that more happens to students at college than improvement of occupational abilities. They refer to these other effects as "externalities," meaning changes in ideologies, opinions, attitudes; political and religious beliefs; leisure, esthetic, and expressive activities; and intelligence and knowledge—to note a few dimensions.

I am sure that neither Mundel nor Hartman coined the term externalities for these effects, but they accept it without question. It is not a value-neutral term: It implies things extrinsic and less vital, at worst, less precisely measurable therefore less important, at best. In any case the use of the word says much about the authors' (or their discipline's) attitude toward the basic purpose of higher education.

These "externalities" are central to higher education, for in a broad sense, such effects constitute the college learning experience. On the contrary, it is the occupational training, mobility, and salaries that are peripheral to higher education. *It never once occurs to Mundel or Hartman to legitimate additional federal funding on the grounds for which higher educational institutions were established and exist: that is, teaching, learning, and scholarship.**

I am disappointed also that neither author realizes that the so-called externalities are themselves societal resources: generalized resources analogous to money that are transferred in larger degrees to those who attend college than to those who do not. Therefore, it might be suggested that additional "expenditures" of public funds be made on the grounds that the government assure the just allocation of these resources as well as those of money or jobs.

Both authors claim that the findings regarding externalities are neither

---

* I wonder if Hartman and Mundel as economists would propose that industry be underwritten by federal support only if it shifted its purposes from production to religious training. That would be analogous to what they suggest for higher education.

precise, substantial, nor plentiful. In truth, this is not the case. We can initially proceed by inference in this area. For example, it is well known that there is a high correlation between social class and years of education and between social class and a vast array of attitudinal and behavioral phenomena. Insofar as a society values a healthy, active, and unalienated population, the results of the studies that follow can be viewed as a resource capitalization, or more simply, as benefits for society.

We know, for example, that those in higher classes have higher voting rates, spend more time in leisure activity, and engage in more diverse leisure activities. They travel more, see doctors more regularly, experience less severe mental illness. When they are ill, they seek help and visit psychiatrists more often. They meet with lawyers more often, belong to more voluntary associations, and are more active in community affairs. They are more culturally humanistic and more tolerant of religious and ethnic diversity.*

Naturally, a good portion of the variation in these findings can be explained simply in terms of having and spending more money than the lower classes. But this hardly explains all of the differences. More accurately, we have come to realize that the middle classes are less intimidated by society and its morals and are more willing to bend morality in their own favor. They stand up for their rights, assert counterpressure in society, and demand justice and service. These aspects of middle-class culture are not simply attributable to money; *they are part of the personality of the middle classes and the societal arrangements the middle classes demand and live in.*

For the moment we will refer to all of this as the "middle-class lifestyle"; it developed out of familial and educational socialization. Those who were raised in lower-class families but completed college tend to manifest the "middle-class lifestyle." Thus, it can be said that, as of today and perhaps for the immediate future, a "middle-class lifestyle" is, in large part, associated with college attendance. In this connection Jencks & Riesman have suggested that the breaking point in terms of lifestyle, the single most important influence and criterion, is college education. Thus, for them college education becomes the basis for dividing the upper-middle from the lower-middle classes (Jencks & Riesman, 1968, Chapter 3).

I do not intend to imply that what has occurred for a subsection of the population (as of today approximately 20 to 30 percent of the age grade complete college) would in the exact same manner and degree

---

* These are called "correlates" of social class and can be found in most discussions on social stratification. See Bendix & Lipset (1953); Blau & Duncan (1967).

be transferred to the whole population if higher education were made available to all. I would like to suggest, however, that this lifestyle could be more fairly distributed throughout the population if greater numbers of the poor were admitted to higher educational institutions.

From a historical perspective, the development of free markets (such as those mentioned by Mundel regarding the economy and a free labor force) can, in their social consequences, be one way of integrating the common man into a more just distribution of society's financial resources. There have been struggles and conflicts, to be sure, but unionization, minimum wages laws, minimum yearly income, and so on, have guaranteed a basic level of access to these "fluid" resources (Marshall, 1965).

The economic case for inclusion can be generalized to other societal institutions. Thus, political inclusion was accomplished with political democratization of society, especially through the elimination of ascriptive bases for political participation (blood and kinship) and through universal enfranchisement.

Societal inclusion is not a familiar conception, but insofar as it can be discriminated from political and economic inclusion, it, too, has occurred, especially since the turn of this century. Societal inclusion means the right of access to those aspects of the society that define each individual of a national state as a member in equal standing, and to facilities of the society that may be partly related to economic and political factors but are also independent. For example, the recent Civil Rights Movement, besides seeking jobs and the vote for minorities, also pressed for the right to eat where one wished, to attend parks, beaches, and libraries without discrimination, and so on. In short, societal inclusion underlies the demand for equal citizenship for all and the absence of structural inhibitions and symbols implying "second-class citizenship," for example, the stigmas of ethnicity, religion, race, poverty, or sex. The assimilation of Catholics, Jews, Irish, Italians, etc., is a good example.

None of these inclusion processes is complete, but they are now taken for granted, and there is continuous pressure to assure their implementation. The contemporary *moral legitimacy* of demands for inclusion and justice in any or all of these areas, (economy, polity, and society) is itself evidence of important historical change.

If one can conceive of markets in these other areas similar to those of the economy, it is also necessary to envision a resource that circulates in these markets, similar to money in the economy. These resources become more justly shared with the inclusion process; segments of the society that were entirely excluded from access to that resource or received unfair amounts of that resource obtain more equitable access to and larger amounts of it. In economics this resource is obviously money; in politics, it is political power; and in society, it is *influence* or *prestige*, as these terms are analytically defined by sociologists (Parsons, 1967).

There is also an educational analogy. I would suggest that the resource available for distribution in higher education is generalized cognitive capacities, that is, the ability to organize one's environment and one's personal life through the use of *intelligence* and *rationality*.

Access to higher education upgrades and more fairly distributes cognitive capacities in society. Certainly, cognitive capacity can be expended (in combination with other factors) to get better paying jobs, but that is not the only way this resource can be allocated (Parsons *et al.*, 1973).

Ego psychology (i.e., psychoanalytic theory) and cognitive learning (i.e., academic psychology) suggest that it is the cognitive capacities of individuals that affect such things as the distribution and sense of loyalties held by individuals—e.g., the importance and distribution of feelings for family, friends, religion, nation, etc.; the ability to make fine perceptual and cognitive distinctions; the degree to which action is under conscious (ego) control; the ability to critically and rationally evaluate the environment; the ability to discriminate and verbalize emotions, including those of esthetic and expressive experiences; and so on (Kohlberg, 1969; Kagan & Moss, 1962; Schafer, 1968; Wolff, 1967; Rapaport, 1960).

In short, particular personality action styles (i.e., emotions and behavior) develop with increased cognitive capacities much as familial or household living and buying styles change with increased financial resources. It is the increased cognitive capacities that undergird the characteristics of the "middle-class lifestyle," but that phrase simply denotes the content for which cognitive capacities are expended. However, such a generalized resource may be used for that style or for any other activity.

Therefore, I wish to avoid the term "middle-class style" because it carries with it a pejorative connection. *I do not advocate access to higher education for the poor to become middle class*—that is only an illustration of where upgraded cognitive spending has been concentrated in the recent past. I am suggesting that the poor have greater access to cognitive resources for *expenditure in whatever area of social, economic, political, cultural, and intellectual life they like,* including the possibility of "middle-class lifestyle" if they so wish.

Government should foot the bill for higher education when it is decided that it is just and right to more fairly distribute these cognitive capacities throughout the total society, even in Professor Mundel's words "at the expense of some decline in output" of other aspects of society.

I am not proposing here that all those who participate in higher education will, in the end, have equal degrees of developed cognitive capacities and that there will be no inequalities in this respect in society. Organic differences will surely lead to variations in the distribution of these resources. However, social and cultural obstacles blocking the poor from those resources must be eliminated.

Mundel and Hartman fail to distinguish in analytic terms the development of more specific technical skills that contribute directly to occupational performance from those of the more generalized cognitive capacities of which we have been speaking. It is this lack of distinction that leads them to slight cognitive capacities and to emphasize the more precisely operational consequences of the development of occupational skill, despite their now obvious circumscribed importance to the central concerns of the educational process. By doing so they have hitched their analysis to a common sense ideology ("I'm going to college—, or we're sending our kid to college—, to get a better job") that is fundamentally *reductionist** vis à vis *higher education and its mission in society.*

In turn, they have drawn their analysis into some very troubling, and especially historically regressive, ideological waters that can have serious destructive consequences for higher education and learning as it has developed and continues to develop in the United States.† First, for example, legitimation of governmental expenditure on grounds of improved occupational abilities rather than on upgraded cognitive capacities will definitely influence the university curriculum. Given the enormous influence of financial expenditures, there would be subtle, and not so subtle, pressure to move the university from an environment of learning and scholarship to one of vocational training.

A second potentially negative consequence is related to the first. By linking expenditures primarily to the lower classes for improved occupational skills, both analysts are suggesting to government officials and legislators:

> The poor and the minorities should go to college and you should foot the bill, but don't worry, they're not going to get involved with any esoteric or useless nonsense at college. They're going to learn how to perform on the job and to contribute to the society in these terms and therefore it's in your long-range interest to hand over the money.

* In order to achieve their analyses both authors have had to caricature the university learning process in terms of an economic model of estimable productivity, rather than dealing with it on its own terms and level.

† Nineteenth-century colleges were undifferentiated from religious and vocational learning. In this century universities and colleges have tended to become autonomous of these other concerns and oriented by their own values. Thus, any suggestion to reintegrate religious or vocational values is historically regressive.

What was once for the upper-middle classes an exciting, stimulating, intellectual experience, a leisurely experience, a short period of irreality to the point that Erik Erikson (1950) could refer to college as a "moratorium from life," will, for the lower classes, mean getting down to business. No wandering off into the library stacks to read what is not required, no late night bull sessions, no changing or playing around with major concentrations, no dropping out of or into college, only enough humanities courses to fill requirements, no panty raids, and especially no political activism.

Thus, perhaps the most naive aspect of both papers is the "black box" conceptualization of higher educational institutions: The young are placed at one end and emerge transformed after four years. How they are transformed and what is learned in college depends upon what goes on in that black box. Mundel and Hartman appear unaware that higher educational institutions are themselves social organizations and thus operate in a particular manner. Like any organization, and perhaps more than many, the college and the university are sensitive to external pressures placed upon them. There is no recognition in either paper that the desire to underwrite the attendance of the poor in college, justified in terms of occupational skills and improved salary—no matter how decent or liberal the sentiment behind it—will pressure higher educational institutions to do just that, to shape their curricula to produce vocationally oriented students.

Negative consequences for the pluralistic and diverse character of higher education will be great. When the university system is moving in the direction of even greater flexibility, more disciplines, more interdisciplinary work, and different fields and programs, there will be new pressure to become technically and vocationally oriented.

Those more vulnerable schools that will need and seek federal funding in order to survive are the very institutions where the poor will likely be concentrated. Thus, lower-income students will not enjoy the experience of sharing increased generalized cognitive capacities, which, as a "liquid" resource, they can expend in many different social realms; rather they will develop vocational skills, which are useful primarily in occupational endeavors.

No matter how diverse the reasons for the poor (or the rich) to attend college, and no matter how diverse the educational environment available as learning opportunities, *it is the development of cognitive capacities, not occupational skills, that should characterize the learning experience.* The university can be diverted from its present mission and still remain a physical entity in society. However, it would then serve a different purpose than that of learning and scholarship, as these have been most broadly defined. Both Robert Hartman and David Mundel are subtly suggesting that higher education move *in a particular direction,* one which I consider historically regressive and of less value to the society and to its participants.

REFERENCES

Bendix, R., & Lipset, S. M. (Eds.) *Class, status and power: A reader in social stratification.* Chicago: Free Press, 1953.

Blau, P. M., & Duncan, O. D. *The American occupational structure.* New York: Wiley, 1967.

Erikson, E. *Childhood and society.* New York: Norton, 1950.

Jencks, C., & Riesman, D. *The academic revolution.* New York: Doubleday, 1968.

Kagan, J., & Moss, H. A. *Birth to maturity.* New York: Wiley, 1962.

Kohlberg, L. Stages and sequence: The cognitive developmental approach to socialization. In D. A. Goslin (Ed.), *Handbook of socialization, theory and research.* Chicago: Rand McNally, 1969.

Marshall, T. H. *Class, citizenship and social development.* New York: Doubleday (Anchor Books), 1965.

Parsons, T. On the concept of political power, *and* On the concept of influence. *Sociological theory and modern society.* New York: Free Press, 1967.

Parsons, T., & Platt, G., in collaboration with Smelser, N. J. *The American academic system: A theoretical perspective.* Cambridge: Harvard University Press, 1973.

Rapaport, D. *The structure of psychoanalytic theory: A systematic attempt.* New York: International Universities Press, 1960.

Schafer, R. *Aspects of internalization.* New York: International Universities Press, 1968.

Spady, W. G. Educational mobility and access: Growth and paradoxes. *The American Journal of Sociology,* 1967, 23: 273–286.

Wolff, P. Cognitive considerations for a psychoanalytic theory of language acquisition. In R. R. Holt (Ed.), *Motives and thought.* New York: International Universities Press, 1967.

Part V

OVERVIEWS

PERSPECTIVES ON THE BENEFITS OF POSTSECONDARY EDUCATION

Fritz Machlup

I propose to address myself to seven issues of various degrees of relevance to the problem of the benefits of higher education: first, the use of the status of parents together with the ability of students as independent variables, separate but equal, in functions determining the "output" of education; second, the concept of educational attainment; third, the estimates of the pecuniary returns to investment in extended schooling; fourth, the assumption that private pecuniary returns reflect accruals to society of at least equal value; fifth, the concept of economic mobility; sixth, the use of the word "measurement" for estimate and for valuation; and seventh, a proposal for survey research on some factors attracting or deterring potential takers of longer education.

The Role of Parents' Socioeconomic Status or Educational Experience in the Explanation of Students' Attainments and Achievements

It has become customary in quantitative analysis of various aspects of education to use either parents' socioeconomic status (SES) or parents' years of education as one of several independent variables in the explanation of a variety of attainments or achievements of students, especially of students in tertiary education. In many, perhaps in most, instances the SES or parents' variable is used in conjunction with some measure of students' ability, chiefly, intellectual ability. I submit that such a procedure of combining a parent's variable with a student's variable is permissible for some explanatory purposes but not for others. It is permissible when the parents' variable is not itself a causal factor in the students' ability but a separate factor in determining the result. I propose two examples where this may be the case: in explaining *admission* to college and in explaining *completion* of college.

An admissions officer in college may be influenced chiefly by some objective or subjective criteria of the student's ability and, conceivably, also by the father's SES. He may, for example, admit the son of a professor, the son of a rich banker, or the son of a minister but reject a blue-collar worker's son with the same SAT and high school record. Most of us would complain about such discrimination, and in many institutions it has been stopped or even reversed. If we attempt to find out what factors are important in ensuring that students complete college instead of dropping out before graduation, we may find that the parents' SES is influential. The theoretical explanation may be twofold: parental moral support and parental financial support. Where a son or daughter of poor parents with little education is likely to drop out rather than go on with borrowed money when he or she is on scholastic probation, the student whose parents shell out the money and share some of his intellectual interests may hang on and complete college.

When we attempt to explain the output of tertiary education, the combined use of a parent's variable along with a variable measuring the student's ability is not legitimate, because the parent's variable may be one of the factors contributing to the student's ability. Thus, ability would appear twice in our function, once measured by some such proxy as IQ or Armed Forces Qualifying Test and again by whatever the parents have contributed through their genes or through their presence, their play in the nursery, and their conversations at the dinner table to the scholarly qualifications of their offspring. The extent these qualifications are innate or acquired is a question that is important, especially if one wants to compensate by educational efforts for what biological heredity may have failed to provide, and if one has established that it can be done and how it can be done. Let me warn, however, against the widespread error that the ability to learn is merely, or even largely, "intelligence," let alone that measured by intelligence tests. No matter which output we want to explain—Graduate Record Examinations, lifetime earnings, occupational status attained, cultural attainments, lifestyles, or attitudes—and no matter whether the qualities of the student that contribute to this output are innate or acquired, there are many more qualities than mental ability. In an article published recently (Machlup, 1972), I listed six qualities. My list has now grown to include eight ingredients of the ability to learn or of the ability to profit from higher education: mathematical ability, verbal ability, creative ability (inventiveness), entrepreneurial ability (drive, daring, and flair), interest (intellectual curiosity), ambition, industry (diligence), perseverance.

To every one of these factors, which contribute *directly* to the output of educational effort, the parents' SES or their educational experiences may have made some contribution. If we put into our function both the ingredients of student quality and the parent variable, the regression coefficients of the factors that operate directly on the output will be confusingly small. Yet we should admit there may be two influences from the parent variable that may work on the output *not via* student ability. One is *pull*, especially in getting the graduate's first job and perhaps also his early promotions. (Pull, as I think of it, includes friendships and good connections.) The other is *finance*, which may have been needed to help the graduate to get the sheepskin. But if these two influences were actually at work, they ought to be specifically ascertained and separated out, not included in a parent variable that works most powerfully through the various ingredients of student quality.

Educational Attainment and the Contents of Education

I cannot suppress a short comment on a semantic aberration. I rise in horror about the use of the words "educational attainment," if no more is meant than "years of school." This is not merely a euphemism; it is deceptive advertising. To sit in school for 9 or 12 or 16 years is perhaps an attainment in patient docility but not an educational attainment. Attainments of educational effort cannot be anything but matters of the mind, of the character, attitudes, working habits, or lifestyles. A *given* level of educational attainment can be the result of a *variable* number of years. One may learn slowly or fast. Some people want to extend school from 12 to 16 years for everybody, even if the intellectual outcome is not perceptibly increased. My own ideal, as I set it forth in *Production and Distribution of Knowledge* (Machlup, 1962), is a system in which an enlarged and enriched curriculum is compressed from 12 into 9 and 10 years. To measure educational attainment in years is a swindle.

Similar in ambiguity is the application of the term "higher education" to any kind of school attendance beyond 12 years. This is misleading.

As far as any honorific connotations are concerned, we need not care. Perhaps it has therapeutic value to call a student who tries to learn at a college what he has failed to learn at high school a student in higher education. However, when we want to study the cost of and benefits from 4 additional years of (postsecondary) schooling, we must not disregard what is done in these years. Would 4 years of Bible reading be equivalent to 4 years of foreign-language study and to 4 years of higher mathematics? Would 4 years of art appreciation be equivalent to 4 years of Marxist–Leninist study and to 4 years of microbiology? I cannot believe that it makes no difference what subject matter, what reasoning techniques, and what ethical systems are being taught in post-secondary schooling.

Pecuniary Returns to Extended Schooling

Most writers on the subject take as an established fact that the pecuniary returns—that is, the differential earnings attributable to four years of tertiary schooling—are not only positive but also larger than the incremental cost. Thus, the pecuniary net returns are believed to be positive, and the rate of return on the private investment is believed to be as high as that on investment in tangible capital.

These beliefs are warranted for the past. The calculations by Gary Becker (1964) are based on acceptable data and supported by acceptable hypotheses. Today, however, the results seem somewhat dated. The cross-section data on incomes of various age groups were from the 1940 and 1950 Census figures, that is, from 1939 and 1949 incomes. The incomes of persons 40 years old were therefore the incomes of those who graduated from college in 1921 and 1931. Giora Hanoch (1965) has more recent data from the 1960 Census, and they confirm Becker's results. Still, the 40-year-old income earners from that Census graduated from college in 1942. At that time only 15 percent of the college-age group were enrolled in college. I question whether income differentials earned at a time when only 15 percent went to college will be valid for a time when 50 percent go to college.

The law of supply and demand is still in effect. Income differentials earned at a time when college graduates were scarce will not hold in times when graduates are plentiful. The Carnegie Commission on Higher Education believes that there is a satisfactory pecuniary return to investment in college education, and they explain their belief with an increase in demand for graduates. I grant that technological and organizational changes in our economy have resulted in increased demand for college-trained personnel, but I doubt that the expansion of demand can have matched the explosion of supply. Thus, I do not share the faith of my fellow analysts of the economics of tertiary education in the persistence of positive net returns. Indeed, I would not be surprised if future income data should show that the positive income differentials of our current graduates have vanished.

Pecuniary Social Returns Different from Private

One may not share my doubts and may prefer to think that the private net returns to investment in college education are continuing at a positive and satisfactory rate. Since I cannot prove my suspicions on this score, I propose that we ask whether the existence of a positive rate of private net return guarantees that the rate of social net return is also positive and even higher, indeed, high enough to support a claim for government subsidies for the promotion of larger enrollments. I shall not repeat what Lee Hansen has argued ("On External Benefits and Who Should Foot the Bill?", pp. 329–333) about comparative merits of claims for public support. Nor shall I stress the fact that at the present rate of support from all levels of government and from private philanthropists, the social costs are greater than the private costs. I want to call attention to a different point regarding any income differentials that may be received by college graduates, namely, whether these income differentials can be taken as safe indication of at least equal accruals to the national product.

It is possible that the improved performance of college-trained personnel produces a net increase in the nation's product exactly equal to the income differentials paid to the graduates. It is also possible that college-trained labor is complementary with non-college-trained labor, so that the incomes of the less educated increase also, and the increase in the nation's product will exceed the income differentials paid to college graduates. There is still a third possibility: College-trained labor, in increased supply, may be competitive with non-college-trained labor. Thus, the incomes of the latter will decrease as college graduates are substituted for high school graduates in many jobs. In this case, the nation's product does not increase as much as the income going to the college graduates. In other words, the social returns on investment in college education would in this case be lower than the private return.

The possibility of competition between college-trained and less-trained labor has been examined. One author spoke of the "bumping" of high school graduates by college graduates in occupations for which the additional four years of education would not have been really necessary. I also refer to Ivar Berg's research, reported in his book with the striking subtitle *The Great Training Robbery* (1971). Allow me to mention also the simple explanations offered in my book on *Education and Economic Growth* (Machlup, 1970). The point is that the private income differentials earned by persons with a bachelor's degree are not at all sure indications of these persons' making equivalent contributions to the national product. Thus, the private rate of return can be attractive, while the social rate of return is zero; and the private investment may be wasted from the point of view of society.

The Concept of Economic Mobility

David Mundel ("Whose Education Should Society Support?", pp. 293–315), has made a good deal of "social and economic mobility." I had not previously encountered (or noticed) the expression "economic mobility" and was puzzled about its meaning. My first guess was that it meant occupational and geographic mobility, which are probably very important among the good results derived from good education. Education is supposed to make people more capable and more inclined to look for better job opportunities, to find the information, to interpret it, and to take advantage of it; in addition, the better-educated worker is supposed to be more adaptable and thus able to do a better job in the better job. All this is part of the total contribution that longer education is supposed to make to the national product as well as to private incomes. In other words, the effects of occupational and geographic mobility are included in the pecuniary private and social benefits of education, and we must not count them twice. Hence, I conclude that something else must be meant if "economic mobility" is given separate billing as a social benefit of longer education.

An alternative meaning of "economic mobility" may be the ease with which poor people can "move up" into higher income brackets. This is a private benefit of the persons concerned and an additional (social) benefit of concerned persons, concerned, that is, about the existence of poorer people in a presumably open society in which people can improve themselves, and the poor can rise to affluence. To the extent that widespread awareness of such opportunities increases the incentives and ambitions of poorer people, and their efforts lead to increased earnings indicative of increased productivity, there may be some additional third-party effects, or external benefits, in the form of material accruals to others. Yet, any social benefits in material form are disdained by many concerned people; they cling to nonmaterial social values.

Some of the "economic mobility" evidenced in upward movements from lower to higher income brackets is a mere *ex post* reflection in the statistics of the distribution of national income. To inspect the statistics and find that such a movement has taken place may be a heartwarming experience both for those who like to see the situation of poor people improved and those who like to see greater equality in the distribution of income. These are two different sentiments—the one being sympathetic (vicarious) enjoyment of greater affluence of previously poor, the other, sympathetic (vicarious) gratification from reduced envy. Both are genuine "social values," and the difference between the two sentiments is operationally testable. If the satisfaction from seeing poor people better off is unabated by observing a similar or even greater improvement of rich men, then we can diagnose the satisfaction as pure sympathy with the poor. If, however, the pleasure of seeing an improvement of the lot of the poor is spoiled by displeasure from seeing rich people getting richer, the case is one of vicarious envy.

This brings me to another meaning of "economic mobility" alluded to in David Mundel's paper: upward mobility of some matched by downward mobility of others. In this case, it seems that some concerned people get pleasure out of observing a redistribution of income among people who trade places, while neither total income nor its dispersion need to change. If we had a "hedometer" to measure and compare the feelings of pleasure and pain of different persons, we would probably find that a cut in income feels worse than an equal rise in income feels good, simply because it is so very hard to give up some of the goodies to which one has become accustomed. Thus, the combined utility or "welfare feelings" of the people concerned would probably be reduced by a trading of places between persons in different income brackets. How strange that concerned persons, self-appointed arbiters of social values, should hold that the upward-cum-downward mobility, where people merely trade their places in a given income distribution, is a good thing for society.

Nonpecuniary Benefits: Measurements, Estimates, Valuations

In an interdisciplinary meeting the mutual suspicions and distrusts of representatives of different disciplines become apparent to all. The economists prefer to concentrate on pecuniary benefits; the sociologists, psychologists, and educationists want to give greater weight to nonpecuniary benefits. The noneconomists are disdainful of the dollar-and-cents values the economists want to put on the social benefits of education; and the economists are somewhat reserved concerning the more esoteric social values that some of the antimaterialists claim are supreme, priceless, and invaluable. The noneconomists get especially

disturbed about economists who seem to accept some of the im-
measurable social values but proceed to measure and enter them in
a formal cost-and-benefit account.

It is a serious obstacle to mutual understanding when economists
in their scientistic zeal talk about measuring where they are merely estimating and, still more, when they use the term "measurement" for more
or less subjective valuation. This is not merely a matter of diplomacy;
we really confuse the public if we call measurements what, in fact,
are rather crude estimates of pecuniary private benefits—estimates based
on raw data of questionable reliability and on sophisticated hypotheses
of doubtful credibility. It is worse still, if we say that we measure where
we simply place a rather artitrary value on any Good Thing that any
Good People—including Charlie Brown or Lucy, and all other social
psychologists—nominate for a prize in a social popularity contest.

The valuation of nonpecuniary social benefits is a delicate matter,
first, because it is based on a prior evaluation of the probabilities that
the claimed benefits are actually achieved as a result of the proposed
social action—in our case, getting more people to go to school for more
years. Then, if these probabilities are judged to be high, the valuation
is either that of a single arbiter, with all his personal biases and preju-
dices concerning societal goals, or that of a social scientist claiming
to know the "social welfare function," that is, the combined preferences
of all the people who belong to the particular society. Finally, it may
be that of a collection of elected legislators who represent the people
and follow some parliamentary voting procedure to enact the "general
will." All these ways of ascertaining the correct value of the social benefits in question are rather far from a process of measuring, but they
are necessary preconditions of rational social action. Indeed, no legislator
who has any sense can deny that in his vote for or against a bill, he
places an upper limit as well as a lower limit on the value of some
social benefits to be derived from the particular action of the
government.

These valuations, for most decision makers, will be a matter of upper
and lower limits, but the compromise on the appropriation of required
funds will be a single round figure. If, for example, an additional $10
billion is appropriated for "higher education," the action implies that
the legislature values the benefits from the extended education to be
worth at least $10 billion. This amount might have bought more hospi-
tals, better roads, faster mail service, safer streets, cleaner air, or many
other types of social benefits among which choices had to be made.
These choices, if they are made not by fools or corrupt pawns of vested
interests but by responsible politicians, reflect comparative values, ex-

pressed in money, of alternative social benefits expected from various social actions.

The social scientist is probably better informed on many aspects of the indispensable and unavoidable cost-and-benefit analyses. If he wants to help the legislators in their deliberations about alternative courses of action, he may offer his own valuations of the respective social benefits. To be sure, the professional educator may be biased in favor of larger appropriations for education, just as the Army Corps of Engineers may be biased in favor of public works on rivers and waterways, and the ecologists may have especially high aspirations concerning measures to reduce the pollution of our physical environment. The exaggerated respect that experts have for their own special fields makes it desirable to restrain them by forcing them to understand the notion of opportunity costs—the values of possible alternatives. Where investment outlays are involved—that is, outlays that do not have their entire payoff immediately—the opportunity costs of any action can be held in view only by insisting on a competitive rate of return secured from the investment. This is a rate competitive not only with all other forms of social investment but also with the returns on investment in private tangible capital.

This requirement sounds terrible to one who puts cultural values above the satisfaction of material wants. Let me reassure him that economists do not put material above cultural benefits. Choices must be made among all sorts of alternatives, and the gratification of cultural desires— music and art, beauty and truth, peace and justice—is not outside economic considerations. We cannot measure such benefits, but we cannot help evaluating them as long as they do not fall like manna from heaven.

Factors Attracting or Deterring Potential Takers of Longer Education

There is a great deal written about the proportion of college-age people that "ought" to attend college or some other school with grades 13 to 16. The extremists want "universal higher education," which I translate to mean "longer education for 90 percent of the age group." The moderates would be happier with something like 50 percent. The elitists hold that really "higher" education is suitable for probably no more than 15 percent of the age group and that longer education of the other possible kinds (broader or thinner) is a luxury, if not a wasteful use of resources. Since I have expressed the unpopular elitist view, I should say a few words of explanation.

Longer education—say, longer than 12 years—can be higher, broader, or thinner. It is higher only if it builds upon knowledge that is absorbed in secondary education and introductory courses but disseminates knowledge that could not have been absorbed at that earlier stage (except by a few geniuses). The simplest example is higher mathematics, but advanced courses in virtually any discipline qualify as higher education: symbolic logic, microeconomics and econometrics, nuclear or solid-state physics, microbiology, quantum chemistry, structural linguistics, classical archaeology, stratigraphic paleobotany, sensory psychophysiology musical accoustics, analytic demography. No curriculum in a liberal arts college offers more than a fraction—perhaps between 20 and 25 percent—of higher education; the bulk of college work is broader education, and some portion is remedial education.

I am neither snooty nor disrespectful of broader or of remedial education. I firmly believe that every scholar needs broader education, much more than he can get in secondary school. Without such broader education the greatest specialist would still be an uneducated man. As far as remedial education is concerned, I hold that everybody who was unable to obtain an adequate elementary or secondary education ought to be given a chance—at any age—to make up for what he has missed. However, it would be ridiculous to plan for 16 years of schooling on the theory that a substantial fraction of students cannot master the normal requirements of secondary school in a shorter time. I submit that the contrary is much more plausible, and that greater concentration (compression of the 12-year curriculum into 9 or 10 years) would be more likely to succeed in achieving mastery of the basic skills and cognitive techniques. To make education longer but thinner would be counterproductive; the graduates of schools designed to teach in 16 years what could be learned in 10 years would be educationally disadvantaged.

Now, assuming that college should and would offer a healthy mixture of broader and higher education, how many students—what proportion of high school graduates—would it attract, hold, and benefit? Since we have no technique to ascertain the degree to which students possess the eight requisite qualities of higher education, we could instead find out what percentage of high school graduates would *elect* to go to college if no pressures of any sort were applied, no disadvantages of staying out were threatened, and no pecuniary or social advantages were offered or promised. Such a test of self-selection could be made only through survey research; replies to questionnaires would be quite unreliable. To find out what factors would attract or deter potential takers of tertiary education one might formulate a series of terms or conditions and then ascertain whether the decisions to go to college would be affected by the presence or absence of any of these terms or conditions.

In an article in *The Humanist* (Machlup, 1972), I listed 11 conditions, but I am sure that my first try at formulating the relevant ones was clumsy and inadequate. I attempted to find out how much it mattered if various traditional requirements (of courses, attendance, examinations, grades) were imposed or dispensed with, if the cost to students were positive or zero (with stipends equal to earnings foregone), and if pecuniary advantages and social discrimination were or were not existent. If no one could expect higher incomes or higher social status as a result of longer education, the benefits from the extended educational effort would be cultural only. It would surely be interesting to find out how many young people want more knowledge for the sake of knowledge, greater cognitive capacities not convertible into money or status, and finer esthetic tastes and ethical discernment just for the sake of a refined lifestyle.

Perhaps I am too pessimistic, but I expect that the number of those electing to enroll and complete college (with a healthy dose of higher education) would be far below present figures. This, of course, is a mere guess, but research to obtain an approximate estimate would not be difficult to execute.

REFERENCES

Becker, G. S. *Human capital, a theoretical and empirical analysis, with special reference to education.* New York: National Bureau of Economic Research, 1964 (General Series, No. 80).

Berg, I. *Education and jobs: The great training robbery.* Boston: Beacon Press, 1971.

Hanoch, G. Personal earnings and investment in schooling. Unpublished doctoral dissertation, University of Chicago, 1965.

Machlup, F. *The production and distribution of knowledge in the United States.* Princeton: Princeton University Press, 1962.

Machlup, F. *Education and economic growth.* Lincoln: University of Nebraska Press, 1970.

Machlup, F. Universal higher education, promise or illusion? *The Humanist,* 1972, 32(3): 17–23.

ECONOMICS OF HIGHER EDUCATION

*The Changing Scene**

Andre Daniere

A good deal has happened to the economics of higher education—or to its practitioners—in the course of the last decade. A reader of the literature in the mid-sixties would come away with the (justified) impression that the single concern of economists in the field was the contribution of educational activities to measured national product. Their policy prescriptions seemed limited to adjustments (increases) in the provision of education in response to "rates of return" achievable through this particular type of social investment. By contrast, an observer of the Woods Hole Conference, July 16–19, 1972, would conclude that contemporary interest lies primarily with the equity or equality of the distribution of education among social groups. The same message can be read in the latest issue of the *Journal of Political Economy* (1972) so often quoted during the course of the conference. The title of the JPE compendium, "Investment in Education: The Equity–Efficiency Quandary," represents a feeble attempt to assert continuity; the contents, however, reveal the birth of an essentially new field of inquiry from which earlier passwords have all but disappeared.

* A shortened version of this paper was previously published in *The Annals of the American Academy of Political and Social Science*, 1972, 404: 58–70.

In retrospect, the excitement engendered around 1965 by empirical findings (Schultz, 1963) of high economic returns from education appears puzzling, for such results were, after all, quite consistent with conventional wisdom. It must be recalled, however, that education had long been left out of the economist's arsenal in quantitative explanations of economic growth. It made its reappearance just as serious questions were being asked about the adequacy of "capital" and "labor" indices in accounting for long-run changes in GNP. There was also a sense of disappointment at the roughness of rate-of-return estimates initially publicized in advanced countries. No apparent effort had been made to distinguish between types or qualities of higher education, and very little was done in the way of separating the effects of education proper from those of student attributes acquired before the college experience. Of course, neither American economists nor their colleagues in Western Europe could expect to be consulted on the details of higher education planning in their respective countries. Under the circumstances, they could not be blamed for devoting their time to theoretical explorations of the revived "education" variable (Solow, 1957) and to encouraging perennial enthusiasts of "more education for more."

On another front, the early record reveals an impressive effort to build detailed education plans for countries in the early stages of their development. A unique opportunity was afforded the frustrated central planner hidden within every economist to prove his mettle, and to do so free of ideological conflict, inasmuch as he was dealing with a traditionally public service. Every country with a per capita income under the world average was soon endowed with its complete education plan, showing enrollments needed at each level and in each major sector of education over the coming decades to fulfill the manpower requirements of planned (or hoped for) economic development. While the calculation of rates of return on educational investment in Western countries gave numerical weight (if not precision) to the argument for education as a priority objective of development, the rates played no practical role in the planning process itself: The approach was very much in the tradition of centralized socialist planning, with dependence on formally rigid "input–output" coefficients linking labor-force requirements to "planned" sectorial outputs and enrollments in each cycle of education to flow requirements into the labor force or into further education. Again, there is reason to be dissatisfied with the unsophistication of much of this work, especially the application of input–output structures from the West to a widely different resource mix and the international equation of educational categories without regard for their actual content. But the context of an urgent shortage of trained manpower, together with the lack of alternative data, provided a sufficient excuse for whatever misdemeanors were committed at the time.

The earliest and academically most productive deviation from the economic-growth approach was heralded by Gary Becker's publication of his fundamental work in 1964. While much of his effort was initially directed at refining concepts and measures of "human capital" and its returns, he was soon led—and inspired others—to study the impact of unequal education among social groups on the income distribution. Much of the early work dealt with racial differentials, and some of the major publications up to 1970 focused on this special area. It was established that one's ethnic, income-class, or geographic origin did affect one's opportunities for education, which, in turn, affected one's future income prospects. It was noted very early with reference to ethnic differentials (primarily the white–nonwhite classification) that the earnings gap was by no means fully explained by differences in educational attainment; specifically, nonwhites earn substantially less than whites with the same number of years of schooling, suggesting that social differences other than education are of influence in the labor market. While the importance of qualitative differences in the average education of blacks and whites is widely noted as a biasing factor of "job-discrimination" estimates, little has been done to introduce the necessary corrections.

The culmination of national concerns with racial discrimination in the mid-sixties was more than coincidentally related to the concentration of economic studies on educational differentials between racial groups. Similarly, the new lines of inquiry developed over the last five years owe much to recent manifestations of "class consciousness" emanating from the poor, women, the young, and a few more esoteric groups.* Much of the work reported at the Woods Hole Conference was devoted to the explanation of earnings differentials in terms of social-class origin, sex, and, marginally, differentials over the life cycle. Partly as a result of the intrusion of "radical economists" bent on demonstrating the perversity of the System—specifically, its resistance to social mobility or equalization—interest centers as much on the earnings impact of social or personal characteristics *independent of education* as on the influence of such characteristics *via* the education they promise. Much of the variance observed in earnings and occupation within age cohorts remains unexplained after account has been taken of education, ability, and

---

* Such manifestations may be viewed as an outgrowth of the earlier (and continuing) racial crisis, and contemporary economic studies of higher education may be interpreted as refinements of earlier investigations in the problem of racial differentials. There is no doubt, however, that race has receded in the hierarchy of "variables of interest" within either universe.

parental characteristics; the latter two may contribute half as much as education itself to what they jointly explain. On another level, radical economists and others are questioning the extent to which the skills acquired in the formal education process contribute to differences in productivity within broad occupational categories. They suggest that education level is, in part, a "certification" of characteristics that employers use as a selection criterion for positions in the production hierarchy.

Education and Productivity: The Theory Revisited

It is evident that the new preoccupation with economic opportunity structures or, for some, the social-class dynamics of modern capitalist countries is leading to a far more detailed analysis of the determinants of occupation and earnings than earlier studies of returns on "human capital" ever did. Measures of student ability (best interpreted as predictions of performance in standard activities under the average sequence of experiences offered by the society), quality scales of the higher education received, and multiple characterizations of family background, all have become regular guests at the statistical tables of economists. Clearly, this should provide the opportunity for a refinement of earlier rate-of-return computations and a better identification of which type of education, applied to whom, is most likely to contribute to GNP growth. Indeed, many of the economists active in the field still labor toward that end. But it would seem that the new insights are eroding existing foundations without, at the same time, providing the means for a better construct.

Part of the problem is the multicollinearity of family background, ability, and education in available samples—or, worse, the near absence of observations for combinations involving wide ranges of each variable—resulting in a high variance of estimates. Moreover, economists are still uncertain of the mechanism by which the labor market assigns occupations with reference to education achievement. They know only that the earnings differentials associated with education, after controlling for the independent effect of ability and family background, can no longer be viewed as proper measures of the productivity of relevant educational increments. They need not accept the radical notion that much of higher (and earlier) education is only meant to legitimize the claim of the well born to high social positions or, at best, to reinforce or produce in each educational stratum the attitudes and behaviors most likely to strengthen capitalist control of the society (Bowles, 1971). It is enough to be impressed by what is now referred to as the "screening" theory of higher education, several forms of which are competing for attention.

In its mildest version, the theory states that higher education does not add to the skills of its clientele as much as it identifies individuals endowed with appropriate characteristics. The less "technical" or work-oriented the education (i.e., the more "liberal"), the more it takes the quality of a testing device and the less that of a training instrument. While there may be no reason to question the allocative efficiency of the labor market proper, differences in productivity associated with differences in education are not fully attributable to the educational increment; similar, if attenuated, differences would occur in the absence of education. The economic productivity of a strictly "screening" education is the contribution it makes to GNP by allowing a better matching of jobs and people than would occur in its absence. We don't know how large this contribution is, and there is reason to suspect that it can be produced more cheaply through alternative testing instruments.

More extreme versions of the screening interpretation—perhaps better described as "ranking theories"—question traditional views of the competitive labor market, including the expected equalization of payments and productivities for all equally skilled workers. All similarly trained foremen in a shop could, indeed, be paid the same, with each sharing in the control and organization of shop activities. However, if one of them acts as shop manager with control over the remaining foremen, productivity increases. Moreover, the productivity of the shop rises with increases in the manager's pay much faster than with comparable increases in the aggregate of foremen's salaries. As a result, a maximum profit is obtained by selecting one of the men as shop manager and paying him a substantial differential. The extra pay serves to increase the "effort"* of the one individual whose effort makes the greatest difference in productivity, not primarily because of his training but because of the specific controls he exercises.

---

* "Effort," in the present context, does not mean simply exertion but includes resistance to sin (subtle and less subtle forms of thievery), as well as the exercise of extra doses of care and loyalty. Payment of a small differential is not sufficient to obtain superior performance, even when added to the prestige of a higher position: The manager would stand to lose little from low performance (if dismissed, he would generally find work at his former occupational grade), and he could gain a lot at the expense of the firm. Furthermore, the costs of ineptitude, negligence, or malfeasance can go very high before they are discovered and the corrective of dismissal is applied—unless even more costly controls are placed over the manager. Finally, a quantum jump in performance is achieved when the differential is wide enough to induce social identification with higher management and, thus, internalization of the latter's goals.

Education enters the process side by side with experience and the qualities it reveals, although in no direct relation to measured "productivity": A preference is given to the more educated, more experienced or ostensibly more able in the selection of shop manager, in part because their performance is expected to be no worse or better, and in part because the elevation of one foreman is more likely to be accepted by the rest of it is based on some objective (unambiguous) criteria. In essence, then, education helps provide a rank ordering of individuals on the basis of which jobs are filled in a parallel ranking of control and responsibility. While the proposed model only acquires validity within classes of manpower sharing similar technical skills—and much of education activity is instrumental in developing such skills—it may well predominate within the broad range of occupations filled by "liberally" or "generally" educated individuals across all economic sectors.

Direct empirical evidence in favor of either theory is meager, and it may remain so until the emphasis of manpower research is shifted from the estimation of statistical "earnings functions" to the longitudinal investigation of careers and the analysis of the promotion process within and across units of the modern industrial state. This is one of several junctures at which the new orientation of research leads to grounds covered earlier by sociologists. Meanwhile, much hangs on the generally perceived phenomenon of *job upgrading,* i.e., the secular increase in formal education requirements observed over the whole array of occupations. Millions of jobs can be counted in successive censuses for which objective skill requirements have not changed significantly; nevertheless, they have been transferred from grade school finishers to high school graduates, or from the latter to holders of college degrees (Berg, 1971).*
While this is evidence of a massive shift in the population distribution by level of schooling—sustained, in large part, by expectations of higher earnings through education and a general disposition of the society to satisfy educational demand—it is not likely that the change in average education within relatively stable occupations has made much difference

---

* I have, unfortunately, not had access to the forthcoming work of Taubman & Wales (1972) concerning the screening hypothesis. What is reported by Lewis Solmon ("Schooling and Subsequent Success," pp. 13–34), however, suggests that their evidence may be more subtle than convincing. Note that the evidence presented *against* the theory is no stronger. For instance, Barry Chiswick argues ("Schooling, Screening, and Income," pp. 151–158) that the declining correlation of earnings with education he observes in groups of increasing work experience (following a slight increase up to the tenth year of experience) supports the "human capital" model more than any screening hypothesis. But if the screening pattern is one of (a) relative standardization of earnings for "first" or "entry" jobs, (b) promotion in early years by main reference to education, and (c) increasing reference to revealed abilities on the job, the expected correlation pattern would be precisely as observed.

to the productivities of those occupations. It is tempting, indeed, to conclude that a general increase in the educational stock of a population simply raises educational requirements for any given position in the hierarchy. From the "proving ground" perspective, it may be that the qualities once revealed by the test of grade school completion need the further test of high school graduation when, some decades later, every child is somehow carried through the elementary curriculum.

A related situation seems to occur in developing countries, India, for instance, where the rapid growth of higher education under the joint impact of competitive social demand and a national will to accelerate economic progress has generated a stock of college graduates exceeding the "objective" needs of the economy. College graduates are distributed along the fairly narrow band of jobs affording a middle- or upper-middle-class status, with a large spillover into lower-middle-class occupations. Because the mass of graduates is relatively undifferentiated, people with the same educational identity find themselves spread over a wide range of occupational status and income, much of it on the basis of luck or family connections, at an unknown cost in social alienation. Again, competitive forces fail to equalize salaries, because production is better served by the existing job structure and because the higher pay received by those in positions of higher responsibility is worth what it generates in the way of exertion, loyalty, and lessened corruptibility.

Under any of the hypotheses offered, it is apparent that rates of economic return on additional investments in higher education cannot be calculated by reference to differential earnings, except in job areas where some identifiable educational sequence clearly stands as a precondition of technical competence. Ways to obtain proper estimates of the true marginal productivity of various educational increments in what may be a very complex market equilibrium have not been devised, and they are not likely to be, as long as that equilibrium remains poorly understood. There has been an unfortunate tendency to discard all deviations from the classical supply–demand model into the limbo of "market imperfections," even though the alternative models are fully consistent with rational profit or utility maximization on the part of all participants and with the efficient allocation of educated manpower.* Many are acting defensively on behalf of "human capital" interpretations, as if the

---

* This does not mean, of course, that our supply and distribution of higher education are optimized; employers may make the best of the rankings or tests education offers them, yet education may be wholly inefficient in providing this service. A hierarchy is less subject to ambiguity the wider its spread. But how much is gained through each extension is not clear. A proving ground is more conclusive the more numerous and difficult its hurdles, but decreasing returns must eventually set in.

new insights meant rejection, rather than refinement, of the older apparatus. While the exaggerated claims of some "screening" enthusiasts have exacerbated the debate beyond reason, one must hope that constructive efforts toward realistic new models will soon drown unseemly controversies.

Short of a quantitative statement, the various "screening" hypotheses do, at least, carry one policy implication: Higher education should continue to identify its products in terms of a well-understood and dependable hierarchy of merit. This is not to say that the information offered by a system of higher education on its graduates (or drop-outs) is the most appropriate for purposes of manpower allocation, but a tool helps, even if it is the wrong tool. In the case of developing countries experiencing a rapid growth of college-level education, it may be that the only (simplest?) way of reducing the perception of intolerable inequities among college graduates is the establishment of a strict hierarchy of degrees that leaves no one in doubt as to where he stands on the educational ladder. All such recommendations conflict with one or several of the ideological fashions of the time: the grass-roots American commitment to individual competition on the basis of true merit rather than acquired titles and the modern liberal vision of a less competitive, less stratified society in which the prime role of education is to reassure each individual of his unbounded capacity for growth. The recommendation will, nevertheless, have to be considered seriously if sufficient evidence accumulates in support of the screening role of higher education.

Meanwhile, some economists exhibit a growing inclination—and others a long-established determination—to look for criteria other than direct economic productivity in evaluating and testing educational investments. Well within the professional universe are so-called economic externalities, i.e., marginal contributions of education to productivity that are not received by the graduate and, thus, are not measurable with reference to his earnings. Unfortunately, they do not seem, in general, to be measurable in any other way, at least in the current state of economic information (Weisbrod, 1964).* Still within the traditional economic province are the "consumption" benefits of higher education, meaning the value to individuals of all outcomes of their education other than the earning of additional dollars. Measurement is again a problem, how-

---

* While David Mundel ("Whose Education Should Society Support?", pp. 293–315) provides a consistent and penetrating framework of analysis, his criteria for distinguishing between "social benefits" and "externalities" are a bit hazy. The first are evaluated by reference to economic productivity, while the second refer to alternate objectives (distribution).

ever, since individuals must somehow "reveal" their valuations in exchanges (substitutions) involving marketed goods or money.

Increasingly, then, economists are turning away from their preoccupation with maximizing benefit aggregates to the consideration of *distributional* objectives, more particularly the degree to which personal incomes, or opportunities for the earning of income, are equalized among members of the national or international community.* Distribution problems are, to a large degree, discussed within the context of a given educational investment, but the maximization of distributional objectives may also serve to determine optimum enrollment under alternative constraints—for instance, an institutional limit on the level of public financing or a determination not to reduce the access of any group to education. In any case, the trend initially identified as a response to growing concerns with inequality in U.S. society reappears in the end as a technical imperative: Having taken another look at the determinants of earnings, economists are forced to question the validity of former measures of education productivity and induced to deal, instead, with more easily related objectives of higher education.

The New Thrust: Studies in Distribution

While problems of distribution have always been part of the domain carved out of the social universe by economists, they have been handled somewhat gingerly. The conventional view is that all reasonable men must welcome an addition to the volume of goods and services available for distribution, but that few will agree on the virtues of any given distribution scheme.† For better or worse, the profession has experienced some degree of "liberation" in the last decade, in the sense that many of its adherents no longer show any reluctance to deal with social distribution. Members of that group have been pleasantly surprised to

* Other sociological (including political) outcomes of higher education are examined in the economic literature at large and by Robert Hartman ("Rationale for Federal Support of Higher Education," pp. 271–292) and by David Mundel. While the resulting commentaries are occasionally judicious and perceptive, their sterility fully justifies Richard Freeman's strictures ("On Mythical Effects of Public Subsidization of Higher Education," pp. 321–328).

† Rankings of economic status in terms of social desirability lose generality—and thus scientific status—to the extent that they rely on a particular set of preferences among income distributions. Furthermore, while a simple system of weights (market prices) is available to build a consistent index of welfare changes associated with shifts in the national basket of goods and services, few individuals or bodies politic can clarify the relative values they place on different levels of some "equalization" index or on increments of "equalization" versus increments of productivity.

discover that nothing, in fact, is more easily measured or more abundantly documented in national statistics. And their elation was complete when they saw the promise of a new family of quantitative models rooted in distributional information concerning such variables as family characteristics, ability, age, sex, education, occupation, related social roles, and income. Sociologists (and worldly philosophers) had, of course, dealt with such a complex in numerous studies of social-class differentiation, class identification, and social mobility. But it was evident that the field would greatly benefit from the keener minds and sharper tools of the economic brotherhood.

The results so far have not been spectacular. No duplication of the well-articulated dynamic models, sophisticated econometric forays, and systematic searches for optimum solutions that distinguish economics from her sister sciences has occurred. Instead, economists have been caught using—possibly for the first time—the methods of "path analysis" lately popularized by sociologists to achieve neat decompositions of the impact of variables linked in recursive systems (Griliches & Mason, 1972). The majority have been content to estimate simple regressions for the few available samples in which income, occupation, or educational attainment are measured jointly with their presumed antecedents, leaving the construction of multistage models to better days, or incorporating selected findings into loose concoctions lifted from the Marxist recipe book. Those engaged in the latter exercise have been under no compulsion to offer "social welfare" judgments: They only have to assert the ineluctability of social-class differentiation and its perpetuation to the benefit of the capitalist class under an educational system evidently built for that very purpose. Others have attempted to trace the impact of existing policies and their alternatives on various measures of social equalization, with the (generally implicit) understanding that more equalization is better than less, at least when moving incrementally from the existing pattern. This particular effort engages most of the resources of individuals presently working in the "economics of education," although along different and unequally promising paths.

HIGHER EDUCATION AS A TOOL OF SOCIAL MOBILITY

The ultimate question is whether higher education does—or can be made to—contribute to an individual's economic achievement beyond what he can expect on the basis of his personal and family characteristics. It is not whether higher education is socially *productive* but whether it helps its pupils, perhaps at the expense of others. Another way to put it is: Can higher education act as an equalizer of economic futures by more investments in education on the part of the less advantaged? This could mean either more resources per unit of time or the same annual resources over a longer period. It may fail to do so because no amount of education may compensate for personal or family handicaps or because no level of performance may compensate for such handicaps in one's ability to succeed economically. The failure of institutional certification to correlate with economic success may, in turn, constitute a shortcoming of the educational system—which may be congenital or amenable to correction—or result from prejudiced (inefficient) behavior on the part of controlling economic agents. The problem, of course, is less to establish that compensation through education does or does not occur than to measure how much is obtained in relation to variable amounts of resources applied in alternative forms of higher education.

It is evident that firm answers cannot be expected in the absence of sizable samples of individuals providing detailed information on their family characteristics, their performance in comparable tests at different stages, their educational history, and a substantial slice of their work history. Even then, the relevance of the estimated pattern for later generations would have to be questioned—as would the stability of estimated parameters under policies generating massive changes in the volume and distribution of higher education. The material available to researchers in the area, however, is a far cry from the "ideal" sample, and the surveys offered by Solmon ("Schooling and Subsequent Success") and Wolfe ("To What Extent Do Monetary Returns to Education Vary with Family Background, Mental Ability, and School Quality?", pp. 65–74) reveal a wide range of interpretations.*

Estimates of the relative roles of ability and education in determining future income vary extensively, but none attributes to ability more than one third of the variance of earnings jointly explained by the two factors. The impact of college education is more pronounced the higher the student's ability. The quality of the education received makes more difference the less able the student—except that very high-level institutions do the most for very high-ability students,† perhaps by giving them exclusive access to the higher rungs of the Establishment. Some studies suggest that the impact of institutional quality is not so much to increase scholastic achievement as to ensure preferential treatment in employment and admission to graduate schools (Astin, 1968), an observation quite consistent with the screening theories.

With respect to family background, it is generally found that educa-

---

* The review of the findings that follows draws heavily from these two surveys.

† This exception was missed by Daniere & Mechling (1970). Solmon, however, gives it excessive weight in his general interpretation of the interaction.

tional attainment is the main contributor to occupational attainment, the socioeconomic status of parents being of influence mostly through its effect on educational attainment and ability. Furthermore, the impact of background on educational attainment is felt primarily through the differential access it procures to various levels of higher education. These findings are favorable, overall, to the expectation of increased social mobility under more equalized opportunities for higher education. From the standpoint of radical analysis, however, the fact that family background *may* explain as much as one half the variance of schooling completed assumes central importance. When associated with extreme estimates of the independent effect of background on earnings (with educational attainment controlled), it gives substance to the position that parental characteristics are the prime direct and indirect determinant of variations in earnings (Bowles, 1972).

Equity of Cost–Benefit Distribution

A more traditional line pursued by economists concerns the degree to which personal benefits and costs of higher education are equitably distributed. Each individual contributes to the aggregate costs of higher education in three possible ways: (1) He foregoes income to the extent that he studies and does not work; (2) he sacrifices present and future consumption to the extent that he pays tuition bills out of present or future earnings; and (3) he pays taxes or makes donations over his lifetime, part of which are allocated to the support of higher education. This raises a number of questions. Looking at higher education as a public service and accepting whatever income distribution results (in part) from its administration, one may inquire as to the "progressivity" of its financing, i.e., whether the contributions listed above increase more or less than in proportion to the lifetime income of individuals. If, instead, the emphasis is placed on education as a producer of greater earnings, reference is made to the public investment–subsidy received by purchasers of education, i.e., the discounted costs of their education net of whatever they, their families, or private donors contribute in support of such costs: What is the size of the subsidy, and why—apart from the support of identifiable external benefits—should it go to a category of investors already favored with superior human (and often material) resources rather than to the less advantaged?* If, finally, the benefits of education are viewed as accruing to families (i.e., if the

---

* The rate of pecuniary returns on the student's own investment (foregone earnings and payments out of own income) is of little interest from the standpoint of equity, but it is worth measuring in any case, since any policy designed to expand educational opportunities must insure that potential new recruits reap a positive return from joining the ranks of the higher educated.

success of their children is an important objective of families), the size of net benefits to families in relation to their income is worth examining.

The major study in this area (Hansen & Weisbrod, 1969) concludes that the cost–benefit structure in at least one major state (California) is seriously regressive (i.e., unfavorable to the lower-income group), but its results are largely based on irrelevant comparisons* and do little more than underline the greater access enjoyed by higher-income families to more expensively produced and more heavily subsidized education. Other calculations (Pechman, 1970) deny any substantial regressivity of the California system, but they suffer from their own conceptual or informational defects.† In effect, the meaningful calculations have not been carried out, a reflection, perhaps, of the low priority they deserve.

EQUALIZATION OF EDUCATIONAL OPPORTUNITIES

The least ambitious, yet most immediately relevant, investigations concern themselves with the equalization of educational opportunities among socioeconomic groups, leaving aside the question of whether these mature into equal economic opportunities, and according only limited attention to the "progressiveness" of the underlying cost distribution.

Two decades of studies of the incomes associated with different levels of education have revealed that, whether or not the educational process is responsible for it, those who go through more education can expect additional earnings of a determinable size.‡ As long as (1) admissions to educational institutions are independent of the student's financial status, (2) the costs to be covered by any student are low enough to provide a positive expected net return on his investment,§ and (3)

---

* Public education subsidies received by individuals are compared with taxes paid out of differential income to obtain a measure of net transfer. Clearly, however, the subsidization cannot be regarded as an individual transfer independently of the income it produces, and the equity of taxes on that income should not be evaluated by reference to its source. The comparison with respect to student families (subsidy per family of students enrolled in different types of institution versus state and local tax payments per family, both on an annual basis) compounds a multiplicity of errors.

† Richard Freeman ("On Mythical Effects of Public Subsidization of Higher Education") sketches the elements of a proper equity evaluation with reference to families, but the empirical work is admittedly incomplete.

‡ The reference is to student expectations, i.e., the mean of their probability distribution of income. The differential is determinable within a small range of probable error, at least in real terms and for the first decade of working life.

§ To the extent that the student has no access to funds for investment in alternative channels, his competitive returns are zero, and any level of expected net benefits in excess of the interest charge is sufficient to make his enrollment "economically" rational.

funds are made available so that the student can cover his costs when required, the financial barrier to equal educational opportunities is effectively lifted: Any "admissible" student is given both the means and the economic incentive to enroll.

One possible approach to the equalization of opportunities, therefore, is a combination of student charges calculated to provide admissible students with an acceptable rate of pecuniary returns, together with the provision of sufficient financing during school years in the form of long-term loans repayable at interest. The peculiarities of the situation make it possible and desirable to minimize both the risk and expected subjective cost of the investment through the institution of "contingent loan" programs, i.e., loan systems under which repayments are calculated as a percentage of the borrower's annual income, whatever that income turns out to be. So far, however, the contingent-loan idea has drawn far more enthusiasm from economists and private educators (Hartman, 1971) than from legislatures, for reasons that have little to do with its intrinsic merits.

The student-loan alternative is fighting an indecisive battle against more traditional policies for the establishment of equal opportunities— free or low tuition in public institutions with compensating tax support and student or institutional grants to the private sector. The rapidly increasing and perversely uneven weight of taxation, however, does generate strong pressures toward the consideration of less painful financing methods—payments (by students) for identifiable individual benefits (increased earnings) are clearly more attractive than unrequited levies on the general population. Additional pressure emanates from private institutions that, because most of the public subsidy goes to support low-tuition public institutions, find themselves increasingly unable to enroll the students they want at the high tuition they must charge to meet instructional costs. Finally, there is evidence that low tuitions, by creating a state of fiscal stringency that discourages public programs of student aid, may distort enrollments away from equalization: Because the cost of going to college goes far beyond the payment of tuition, low-income students are induced to attend schools within commuting distance (to save on expenses) and to limit their attendance to two years (to reduce their earnings loss). Thus, under a sustained policy of low public tuitions, and with the encouragement of new, but timid, programs of federal student aid inaugurated in the mid-sixties, the number of high school graduates from the lower-income quartile going on to college has increased dramatically over the last seven years. But it is also true that most of the additional enrollment has been funneled to two-year institutions with a relatively low rate of transfer, while the proportion of low-income students in four-year public institutions appears to have registered a slight decline. There is little expectation of a change in this trend until the prevalent free-tuition ideology is replaced by a realistic commitment to adequate student financing under a more equitable sharing of higher education costs by those who benefit the most.

REFERENCES

Astin, A. W. Undergraduate achievement and institutional "excellence." *Science,* 1968, 161(3842): 661–668.

Becker, G. S. *Human capital, a theoretical and empirical analysis, with special reference to education.* New York: National Bureau of Economic Research, 1964 (General Series, No. 80).

Berg, I. *Education and jobs: The great training robbery.* Boston: Beacon Press, 1971.

Bowles, S. Unequal education and the reproduction of the social division of labor. *The Review of Radical Political Economics,* 1971, 3(4): 1–30.

Bowles, S. Schooling and inequality from generation to generation. *Journal of Political Economy,* 1972, 80(3, Pt. 2): S219–S251.

Daniere, A., & Mechling, J. Direct marginal productivity of college education in relation to college aptitude of students and production costs of institutions. *The Journal of Human Resources,* 1970, 5(1): 51–70.

Griliches, Z., & Mason, W. M. Education, income, and ability. *Journal of Political Economy,* 1972, 80(3, Pt. 2): S74–S103.

Hansen, W. L., & Weisbrod, B. A. *Benefits, costs and finance of public higher education.* Chicago: Markham, 1969.

Hartman, R. W. *Credit for college.* New York: McGraw-Hill, 1971. *Journal of Political Economy,* Investment in education: The equity-efficiency quandary, 1972, 80(3, Pt. 2).

Pechman, J. A. The distributional effects of public higher education in California. *The Journal of Human Resources,* 1970, 5(3): 361–370.

Schultz, T. W. *The economic value of education.* New York: Columbia University Press, 1963.

Solow, R. M. Technical change and the aggregate production function. *Review of Economics and Statistics,* 1957, 39(3): 312–320.

Taubman, P. J., & Wales, T. Earnings: Higher education, mental ability and screening. Unpublished manuscript, University of Pennsylvania, 1972.

Weisbrod, B. A. *External benefits of public education: An economic analysis.* Princeton: Princeton University Press, 1964.

SELECTIVE REMARKS AND SOME DICTA

Mary Jean Bowman

These notes are based on the taped record of the proceedings of the Woods Hole Conference on the Benefits of Higher Education. In part they are responses to other people's comments and in part self-generated. They fall naturally in four main sections:

1. Questions concerning the noncognitive effects of education on students and the subsequent significance of such learning;
2. Remarks concerning analysis of higher education in a career perspective and the importance of looking at both alternatives to higher education and the postschool learning that is complementary to higher education in the unfolding of a career;
3. A brief statement concerning earnings expectations as distributions;
4. A set of assertions that seemed to me to be especially worth stressing in the closing session of the conference. This was not in fact or by intent a balanced general view, and I have made no attempt to write down later reactions in retrospect.

Throughout, these notes are as close to the tapes as possible. However, given that discussions are not being reproduced as such, I have inserted statements at the beginning of the first two sections for general orientation, and I have added occasional transition sentences to replace a dialogue. Also, in the third section I have inserted a summary statement of the gist of a hand-out circulated at the conference.

Concerning Noncognitive Attributes and Causation

Few would challenge the general proposition that success in life as measured by external criteria (whatever criteria we may reasonably pick) depends in part, but only in part, on family background, intelligence, cognitive achievement, and educational certification. Neither will most people deny the proposition that among the other things that affect a student's later life, including his outward "success," are his attitudes, values, and self-image. So much, whether made explicit or not, I take to be common ground of most if not all behavioral scientists. Where one goes from this point, and what may be the implications for research concerning benefits of higher education, is another matter. Furthermore, the social–psychological domain is a problem area in which communication can be especially difficult and especially sensitive. One of the communication problems at the conference was attributable, in my judgment, to the fact that some people started off by thinking about simple association, and even among those who were thinking in terms of causation there were widely differed referents with respect to focal links in a presumed causal chain.

It would seem, to start with, that when we are talking about the "benefits" of something we must be looking for causal relationships. This applies whether the benefits are single or multiple variables and whether they are perceived primarily in terms of individual subjective experiences, individual "objective" performance, or societal processes and welfare (in whatever dimensions). The causal emphasis may then lead to talk about "production functions" or about recursive models and path coefficients, with emphasis on what seem to be the most powerful explanatory factors. But we may also be trying to frame our analysis to make it as relevant to policy matters as possible. If so, we want to know not just what causes what, but which causal variables are maneuverable—which are instrumental variables not in the technician's econometric, statistical sense but in the sense of variables that can be used to change things. If we put questions in these terms, perhaps we can clarify the discussion a bit. In particular, this may help in talking about the "psychological" variables; many such variables—not just ability—may, indeed, have a lot to do with what people do in life, including what occupations they pursue. I don't think that this is what was being challenged.

The question is: How far do schools, or can schools, alter the more subtle psychological attributes? And in particular, at what stage may they have such effects? We have been talking about schools all the way up and down the age scale. In higher education, how far can we expect what kinds of changes? Do we already have evidence that the more fundamental effects that will carry over into later life will be so small that Herbert Gintis and his associates* are just pursuing an ideological will-o-the-wisp? What are the judgments among the members of this conference? Are most of the educational sociologists here today, and in particular those who have studied the question intensively, willing to accept as confirmed the hypothesis that noncognitive personal traits are important for postschool performance but not optimistic about research payoff from testing whether colleges can do anything fundamental to alter those traits? This is an honest question, not a rhetorical pronouncement.

The suggestions for before-and-after tracing of noncognitive characteristics of college youth leave me somewhat disturbed in terms of research design; they lack the essentials for even a preliminary identification of causes. Are observed changes in attitudes and behavior a result of going to college (or to a particular kind of college), or are we observing simply changes with growing up? And how may the answer to this question differ with the kinds of attributes with which we are concerned?

When we first started discussing noncognitive outputs of the college experience, implicitly at least we were defining noncognitive in a pragmatic way, to include everything not measured by achievement tests. We haven't tried to distinguish the cognitive learning that has thus far eluded those tests; but let that question pass. Our initial discussion was very general also in that it cut a wide swath through an unspecified domain of relevant ultimate benefits—positive or negative, to the individual or the society—associated with the equally unspecified noncognitive attributes. A more explicitly focused part of our discussion has pointed to associations between noncognitive attributes and occupational choice. To argue that college may indeed socialize people into particular occupations, and that professional schools especially do this, is not at all the same thing as to argue that college experience changes basic personality attributes and self-conceptions at a more general and fundamental level. When we come to professionalization, my question would bring us back to studies of why people go into one sort of occupation rather than another in the first place and to what extent the attitudes that go with a particular occupation also preexist in the positive selection

---

* Among members of the Union of Radical Political Economists (URPE), a group centered mainly at Harvard has been giving increasing attention to noncognitive traits, both as determinants of career prospects and as outcomes of schooling experiences. Herbert Gintis has been the leader in this development. For an early statement, see Gintis (1971).

of people preparing for it. It seems important, if we are to understand
the impact of the college experience, that we keep very clearly before
us the distinction between what is associated with college education
and how far the college experience can account for this association.

Learning Complements and Substitutes in Career Perspective

*It is hardly surprising that the Woods Hole Conference should see
reenacted some of the skirmishes and confrontations that have characterized interchange (and miscommunication) between economists starting from a "manpower planning" perspective and the neoclassical
theorists of human investment. The interchange at Woods Hole was
also constructive. Indeed, as a long-time participant in this arena, and
a sometimes renegade associate of the neoclassical contingent, I found
the Woods Hole discussions refreshingly free of dogmatic stereotypes,
with an emphasis on research priorities that had received insufficient
attention from the neoclassical, the manpower, or any other perspective.
The discussion of these issues was set off by a series of remarks by
Carl Kaysen (formalized and modified in his "New Directions for Research," pp. 147–150) that sounded initially like a typical manpower planner's onslaught on rate-of-return analysis but ended up being something
quite different. The first remarks below were a response to Kaysen.
Following these are some comments that underline Harbison's emphasis
on the importance of learning at work.*

Kaysen has provided us with a combination of high entertainment,
an absurd stereotyping of people who talk about investment in human
beings, and a constructive set of ideas and suggestions concerning career
perspectives in the study of economic benefits of higher education. His
comments illustrate, at the same time, that real disagreements and disagreements that arise from poor communication are not merely interdisciplinary problems; there are plenty of examples within disciplines (or
at least within economics) as well. I have vigorously challenged much
of the "manpower requirements" activity, but I do agree with Kaysen
that when we talk about the economic effects of education, the emphasis
has to be on careers, not on a particular part of a career or of an
earnings stream. A career emphasis is entirely consistent with human
investment theory, though not necessarily consistent with Mincer's empirical assumptions in his ingenious attempt to measure the amount
of on-the-job learning by analysis of the time shape of a life-income
stream (Mincer, 1962). The tendency of many practitioners and critics
alike to identify on-the-job training in the neoclassical theory of invest-

ment in human beings with what Becker calls "general training" and to measure it as Mincer has done ignores all of the "Becker-specific" on-the-job training in the firm.* But both Becker and Mincer are key contributors to theoretical developments that go far beyond the particular application in Mincer's computations. Part of this development is concerned with investments by the firm in the training of its personnel and how the costs of such training and learning are divided between the firm and the individual. That line of research can lead quite directly to something on which I think Kaysen has put his finger and that has indeed been seriously neglected—the time horizon of decisions and commitments on the part of both individuals and employing agencies. Career choices that entail on-the-job learning, and especially Becker-specific training, entail decision making under some kinds of uncertainty, not only because all career decisions look to the future but also because long-term quasi-contracts are implicit in the Becker-specific situation with respect to investment in human beings. That the analysis of on-the-job training that Kaysen has challenged is just the Becker-general variant with Mincer's empirical estimates becomes clear enough when we look at Kaysen's illustrations. Kaysen has argued that the firm, rather than the individual, pays for most of the training; this situation is a characteristic of the Becker-specific model. And no investment economist worth his salt would argue that the graduates coming out of a particular level of school are all the same; most decidedly they are not a homogeneous collection. This does not preclude the use of averages, but it does invalidate generalizations about what schooling does from data for particular occupations; Ivar Berg is clearly to be faulted on this score.

For some years I have been stressing the importance of getting into analysis of communication networks and communication fields as a part of the theoretical and empirical study of the economics of investment in human beings. This applies to explanations of the diffusion of schooling in a population at a particular time and through time. It applies also to postschool job search and career development. One view of the communication network as a sorter and distributor of learning opportunities in the postschool years would regard all this as a sort of nepotism, but it can be seen in a less pejorative context; which information network a young man manages to get linked into can make a lot of difference in whether he will have a chance to show what he can do. Furthermore, it is not accidental that the association between ability and earnings

---

* I use the term "Becker-specific" (Becker, 1962), instead of simply specific, because those who are unfamiliar with Becker's theory frequently misinterpret the word specific. "Becker-specific" human capital refers to human capital that is attached to the firm. This is not a matter of technical specificity.

seems to increase with experience; the selection process and the weeding-out process continue far beyond the school years. Ability, I believe, tells more about income later than earlier in working life. You don't have to force this into a Mincer model. I think it is more a Kaysen model, though I really claim it for myself. By all means, let's look at careers, let's look at decision making under uncertainty, and let's look at the communication nexus.

At an early stage two Americans, Fredrick Harbison and Herbert Parnes, were top claimants internationally to the title of Mr. Manpower Planner, with Harbison the first on the scene. But way back before that, Harbison gave us an extraordinarily insightful (and too little known) study of on-the-job training and learning for management in Egyptian enterprise (1958). His emphasis on this aspect of manpower problems and policies is something that I strongly applaud, as I applaud also his warnings against the more technocratic styles of manpower analysis. I remain convinced that one of the main explanations of dualism in developing economies has been gaps in the sorts of knowledge that you don't acquire and probably cannot acquire efficiently (if at all) in school. Furthermore, I have taken this position for the past decade (Bowman, 1965), and I find nothing in it that is in conflict with the modern theory of investment in human beings. It seems to me unfortunate that several people at this conference are simply distorting the human investment theory in its broader formulations, looking only at a particular subcase—the empirical estimation of opportunity–cost general training under pure competition with constant internal rates of return. That is a useful special case for some purposes, but there is no point in flogging the theory of human capital because a particular case is not the whole. There can be the question: Have we put enough emphasis on certain aspects of relationships between schooling and careers and on the unfolding of career patterns? I would in fact agree that treatments have been lopsided. But this does not mean that the basic theory of investment in human beings and the positions taken by Kaysen are necessarily in conflict.

It is not just on-the-job learning, job search, and communication networks that may call for more attention, however. I suggest that we need to look especially also at (a) proprietary schools and (b) associations between youth unemployment and rates of college attendance. The proprietary schools are a much more substantial part of postsecondary training than most of us, especially most university academics, usually assume. Presumably they have been doing this big job because they are placing people. But in conversations with some specialists in *adult education* who have been very aware of what is happening in some of the proprietary schools, I have found grave concern. They say that serious distortions are taking place because of the profit-incentive aspect of student subsidies. Some of the proprietary schools are turning from an emphasis on placement as the way to attract paying students to say to themselves: The best way for us to make money is to seek out ways we can get students who will be financed by the government, regardless of how well we can place them afterward.

In connection with unemployment and college attendance, I want to underline Barry Chiswick's remarks ("Schooling, Screening, and Income," pp. 151–158) about the importance of foregone earnings and also to throw out a little piece of information that may be interesting. In a very tentative study, a young economist I shall not identify found that increasing general levels of unemployment increased rates of college attendance among people from lower- and middle-income ranks, but it diminished rates of college attendance among youth from families in the higher-income brackets. The increased rates of attendance for the middle and lower groups confirm other studies, which consistently show that reduction of job opportunities for young high school graduates, which reduces their foregone earnings in continuing in school, does in fact increase college going. The puzzle is the finding for children of the relatively well-to-do; I have some notions as to what may be going on, but you can make equally good (or bad) interpretations, so I leave it at that.

Earnings Expectations as Distributions

In connection with disputes about the relevance of "rates of return," I draw attention to an excerpt from an article I wrote with C. Arnold Anderson, which was on the table of goodies. This was written in response to the challenge that "the investment view of education is inappropriate because education accounts for only a small fraction of the variance in earnings, even controlling for age."

I summarize briefly: Suppose two sorts of people at an educational decision point, people with characteristics A and with characteristics B, and two levels of schooling, 1 and 2. This gives four different combinations, but only two sets of decisions: the decisions of the A's and those of the B's. If earnings are determined by factors in addition to schooling and the traits defining A and B, we have four distributions of earnings. For simplicity of exposition, assume first that each of the four distributions is normal, giving straight lines on probit paper. Also, for convenience, assume no change in earnings over the postschool years. Favoring our opposition, we take an extreme contrast between the A and

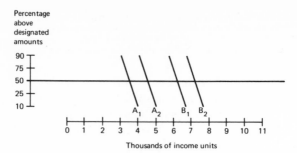

Fig. 1. Hypothetical income distributions with low within-cell variances. (Reproduced by permission from Bowman & Anderson, 1969, p. 102.)

the B populations as compared with the contrasts by schooling. This means that schooling can explain statistically much less of the total variance in earnings for the four groups combined (A1, A2, B1, B2) than can be explained by the characteristics distinguishing A and B to start with. Nevertheless, schooling can make a real difference for each set of men. We take two comparisons, shown in Figures 1 and 2.

In Figure 1 the within-group variance is comparatively small and over the range from the tenth to the ninetieth percentile there is no overlapping between distributions for men with schooling 1 or 2. Taken together, knowledge of a man's categorization (A or B) and his schooling would explain a large share of variance in earnings even when such variance was large. In Figure 2, by contrast, the within-group variances are high, and there is substantial overlapping of the distributions. Schooling and characteristics A and B will explain a much smaller proportion of the variance. But this changes the decision situation hardly at all.*

* Note that an assumption of diminishing marginal utility of income does *not* bias against the investment decision under these circumstances, as has sometimes been argued.

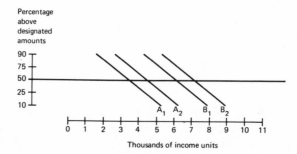

Fig. 2. Hypothetical income distribution with high within-cell variances. (Reproduced by permission from Bowman & Anderson, 1969, p. 103.)

An A who looks forward to earnings prospects with schooling 2 may recognize that there is a chance he will make less with the second increment of schooling if he is exceptionally unlucky than he might make without it if he were exceptionally lucky. But the whole probability distribution for his earnings has moved up (to the right) all along its course. The rates of return at the means (medians and modes) are the same in Figure 2 as in Figure 1. Excluding tuition payments, as we have drawn these curves in both figures, the private rates of return at the median would approximate 20 percent for the A's and 11 percent for the B's. If we had assumed parallel distributions in logarithmic form, the private rates of return would be the same at each likelihood or probit level as the rates at the median or modal values.

It may be that a man (or woman) can't change his inherited ability or his parents, but he can change his income nevertheless. The important thing is not how much of the variance in earnings we can explain but how and by how much distributions of prospects and results can be changed. Education can make a big difference in prospects of individuals even when expectations are far from single valued; the schooling simply shifts the whole set of probabilities. I don't see why we so persistently come back to talking as though all of these variables were single valued, completely forgetting that decisions are made under conditions of uncertainty in a world that is certainly going to change.

Eight Dogmatic Statements

There are several things I would especially like to say in this closing stage of the conference. I set them out as eight rather dogmatic statements.

First, I want to stress June O'Neill's warnings against assuming that wider diffusion of schooling will make for reduced inequality in earnings. Moreover, since Mincer has really not had his due here, I would like to point out that not only has he been an early and seminal contributor to the most basic developments in the modern theory of human capital, he has led all others in applying it to the empirical analysis of personal income distributions. Beginning with a classic article in 1958, he has shown repeatedly that expanding education does not produce equalization of earnings (Mincer, 1958).

Second, too often we look only at individuals, disregarding the importance of developing leadership within distinct subgroups in the society. It can be argued that further expansion of higher education in the United States is going to yield us no net social marginal returns over private ones; we already have so many college people. It doesn't follow, however, that it is not important to increase education for members of certain groups—and I'm thinking about black males in particular—to raise the level and the pool from which leadership of the group comes.

Third, I think that people were jumping on Solmon's use of dummy variables (see Lewis Solmon, "The Definition and Impact of College Quality," pp. 77–102) in connection with occupations in a way that failed to recognize the point of what he is doing and what it means. Actually, with use of those dummy variables he is introducing two things: (a) a kind of taste variable, associated with the idea of "equalizing differences" in wages across occupations where there are systematic preferences in conditions and nature of work; and (b) distinction of major contrasts in market structures associated with types of careers. Without trying to introduce everything at once, this was recognizing some of the very things that he has been chided for omitting or ignoring. The problem seems to be one of noncommunication rather than of disagreement in substance.

Fourth, I become disturbed when some of my economist colleagues make the conventional assertion that the efficient way to redistribute income is just to do it with dollars and leave it at that. Often they ignore the fact that it is not true that regardless of the problem at issue, a dollar is a dollar is a dollar. Perhaps a dollar earned has more value than a dollar you receive because you're poor. Such is my belief, and if I am right it follows that the redistribution, or equalization, of opportunity to earn those dollars has a value in itself. This ties in with the remarks that have been made about screening and opportunity to learn at work, which brings us to my next point.

Fifth, one of the main things that schools do is to channel people to greater or lesser future opportunities to learn over the course of their careers. But labor markets also have something to do with career development, and we must therefore ask: Does the labor market foster or impede the realization of career objectives, and does it widen or narrow the distribution of career opportunities?

My sixth point concerns social mobility. Several people have suggested that mobility defined as circulation in the system is a value in itself, even if there's no net upward mobility, but we seem to have let that point slip back into oblivion. Surely a significant quality of a society is the openness of its processes. Can people move around? Even if there were little change over time in occupational structure, and hence mathematically little possible net upward mobility, there could be substantial freedom of movement. What part may and do educational institutions and educational systems play in this process?

Seventh, I suggest that we have put too little stress on the question about discrepancies (positive or negative) between social and private benefits, or the economist's "externalities." In essentials, externalities refer to those effects that produce no incentives for individuals to modify their behavior because the benefits or the costs accrue to someone else. I believe that if we carry our thoughts about incentives further, we will look into some things that have been very much missing from this meeting.

Finally, following upon point seven, it is notable that we have almost totally ignored the nature of collective choice. Also, we've had virtually no analysis of the ways in which incentives are structured within institutions of higher education and what this does to the way the system of higher education itself develops, changes, or stagnates. It seems tremendously important that we take cognizance of the fact that institutions of education have an almost organic quality with a life of their own and that we seek more understanding of both the inner and outer processes that shape them.

REFERENCES

Becker, G. S. Investment in human capital: A theoretical analysis. *Journal of Political Economy*, 1962, 70(5, Pt. 2): S9–S49.

Bowman, M. J. From guilds to infant training industries. In C. A. Anderson & M. J. Bowman (Eds.), *Education and economic development*. Chicago: Aldine, 1965.

Bowman, M. J., & Anderson, C. A. Relations among schooling, "ability," and income in industrialized societies. In K. Hümfner & J. Maumann (Eds.), *Economics of education in transition* (Essays in honor of Friedrich Edding). Stuttgart: Ernst Klett Verlag, 1969.

Gintis, H. Education, technology, and the characteristics of worker productivity. *The American Economic Review*, 1971, 61(2): 266–279.

Harbison, F. H., & Ibrahim, I. A. *Human resources for Egyptian enterprise*. New York: McGraw-Hill, 1958.

Mincer, J. Investment in human capital and personal income distribution. *Journal of Political Economy*, 1958, 66: 281–302.

Mincer, J. On the job training: Costs, returns, and some implications. *Journal of Political Economy*, 1962, 70(5, Pt. 2): S50–S80.

INTERDISCIPLINARY RESEARCH ON OUTCOMES
OF HIGHER EDUCATION*

C. Arnold Anderson

Formal education—indeed any sort of education—is multifunctional. Inasmuch as different educational processes are carried out in varying degree and with varying effectiveness, and since the outcomes are in part offsetting, an educational system is partly autonomous. Its functioning is not by any means wholly determined by relationships to other sectors or institutions of a society. Unfortunately, most of the stipulations as to how an educational system should function are ambiguous, and measurements of performance are usually vague. Tests of pupils' "educational achievement," for example, relate usually only to conventional outcomes such as scores on a test of arithmetic. Moreover, the part played by schools in effecting this achievement (in contrast to observation of current events, watching TV, or home background) remains uncertain. The contribution of "knowledge acquired" or "habits of work" possessed by a youth on leaving school to his vocational success or his income is even more difficult to identify. Measurement of the effects of schools is frustrated even more by the lack of longitudinal measures of what pupils learn in successive years of school.

* The first version of these notes (circulated to participants in ditto copies during the summer) was prepared for the conference a day before it ended. In the present version those comments are arranged and systematized.

We could do a more thoroughgoing analysis of "the educational institution" if we had more complete knowledge of how other "people-serv-
ing" agents and institutions operate. We are quite uncertain, for example,
about the effect of direct physician–patient therapy as compared with
the benefits of piped water and sewage systems or improved diets. A
reanalysis of the effects of psychotherapy or of penological confinement
could contribute to our judgments about schools. Similarly, systematic
assessment of advertising in comparison with the work of schools would
help us to choose a better strategy in pedagogy. It seems to me warranted to assume that education is the sort of industry in which we
may not anticipate the occurrence of major breakthroughs in productivity. Rather, as in the past, we may look forward to accumulation of
many small improvements on the order of movable desks or replacement
of slates by pencil and paper.

The importance of seeking longitudinal measurements of attributes
of students and graduates attributable to school experience is underlined
by considering how little we know about the changes occurring in students as contrasted with changes in youth of the same age span who
are not attending school. Virtually no data exist for this comparison,
whether we are interested in skills in arithmetic, in political attitudes,
or in esthetic tastes. It is intriguing to learn that the drop-out rate from
college (and the imputed or reported reasons) have changed little over
a half-century. No less interesting is the fact that the percentage of
college students crossing state lines to attend seems also to have been
constant for several decades.

It is easy to persuade me that the economics of education is not
committed to a "productionist" viewpoint. And economists are as ready
as are sociologists to take full account of our national commitment to
equality of opportunity in education. Just as many economists as sociologists concede (or deny) that major gains in distribution of housing,
health, or adequate income will not result automatically from more equal
distribution of more years of schooling. There are indeed many prevalent
sophistries about relationships between schooling and mobility or opportunity, of which a few are commented on in this paper.*

---

* I deplore the contention (Folger et al., 1970, p. 43) that "the most pressing
problem appears to be that of getting young people to choose the career areas
where future demand is likely to be the highest." I view a taste for "better"
education as desirable, else why be so eager to give that boon to those who
must overcome a deprived background in order to benefit from it? Perhaps the
Committee on the Benefits of Higher Education would profit from touring representative campuses solely to observe the renaissance in painting among American students.

Today it is the vogue to uphold the application of universalistic princi-ples for allocation to jobs or schooling. Seldom can one obtain any serious attention to the dysfunctionalities in that procedure. But it is interesting to notice how askance the populace views people who live by the appli-cation of "specialized intelligence." When is "an unpleasant personality" justifiable grounds for not appointing a man to a given position? What are the consequences of the fact that "vocational" students are most like the populace in views and conduct? If college graduates did uni-formly get a sizable payoff in mobility, would the disjunctive effects upon society outweigh the favorable effects?

In any broad assessment of research potentialities (such as was em-bodied in the Conference on the Benefits of Higher Education) one needs to be alert to the limitations on his intellectual horizons. Not only are the effects of formal or informal education elusive because they are distributed over large spans of time. Expectation of novel out-comes from institutional operations is seldom voiced: Few observers anticipated the appearance of student unrest in the mid-1960s or the spread of drug-taking.

The remaining sections of this paper deal with four broad topics: 1. the isomorphism of sociological and economic approaches to educa-tion; 2. the need for collaborative micro studies; 3. comparative perspec-tives on mobility; and 4. the utility of intercountry comparisons in higher education.

Isomorphism of Sociological and Economic Approaches to Education

Evaluating the payoff from headstart programs or from junior colleges, each being enormously costly on an optimum scale, illustrates one sort of problem most suitably approached by joint efforts. Then there is the practice of staffing junior colleges with ex-secondary teachers rather than drawing upon the expanding supply of persons with doctorates. We are unlikely to understand the compulsion to convert "community colleges" into transfer institutions until we supplement studies of educa-tional aspirations with scrutiny of alternative ways to finance postsec-ondary education. Neither sociologists nor economists apparently have as yet appreciated the importance of following up the recent identifica-tion of underused colleges (Astin & Lee, 1972). The possibilities for fusing work on the politics of education, new hypotheses in educational finance, and sociologists' studies of urban communities have remained unnoticed. Only by making use of such economists' tools as the distinc-tion of public from private goods or the computation of benefit/cost indices will we decide how to compare the utility of different services, such as more places in college or better care in mental hospitals. But economists are sometimes timorous in taking up such questions; perhaps they really are "productionist minded."

Both sociology and economics can disaggregate their data from the society or school system down to the individual while retaining units that can be reaggregated. This sort of analysis is rarely possible in other social sciences. Unfortunately, political considerations often stultify those potentials. Because the ongoing "national assessment of school progress" does not obtain data for actual school systems, its findings have little usefulness for evaluation. The balancing of equity against efficiency can be carried out in either the economists' or the sociologists' domain. Imperfect capital markets and external effects are equally open to parallel interpretation for either field. The recent study for the Carnegie Commission of accessibility effects in college attendance has many parallels to analyses of markets (Anderson, Bowman, & Tinto, 1972).

The literature on socialization is by no means confined to young children: readiness to make best use of quality schooling, learning of work habits through study of school lessons, learning the folkways of work groups after completion of schooling. A study of the market inducements to individuals for acquiring skills can readily be linked to studies of job aspirations and of vocational recruitment. On-the-job learning can be rephrased as socialization into the culture of an occupation. Efforts to understand the ineffectiveness of vocational guidance link up neatly with sociological inquiries into the influence of "significant others," including their serving as role models.

On the present evidence "the school factor" explains only a small part of individual differences in educational achievement, at whatever level of school we observe. Our difficulty with this topic is due partly to the fact that we have little information about "value added" cumulatively during the span of one, four, eight, or more years of schooling. We will be unable to measure the feedback effects of well-educated mothers upon children's readiness for school until we do have these cumulative test data put in absolute units. The lack of such data also precludes our finding out how much learning goes on in graduate or professional schools when allowance is made for the capability of entrants to those schools. We will continue to speculate as to whether it really is the more enterprising persons who drop out of college until we have follow-up data into the peak years of occupational performance. Perhaps we finally can put discussions about alienation among college students into perspective when we are better informed about individuals' difficulty in learning to be prompt in reporting for work.

The Need for Collaborative Micro Studies

Macro studies may be quite serviceable in identifying correlations, but they yield little of the insight into processes that can be obtained with micro data. Macro data tend to be average for vaguely defined aggregates within which we know dispersion to be large. That we can predict individuals' occupations better than their incomes, for example, may well be due largely to the fuzzy definitions of occupations. We are unlikely to make rapid advances in discerning how education modifies "the culture" of an occupation until we take onto account pertinent labor-market factors.

Our understanding of how education contributes to status mobility or occupational transformation is blocked by the persisting utopian aura of much writing about education. No sooner did we become comparatively skillful in identifying and measuring "equality of opportunity" for schooling than an elision was made to talking about "equal quality of schooling." But we are as yet unable to agree on a definition of quality, and we have been unable to relate available measures of this quality to differences in what pupils learn. And then before we have even clarified our thinking on this last point we are being pushed to talk about assuring everyone "equal benefit" (or payoff) from schooling. Clearly this last aim cannot be assured under any imaginable circumstances. All social scientists would benefit if we could disentangle the ambiguities in these statements of goals while at the same time pointing out promising new investigations of occupational structures and other status systems.

Presumably priority should be given to assembling data about how skills are utilized in our economy. [Though I dissent from much of his analysis and most of his conclusions, Ivar Berg (1971) has raised basic questions.] We especially need measurements of individuals' capabilities of various kinds at the time when they move from schooling into employment and on the ways that different capabilities and jobs are combined. It is of interest that for national samples of youth from the advanced economies scores on mathematics are, if anything, lower in the more prosperous and technological societies. So we face the query: To run an economy effectively what proportion of workers need to know what school subjects to what level of competence?

The foregoing question actually is equally related to evaluations of nonformal education. Not only do the individuals with the most and best formal schooling also receive more nonformal training, there are also diverse patterns for the cycling of training over the working life. Concealed in this bundle of topics are some of the most complex forms of "anticipation," including subtle interactions among occupational motivations, structures of social status, and occupational structures.

If one is speaking of education generally, it is a truism that the labor force of an economy possesses (at least) the education needed to operate the economy on which their society subsists. But if one is speaking about formal schooling, one can say that every society has distinctive institutional arrangements that both enhance and attenuate the correlation between schooling and later occupation or income. If a society has tough standards for moving from one grade to another in school, individuals who survive to the higher levels will be comparatively uniform in competence, but a large proportion of youth will have been dropped from the schools along the way. In such circumstances one could also expect the association between amount of schooling and occupational success to be rather close. In the United States, on the contrary, we have for some years been moving toward a situation in which survival in school is only loosely related to tests of competence. We have arranged matters so that there is comparatively little scope for schooling to determine adult destinies—after "ability" is allowed for.

Finding that amount of schooling is only loosely correlated with jobs or incomes, some investigators are contending that it is the "hidden curriculum" and (biased) "personality training" by schools that mainly determine vocational capability. It would be my wager, however, that if we developed personality tests for pupils we would not greatly improve our predictions of adult success. This disappointment would be due partly to the fact that no separably identifiable and controllable factors in early rearing play a dominant part in adult success, partly because the various categories of relevant independent variables overlap greatly. (This is not to denigrate the importance of studying educational milieus; I am expressing skepticism about the utility of burrowing deeply into pupils' personalities.) It would seem to follow also that proposals to give educational certificates for community service or for off-campus activities will not improve the validity of diplomas as predictors of vocational competence. But even if I am wrong on the latter point, that policy would stultify our efforts to find out what can and what cannot be done well in formal schools. This latter task must be coped with however many devices we think up to substitute for evidence of school achievement.

Perhaps the most fruitful collaboration would be in the identification of "production functions" for schooling (or other education). Only thereby will we identify the components in quality of schooling and establish levels of payoff from different arrangements for instruction or learning. Leaving aside the familiar examples from the sphere of elementary education, we have as yet hardly begun the task of ascertaining whether one college is better than another or how to improve learning in a particular curriculum. The potentials of the low-quality colleges (Astin & Lee, 1972) or the merits of preserving Negro colleges illustrate the sorts of questions that deserve priority in research.

There is abundant scope for building that sociology of pedagogy about which so many men have speculated for over a century. At the same time we must tackle the complementary problem of analyzing the educational milieu, the school as a total environment. But we have only a faint notion of how to construct those indices. Even within the comparatively rarified air of colleges, we do not know how to identify features of classroom climates that strongly affect adult careers over and beyond enjoyable or miserable experiences during college. One may hazard the guess that school climate will prove to be a weak determinant of adult careers. To the extent that conclusion is warranted, study of production coefficients with combinations of less subtle elements will prove more manageable. In the process, the economist can make a major contribution to our techniques for deciding on the worth of educational innovations.

Comparative Perspectives on Mobility

Discussions of mobility are not always characterized by tight logic. Many generalities would resist definitive testing. Thus, when Karabel (1972, p. 31) writes that "the present educational system perpetuates existing differences between rich and poor," readers may be confused. As a member of a society that is distinctive for the openness of its universities, one is disconcerted to read "at stake, then, in who is given access to the university is nothing less than the distribution of privilege in contemporary America." This could be a truism, but just now we are worrying about an oversupply of college graduates.

There is a wide range actually among "advanced" and "democratic" countries in the degree of opportunity for secondary or college education. For the mid-1960s we have some ratios of university students from "upper-class" homes to the proportion of such homes in several societies Spain and Portugal were, as one would expect, rather "closed"; but so was Sweden; for all three countries the ratio was about 8:1. The United Kingdom, Greece, Norway, and Belgium had ratios of about 3:1. For the United States and Yugoslavia the indexes were 2:1. As yet no economist can indicate how to relate these disparities among countries to the operation of their labor markets or to their levels of income. How much mobility is "much"? If the upper stratum were wholly replaced from below in a generation, only a small faction of those with lower status could be promoted. Economists can help to make sociological studies of mobility more full-bodied. In particular there can be collaboration in studies of mobility, of access to directing positions, in analyses of sticky labor markets, or in studies on the incidence of poverty.

On the broader issues of the profile of our status system, I read few challenges to the main conclusions of Blau & Duncan (1967). I read them as confirming what I wrote in 1961: that son's schooling outweighs paternal status in determining the adult status of the son. It probably will be only when econometricians join sociologists that many behavioral scientists will appreciate the simple fact that if educational opportunities were indeed equal, education would cease to be a factor in adult status. Similar collaboration and the use of better data will be needed to forecast when output of college graduates will lead to a shrinking differential in their prestige and incomes over those of secondary graduates.

Historically our present sort of schools developed just because the traditional nonformal kinds of education had proved unsatisfactory. It would indeed be ironic if we arrived at a situation in which all individuals received equal schooling but found their ultimate positions in life determined by the many kinds of nonformal training that had grown up to perform training and certifying functions that schools no longer would carry out.

Great progress has been made in the last couple of decades in analyzing intercountry differences in levels and growth of income. Progress has been made also in mapping the status structures of many countries. As yet, though it was Cairnes and Taussig who set the problem of "noncompeting groups," the two disciplines continue to find it difficult to join efforts in study of this common topic.

The Utility of Intercountry Comparisons in Higher Education

Mobility is not the only useful bridge between economics and sociology. Studies of higher education are proliferating in most countries of the world, and universities are the producers of that critical category called "high-level manpower." But comparisons between states are no less fruitful.

For example, California and Massachusetts send about the same proportion of high school graduates to college. But while in the former nearly all go to public (and cheap) colleges, in the latter the majority enroll in private (and often expensive) colleges. Nor is the social-status profile of college students vastly different in the two states. Seemingly cost is a less weighty factor than one would infer from the literature, especially that written by sociologists. In California, moreover, while a comparatively large proportion of less able youth enroll in college, that state's percentage of entrants who obtain the baccalaureate is below the national average. As "production systems" the structures of higher education in the various states are rather dissimilar. Without pausing for illustrations, it may be said that internation differences of the foregoing sorts (as of the status composition of students) are no less striking than among our states.

One can find equally impressive differences in the way that lower schools operate in different countries. In the international mathematics study lower-status pupils in some countries scored higher than did upper-status pupils in other countries. The score of a typical Japanese pupil was twice that of an American pupil, yet the correlation between score and parental status was about .30 in each country. Seemingly the two school systems are equally unsuccessful in overcoming the handicaps of family background, yet the Japanese system instills much more knowledge or capability with no identifiably superior resource inputs.

The "mix" of elements in the educational process differs greatly from one to another of the "advanced" countries. No one has made even a beginning in showing how these different systems of higher education came to have their distinctive forms. No one can trace the effects in the economy of the differing profiles of capability generated by the several systems of higher education. The percentage of university graduates who obtain "top-level" jobs is distinctively low in Japan and rather low in the United States. In Sweden and Norway the top jobs are considerably more confined to university graduates. What, then, is a meritocracy? What is the payoff, either economically or politically, of the pattern of using university graduates in Japan or the United States as compared with that in other countries?

REFERENCES

Anderson, C. A., Bowman, M. J., & Tinto, V. *Where colleges are and who attends: Effects of accessibility on college attendance.* New York: McGraw-Hill, 1972.

Astin, A. W., & Lee, C. B. T. *The invisible colleges: A profile of small, private colleges with limited resources.* New York: McGraw-Hill, 1972.

Berg, I. *Education and jobs: The great training robbery.* Beacon Press, 1971.

Blau, P. M. & Duncan, O. D. *The American occupational structure.* New York: Wiley, 1967.

Folger, J. K., Astin, H. S., & Bayer, A. E. *Human resources and higher education.* New York: Russell Sage Foundation, 1970.

Karabel, J. Perspectives on open admissions. *Educational Record,* 1972, 53(1): 30–44.

PREREQUISITES FOR FURTHER RESEARCH ON THE EFFECTS OF HIGHER EDUCATION

Lewis C. Solmon

It is apparent that a clear explication of the issues involved in any study of the effects of post-secondary-school education is greatly needed. What do we mean by "costs and benefits" in higher education? What exactly are the principles upon which future research in this area must be based? What directions need to be explored?

First, it should be obvious that "benefits," in this sense, might be positive, negative, or even nonexistent. In other words, we must look at both the costs and benefits of higher education and also realize that in certain areas education might have no impact at all.

Studies of postsecondary training must examine other institutions besides formal universities; these include two-year colleges, adult education, vocational training, and many other activities after high school for those seeking to improve themselves. Moreover, in order to fully understand the effects of higher education, we must look at groups who do not take additional training beyond the twelfth grade.

Any type of training after high school, and college attendance in particular, imposes costs and yields benefits. The costs to the individual student or his family may be direct—money for tuition, books, transportation to and from school, and the like—or indirect—increased taxes to support institutions of higher education, for example. The largest cost is generally considered to be the opportunity cost, that is, earnings lost by staying in school instead of taking a job.* Private nonpecuniary costs also can accrue, such as loss of self-confidence after attending a competitive institution.

Of course it is the benefits—both monetary and nonmonetary—that draw an individual to higher education. A literature is developing on what aspects of the educational experience enable students to subsequently earn higher incomes. Certainly, increases in knowledge gained in school are productive. However, increased socialization, willingness to take risks, and willingness to innovate are other income-incrementing characteristics that might be obtained from the educational experience. Higher earnings in themselves may not benefit individuals, since money does not guarantee happiness. However, we should be guided by the proposition that the objective of more post-secondary-school education is not increased happiness, but increased range of choice. A greater income definitely accomplishes that.

More and more, nonpecuniary returns from extra schooling are also being recognized. It has been argued that those with more education are more efficient consumers, that they use their time more effectively. Others claim that enjoyment from reading a good novel is higher for those with greater education.

Several caveats must be inserted at this point: First, it has been alleged that incomes are larger for those with longer education, not because of increased skills and productivity obtained in school, but merely because educational attainment is a credential for which employers will pay more, despite the fact that there is no real difference between an educated and a less-educated man. Thus, lack of education may be a barrier to entering high-paying occupations. Second, it is important to analyze what characteristics distinguish better- from less-educated persons. Would these same differences between the samples have been apparent even if the groups had ended up with the same amount of education? Perhaps the traits that led particular individuals to opt for more schooling would have been influential with or without the education. We must also distinguish between the effects of aging versus the effects of going to college. The necessity of comparing college attenders

---

* The practice of adding lost earnings to educational costs is valid only if the student could have obtained a job. However, individuals may estimate opportunity costs on the assumption they are foregoing income even if the assumption is incorrect. For those who might be unemployed, the cost is zero or even negative, since idleness and frustration may lead to unlawful activities and subsequent legal penalties. This has led some to point out that one benefit of higher education is the extension of the babysitting role played by schools in keeping children off the streets. This is a social benefit that will be discussed in detail later.

with those who did not attend college is evident. Finally, we should distinguish between aging and maturing. People mature at vastly different rates. For some, college may offer a shelter that retards their maturation, while a different experience, such as military service, might speed it up.

In short, we must look beyond an individual's level of income or occupational status as the goals of tertiary education. We must analyze the impact of education in terms of the subject's psychological development, feeling of identity, and spiritual development. We must investigate the process by which education affects the individual. Is schooling important because it changes cognitive or affective abilities or because it imparts specific knowledge? Does education really do anything beyond serving as a credential, a screening device to allocate individuals among occupations?

There are also costs and benefits of higher education that accrue to society as a whole. Some of these are shared between the student and society in general. Others accrue more to society and less directly to the individual. Traditionally, for example, the more-educated society is, allegedly, a better functioning democracy. This might concretely benefit the educated individual only slightly. On the other hand, it has been argued that education, particularly of women who later become mothers, provides benefits to subsequent generations of children. There is evidence that children of more-educated mothers ultimately become more successful than children of less-educated mothers (controlling for a large number of other factors). In a sense, this is a social return. However, the mother certainly gets something out of both training the child and observing later success.

Potential social costs of higher education include "negative social benefits"—undesirable or harmful attributes of society brought about by higher education—and alternatives foregone when resources are directed into higher education rather than defense or urban renewal, for example. More thought has been directed toward the second type, which is easier to put in monetary terms. But the other costs do exist. Some claim that a more-educated society is a more-alienated society or even that more-educated people better recognize differences among individuals and ultimately tend to become less tolerant. Moreover, the uneven distribution of income due to varying degrees of education eventually might result in widespread social discontent, as we have observed in this country over recent years.

A related phenomenon is the distortion of values by higher education. White collar and production work, for example, have been extolled to the point where manual skills, craftsmanship, and work in the service industries appear to many as unappealing, resulting in shortages in the labor force.

Government support and financing of higher education is rationalized by the benefits education yields to society at large: Without subsidization, individuals would base their educational decisions only on returns to themselves, resulting in less education than is socially optimal, as suming social benefits do exist.

The federal government offers extensive subsidies to stimulate college education: The Office of Education's total budget allocation for higher (primarily undergraduate) education is $1.3 billion in fiscal year 1972. From this, that office provides direct student aid, ranging from 100 percent grants to partial-interest subsidies on loans, on the order of $800 million. Indirect student aid is available through institutional support. Recent legislation passed by Congress (including a general higher education institutional support program) will increase the magnitude and scope of federal involvement.

Although the existence of social (versus individual) benefits is continually used to argue for governmental support of higher education, the discussion has been primarily limited to conjectures on their nature and scope. Little effort has been directed toward measuring these returns. Such a study would be of major interest.

Social effects are quite difficult to quantify: After all, what exactly are social benefits? Even if they can be identified, who can put a price tag on such things? One important approach is to identify those benefits to individuals that benefit or impose a cost on society as well. We must also ask: Is additional schooling associated with the evolution of these effects? After these questions are answered, perhaps we can turn our findings over to politicians for an "evaluation."

The scanty work in this area may result from the fact that cost-benefit analysis has traditionally been a tool of economists, whereas many of the social returns to education are more easily identified, discussed, and perhaps quantified by sociologists, psychologists, educators, and political scientists.

It is apparent that different attitudes and policies toward higher education will yield widely varying problems and consequences. A society where higher education is considered a right for all will not resemble a society where higher education is only for the elite. Of course, the direction of these differences is not clear: We would expect less divergence of income and less social discontent where there was mass higher education. On the other hand, unfulfilled expectations from mass higher education might result in great discontent. Of course, entirely different institutional structures are needed to operate the two dissimilar systems.

The private and social costs and benefits of higher education are clearly a function of both the quantity and quality of schooling. Thus, it is necessary to study separately private and public institutions of higher education, the effects of different types of colleges, and indeed the effects of all kinds of post–high school experience (adult education, on-the-job training, vocational training, apprenticeship programs, etc.). We must examine the effects of each type of college: a sexually segregated school, a racially segregated school, a religiously controlled school, a college emphasizing extracurricular activities, an institution with students directly from high schools or one dominated by transfers or re-entrants, a large versus a small school, a residential versus a commuter college. We must explore the meaning of "quality" in education, whether faculty quality is best measured by teaching capabilities, attitudes, training, or research activities, and the relation of these factors to the benefits we are discussing.

We have been confronted in the early seventies with conditions that were "produced" by the dramatic developments of the post-World War II period and especially the sixties. The higher education boom of the last decade has substantially distorted private and public choices, particularly in terms of college and program availability. We must now reckon with these distortions. What are the adjustments that will best get us onto a steady path with respect to higher education opportunities? The simplistic enrollment projections of the late sixties are far off the mark. But we must clarify why they are wrong if we are to learn from our past mistakes. Our major campuses have invested heavily in structures and equipment. In view of the slack in the demand for these things, can they, and should they, be maintained intact, awaiting a revival of interest? In private economic affairs, sunk investments are bygones that are written off appropriately as adjustments are made to new circumstances. Is this also "public" wisdom, considering the serious diseconomies associated with the scale of such large campuses?

So far the concept of time has not entered into the discussion. Obviously most of the private costs, those to the student or to his family, are incurred at the time of education. However, graduates' initial incomes might be lower than those of less-educated peers because of their lower work experience or a decision to take lower earnings in exchange for on-the-job training. Social costs from education might also linger over a longer period of time: Social discontent can rage for many years after attempts to upgrade the education of poor minorities.

Similarly, educational payoffs can appear during the schooling experience, immediately thereafter, or over a period of years. Chopin might be better appreciated after a freshman music course. An individual's college degree might move him into a higher-status job immediately after graduation. However, the quantity and quality of education explain varying incomes among individuals much more clearly after 20 years than immediately upon leaving school. One reason may be that the better-educated spend more time (and take lower-paying jobs initially) to acquire on-the-job training after their formal education and are better trained to earn more later on. Finally, benefits from a better-informed electorate—if these exist—may persist for a generation.

The issue of time is particularly important when attempting to evaluate the effectiveness of educational inputs. It is not enough to analyze the change in a student between the time he entered college and the time he left in order to evaluate the effectiveness of the institution; the effects of schooling are not all immediately realized when the diploma is received. On the other hand, postschool factors will affect an individual's earnings, for example, 20 or 30 years after graduation, rendering any measurement of educational benefits extremely difficult.

Even for some of the immediately obtainable benefits from higher education, such as personality changes or increases in knowledge, several additional questions must be asked: To what extent do the trait changes persist? If we observe energetic entering freshmen becoming lethargic graduating seniors, can we predict that this lethargy will continue throughout life, or will it become even greater enthusiasm once the graduates have rested from their final exams?

Researchers have generally implied that it is good to see increased liberalism and other positive changes persist after leaving college. (Is increased liberalism necessarily positive?) However, persistence of college changes really means no further changes afterward. Is this necessarily worthwhile? Does college effect change in a student's productivity, psychology, or physiology only during the four or more years of attendance, or does college stimulate continued flexibility? If a student who was liberalized by college is studied 20 years later, should we expect him to be as liberal as he was upon graduation, more liberal than he was as a freshman but not necessarily as liberal as upon graduation, or much more liberal now? If he has moved, through intellectual considerations, to a conservative outlook over 20 years, does this imply college has had no effect? To what extent are character or other changes during the educational experience of value to the individual and to society? Increased socialization may be good, since the socialized individual is a more cooperative and productive member of society; or it may be bad, since the more socialized graduate is less freethinking and less innovative.

There is much debate over the need to quantify in order to study higher education. On the one hand, those effects of higher education that are amenable to quantification should be studied in this way, at least as a part of any research program. There is nothing inherently evil in quantification or in statistical analysis. On the other hand, there is no need to exclude those items that are not quantifiable, many of which are important, from any study of the effects of education; humanistic attitude is also necessary. It has been proposed that only personal interviews will reveal identity changes effected by college, that we cannot generalize results from large samples. Certainly, if we do not always meet our subjects personally, at least we must go beyond studying nationally representative populations of individuals. We must look at subgroups in our society—blacks, women, ethnic groups, and disciplinary and professional divisions—and at the effects of education upon them.

Finally, we must be cautious about predicting future impacts of postsecondary education by extrapolating from the past. Previously only small numbers attended school beyond the twelfth grade. Today many aim for universal higher education; the availability of highly educated manpower, social interaction, and other phenomena will never be as they were. Moreover, we can fully understand the impact of higher education only after seeing how the educated progress through the occupational structure and how they change the nature of jobs themselves.

There is much more work to be done before a satisfactory evaluation of postsecondary education can be made. The Panel on the Benefits of Higher Education hopes to be a catalyst in this effort.

AUTHOR INDEX

Numbers in italics refer to the pages on which the complete references are listed.

A

Aaron, H., 281, *290*
Adorno, T. W., 60, *61*
Alwin, D., 103, *104*
Anderson, C. A., 388, *391*, 396, *401*
Armer, J. M., 103, *104*, 130, *144*
Arnold, M., 278, *290*
Arrow, K., 151, *158*
Ashenfelter, O., 19, *32*, 71, *73*
Astin, A. W., 15, *32*, 36, 53, *61*, 78, 99, *101*, 107, 109, 114, 123, 124, 125, *127*, 130, *144*, 165, *171*, 375, *379*, 395, 399, *401*
Astin, H. S., 226, 228, *229*, 394, *401*
Atkinson, R. C., 166, *171*

B

Bacote, C., 245, *249*
Banfield, E., 280, *290*
Barron, F., 113, *127*
Battle, E. S., 43, *62*
Bayer, A. E., 226, 228, *229*, 394, *401*
Becker, G. S., 19, 30, *32*, 66, 68, *73*, 86, *101*, 151, *158*, 274, 276, *290*, 299, 300, *314*, 356, *363*, 367, *379*, 385, *391*
Bendix, R., 344, *349*
Bereiter, C., 44, *61*

Berg, I., 24, *32*, 151, *158*, 262, *268*, 357, 358, *363*, 370, *379*, 397, *401*
Berls, R. H., 16, *32*, 279, *290*
Birnbaum, M., 77, *101*
Blaine, G. B., 49, *62*
Blau, P. M., 25, 30, *33*, 130, 131, 142, *143*, *314*, 344, *349*, 400, *401*
Blum, Z. D., 27, *33*, 225, *229*
Bock, R. D., 170, *172*
Bowen, H. R., 278, 281, 287, *290*
Bowles, S., 30, *33*, *101*, 151, 158, 368, 376, *379*
Bowman, M. J., 386, 388, *391*, 396, *401*
Break, G., 285, *290*
Bridgman, D. S., 17, *33*
Brisbane, R. H., 245, *249*
Brimmer, A., 232, *237*
Bullock, H. A., 243, *249*
Burt, C., 170, *172*

C

Carson, W., *249*
Cass, J., 77, *101*
Cattell, R. B., 170, *172*
Centra, J. A., 15, *33*
Cheit, E., 284, *290*
Chickering, A. W., 48, 50, 51, 53, 55, *61*
Chiswick, B. R., 157, *158*, 274, *290*
Christie, R., 52, *62*

411